THE COMPANION GUIDE TO

The West Highlands of Scotland

THE COMPANION GUIDES

GENERAL EDITOR: VINCENT CRONIN

*It is the aim of the Guides to provide a Companion,
in the person of the author, who knows intimately
the places and people of whom he writes, and is able to
communicate this knowledge and affection to his readers.
It is hoped that the text and pictures will aid them
in their preparations and in their travels, and will
help them to remember on their return*

SOUTHERN GREECE · THE GREEK ISLANDS
BURGUNDY · PARIS · THE SOUTH OF FRANCE
ROME · FLORENCE · VENICE
UMBRIA · TUSCANY · SOUTHERN ITALY
JUGOSLAVIA · THE SOUTH OF SPAIN
MADRID AND CENTRAL SPAIN
EAST ANGLIA · IRELAND · LONDON
KENT AND SUSSEX · NORTHUMBRIA
DEVON AND CORNWALL
NORTH WALES · SOUTH WALES
THE WEST HIGHLANDS OF SCOTLAND

In preparation
SOUTH WEST FRANCE · THE ILE DE FRANCE
THE WELSH MARCHES · MAINLAND GREECE
EDINBURGH AND THE BORDER COUNTRY
TURKEY · NORMANDY

THE COMPANION GUIDE TO

The West Highlands
of Scotland

W.H. MURRAY

A SPECTRUM BOOK

PRENTICE-HALL, INC.   COLLINS
Englewood Cliffs, New Jersey 07632   St. James's Place, London

Library of Congress Cataloging in Publication Data

Murray, W. H. (William Hutchison)
    The Companion guide to the West Highlands of Scotland.

    "A Spectrum Book"
    Bibliography: p.
    Includes index.
        1. Highlands (Scottland)—Description and travel—Guide-
books.   I. Title.
DA880.H7M95   1984   914.11'5   83-27072
ISBN 0-13-154782-8
ISBN 0-13-154774-7 (pbk.)

ISBN 0-13-154782-8

ISBN 0-13-154774-7 {PBK.}

ISBN 0-13-154774-7 (p)
ISBN 0-13-154782-8 (c)
ISBN 0 00 216813 8 (Collins limpback)
ISBN 0 00 211135 7 (Collins hardback)

First published in 1968
Made and printed in Great Britain by
William Collins Sons & Co., Ltd., Glasgow

U.S. edition © 1984 by Prentice-Hall, Inc., Englewood Cliffs, New Jersey 07632;
William Collins Sons & Co., Ltd.; and W.H. Murray

A SPECTRUM BOOK

Printed in the United States of America

10 9 8 7 6 5 4 3 2 1

Prentice-Hall International, Inc., *London*
Prentice-Hall of Australia Pty. Limited, *Sydney*
Prentice-Hall Canada Inc., *Toronto*
Prentice-Hall of India Private Limited, *New Delhi*
Prentice-Hall of Japan, Inc., *Tokyo*
Prentice-Hall of Southeast Asia Pte. Ltd., *Singapore*
Whitehall Books Limited, *Wellington, New Zealand*
Editora Prentice-Hall do Brasil Ltda., *Rio de Janeiro*

Contents

Contents

Illustrations

Illustrations

THE COMPANION GUIDE TO

The West Highlands of Scotland

The Seaboard of the Gael

My purpose in writing this book is to help you to know the west highland coast; my hope, that you will enjoy it as much as I have. I write specifically of the mainland coast, but include many islands that are virtually part of it because they lie close offshore and are so easy of access, like Skye. I do not include the main Hebridean archipelago. The Hebrides comprise more than five hundred islands forming a geographical and historical unity, whose thorough description needs a long book to itself (see *The Hebrides*, by W. H. Murray).

The Highlands have only one coast: the West. Scotland's northern and eastern seaboards are Lowland. Among the several geological freaks that captivate eye and mind in the Highlands, none is more extraordinary than the coastline itself. From the Mull of Kintyre to Cape Wrath, it extends 225 miles by crow-flight, but in outline measures 2000—and this does not include a thousand minor involutions. This crazily indented coast was not 'eaten out' by the sea. The events causing it were much more dramatic.

Around thirty million years ago 'Scotland', then a nearly sea-level plain, rose up as a high plateau, a solid block free of folding. The land mass then extended westward far beyond the present Hebrides. But the natural forces had barely begun their work. Water and ice eroded the plateau into a complicated mountain-land, in which 543 tops stand today clear above 3000 feet. The western half of the land then took a seaward dip. In this huge subsidence the old coast-line was submerged. The sea flooded into the long, westward-running glens, filled the rift valley of the Minch to isolate the farther hills as the Hebrides, and gave Scotland her five hundred offshore islands and that wildly serrated coastline, where the fiords run twenty, thirty, and forty miles into the mountains. Together they form a sea- and land-scape which, in beauty and variety over so long a stretch of coast, is without parallel in Europe.

The varieties of scene are more readily distinguished if at the outset one takes a wide sweep of the eye and surveys the scene whole. And this will be helpful too in a practical way. Choice can be embarrassing on a first visit. No man can hope to see and know the entire west coast on one summer's journey. He must know in advance which district he prefers to see first, go there, and truly come to feel that he knows it before moving on to another. Indiscriminate long-distance touring by car is a folly of our age that brings small reward. It congests the mind with an undigested wealth of visual experience. The truth is that no bit of Highland country will ever be known until a man walks in it and walks far, speaks to the people, and gets well off the main roads on foot. Otherwise the life of that country will pass him by, and he will know nothing of it. To choose well, he must know what is offered.

When the Picts occupied the Highlands, the country's name was Alban, meaning Mountains. But the Scottish Highlands' true point of scenic distinction will not be found in mountain shape as in the High Alps, nor in the leagues of heather rightly beloved of the August visitor (October is much more colourful). In what, then, does it lie? To understand the answer you must let me go a little further into the geography of the region.

The main geographical feature, the jagged coastline, is also the origin of several of the main diversities of scene. Through the long sea-lochs the waters of the Atlantic Drift penetrate far inland. Their shores and the glens of the seaboard thus enjoy a relatively mild climate. Mean temperatures in mid-winter are several degrees higher than those of the east coast; but this warmth is confined to low ground, for temperature is less determined by nearness to the sea than by height above it. The hills rise from the sea abruptly, hence mean temperatures for the west are low while at the same time the coastline strips are milder than anywhere in Britain save the south of England and the west fringe of Wales. In Argyll you will thus find palms and figs, and many other exotic and flowering shrubs that do not thrive elsewhere in Britain outside south-west England.

The area as a whole gets less snow than the Pennines of England or the Southern Uplands of Scotland, but this general truth must again be balanced by excepting the high tops, where snow in great quantity comes earlier and stays later, notably in Lochaber.

The Seaboard of the Gael

The thirty big sea-lochs are one and all names of international repute: Fyne, Etive, Linnhe, Sunart, Nevis, Hourn, Ewe, Broom, Torridon—these are just a sample. Their typical form is that of a wide outer loch separated by narrows from a narrow inner loch, otherwise no two are like. The peculiar character of the western sea-lochs owes much less to their own or to mountain shape than to their channelling the Atlantic Drift. Some of them, notably Loch Hourn, have been likened to Norwegian fiords, narrow and twisting with craggy flanks and tall walls. The likeness goes no further. The scale is not Norwegian. The detail when examined is peculiar only to the Scottish west coast, whose hills are 'clothed' by this Atlantic atmosphere. Rain, mist, and cloud form a large part of summer and winter wardrobe, but the bright dress of spring and the rich of autumn, even the winter nakedness in frosty morning air, all have a beauty so exhilarating that days of rain are forgotten.

This cloth of colour and atmosphere, given by vegetation and climate, drapes even the low southern hills of the Cowal and Kintyre peninsulas and Knapdale, which are not inferior to the tumultuous north but different in kind. These low hills and moors of south Argyll have the delicate colours of an ancient tapestry, whereas if one moves farther north into the more 'highland' country of Lorn, Appin, Lochaber, Moidart, Kintail, the scene has not more elegance but more power. The mountains do not take the eye by storm like the world's great ranges, but by grace of line and colour and haze of enchantment. Although near, they look remote, more mysterious than the unchanging Himalaya.

The rocks of the seaboard from Kintyre to Kintail are largely schistose and their hills grassy. Variety is given by areas of pink granite in the Black Mount and Lochaber, quartzite crowning the pointed tops of Mamore, basalt in Mull and Skye giving a friable soil and good grass for cattle. Beyond Kintail, the North-west Highlands (Ross and Sutherland) are distinguished by ranges of gneiss and sandstone, often wrongly described as the oldest mountains in the world. They were raised as a plateau about the same time as the Alps and carved since to present shape. It is not the mountains that are so very old, but the rocks of an earlier chain now exposed on the moors and hills to give—when seen from high ground—a lunar landscape.

This effect is more usually associated with the gneiss moors of Sutherland, but is found too in Ross on hills of Torridon sandstone as far south as Applecross. Neither rock breaks down into good soil. But that is only one aspect of the North-west, where a southern softness overlaps northern harshness, the two providing startling contrasts, especially in Ross. In well-marked degrees or steps the landscape hardens northward to ruggedness. Around Loch Torridon and Loch Maree the mountain land is full in stature and variety. To my own eye (for this is always a matter of opinion) it exhibits more of mountain beauty than any other region of Scotland. The lands to the north, and Skye to the west, are unrivalled of their own kind, a more special kind—naked rock and barer ground.

On crossing the Sutherland border one penetrates country so distinct from any other that one feels as if entering a new land. The mainland's most wind-tormented coast, it is very much the northern promontory of the British Isles, and save in protected glens it is bare of trees. Everywhere the land is more openly wilderness; the sandstone mountains low but seeming twice their real height as they spring out of their rolling floor of archaean gneiss, the waterways between meandering in maze-like spread.

The points of true distinction on the west seaboard are first the singular variety of scene from region to region within a small country, which may owe its disjointed skeleton to numerous geological accidents, but shape, flesh, and clothing to a much maligned Atlantic atmosphere. This humid climate gives the Highlands the variety and subtlety of colour so relatively absent in the countries of the sun. They too have colours, strong in contrast but few in number. The Highlands are richly apparelled: granted sun, one of the most colourful countries of all. The coat of many colours costs a high price in days of rain, but only thus can you have it to enjoy.

Weather has given the myriad waterways, and that brings me to the second point of true distinction: the Atlantic and the lochs, of all mountain settings the most brilliant. The sweep of sea and winding loch, which bursts on the traveller when he breasts a hill, has its counterpart in every glen where a burn storms under a Highland bridge and on every moor where water lies at peace in brown pools. This wedding of rock and water, embellished by a wealth of living things from old Caledonian pine to sphagnum moss, gives rise to the particular kind and colour of Highland landscape for which Scotland is unexampled.

The West Highlands are notoriously wet. The very high rainfall comes not on the coastal fringe (with which this book mainly deals) but several miles inland, extending in a broad belt from the

The Seaboard of the Gael

Affric hills of Ross to Cowal in Argyll. The mountains take the blame for this precipitation of 80-120 inches and more, but on the coastal fringe it drops markedly to 60-80 inches. The best, driest, and sunniest time of year is from mid-May to the end of June; the next driest (although not sunniest) is from mid-September to mid-October. A drought of six to eight weeks occurs in the West most years, but may arrive at any time between February and November. While hoping for the best, come prepared for the worst.

Preparation means not only oilskins and rubber boots, but knowledge of how to mitigate the penalties of unreliable weather, the worst of which may often be escaped. Along the great length of the riven coast many low-lying peninsulas project seaward, like Kintyre, and Keills of Knapdale, the Ross of Mull, Ardnamurchan, Arisaig, the north wings of Skye, the Gruinard and Rhu More of Wester Ross, the Stoer of Sutherland, and a score of lesser ones. When storm clouds sweep in from the west they often pass over these outlying lands, leaving them in sunshine, or in blinks of sunshine, to precipitate on the hills behind. If rain does fall on them it is likely to be showery rather than continously wet. Your best policy is then to make for the promontories, where you can enjoy the exhilaration of walking the cliff-tops in wind, watching the great Atlantic rollers crash across the reefs, reconnoitring sandy coves and beaches to which you would like to return in fine weather, exploring caves and natural arches, visiting the nesting cliffs of fulmar and guillemot, discovering little crofting communities in unexpected bays, where salmon nets and lobster creels drape the foreshore. The interest of these bare promontories is unending if only one will walk and look. If foul weather comes instead from north or east they will not escape their share of it, but even then the rainfall will be less than inland. The air will be lighter and freer. Few people are aware of these truths, which do need remembering: there is a grimness in the rain that settles into a Highland glen, convincing the mind that all the world must be inundated. Five miles away it can be dry. It is worth investigating.

Encourage the West Highlander to talk to you. During this century there has been a fairly large influx of men and women from the south, both from England and the Scottish Lowlands, but the people remain predominantly the Gael of Celtic race. The dour, silent Highlander is largely a creation of fiction, or where not is likely to be an incomer. The Gael are an intensely social, communicative people, with high standards of domestic custom and

13

hospitality, which are among the better products of the old clan system.

The Gael of the Bronze Age arrived in Britain nearly a thousand years before the Britons of the Iron Age. They colonized Ireland around 1,300 BC and are thus the oldest ethnic group in Britain. One of their tribes, the Scots, began to colonize Alban in the period AD 250-500, when they occupied Argyll. In the mid-ninth century they finally overthrew the power of the Picts, and by the mid-thirteenth century had conquered the Viking colony of north Scotland and seized the Hebrides. The Norse occupation of the islands and northern mainland had lasted four centuries. It permanently affected the character and physical features of the Celtic people of the seaboard, where the combination of fair hair and blue eyes remains prevalent and the men are still daring seamen. A big proportion of youths, especially from the Hebrides, enter and rise high in the merchant navy and Royal Navy.

The Gael has always had a two-way passion, one an inborn reverence for scholarship, song, and poetry, the other a reckless bravery in battle as famed as that of the Viking at sea. His impetuous nature has often led him to extremes, and when matters of honour and loyalty could be invoked, made him too easily led to disaster, as during the rising of 1745.

At the present day the people are well-read and imaginative. A high proportion of the youth of both sexes graduate at universities. The Gael has inherited no respect for class distinction. The early Celtic people were freemen unbound by the principle of primogeniture in selecting a chief. A clan's land belonged to the clan (family) not to the chief. The people gave him the free allegiance of a family to its head, who had thus no need to rule by force. They loathed the stratification of society into classes, which feudalism entailed, and which, forced on them by kings from the twelfth century onward, never won their inner assent. It is still abhorred in its surviving forms.

You should take every chance of speaking to the people, whether in your spare time or in any doubt or difficulty. They will instantly respond, and give you a generous interest and practical help, and give it with a natural courtesy that has been a trait of the Gaelic Scot since earliest known times.

CHAPTER 1

Loch Lomond and Arrochar

Not even the Nile is so thronged by crocodiles as Loch Lomondside. They appear in summer only, crawling in file along the west bank: cars nose to tail northbound to week-end freedom. Three-fifths of Scotland's population live in the Central Lowlands and Loch Lomond is the royal route to the West Highlands. The traveller here should, if he can, avoid Saturday afternoons and Sunday mornings.

The Highland Line stretches north-east across Scotland from the west coast at Loch Lomond's foot to the east at Stonehaven (near Aberdeen). The name is given to the geological boundary caused by a great subsidence, which left the Central Lowlands as a rift valley and the Highland Line as the south base-line of the Grampian mountains—in which Loch Lomond is the best and biggest breach. The loch is also Britain's largest sheet of fresh water, 27½ square miles in a length of 21.

In approaching the West Highlands by road from Glasgow, you have to make a choice of route near Dumbarton. You can fork left for Gare Loch and upper Loch Long, or strike north to Loch Lomond. The Loch Lomond route is shorter, faster, and scenically superior. The route by Gare Loch is in every respect inferior—passing through towns at Dumbarton and Helensburgh, hideously marred at Faslane near Garelochhead by a huge ship-breaking yard and the development of a nuclear submarine base, and at Finnart, Loch Long, by oil tanks. It is worth travelling only for one excellent view. From the hill-top at Whistlefield one can look down upon Loch Goil, the only truly mountainous fiord of Argyll, corkscrewing into the Cowal hills. You should accordingly take the north road, turning sharp left across the river Leven to Alexandria, thus by-passing the town of Balloch to Loch Lomondside.

Loch Lomond discharges into the Clyde estuary by the river

15

Leven, named thus from the loch itself, which was called Leven prior to the thirteenth century. The new name Lomond came from the mountain that dominates every view of the loch—Ben Lomond, 3,192 feet, Scotland's most southerly *Munro* (a title given to 276 separate mountains of 3,000 and over, first listed by Sir Hugh Munro). Few people recognize Loch Lomond for what it is, a seaboard loch. They think of it as inland, enclosed by 2,000-foot hills; at the upper end flanked and ringed by *Munros*: Ben Vorlich, Oss and Dubhcraig, Beinn Chabhair and Ben Lomond. In fact, the loch's foot is only four miles from the sea, and the upper loch one and half miles. At one stage in its history it may well have been a sea-loch, and some 12,000 years ago its site was occupied by a big glacier. The ice helped to scoop out the vast rock-basin in which it now lies: traces of the old moraine may still be seen between Alexandria and Balloch. The water's surface is only 20 feet above sea-level. In the narrow upper section the bottom plummets to 653 feet.

At first the main road north keeps well back from the loch-side. Less than a mile from the Balloch fork a side-road leads to a bear park at Cameron House (signposted). Better access to the shore may be had half a mile farther at Duck Bay, where there is a car-park, picnic site, and an inappropriately sited restaurant. The view shows all lower Loch Lomond. The loch is shaped like a tadpole. The tail, barely a quarter of a mile wide and from here invisible, flicks fifteen miles into the mountains. Where it joins the body near Luss it widens to a mile, the body then swelling to four and a half miles. More than thirty islands dot the surface. Most are tiny, but by good fortune the dozen largest and best wooded are all in the lower part, where most needed, dispelling any monotony of aspect that might have been caused by so great a width of water.

The nearest and largest is Inchmurrin, named from St. Mirren, the patron saint of Paisley Abbey. The ruined castle on its south shore was once the seat of the Earls of Lennox. The five islands stretching beyond it towards Balmaha on the loch's far side, named Creinch, Torrinch, Clairinch, Aber Isle, and Inchcailloch, form a nature Reserve of 600-odd acres, which includes a part of the mainland shore south of Endrick Water. Inchcailloch once had a nunnery and church, both now abandoned. All are thickly wooded in oak. The Reserve is famous for its wintering wildfowl. Autumn brings a big invasion by wigeon, and by other duck including goldeneye, pintail, teal, and scaup. A thousand head of goose fly in, mostly

16

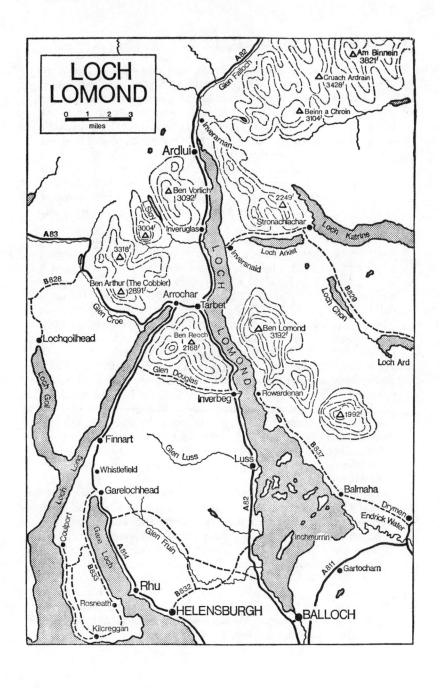

grey lag with a few barnacle, brent, and pink-footed. The great northern diver appears and numerous whooper swan, and grebe, both Slavonian and crested. Among the passing birds of prey are osprey, marsh-harrier, goshawk, and more rarely a peregrine falcon. A little islet is the only one in Scotland where the capercaillie is known to breed. The slow coils of the Endrick Water and the lagoons of its south shore are rich in aquatic life.

Far behind the isles, Ben Lomond's broad but low brow appears above massive shoulders. The name means Beacon Hill. Even at twelve miles' range it imposes its presence not by raw shape or startling beauty, for it is an old and worn mountain, but by gentle boldness of line and colour.

The banks of Loch Lomond are clothed by deciduous woods. Oak, beech, chestnut, larch, and birch predominate. Caledonian pine and most other coniferous evergreens are present but not much in evidence. Loch Lomond thus appears most colourful in spring and autumn when leaf is either bursting or dying. One of the more enthralling sights of June is the bluebell wood north of Luss, or in May the azaleas and rhododendrons brightening cottage gardens, and in autumn dead bracken, sun-stricken on the hillsides and blazing like a Viking's pyre. These woods of Loch Lomondside are becoming more highly prized as the work of the Forestry Commission, whose appetite for ground is insatiable, spreads a coniferous monotony across the face of Scotland, for broad-leaved trees and hardwoods are not a rewarding crop. That the banks of Loch Lomond have remained so long free from the forester's axe and from impairment by tourist development appears well-nigh miraculous. Their preservation has been due to the rule of enlightened landowners, principally the Colquhouns of Luss, who have sacrificed personal profit.

The Colquhouns (pronounced Cahoons) alone survive among the several clans who once lived and fought around the loch. Their territory extended west to the Gare Loch and Loch Long, and included Helensburgh, which Sir James Colquhoun planned and built in the eighteenth century, and named after his wife. Their notorious neighbours were the Clan Gregor, who held the upper east side from Ben Lomond to Inverarnan in Glen Falloch, and the MacFarlanes, who held the upper west side from Inverbeg at Glen Douglas to Inverarnan. Both were incorrigible cattle-rievers: throughout Loch Lomondside the moon was called 'MacFarlane's Lantern' and the name has lasted to this day. As for the MacGregors, their name became a byword for brigandage. Their ill-repute came to a climax in 1603, when they raided Glen Fruin (after an attack by the Colquhouns). This glen runs westward into the hills at Arden, just a mile beyond Duck Bay. Two roads now give access with a fork to Helensburgh. In the upper glen the MacGregor force slaughtered nearly three hundred Colquhouns in battle, then plundered the fatter lands around Luss. Colquhoun led two hundred and twenty widows before James VI at Stirling. In their hands they carried the bloody clothing of their dead men. The outraged king outlawed the Clan Gregor, proscribed their very name, and forfeited their lands forever, both here and at the head of Loch Awe.

A hundred years later the MacGregors were still on the warpath, ironically enough in support of Stewart kings, who having outlawed them were now outlawed in turn. In the Jacobite rising of 1715 the MacGregors seized all boats on Loch Lomond and raided up and down the shores. A warship had to be sent to the Clyde, but by the time the sweating seamen had dragged small boats up the river Leven to the loch, the MacGregors had vanished into the hills.

A mile and a half beyond Arden you pass the great iton gates ol Rossdhu House (open to the public), the home of Sir Ivar Colquhoun. Two miles farther the road turns at last to the edge of the loch and thenceforward becomes one of the two or three most beautiful highways of all Scotland. The very twists that madden the road-hog are an essential part of its excellence. Let us pray that they may never be made straight.

At **Luss**, peacocks may be admired in a house-garden facing the Colquhoun Arms Hotel, but you turn past these down a side road, for the village between the main road and the shore is the prettiest of West Scotland. It was just a miserable collection of huts in 1850, when it was rebuilt by the Colquhouns. The mellow stone of the cottages is covered in climbing roses. A narrow strip of sand edges the gentle curve of the bay. Offshore lie the main mass of wooded islands. The nearest, Inchlonaig, was planted with yew trees by Robert the Bruce to provide bows for his archers. The derelict pier is no longer visited by the paddle-steamer *Maid of the Loch*, which daily in summer (May to September inclusive) sails from Balloch to the head of the loch, calling en route at Balmaha, Rowardennan, Tarbet and Inversnaid. This sail is the best way of enjoying Loch Lomond. It is seen whole and in greater beauty than by road. Ideally, it should thus be seen first, and the detail by road later.

Three miles north of Luss, Inverbeg Hotel at Glen Douglas provides a ferry service across the loch to **Rowardennan** (more usually approached by road up the far side). Rowardennan is the starting point for the ascent of Ben Lomond. With the possible exception of Ben Nevis, it is the most frequently climbed and popular mountain of Scotland, and one of the few with a path all the way to the top. The gradients are easy, the distance four miles, and the time needed between two and three hours according to pace. Being so near the Highland Line the summit is the best vantage point of the Southern Highlands. It allows unusually wide views far across the Lowland plain to Tinto Hill in Lanarkshire, to Stirling and the Forth estuary, and south-west across the many arms of the Firth of Clyde to the Arran hills, to Kintyre and Jura, even to the Atlantic beyond. Forty-five miles away to the north, the broad back of Ben Nevis emerges from a turmoil of mountains like a whale from a stormy sea. Close below, Loch Lomond gleams placidly, silver grey, or blue, or black as gun-metal.

Loch Lomond offers good fishing. Boating, dinghy-sailing, canoeing, and water skiing are centred at the southern end around Balloch; at Rowardennan the Scottish Youth Hostels Association organizes canoeing courses. Swimming in the loch is dangerous and many people have been drowned. One expert swimmer recently had a narrow escape after a long and exhausting struggle with a gigantic eel, which had wrapped itself around his body. The fish of the loch are brown trout, sea-trout, salmon, perch, and pike. The pike are numerous and grow to a great size—one of 74 lb, has been caught. They make heavy killings of duckling and thin out the trout. A rare fish, peculiar to this loch and to Loch Eck in Cowal, is the powan, called 'a fresh water herring' but closely allied to the salmon, which perhaps became landlocked many thousands of years ago.

Good walks may be enjoyed on the region's innumerable tracks. One of the more delightful goes from Rowardennan fourteen miles along a path through woodland to Inverarnan Hotel in Glen Falloch. At the half-way mark is **Inversnaid Hotel,** where a road strikes in from Loch Katrine. This is the old MacGregor country and is now as it was then, a place of refuge. By the shore three-quarters of a mile north is Rob Roy's cave, which had been used before him, for one night only, by Robert the Bruce in 1306. The MacGregors met there before raids. The old fort at Inversnaid, on top of the hill-road near Loch Arklet, had to be built in 1717 to try to subdue them: vain hope—Rob Roy surprised and sacked it.

Loch Lomond and Arrochar

When Wordsworth stayed at Inversnaid in August 1803, he unluckily saw the ferryman's daughter, that 'sweet Highland girl' the vision of whom incited one of his worst poems. In 1881, Gerard Manley Hopkins was able to make a truer response. The opening couplet of his *Inversnaid* depicts accurately the falls of Arklet Water:

> *The darksome burn, horseback brown,*
> *His rollrock highroad roaring down . . .*

The last two stanzas would be true of any Loch Lomond hillside on a summer's morning:

> *Degged with dew, dappled with dew,*
> *Are the groins of the braes the burn treads through.*
> *Wiry heathpacks, flitches of fern,*
> *And the beadbonny ash that sits over the burn.*

> *What would the world be, once bereft*
> *Of wet and of wildness? Let them be left,*
> *O let them be left, wildness and wet;*
> *Long live the weeds and the wilderness yet.*

Back at the west side of the loch, you may notice by the roadside a mile north of Inverbeg a signpost to the 'Fairy Loch'. The route goes steeply uphill through woods to a lochan at 600 feet. In its delicate green water, tradition alleges that fairies wash their clothes. The walk can be enjoyable in fine weather.

North of Inverbeg, the now violently twisting road straightens into **Tarbet** village. The name Tarbet, in its more usual spelling of Tarbert, will often be found on the west coast. It means a neck of land over which ships can be dragged from sea to sea. At this isthmus the head of Loch Long lies only one and a half miles to the west. The name Tarbet is here historically apt. In 1263 King Hakon made his last effort to assert Norwegian suzerainty over the Scottish islands. He sailed with a fleet of 120 ships to the Firth of Clyde. While waiting for Alexander III, the young King of Scots (then aged 22) to come either to terms or to battle, he sent his son-in-law Magnus with forty ships up Loch Long (the Ship Loch) to Arrochar, whence he dragged some of his galleys across the Tarbet isthmus to Loch Lomond. Luss and several of the inhabited islands were then ravaged by fire and sword. At the end of September the forces of Scotland and Norway met at Largs on the Ayrshire coast. The land-battle went to the Scots. Violent storms damaged the

Norse fleet, forcing Hakon to withdraw to the Orkneys, where he died in December. In 1266 the Hebrides were ceded to Scotland.

At Tarbet you have your best view of Ben Lomond, whose head has become a steeply pointed pyramid. The seven miles of Loch Lomond beyond Tarbet are less excellent scenically, for the hills crowd too close. At Inveruglas four big pipelines run down the hillside to a powerhouse faced with pre-cast slabs of Aberdeen granite. It faces the Clan MacFarlane's old castle on Inveruglas Isle, which they occupied until it was sacked by Oliver Cromwell. They used to keep their stolen cattle behind Ben Vorlich in the hidden corrie of Loch Sloy, which is now dammed.

If you ask permission from the office adjoining the powerhouse, you may be allowed to drive your car up the glen to **Loch Sloy** at 800 feet. The dam, 1,160 feet long and 160 feet high, was opened in 1950. The catchment area between the heads of Loch Fyne and Loch Lomond covers 32 square miles of mountain, from which water is diverted to Loch Sloy by numerous tunnels and aqueducts. The Clan MacFarlane's ancient battle-cry, *Loch Sloy!* might now well be appropriated by the North of Scotland Hydro-electric Board.

Among the wildlife of Loch Lomondside, the animals and birds most likely to be seen by the roadside are roe-deer, grey squirrel, pheasant, jay, and owl. There used to be red squirrels, but these were driven off by the American grey squirrel, a single pair of which were released at Loch Long in 1890 and have since spread across the hills. Fallow deer swim from island to island.

Glen Falloch, rising into the mountains at the head of the loch, gives the pass into Perthshire and to north Argyll and is an integral part of the Loch Lomond basin. Beyond Ardlui it enters Perthshire at Inverarnan, landmarked by the Grey Mare's Tail where the Ben Glas Burn foams down a cliff on the hill-flank. The old hotel there, white-washed in the best Highland tradition and set among natural woods on the bank of the river Falloch, is in season a head-quarters for climbers and skiers. The hills close around are the province of the walker, but an hour's run in a car brings the rocks of Glencoe and the ski-slopes of Ben Lawers and the Black Mount within reach.

From Inverarnan, the road climbs steeply up the glen, rising from near sea-level to 600 feet. The Falls of Falloch lie a third of the way up. Unsuccessful attempts were once made to blast them to allow fish a passage to the upper reaches. If the river is in spate the falls are worth inspection. A mile beyond them, a straggling rank of old Scots pines on the east side is one of the last remnants of the ancient Caledonian forest. The crossing of the pass often brings one into a weather system different from that operating southward; the rapidity of change can be startling. The northward descent falls to Strath Fillan.

Bound not for the north, but for south Argyll, I now return you to Tarbet and move west to **Arrochar** at the head of Loch Long. The village nestles under a range of mountains known as the Arrochar Alps: the Cobbler, Ben Narnain, Beinn Ime, and others close to or above 3,000 feet. Most eye-catching by far is the Cobbler, 2,891 feet, whose wildly broken crest of mica-schist has made Arrochar a popular rock-climbing centre. The mountain's official name, Ben Arthur, is long obsolete, but still appears on maps. There is written record that the name Cobbler was used by the local people as early as 1799 in its Gaelic form *An Greasaiche Cròm*, meaning The Crooked Shoemaker, because the rock of the north top overhangs, appearing (by a stretch of imagination) like a cobbler bowed over his work.

The village has several hotels, a railway station, camping and caravan sites, a youth hostel, and a pier. An ugly torpedo-testing station of the Royal Navy mars the west shore. On rounding the head of Loch Long you pass from Dunbartonshire into Argyll and enter the Argyll National Forest Park, which extends south through Cowal to the Holy Loch. Two miles south at Ardgartan, the road swings west into **Glen Croe**. Ardgartan has good camping and caravan sites run by the Forestry Commission, and a youth hostel. Ponies may be hired for trekking on the hills behind which have 25 miles of forest roads and rides. Visitors on foot or pony are encouraged to explore, but not to leave the confines of the tracks until above the plantations. In order to follow this maze of track, it is best to buy a local guide book at Arrochar.

Glen Croe, lifting in four miles to the saddle between Beinn Ime and Beinn an Lochain at 860 feet, is one of the most important hill-passes of Argyll. It leads to the principal county towns, to the open coast, and to the ports for the southern Hebrides. The old road, which runs below the new in the bed of the glen, was one of the many highland tracks reconstructed by the Army under General Caulfeild after the Jacobite rising of 1745. It is still used annually for motor-car trials, for the upper section mounts a long steep hill to a bad hairpin bend near the top. The pass was named Rest and Be

The Companion Guide to the West Highlands of Scotland

Thankful from a stone seat thus inscribed, which has now vanished.

The new road, cut along the north flank of the Cobbler and Beinn Ime, is easily graded. The lower hill-flanks are wooded heavily in Sitka and Norway spruce, but their upper halves rise clear to craggy summits. The long narrow crest of the pass, flanked by Beinn Ime to the east and Beinn an Lochain to the west, is in winter the windiest pass crossed by road in West Scotland. In north-west gales the wind can be funnelled to a blast of enormous velocity, which has overturned heavy lorries and forced buses off the road. From Rest and Be Thankful a still higher road-pass forks south-west to Loch Goil in Cowal. The main road carries straight on to Loch Fyne. The official boundary of Argyll may be set farther back at Loch Long, but geographically, this pass is the threshold.

CHAPTER 2

Cowal

Cowal, a hilly and riven peninsula thirty-two miles long, divides Loch Fyne from the Clyde estuary. Three minor peninsulas form its south coast; they appear on the map like a trident poised above Bute, as though that island were a salmon about to be gaffed. The Island of Bute, politically a separate county, is virtually a part of Cowal, from which the narrowest of straits divide it. Around this south coast lie the townships of Dunoon, Innellan, Tighnabruaich, Rothesay, and others, all of which have been developed since the industrial revolution from obscure or even derelict villages to famous Clyde resorts, the holiday homes-from-home of the people of Glasgow and the Clyde valley.

Cowal was the land of Comgal, grandson of King Fergus of Dalriada, hence took his name. The modern pronunciation groups the syllables wrongly as *Cow*-al, when they ought to be Co-*wal*. The traditional approach from Glasgow to south Cowal is by sea and ship. The land-route is over the pass of Rest and Be Thankful—and that is the only way to reach north Cowal, which has recently been shorn of its steamer service to Loch Goil.

From the summit of the pass, a secondary road climbs south-west over a still higher saddle at 983 feet between Beinn an Lochain and Ben Donich. From there it twists steeply down Gleann Mor (Great Glen), at the same time taking a full semi-circular sweep around Ben Donich to arrive on the flats of the river Goil, which it follows to the head of **Loch Goil** on Cowal's east coast. There is no through road, but the end is sufficient in itself, for Loch Goil is the most beautiful sea-loch of Cowal or the Clyde coast.

The Great Glen above Loch Goil is Y-shaped. The other, lefthand branch is Gleann Beag (Small Glen) always called Hell's Glen. It leads to Loch Fyne, from which it gives an alternative route to Loch Goil, and this route is lower (719 feet) with easier gradients.

Despite the ominous name it affords a surer winter route when Gleann Mor is blocked by snow-drifts.

High up in Gleann Mor the hill-flanks are planted in Sitka spruce, but lower down at the fork of the Y, natural oak-woods lighten and relieve the scene. Below the fork the glen widens to a wooded strath, and by strath and lochside the hills are planted in big clumps of larch, pine, spruce and cypress, the clumps mixed in irregular patterns free of straight lines or 'regimentation'. Here is the finest example of landscape planting to be seen along the entire western seaboard of Scotland. The same discrimination and judgment is not seen again in the Argyll National Forest Park. But there is no reason why it should not be repeated in future, if only the officers of the Commission would take thought.

At the head of Loch Goil the road forks down either side, one branch to Lochgoilhead village (east bank), the other six miles down the west shore to Carrick Castle, where it ends. Loch Goil (from Gobhal meaning Fork) is a branch of Loch Long. It takes an elegant twist through beautifully wooded hills of 2,000 feet, which on the east side form the broad spine of Ardgoil peninsula. The skull is Ben Donich, rising in one clear sweep to 2,774 feet at the head of the loch. The spine trailing south is knobbly with great outcrops of mica-schist. This rough and bumpy range is called Argyll's Bowling Green, a name often wrongly ascribed to the Gael's ironic humour. It derives in fact from a Lowland jocularity in mistranslating the Gaelic Buaile na Greine, meaning Sunny Cattle Fold, a name originally applied not to the rugged crest but to a grazing ground on the south-east side above Mark.

From the fifteenth to twentieth centuries the whole of central and northern Cowal was Campbell country. When the Campbells of Loch Fyne used to travel to their castle at Rosneath, built in 1803 at the mouth of the Gare Loch, or in earlier days drove cattle south to the Clyde, they used not the Rest and Be Thankful but the much shorter route through Hell's Glen to Lochgoilhead, thence across the Ardgoil peninsula by a route still called the Duke's Pass (immediately to the south of the Saddle, 1,704 feet) to Mark on Loch Long. From Mark they ferried across to the Rosneath isthmus. The names Buaile na Greine and Hell's Glen both arose from their use of the route over a period of five hundred years. Hell's Glen, being a steep-sided defile, was approved by the MacFarlanes of Loch Lomond, and no doubt by other tribes with small love for the Campbells, to be a good place for attempting an ambuscade.

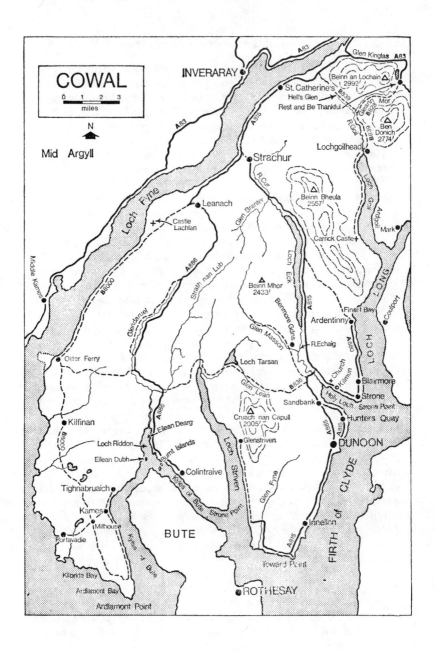

In 1905 the Ardgoil estate of 15,000 acres was bought by Lord Rowallan and donated to Glasgow Corporation as a place of recreation for the citizens. In 1965, after large annual losses, Glasgow feued the ground to the Forestry Commission. The transfer of interest has most unhappily brought the closure of the pier, which had for generations been served by Clyde steamers.

No record survives of the early settlement at **Lochgoilhead**, formerly called Kinlochgyll. The modern houses, extending a mile down the east shore, were built in Victorian days for Glasgow business men. The main village clusters at the head of the loch and is still expanding. Its ancient, white-washed church has first mention in papal records of 1405, and more importantly in 1442 when it was named as the 'Church of the Three Holy Brethren at Kinlochgyll'. The original church would be very much older, traditionally of the seventh century. The dedication is thought to be to three Irish saints, sons of Nessian, who appear in the Drummond Calendar. The walls now standing date in different parts from medieval time to the nineteenth century. The Campbells of Ardkinglas have been buried here since around 1400. A right of way from the churchyard leads into the garden of the doctor's house, where an obelisk sundial, carved in red stone and dated 1626, stands ten feet high on an elegant shaft and stepped plinth. The shaft and its bulged octagonal capital, topped by a slender pyramid, are curiously hollowed with bowls, cups, and hearts. Several metal gnomons formerly projected at right-angles from the faces, and their broken-off stumps can still be seen, but no one now knows how the dial was read. The shaft bears a shield and the intials of Sir Colin Campbell and his wife (Helen Maxwell) who had a manorhouse at Lochgoilhead, presumably at this site. A dozen obelisk sundials survive in other parts of Scotland. They rank among the most important monumental works of art bequeathed to the country by seventeenth-century sculptors. The Loch Goil specimen is one of the best.

The road down the west side of the loch passes through a long stretch of land that was luckily kept out of the hands of the Forestry Commission until 1966, and thus still allows a glimpse of open farmfields, bare hillsides, and natural birch and oak woods: but their good appearance has now been impaired by a too large and ugly caravan park. Half-way down the loch you pass Douglas Pier, a small naval base for testing submarines. Loch Goil is forty fathoms deep, steep-sided, with a bottom free of obstruction, and therefore suitable for underwater runs. At **Carrick Castle** the road ends. The little village behind the castle is busy and popular in summer: it enjoys a more open, sunny position than Lochgoilhead, a slightly lower rainfall, and a superior view out past the old castle and up Loch Goil, where the hills recede in craggy ranges.

Carrick Castle, standing four-square on a rock by the shore, dates from the fifteenth century or earlier. Although a ruin, having lost its roof and interior floors, the walls are intact. They are the home now of white fantailed doves, whose burbling moan and high-winged glide are here unique among the castles of the west. From the first floor level a stair runs up within the hollow east wall on to the battlements. To reach its start from the ground floor one must climb ten feet up the wall on good holds; the stair if attained is sound, and the view from the battlements better than any other castle of Cowal. The name Carrick is a corruption of Carraig, a Gaelic word for Rock, on which the castle stands above deep water. It was originally isolated, an islet rock reached by drawbridge. The natural moat has long since been filled in and grassed.

The castle was built, perhaps by Argyll who became its keeper, as a hunting seat for Stewart kings—most likely for James IV, who in Cowal hunted wild boar. Quick of foot and tusked, it was dangerous game. It became extinct in Britain when the last boar was killed in Cowal around 1690. At Carrick Castle the Campbells interned political prisoners. In 1651 it was garrisoned and fortified by Archibald, the eighth earl, to resist an unexpected siege by Cromwell, while Campbell held out in Inveraray Castle for nearly a year. Carrick's downfall came in 1685. Archibald, the ninth earl, was then leading an invasion of Scotland in support of the Duke of Monmouth against James II. He sailed from Holland to his castle at Dunstaffnage, near Oban, and raised a few thousand of his clansmen, but the response to his fiery cross was not good (clansmen would not rise against the Stewarts); his naval attacks on the mainland were beaten off, and he had to take refuge at another of his castles on Loch Riddon in south Cowal. Ousted from there by the Royal Navy, he was finally captured near Renfrew and beheaded at Edinburgh. Meanwhile, Argyll was invaded by the Murrays of Atholl, acting for the Crown. Under John Murray, the Marquis of Atholl, they thoroughly devastated all Campbell country, reducing their strongholds of which Carrick Castle was one of many. It was never restored.

Loch Goil is not, like the Cowal shore of Loch Fyne, noted for its seals. Instead, heron, eider duck and red-breasted merganser abound. The herons are usually seen singly, fishing off the rocky shores, but flocks of ten may take the air briefly and I have counted twenty-seven crowded on pine-tops. In summer, schools of rollicking porpoise chase herring, sometimes with common seal in attendance. In the winter of 1965 the loch was much frequented by a big white whale—a white not creamy but as cold as quartzite. In late summer the water livens with leaping salmon, which move up the river Goil on the flood. No sooner are the pools full than they are blown by poachers from Glasgow using carbide. Despite this, good angling may be had on occasion. The Forestry Commission controls permits.

The hills of Loch Goil, bridged only by high passes and trenched to either side by lochs, retain an undisturbed wildness. Wild cat are numerous (for their rare species), the golden eagle builds an eyrie on the flank of Ben Bheula (2,557 feet), the peregrine falcon nests on crags above the river Goil, and buzzards abound, drawn by the voles that breed in young forests. Small herds of red deer graze on Argyll's Bowling Green, and roe-deer in the Carrick woods, from which they emerge in hard winters to raid house-gardens at the lochside.

To explore the rest of Cowal you must first go north through Hell's Glen. On crossing the first bridge of its river you will see on the left-hand side of the road a large rock, from which water spurts through the mouth of a bronze lion's head. Known as Moses' Well (from his striking of the biblical rock), it was contrived last century by a local minister. The descent from the pass gives a clear view of Inveraray set in its little bay on the far side of Loch Fyne. At the junction with the old main road to Dunoon, a heart-shaped ring of white quartzite stones at the crown of the road is the Wedding Ring of the Argyll tinkers. When the road was first laid with tarmac they asked the county's road engineers to preserve the ring at which they still held marriages. This was done and the agreement has been honoured ever since. The site is omitted by the new main road made in 1967.

The whole eastern fringe of Loch Fyne down to Ardlamont point is wilder ground than the west side and the villages are accordingly smaller and fewer. From the first, St. Catherines, a ferry used to cross the loch to Inveraray directly opposite, but this service was withdrawn in 1964. A few miles farther, **Strachur** is the largest village of the coast. The Cowal hills at this point are split from coast to coast by a continuous valley with Strachur at one end and **Dunoon** at the other. Midway between stretches the largest freshwater loch of Cowal, Loch Eck, preceded and followed by broad straths. The upper strath, threaded by the river Cur, gives Strachur its name, although the village is set well back on the Loch Fyne side of the low pass between loch and river. The heart of the village is thus not at the lochside, where there are none the less numerous houses and the Creggans Hotel, which has a deservedly high reputation. In a wooded park close to its south is Strachur House, built in 1783 by General John Campbell. The estate and house (and Creggans Hotel) were bought by Sir Fitzroy Maclean in 1957. The Campbells of Strachur, who once lived at Succoth by the river Cur, are of different family from the Campbells of Succoth living at Crarae (see page 69) where they created their famed garden.

The oldest family of Cowal still occupying their home ground are the MacLachlans of **Castle Lachlan**, six miles south of Strachur. There was once a Norse settlement here and the name MacLochlainn means Son of the Norseman. The road goes inland for a few miles through Strathlachlan to rejoin the coast beyond. The strath is heavily wooded. A mile-long line of mature beech shades the road and partially screens the castle, which stands on a promontory by a sandy bay of Loch Fyne. Although ruinous, much of it still survives, beautifully set on green fields between wood and water. The modern house of the family is the big one half a mile inland. The MacLachlans have held these lands for seven hundred years—long before the Campbells found footing in Cowal. The fifteenth chief had the courage to answer the summons of Prince Charles Edward in 1745, and to take with him 250 fighting men, despite Campbell of Argyll's near presence and hostility. His successor, discreetly anti-Jacobite, was re-granted the forfeited estate. The present owner is the twenty-fourth chief.

The south-going road, narrow, twisting, and well-wooded in scrub oak and birch, holds closely to the shore for nine miles to **Otter Ferry**. Thereafter it climbs high away from the sea, not to rejoin it again till it falls to Ardlamont at the end of the peninsula. Otter Ferry marks the narrows between upper and outer Loch Fyne, which now widens to nearly four miles. There is no longer a ferry, only a derelict pier, a few houses, and a hill-road striking east across moors to Loch Riddon at the head of the Kyles of Bute. This side-road is important to the people of Ardlamont in that it gives a short-cut to Dunoon. Apart from such practical consideration, it is a road to be followed: the view from the bare summit at 1,000 feet is the best of the Cowal coast, extending west to the Hebrides at

Jura and Scarba. In the foreground, now far below, Loch Fyne is patterned by islands and sculptured along its farther shore by Loch Gilp and Loch Gair. The towns of Ardrishaig and Lochgilphead at the head of the former, plain to unprepossessing as they are at close-quarters, seem from here like the purlieus of paradise. Loch Gair close to their north is mantled by fields of bright green and crowned as if by halo with the shine of Loch Glashan nestling in a hill-corrie 300 feet above. Between the two inlets of Gilp and Gair, and beyond the rolling backs of their hills, the Sound of Jura flashes whitely, dimmed by sixteen intervening miles, like a river of soft light washing celestial islands. I have watched the scene in wild weather, when clouds raced overhead trailing curtains of rain, and wind flattened the grasses of the desolate moor, and found it no less splendid.

The Ardlamont road continues south through alternating farm-land, woodland, and moorland. The farms, as everywhere in Cowal, are mostly sheep farms, using only a few acres of arable ground for root-crops, and raising cattle on the side. Afforestation grows year by year in importance as more hill-farms are bought by the Forestry Commission, whose activities are putting a check on depopulation. After passing through the village of Kilfinan the switchback road climbs to 500 feet over heather-red moors, which give an unexpected view of the Arran mountains, then falls to a cross-roads at Millhouse. The choice offered is east to the Kyles of Bute, west to Portavadie, or south to Ardlamont peninsula. Southward the farmland sprawls wider and the coast grows much more interesting at several sandy bays. Some of these can be reached at once if you take the road to Portavadie.

Portavadie faces Tarbert across Loch Fyne. Its dozen houses are now mostly holiday cottages rented by townspeople, whose delight is in low heathery hills, wooded glens by the sea, and the small sandy bays to north and south of Glenan and Asgog. Offshore islets teem with gulls, on the nearer rocks bask seals; several pairs of eider paddle the water between, their low *oo-oooee* sounding a perfect counterpoint to cuckoos calling from the birchwoods. Prehistoric man has left his mark in a vitrified fort by the shore near Glenan and standing stones on the lonely moorland track to Asgog Bay. Portavadie has recently become the site of a yard for the construction of concrete oil-production platforms. This has destroyed the region's former character.

Travelling south from Millhouse, you come again to the coast a

Kilbride Bay, known locally as Osda Bay from the name of its river. The beach is a big one by Argyll mainland standards—a sweep of sand three-quarters of a mile wide. Flat grassland backs it, but the side arms are moorland and birch-scrub. Access to the beach is not from the nearest point on the road (200 yards) but a mile back at Kilbride Farm, where there is a parking place beside the church. The beach road is marked *Private—no motor cars—privilege of entry on foot granted*. The beach and farm belong to Ardlamont House, and the discipline maintained from there rewards everyone with a clean shore.

Next down the coast comes **Ardlamont Bay**. It has much sand but a beach too open and featureless to entice sun- and sea-bathers. On the hillside above, Ardlamont House hides itself behind a screen of broad-leaved trees and rhododendron thickets. This ground formerly belonged to Clan Lamont, who gave their name to the peninsula. Their territory covered the whole of south Cowal from the Holy Loch to Otter Ferry.

Ardlamont Point, a huge grassy bluff, projects south into the Sound of Bute. Four great waterways there diverge: Loch Fyne, the Kyles of Bute, the main channel of the Firth of Clyde, and Kilbrannan Sound, whose wide stream is seen opening out between the Cock of Arran and Skipness Point of Kintyre. These wide seas and great islands make a spacious seascape in fine weather, in contrast to the more confined delights of the narrow Kyles to which you now turn.

The road passes east through the policies of Ardlamont House on to farmland, thence up the Kyles between a stony shore and scrubby moorland. During the second World War all the inhabitants of Ardlamont peninsula were evacuated and the ground given over to 25,000 British and American soldiers, who were in training for the Normandy invasion of 1944. Unlike so many other training areas along the Highland seaboard, no ugly huts and concrete emplacements remain to offend the eye, but this coast does still have a derelict air, which vanishes only when you enter the township of Tighnabruaich.

Tighnabruaich (pronounced Tinnabrooach), meaning the House on the Hill, may be approached more directly from Millhouse. Its south end merges with two other villages, Auchenlochan and Kames, whose piers are now disused. Kames seems dull, quite overshadowed by her sister villages, which are really one. Tighnabruaich is the most beautiful village of the Clyde. It is relatively sheltered within the Kyles. Tropical plants flourish in the open, as in many other pats of Cowal and Bute. The hills cradling Tighnabruaich, and the low, uninhabited hills of Bute so close across the water, are in spring smoothly green, in late summer purpled by heather, coppery gold in autumn: at all times craggy with outcropping rock, wild yet gentle. The sea-front houses are not arrayed in a long single line, as in so many Cowal resorts; the siting pattern is broken, broken too by large clumps of trees of varied species, which spread up the hill to the heather-line, and by differing designs of house, mostly of stone, sometimes painted. At the north end they look down the Firth of Clyde to the high hills of Arran. The village may be the best of its kind in Cowal, but fortunately not everyone will want to stay here. It lacks the play-amenities of the bigger Clyde resorts. Tighnabruaich is quiet. Only its waters are busy, for it is a most popular sailing centre. Even in the off-season one may expect to see a dozen white or coloured sails out on the Kyle, which in mid-summer can look crowded.

From Tighnabruaich a road made in 1969 goes seven miles north up Loch Riddon to Glendaruel, where it joins the Dunoon road. Above Tighnabruaich it rises to 614 feet, where lay-bys give excellent views over the Kyles of Bute to the Arran hills and Ayrshire coast. You may also walk up Loch Riddon by the shore. A footpath leaves Port Driseach by the yacht-yard, rounds the point of Rudha Bàn, then goes through birchwoods facing the north point of Bute. On the hillside there you can see the two Maids of Bute—boulders painted to resemble two old women. They appear on all maps, for the paintwork has been renewed throughout the present century. By whom it was started and maintained is something of a mystery, for north-western Bute is uninhabited.

As you approach the great bend of the Kyles, **Loch Riddon** opens out to the north, forming the shaft of an inverted Y. At the mouth lies the craggy Eilean Dubh (Black Isle), bearing two stands of conifer, which seen against the light from Loch Riddonhead look exactly like a castle. Until recent years there was a castle on the shore facing Eilean Dubh named Glen Caladh Castle, which still appears on the maps although now demolished. The Forestry Commission have a wildlife centre here with photo-safari hides where roe-deer, Soay sheep, ducks, and blue hares may be observed.

Within Loch Riddon, Eilean Dearg (Red Isle) bears the ruin of a more famous castle, an ancient Campbell stronghold, which fell in the same year as Carrick. When Archibald, the ninth earl, arrived off the Scottish coast in support of Monmouth, and found that he was failing to raise the country, he sailed into Loch Riddon and occupied Eilean Dearg. He thought he was safe from the Royal Navy, for Loch Riddon is shallow and the isle screened by a reef. But he underestimated: three warships closed in, the castle was taken, and Argyll fled.

Loch Riddon, Tighnabruaich, Bute, and Dunoon may all be approached by road from upper Loch Fyne down Glendaruel. The Glendaruel road starts at Strathlachlan across brown moorland hills. On the southward descent, woods thicken as larch and beech reinforce the birch, until the narrow glen opens out to a strath. This farmland of standing corn and hay and of root-crops, sheltered by tree-belts, appears like an oasis among the jumbled hills. In the lower strath you pass an old bridge across the river Ruel (where a fork goes west to Otter Ferry). Around this bridge a battle was fought in 1110 between the Scots and invading Norwegians commanded by the son of Magnus Barefoot. The Scots won and threw the bodies of their slaughtered enemies into the river, which, formerly called the Red Water (Ruadh-thuil) from its peatiness, was known ever after as Bloody Water (Ruith-fhuil). The subtle play on words has been lost in the anglicised Glendaruel.

Above the head of Loch Riddon we pass the Dunoon road-fork and continue down the loch to the narrows of the **Kyles of Bute**. The narrows are caused by the Burnt Islands, a cluster of flat-topped islets peppered by heather and stunted trees. Passing steamers almost scrape the barnacles off the rocks, but the true land-narrows are not the islands; they come nearly a mile south at **Colintraive,** a name meaning the Strait of Swimming, where in former days the drovers swum their cattle to and from Bute. Colintraive has a car-ferry, the only one across the Kyles.

The village fills a hollow in the hills where the Milton Burn joins the sea. A couple of dozen houses line a clean stony shore fringed by irises. Green fields slope steeply up to rough hill pasture, giving the site almost oppressive shelter. The southward road is more open, and much quieter since it goes 'nowhere'—just four miles to Strone Point, where it turns the peninsula into Loch Strivenside and ends there among a blaze of yellow whin. The Kyles' shore is beautifully scalloped by small bays haunted by eider-duck—I have counted over a hundred in one of them. Black shags stand sentinel on Strone Point, and swans may be seen flying up Loch Striven, their thrashing wings sounding like a whine of electric dynamos. At Southhall, on the low hills near Strone Point, a sprinkling of trees are all that remain of a once famous wood grown last century by Campbell of Southhall. He had planted the trees in shape of the British and French army formations at Waterloo, at which he had fought. When Norwegian commandos were trained at Southhall during the last war they destroyed the old wood with flame-throwers.

The full scenic excellence of the Kyles of Bute cannot be known from the shores alone. To complete the experience one must sail through them on the steamer from Rothesay or Dunoon.

You have now seen the west and central prongs of the Cowal trident. The eastern or **Dunoon peninsula** is the greatest of all, extending sixteen miles from Loch Goil to Toward Point. The approach from Strachur on Loch Fyne passes at first through the farms of the river Cur. The hill-woods lie well back and the valley-woods are no heavier than shelter-belts. Then the strath narrows to a glen, the packed conifers of the Forestry Commission close in, and you enter the most densely forested part of Cowal.

Glen Branter opens out to your right-hand side, thrusting deep into jungle hills. The Forestry Commission have a new wooden village at the foot of the glen, still pleasantly wooded with deciduous trees, for this was the ground of Glenbranter House, now demolished, where Sir Harry Lauder lived for some years. One mile farther, **Loch Eck** fills a deep, six-mile trough between hills of 2,000 feet. The hills being so heavily wooded in spruce and pine seem very dark, and the loch, just 400 yards wide, gloomy except in bright weather. Along the roadside the Forestry Commission have retained a narrow belt of birch, rowan, and sycamore, and to this mercy the western hills add their own cleanly craggy tops, which rise to 2,433 feet on Beinn Mhor.

A third of the way down the loch, at Whistlefield Hotel, a side-road strikes east over the hills to Ardentinny on Loch Long, then down the coast to Dunoon. On this excursion you rise rapidly to 500 feet through pine forest, which being young is not yet overpowering. The pass is bare ground newly planted. On the far side Glen Finart falls to small farms, the conifers withdraw to the hillslopes, and broad-leaved trees lighten the flat floor. At Finart Bay the glen spreads wide on the fields of Glenfinart House, whose Forest Nursery comprises 42 acres with an annual production of seven million plants. They are used throughout the United Kingdom to plant an annual 2,500 acres of land. The nursery is open to the public.

At the south point of the bay, Ardentinny is a clean, neat village of stone-built and white-washed cottages. They line both sides of a twisting road, hotel at centre, and look straight across Loch Long to Coulport on the Rosneath peninsula. Since 1966, Coulport has been 'developed' as an armament depot for Polaris missiles. The odd-looking framework overhanging the shore is an Admiralty launching chute for testing torpedoes. In happy contrast to this ugliness, woods clothe the hills behind you, palm trees grow in the gardens, cattle graze on the flanking fields, and swans paddle off the shingly sea-front.

Three miles down the loch you enter **Blairmore, Strone,** and **Kilmun,** once separate villages, which like other Clyde resorts now form an unbroken line. All three have piers, but Strone is no longer used. The ribbon development typical of the Clyde coast began last century as prospering Glasgow business men built summer villas along the shores. It has been most fortunate that such development was not deferred to the present day, but occurred when money had value and architects imagination. The potential disaster avoided is made plain at Blairmore, where a new extension northward, all pebble-dash on match-box, appears nasty and (however expensive) cheap in its very uniformity.

Blairmore extends to Strone Point, Strone turns the corner into the Holy Loch, and there Kilmun takes over nearer the head. The houses are big, many have the stone painted, and all display fine gardens. The Holy Loch runs two miles into the land, where it receives the outflow of Loch Eck. The wooded hills to either side are grass-covered to their tops, but those circling the head rise much higher and wilder. The loch is divided into outer and inner halves by Graham's Point (between Strone and Kilmun) and by White Farlane Point on the far side. In the inner loch near Kilmun pier is moored the American depot ship for nuclear-powered submarines, one or two of which are usually lying alongside. In close attendance is a big floating pier, and in the outer loch a huge dry dock. Both sides of the loch are lined with houses for this is the most populous part of Argyll with 15,000 inhabitants, two-thirds of whom live in Dunoon.

Kilmun takes its name from St. Mun, a younger contemporary of St. Columba and like him a Gael born in Ireland. His monastery at Kilmun was the first-known Christian building in this part of Cowal, and together with his missionary work it gave the loch the name of Holy. He died in 635. His crosier was held until the sixteenth century by a hereditary custodian, who by virtue of office held hereditary lands at the foot of Loch Eck. Around 1235 the monks were granted a charter by Clan Lamont, then pre-eminent in Cowal, for the Campbells were only beginning to emerge from obscurity at Loch Aweside. When Campbell land and power at last extended to the Holy Loch, Sir Duncan Campbell founded there a Collegiate Church in 1442. For nearly a thousand years the community of Kilmun had a career of first importance and usefulness to the people of Cowal. This ended at the Reformation of 1560, when the Collegiate Church was dismantled.

In 1490, Colin, the Earl of Argyll, obtained from James IV a charter raising Kilmun to a burgh, despite which it never functioned as a burgh and the charter lapsed. The Campbells never made Kilmun one of their seats, although they have used it as their burial ground since 1442. The first modern houses were built in 1829 by the famous engineer David Napier, who bought the land from the Campbell family. His houses are called 'the six tea-caddies' from their square design. The new church, built in 1816 of warm grey stone, is of plain design with a tower. Behind it lurks the domed mausoleum of the Campbells of Argyll. The graveyard runs far up into the heavily wooded Kilmun Hill. Close beside the west door stands the ancient, ivy-covered tower of the ruined Collegiate Church. Propped against its north wall are two iron frames, used in the early nineteenth century to secure coffin lids from body-snatchers, who supplied anatomists.

The interior of the new church is excessively dingy and gloomy, but the grounds are immaculate. Those who take interest in tombstones may be puzzled by the inscription *Free for a blast* carved on numerous stones in the old churchyard. The local story is that these commemorate the dead of Clan Clark, who owned the land around Loch Eck. When James IV came as their guest to hunt deer on the slopes of Beinn Mhor, Clark, seeing that his own hounds were over-taking the stag, called them off with a blast of his horn, thus allowing the king's dogs to close in and bring the beast down. The king, moved by Clark's generosity and always of a generous disposition himself, declared, 'Henceforth you are freed of all taxes.' *Free for a blast* thus became the family's motto.

Driving down Loch Eck from Whistlefield, you can see where this incident occurred at Coire an t-Sith (Corrantee), the glen across the loch on the left-hand flank of Beinn Mhor. On the south slope of this same glen is Paper Cave, where the Campbells of Argyll hid their important title deeds and documents at rare crises, notably when Murray of Atholl invaded in 1685. The cave is hidden by trees but one-inch maps mark the site. An islet close offshore, where seagulls nest in spring, was used by the chief's agent when approaching or leaving the cave. He lay hidden there to watch for enemy spies.

A mile south of Loch Eck the **Younger Botanic Gardens** stretch from the river Eachaig to Glen Masson. These woodland gardens of 85 acres were planted between 1889 and 1925 by Mr. H. G. Younger and his father, then donated by the former to the nation in 1925. They are now an outstation of the Royal Botanic Gardens of Edinburgh, who have used them to build up a national collection of rhododendrons. More than two hundred species are represented. Trees and plants from all parts of the world are growing well in the mild damp climate. An exceedingly fine specimen of tree rhododendron (*Arboreum hybrid*) grows on the lawn in front of Benmore House. It should be seen early in June almost hidden under its burden of bright red blossom. Despite the many good things in the garden, it does not compare with Crarae at Loch Fyneside. The most impressive sight of all, not matched in any other west coast garden, is the main avenue of redwoods (*Sequoia gigantea, Wellingtonia*), each more than 100 feet high. A pond full of golden carp lies in the woods to the north.

At the Glen Masson entrance to Benmore are beautifully wrought iron gates, locally known as the 'Golden Gates'. They bear the monogram of James Duncan, who owned the estate before the Youngers and planted 1,000 acres of hill ground. The Golden Gates are a private entrance, not to be used by visitors. In 1925 the mansion house of Benmore was given by Mr. Younger to the Forestry Commission, who used it from 1929 as a foresters' training school. In 1965 it was bought by Edinburgh Corporation, whose Education Committee run it as a residential centre for courses in mountaineering, sailing, and canoeing. It accommodates sixty pupils and their teaching staff. The gardens remain a public property, open daily from 10 a.m. till nightfall.

Less than a mile down the Dunoon road from Benmore, stone-flagged steps lead up the hillside to Puck's Glen, another part of Mr. Younger's Benmore gift. The climb is steep and long, at first through mature forest of pine, larch, cypress, and redwood whose bark is very thick and soft. The trees are well-spaced with rhododendrons between. The path leads to a dome-roofed hut on a hill-top, and then meanders among outcrops of rock festooned with trees and shrubs to the upper, heather-clad slopes. There are many side-paths, small waterfalls, and rustic bridges across the streams. The wood is entrancing in fine weather, gloomily dripping in bad.

Three great glens converge on the flat strath at the head of the Holy Loch. The first holds Loch Eck, the second is Glen Masson, penetrating deep into the Beinn Mhor range, and the third Glen Lean, which gives the westward pass to Loch Striven. In spring, **Glen Masson** is one of the most beautiful glens of Argyll. Its road diverges rightward after you pass the head of Holy Loch, winds through the flats of the river Eachaig, then past the Golden Gates where redwoods again gladden the eye, and finally up a steep and narrow glen. Two and a half miles from the main road the glen levels out again and runs to the foot of Beinn Mhor. Just below this final levelling, where the road takes an abrupt treble bend, the river falls through a gorge and cauldrons, fringed by birch and alder, hazel and rowan. The waterfalls are not high, but the river thunders over them through deep pots, writhes down a twisted rock-gut, and where rock curtains bar the bed from wall to wall, bores through them by underwater arches.

The hillsides are darkened by pine forest, lightened by birch. The glen plunges in V-shape to the Holy Loch, to which you look across crowded tree-tops. As seen from here the glen is peculiarly like a Pyrenean gorge—the same shape of ravine, rock-gorge, and rough, pine-clad hills with bare tops. The likeness extends to the fishing, for the Masson is one of the best rivers of Cowal for salmon and sea-trout.

Glen Lean is likewise wooded on the ascent from Holy Loch, but very bare and bleak on the high middle part, where the west end has been dammed to create Loch Tarsan, which the North of Scotland Hydro-electric Board stocks annually with 3,000 yearling trout. The new power house at the head of Loch Striven is fed by great pipes left exposed on the hillside. It is not a pretty scene. You will leave it without regret to cross moor and bog to Loch Riddon, your pleasure increasing as woodland thickens, especially as you pass through a beechwood avenue to the more spacious farmland of Glendaruel. This region is richly colourful in autumn and gay in spring, for it carries much oak among the beech and birch.

Returning to the **Holy Loch**, you approach Dunoon through Sandbank. Huge corrugated-iron sheds by the shore are the site of Cowal's best-known yacht-yard, which built the America Cup challengers *Sceptre* and *Sovereign*. At Sandbank the road divides. The direct route goes inland by Loch Loskin, which is better for bird-watchers, who will see many wild duck, water-hen, and swan among its waterlilies and reeds, than for anglers, who will catch only pike and eel. The more interesting road goes by the shore round White Farlane Point, marked by a pointed tower of grey stone—a war memorial of 1939-45. A car ferry sails every half hour to Gourock and motor boats cruise to the U.S. depot ship and its Polaris submarines or as far afield as Carrick Castle on Loch Goil. The point is often called Lazaretto Point from a quarantine station of 1807-40, which was built to expose imported cotton to the air and thus to free it of plague-germs before the ships sailed up the Clyde.

The shore road continues through Hunters Quay and Kirn, now simply outlying suburbs of Dunoon. Hunters Quay is named from a former landowner, Robert Hunter, who built the original pier. It became one of the principal yachting centres of the Clyde coast, from which regattas started at summer week-ends. The presence of the American Polaris base has killed all this activity. The Clyde Week, held in July, is one of the great yachting events of the United Kingdom. At Hunters Quay the opening and closing musters made an enthralling sight. Regatta headquarters are now based in successive years on Rothesay, Helensburgh, Largs and Gourock.

Along the sea-front, villas and mansions and cottages, most of the larger now hotels and boarding houses, extend to Dunoon pier and far beyond to Innellan. **Dunoon** is built around a double bay, called East Bay and West Bay, divided by the low headland of Castle Hill. On top of the grassy hillock stands Dunoon Castle, now a mere ruckle of stones; on the point is the pier, originally built by Robert Louis Stevenson's father and uncle, famous for their engineering feat in building the Skerryvore and Dubh Hirteach lighthouses in the Hebrides. The present pier is a later reconstruction. Near it on Alexandra Parade are heated swimming baths.

The best place to view the town is from Castle Hill. The hills behind it are of wholly undistinguished appearance, but they roll spaciously. From East Bay the town has crept up to them half a mile to a height of 200 feet. Dunoon owes its good general appearance largely to a heavy studding of broad-leaved trees. The sea-front has a dignity of building and plan absent in the town behind. The main street is Argyll Street, running parallel to the esplanade

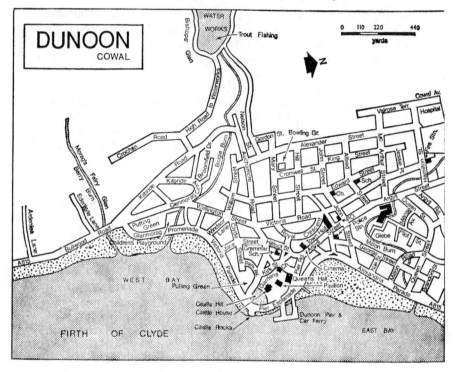

of East Bay. The shops lining its sides sell everything that man on holiday is likely to want.

Seaward, your view is to the famous Cloch lighthouse on the Renfrew coast, where ships (fourteen million tons annually) swing east to the Clyde estuary. Its white, 80-foot column flashes its light fifteen miles south to the mouth of the Firth. Close in to Dunoon, just a few hundred yards off the point, another smaller lighthouse, or red beacon, marks the Gantocks, notorious rocks that have sunk many ships.

The lower slope of Castle Hill carries the bronze statue of Highland Mary. She stands on a red sandstone pedestal and looks down the Firth to Ayrshire, where she and Robert Burns were lovers. Mary Campbell was born in Dunoon at Auchamore Farm. She took service in Ayrshire at Montgomerie, probably as a dairymaid, met and loved Robert Burns with whom she exchanged bibles over

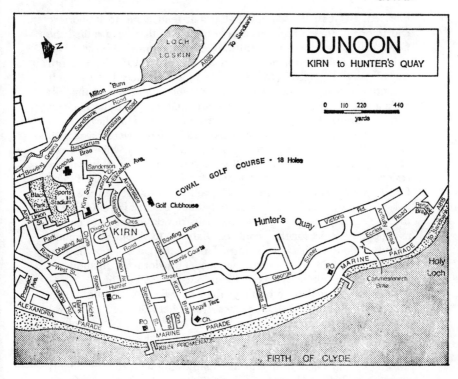

running water (an old Scots marriage rite), but died of a fever at
Greenock while travelling to Dunoon. Burns never forgot her. He
wrote his poem to Mary after he married Jean Armour.

On the grassy crown of Castle Hill only a few stones still stand
to mark the site of a once important fortress. Traditionally there
was a castle here from the early days of the Dalriadan kingdom, but
no date of foundation is recorded. In 1334 Dunoon Castle was
captured by the English, but they were expelled by Robert the
Steward, grandson of Robert the Bruce, who was aided in this
operation by Sir Colin Campbell of Loch Awe. When Robert
came to the throne as the first Stewart king, he named Campbell
hereditary keeper of Dunoon, an appointment fraught with trouble
in land that belonged to Clan Lamont. Feud to the death resulted.
The Campbells settled in. Mary Queen of Scots stayed at the castle
in 1563 while visiting her sister, whom the fifth earl of Argyll had

43

married. In 1646 the Campbell–Lamont feud came to its horrific end in one of these numerous acts of treachery that have sullied the Campbell name down the centuries. The Lamonts' chief seat was only seven miles south of Dunoon at Toward Castle. The eighth earl of Argyll besieged it, failed, and proposed a truce. The Lamonts accepted and let down their defences, whereupon the Campbells sacked the castle, plundered the land, and returned to Dunoon with hundreds of prisoners. On one tree on Castle Hill they hanged the thirty-six leading men of Clan Lamont. The rest were massacred. One feels that Dunoon Castle had earned its doom when Murray of Atholl made an end of it in 1685. He gutted it by fire. It was never restored and a mere vestige remains of what was once called 'The Capital Castle of the Lordship of Cowal'. Following its fall the town fell into sorry state. Its later prosperity and present high standing as the *de facto* capital of Argyll followed its development last century as a holiday resort for the people of Glasgow, to whom, in summer, it truly belongs. The town's normal population is 10,000. In July and August it jumps to above 30,000. This does not include the huge number of holidaymakers living outside the burgh.

West Bay is smaller and quieter than East Bay. A bathing station here has a little sand—the beaches everywhere on the east Cowal coast are shingle or stone, save for one strip of sand at Innellan. At the south end of the bay, Glen Morag on the slope of Kilbride Hill offers wooded paths by small waterfalls. It is now called 'Morag's Fairy Glen' from a local ballad, hung with coloured lights among the branches, and (final degradation) a charge made for admission.

From Dunoon four miles south to **Innellan** the housing strip is almost continuous: any gaps are being closed by further building. This long line of houses is anything but dull. No two are alike, most are large, and this diversity of architecture is displayed amid larger gardens that give Innellan housing a more handsome appearance than other villages of Cowal. Everywhere palms grow. The seashore is rocky. The hills behind carry conifer plantations close to their 1,000-foot summits. The centre of Innellan near the pier suffers from a congestion of small ugly houses, for which the only cure is demolition.

At Toward Point you arrive at the southward tip of the peninsula. The road goes close alongside Toward lighthouse sitting on the last flat rocks. Bute is now only two miles to the south-west. Across its low back rise the Arran mountains and down the Firth the Great and Little Cumbrae. When you move a mile or so farther west below the farmland of Toward Hill you can see into Rothesay Bay, which enthusiastic writers liken to the Bay of Naples. So huge is the difference in scale that such comparison is an absurdity. But if one is thinking simply of grace of line, both of the bay and its background hills, then the miniature is not inferior.

Half-way along the blunt snout of the peninsula, Castle Toward and Toward Castle lie buried among the woods between the lighthouse and Loch Striven. Castle Toward is a mansion-house built in 1832 for the Lord Provost of Glasgow, but now a residential school maintained by Glasgow Corporation for children in need of special care. Each summer, pupils give an admirable musical concert at Dunoon. Within the grounds stand the ivy-shrouded ruin of the Lamonts' old castle, thought to be of the fifteenth century with additions of the seventeenth. It was never re-occupied after the Campbells' rapine of June 1646. One wall of the square tower still stands to full height.

On the west side of the peninsula, **Loch Striven** stretches ten miles into the hills. Its Ardyne Point has been devastated by a big oil-production platform yard. The shore road passes a new N.A.T.O. petrol-storage base with pier and pipes and with tanks buried in the hillside. The south part of Loch Strivenside has the best farmland to be seen on the three Cowal peninsulas; northward the hills rise higher and barer to 2,000 feet on Cruach nan Capull. Their feature in late August is the sweep of heather covering the southerly flanks. Nothing comparable is seen in Cowal and but rarely elsewhere on the west coast, for the greater heather displays are reserved to the Central and East Highlands.

The road ends five miles from Port Lamont near Glenstriven House, but a public footpath continues four miles along the shore to the Dunoon road at the head of the loch. The walk can be recommended. Of all the Cowal sea-lochs, this shore is the least marked by the hand of man. The path is at first wooded by alder, beech, sycamore, and ash, later more exclusively by birch.

Cowal offers satisfactory angling on both loch and river. The principal fishing rivers are the Kinglas, Cur, Ruel, Masson, Little Elchaig, and Goil. The more convenient lochs are the Eck, Tarsan, Restil (on the Rest and Be Thankful), and the reservoirs behind Dunoon. Permits vary in cost from 2/6d to 12/6d per rod.

The great annual event of Cowal is the **Cowal Games** held at Dunoon on the last Friday and Saturday of August. Highland

Games are a feature of every important Highland centre during the summer months. The main events are dancing, piping, and athletics. Chief among the latter are tossing the caber, in which a tree-trunk, often 20-feet long, has to be up-ended and tossed to turn in the air and to fall as far as possible from and in straight line with the thrower; and putting the shot, which long before it became a 'heavy' event at Highland Games was a popular test of strength among young Gaels. They used stones. The Cowal Games, one of the biggest of Scotland's Highland Gatherings, has for its grand finale a march of a thousand pipers.

CHAPTER 3

The Island of Bute

The Island of Bute lies astride the Highland Line, which cuts through it from Rothesay to Scalpsie. The northern two-thirds is thus (in theory) Highland, the southern part Lowland; but the point is academic. The island is Lowland country. It belongs firmly to the lower Firth of Clyde. I add Bute to your Highland journey because it is there: immediately accessible, only five minutes' voyage in a ferry from Cowal.

Sixteen miles long by four wide, Bute tapers at the ends, giving two coasts only, the east and the west. The northern head burrows five miles into Cowal, while the tail lies free on the open sea, its Garroch Head a landmark for Clyde-bound ships. Head and tail are hilly—Windy Hill at the north end is Bute's highest at 911 feet—but in between spreads the belly of the Clyde's most fertile island, swelling grassily to 500 feet, flattening to the cornland of the coastal strips. Sandy bays improve the shore-line. These beaches are rock-sand: Bute has none of the shell-sand with marram dunes and flower-bedecked machair for which the Hebrides are renowned. The distinctive feature of Bute, compared to most Hebridean islands, or to Highland islands close inshore, is the richness of her farmland and her big fields of golden corn.

EAST COAST

Nearly all Scottish islands carry the bulk of their people on the east coast, where the sheltered ports lie. Bute is no exception. Her population is 9,800, most of whom live around the three east coast bays of Kames, Rothesay, and Kilchattan. Rothesay has the lion's share—7,656.

The traditional approach to Bute is by steamer from Wemyss Bay on the Renfrewshire coast. If you come by road you cross the Kyles ferry from Colintraive to Rhubodach at the island's north end. The five-mile stretch of coast leading south to Kames Bay is rough pasture interspersed with green fields and half a dozen farmhouses. The gentle hills are grazed by cattle and sheep. On turning Ardmaleish Point into Kames Bay, Port Bannatyne on its far side confronts you with grey tenement houses. They wear a grim aspect and the shops below them have dull frontages. Their seaward view is across the outer Kyles to the Toward Peninsula, on which the brilliant lights seen at night mark the N.A.T.O. petrol-base and platform yard. The bay is crowded with yachts lying at moorings: sailors prefer to lie off Port Bannatyne rather than Rothesay, which they find plagued by steamers. In contrast to the grey town, the bay's head shines emerald in broad fields; bordered, backed, and divided by lines of trees. On this ground stands Kames Castle, and four hundred yards to its north the seventeenth-century keep of Wester Kames.

Kames Castle was built in the fourteenth century by the Bannatyne family, who came from Ayrshire around 1220. They lived in Kames Castle for five hundred years and built Port Bannatyne early last century. Their castle and lands were bought by the Marquess of Bute in 1863. In 1910 the marquess built a new house around the original fourteenth-century tower, which thus ranks among the oldest of Scotland's inhabited castles. Since 1965 he has leased the castle and nineteen acres of parkland as a home for spastic children. Wester Kames, which can be approached along an avenue of elm and beech opening off the north side of Kames Bay, is leased to the Sheriff of Greenock.

The farther east you move the more Port Bannatyne improves. The big Hydropathic Hotel among the woods above the pier gives the south side of the bay a handsome face as seen from the sea. On rounding Ardbeg Point you pass the Skeoch Wood, tunnelled by paths, and so enter Rothesay.

Rothesay is superior to all other Clyde resorts on several counts: in its shapely bay, to which Barone Hill (530 feet) gives a bold background; in the wealth of steamer services to all parts of the Clyde—cruises to Arran, Inveraray, Loch Long, the Cumbraes, Kintyre, the Kyles of Bute, and Loch Goil; in amenities such as large indoor swimming baths, in which sea-water is heated to 72 degrees Fahrenheit, a ballroom for 1,400 dancers, cinemas, concert hall, and curling. Outdoor recreations include golf on an eighteen-hole course designed by James Braid on Canada Hill above the bay, tennis, bowls, boating, and bathing from sandy beaches in several

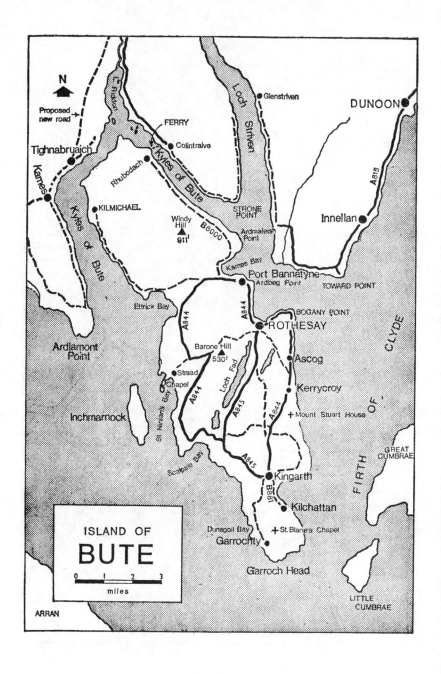

N

Proposed
new road →

Glenstriven

DUNOON

Loch Striven

Tighnabruaich

FERRY

Colintraive

Kyles of Bute

Rhubodach

Kames

KILMICHAEL

Windy
Hill
911'

B8000

STRONE
POINT

Ardmaleish
Point

Innellan

A815

Kyles of Bute

Kames Bay

Port Bannatyne

Ardbeg Point

TOWARD POINT

Etterick Bay

A844

A844

BOGANY POINT

ROTHESAY

Ardlamont
Point

Barone Hill
530'

Loch Fad

Ascog

Straad

A844

Chapel

Kerrycroy

Inchmarnock

St Ninian's Bay

A844

A845

A844

Mount Stuart House

FIRTH OF CLYDE

GREAT
CUMBRAE

Scalpsie Bay

A845

Kingarth

B881

Kilchattan

Dunagoil Bay

St. Blane's Chapel

Garrochty

Garroch Head

LITTLE
CUMBRAE

ISLAND OF
BUTE

0   1   2   3
miles

ARRAN

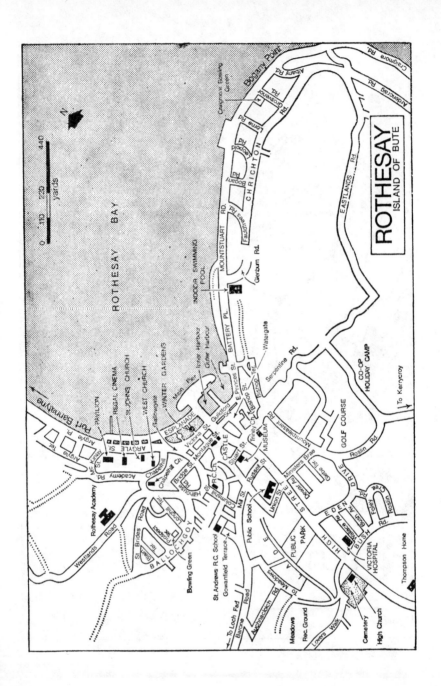

different parts of the island, to which bus services give easy access. Even more than Dunoon, Rothesay specializes in catering for the holiday-maker, and appears bigger although its population is less. The back part of the town away from the sea-front has much more character than that of Dunoon, and in no small part it owes this to Rothesay Castle.

The castle is one of the most important medieval castles in Scotland, where its round form is unique in combining the old Celtic design with the new Norman. It stands three hundred yards up the hill directly behind the pier, completely hidden from below by old houses of three or four storeys. The main building is a huge circular curtain-wall of pink and grey sandstone set on a broad grassy plinth and moated. Four massive drum towers project from the wall. On the north side (facing the bay) the moat is spanned by a wooden bridge built in 1900 but copied from the old bridge, whose burnt timbers were found in the moat. It leads into the great entrance *donjon* or fore-tower built by James IV.

The castle is thirteenth century or earlier, for it first appears on record as a royal castle defended by the High Steward of Scotland in 1230 against the Norsemen, who captured it. The more likely foundation date would be around 1156. In that year Somerled and his three sons had defeated the Vikings at sea. As King of Argyll and the Isles he then gave the Lordship of Bute and Arran to his son Angus (Kintyre and the Isles going to Ragnall and Lorn to Dughall). The House of Islay was far in advance of others of the time in introducing to the West the Norman ideas in castle-building. King Hakon held Rothesay Castle when his fleet invaded the Clyde in 1263. His defeat at Largs brought its prompt return to the King of Scots. It appears to have changed hands during Bruce's war with England. When Bruce's daughter married the High Steward, and the Stewarts finally came to the throne, the castle was much used by Robert II and Robert III. The latter created his son Duke of Rothesay, which has ever since been the principal Scottish title of the male heir to the throne. The town then became a Royal Burgh. In 1498 the Bute family of Stuart were appointed hereditary constables of the castle, which became of great importance in the sixteenth century during the reign of James IV and James V while they tried to subdue the Hebrides. The castle was held or fell in several risings and rebellions, notably when Cromwell's army seized it in the period of 1651–59. Its final downfall came at the Monmouth rebellion of 1685. Campbell of Argyll attacked and was beaten off, but a few days later his brother caught the garrison by surprise. The castle was sacked, burned, and never again occupied. Last century extensive repairs were made by the marquesses of Bute, who in 1951 placed their castle in the care of the Ministry of Works.

The castle to-day presents a picture of peace, complete with pigeons in the north-west tower. The moat, supplied with water by a stream from Loch Fad, is indented with little bays on which ducks swim, and has several islands bearing flower-gardens. On the grassy banks flowering shrubs and weeping willows grow by the waterside, ash and sycamore by the street. Within the curtain-wall the court-yard grass is short and clean. There were formerly several buildings here; the only one remaining is the Chapel of St. Michael the Archangel (patron saint of warriors). Between the chapel and curtain-wall are the delapidated ruins of the Bloody Stair, on which, in 1230, the daughter of the High Steward thrust a dagger into her heart rather than fall into the hands of the Norsemen. She had seen her father and brother butchered below.

From the vaulted passage of the fore-tower, by which you entered the courtyard, you can climb a stair to the great hall on the first floor. On a table there stands a model of the old castle showing the buildings in the courtyard as they were before destruction. The fore-tower was originally a gatehouse with portcullis, developed to provide accommodation for king or constable.

The castle is closely ringed by four narrow streets. Some of the houses have been mellowed by time, adding, like the municipal buildings, a touch of dignity when in good condition, or of honest age when not. The circus is seriously marred on the west side (King Street) by a new block of modern office flats, which house the Inland Revenue and government ministries. The design might have been good anywhere else in town. Here it is a breach of taste. Mistakes that could still be rectified are the decoration of two pubs, one dingy and the other (facing the castle gate) garish in red and yellow.

When Argyll's men burned the castle in 1685 they also burned the town. Like Dunoon, it remained in miserable state for a century. The Bute family rescued it. The burgh was rebuilt. Shipbuilding, herring fishing, cotton spinning, weaving, and farming were either introduced or developed, and although the first three eventually died out, the arrival of steamships in the early nineteenth century made Rothesay the Clyde's most successful holiday-resort. Behind the castle in Stuart Street, the Bute Museum ought to be visited for information on the island's fauna and history. Bute has been continuously occupied since at least 4000 B.C. as attested by middle Stone Age remains and the relics of Bronze and Iron Age settlements. You will see more of these on the ground when you tour the island.

The houses circling the bay are of tawny and reddish sandstone, mostly four storeys high, many now painted cream, pale blue, white or pink. The big pier at centre has an inner and outer harbour, favoured by swans and small ships. The outer pier takes a continuous procession of passenger steamers. They come and go day-long. Promenades stretch round the bay, but the heart of the sea-front is the esplanade, immediately west of the pier. No wheeled traffic is allowed on to it.

The esplanade is set out as a garden with flower-beds, putting greens, clumps of pampas grass, and palm-trees around a fountain. Nearest the pier is the Winter Gardens concert hall.

Much is done for Rothesay's good appearance by St. John's Church of Scotland. Built of tawny sandstone in spired Gothic style, it rises from the junction of the esplanade with Argyle Street, pulling the sea-front together and giving the needed focal point. For this reason, no doubt, it is floodlit at night. The night-scene is gay: an arc of coloured lights extend two miles from Ardbeg Point to Bogany Point. The floodlit fountain changes colour every few minutes. The bay and harbour come alive with trembling pencil-lines of green, red, blue, and yellow. Beyond the flashing lighthouse on Toward Point shine the long-drawn, clustered lights of Wemyss Bay and Skelmorlie across the Firth. Light is everywhere, even the Skeoch Wood is alight with gigantic coloured peacocks among the trees, no doubt to the irritation of dark-seeking lovers, whose preserve this traditionally is.

Rothesay has sand on the shore of Argyle Street between pier and jetty. It is not a big area, but Bute has plenty more and these are quickly reached by bus or car. Full information about transport and tours by sea or road, and of the town's amenities and accommodation, can be had at the information office beside the pier.

Rounding Bogany Point, you continue down the east coast to Ascog village. Its little bay has dun-coloured sand, but drain-pipes emptying into it discourage bathers. A mile farther, the pink sands of Kerrycroy Bay are much more pleasing, and are protected from the south by a stone jetty. Seven houses circle the bay—a model village built by the Bute family at the main gate to their home,

Mount Stuart House. Between them and the shore, tall sycamore fringe a greensward fifty yards wide. Behind the gates an avenue of beech and lime runs a mile to the house, a Gothic style mansion of three storeys built last century at a cost of £200,000. Ten times that sum would not build it to-day. Beside it stands a splendid chapel, which survived when the original Mount Stuart was burned down in 1877. The marquess still lives here and the house and grounds are not open to the public. The road accordingly leaves the coast and makes a three-mile detour inland through delightful woods to Kingarth, where the main body of Bute narrows to an isthmus of one and a half miles. Beyond lies the great tail of Garroch Head. At Kingarth you turn east to the coast at **Kilchattan Bay.**

The bay bites deep into the isthmus of corn- and grass-land. Its wide pink sands curve more than a mile and face to the Cumbrae. The village of Kilchattan (pronounced Kilcattan) is named from Cattan, a saint of the sixth century who built his cell here. The village shelters under a wooded and heathery hill on the south side of the bay. The houses are substantial sandstone buildings of three storeys, some of them tenements and almost all with tiny rose-gardens. They stand in a single line facing a shore of red sandstone rock. The road ends at the pier, which is closed to steamers, but still used by fishing boats. Kilchattan is small, remote from Rothesay's crowds, therefore all the more popular with the large minority who enjoy relative quiet. In high summer, of course, its famous beach is invaded from all parts of the island. Southward, a good walk may be had along the rocky coast to a lighthouse on the point nearest to Little Cumbrae.

WEST COAST

Kingarth, at the isthmus's centre, has a hotel, a farm, a church, and cottages sprawling where five roads meet. You take the south road to the west coast, bound for St. Blane's Chapel near Garroch Head.

Half a mile south of Kingarth Church you can visit an early Celtic sun-circle in the woods on the left. There is no sign-post, but the place is easily found: at a wide opening in the roadside wall a forest track divides a plantation of Sitka spruce from larch. In among the larches, fifty yards to the right of the track and seventy-five yards from the road are Bronze Age standing stones set in a circle. Most standing stones are of straight clean line, but here the shapes are weird, rising seven to nine feet high, posed like ghosts in this twilit wood. The stones, of reddish colour, have been standing here for three thousand years.

Two miles on towards Garroch Head, the land rises in abrupt hills of 400 feet—wild scenery compared to the rest of Bute. At the road-end before Garrochty Farm, a sign-post points left up the hill to St. Blane's Chapel, which from here is hidden, for it lies three or four hundred yards off the road in a green hollow on top of a hillock, and is surrounded by tall beech, sycamore, and ash. Pass through the iron gate on to the farm-road, but instead of following it, turn sharp left by a footpath along the stone wall. This route leads through a field and swing-gates to the chapel.

The site is one of the few places on Bute to retain an air of magic. To appreciate that 'out of this world' atmosphere one must come alone (or with a friend) and not with a bus-party. The ruins date from the twelfth century. The walls have fallen low but the two gables and a Norman arch still stand. As always in Bute the stone is sandstone, but here it is yellow, red, grey, and pink. A few yards to the south-west of the Norman arch, the ruin of a round cell is thought to be St. Blane's. A few yards from his cell are Celtic stones of the ninth century.

The great green hollow in which the chapel stands is enclosed by a flat-topped cashel wall. The graveyard is unusual in that the dead are segregated according to sex, the men in an upper yard lording it over the women in a lower, to which one descends by stairway. The story goes that when consecrated soil was brought from Rome for the graveyard it was landed by ship and carried to the chapel in creels. When one of the head-bands broke, the abbot in charge asked a woman to lend her belt as a substitute. This she refused to do. The incensed abbot directed that the graveyard be made on two levels, all holy earth reserved for the upper, and women consigned henceforth to the lower. This stern order was not relaxed till the Reformation. A few women now enjoy (we hope) their upstairs lair.

A circular enclosure of massive stones near the chapel is called the Devil's Cauldron. It is thought to have been a place of confinement for confessed sinners, who were committed to it for a few days by way of penance. The site is conducive to a contemplation of man's follies. The outlook to the Arran mountains across the Firth, is one of the best in Bute, and in these silent woods the only harsh sound is the *Korr-kok* of pheasant.

Blane was born in Bute in the sixth century, a nephew of Cattan.

Brought up in Ireland, he returned to Scotland to found monasteries in Bute, Dunblane in Perthshire, and Strathblane in Stirlingshire. At St. Blane's of Bute seven abbots succeeded him. The monastery was destroyed by the Vikings in 798, but restored and rebuilt. The Norman arch is eleventh-century work, the surviving walls twelfth century. The church remained in constant use until the seventeenth century, the last minister being ordained in the eighteenth.

Less than half a mile north along the road, a field-gate gives access to **Dunagoil Bay**, which looks to the Cock of Arran and Kintyre. Its sands are pink. Although no more than a cove and only a couple of hundred yards from the road, the bay stays unspoiled, secluded, and backed by clean turf. On its south side a flat-topped hill is buttressed by sea-cliffs of fifty feet. Perched on top are the remains of Bute's best-known prehistoric fort, a vitrified fort of the Iron Age, which has yielded numerous relics to excavators. It was occupied for at least two hundred years during the period 100 B.C. to A.D. 500. Its site gives an excellent view up the west coast to Inchmarnock and Scalpsie Bay.

The broad coastal strip running four miles north to **Scalpsie** has a pancake flatness; its several shallow bays are thus shelterless and featureless, and the first worth visiting is Scalpsie. Clean sands there lie red against a background of green or gold according as the corn is springing or ripened. Scalpsie is the south end of a trough that runs through the island north-east to Rothesay. This deep fold of the hills is the line of the Highland Fault.

The south flank of the trough carries the main road across the island through rich and swelling farmland. In the bed of the depression lies Bute's biggest loch, **Loch Fad**, two and a half miles long, but so deeply sunk as to be invisible from the road except at the north-east end. All that you can see are steep, thickly wooded slopes on its far side. These woods at the water's edge can be approached from Rothesay by the road to Barone, and then by a side-road to Woodend, half-way down the loch. There you can still see the house built by Edmund Kean in 1827. The famous actor, like many another man, hoped to escape from the hurly-burly of this world, and found when he tried that he was even gladder to escape from himself by a return to London's fleshpots. Drunkenness and extravagance brought him low in his last years. How ill-fitted he was for the loneliness of Loch Fad is exhibited by busts he put on his gateposts: Shakespeare and Edmund Kean.

Some two miles to the north of Scalpsie, **St. Ninian's Bay** has a deeply inset beach facing south and guarded on the west by the island of Inchmarnock a mile offshore. The bay is named from its western point, which once bore a chapel founded in the fourth century by St. Ninian. Your approach to the bay goes through the clachan of Straad, which is no beauty spot. Here the road divides. If you go straight on you arrive by a rutted track on a boggy foreshore, weedy with thistle, bramble, gorse, and iris, and churned by tractors. The east arm of the bay has been used as a rubbish dump. The sand is covered with cockle-shells, sore on bare feet. If instead you turn sharp right at Straad, you emerge on clean grass at the true back of the bay, whose sand, unlike the more southerly beaches, is not red but tawny. The low rocks of St. Ninian's Point take a half mile sweep to seaward, grass-topped for good walking.

The ancient chapel, of which nothing remains but a low, grassy ridge, had a free, airy site, looking down the Sound of Bute and the Arran coast to Holy Isle. St. Ninian was a disciple of St. Martin of Tours, and one of the first preachers of Christianity in Scotland. The Pope ordained him Bishop of the South Picts. He died in 432. Although he founded this chapel, his centre was not here but at Wigton. Do not mistake for the old chapel another more recent ruin on the point. Its cemented walls stand several feet high, tumbled and ugly, urgently needing, together with their sheep-fouled floor, to be uprooted and cast into the sea.

Inchmarnock, the Island of Marnock, is named after yet another saint, who built his chapel there in the seventh century. Later it was owned by the Cistercians of Saddell in Kintyre, and later still was used by the people of Bute for curing habitual drunkards by isolation. During the last war the Army used it for assaults by landing craft under fire. To-day the island is farmed, as it has been for several thousand years. The body of a Bronze Age woman has recently been found in a stone coffin. She was wearing a jet necklace, which may now be seen in the Bute Museum; at her hands lay a flint knife. She had been there for three thousand five hundred years.

Three miles to the north of St. Ninian's, Bute is pinched to a two-mile isthmus by Kames Bay on the east coast and Ettrick Bay on the west. Between spreads the waist of Bute, all green farmland, a most beautiful sunny strath, open to Cowal on one side and the jaggy outline of Arran on the other. Your approach is made by the road from Port Bannatyne.

Ettrick Bay has Bute's most popular beach, one and a quarter miles of curving sand, stony at the upper fringe. Dairy cattle graze on the fields behind; September corn stands in golden stooks; and three miles out to sea Ardlamont Point thrusts a dark finger, beyond which you see the low grey back of Kintyre. Eider-duck paddle the water, except when the beach is invaded. The one eyesore is a big tea-room pavilion on the foreshore, gaudy in yellow, blue, and white. One should be thankful that no worse has befallen, for in earlier days, when electric trams ran to the bay from Rothesay, there were plans to develop the site as a new resort.

From Ettrick Bay a road runs four miles up the coast to Kilmichael Farm, where it ends. A few hundred yards south-west of the farm, **St. Michael's Chapel** stands by the shore. Visitors are often recommended to drive to this ancient chapel. They should be wary: the chapel is not worth inspection. But if you leave your car at Ettrick Bay, you will find the road worth walking, at least until you tire: it is narrow, quiet, and wild, passing much of the way through woods of oak and birch.

At Kilmichael, gates give access through two fields to the chapel, which crouches on a bank above a stony shore. The ruins lie low to the ground: a good marker is a tall pole to which electric cables cross the sound from Ardlamont peninsula. The old altar stone still stands in the circular chapel, which has a fine view down the Kyles and across the flat back of Inchmarnock to Arran. An old oak in the graveyard lends a potential dignity. But all is spoiled by the dirty state of the ruin: the surrounding wall has been breached and not fenced; sheep-droppings cover the altar, the floor, and any part of the graveyard not already deep in bracken.

Bute offers coarse fishing, good of its kind. Pike and perch of large size may be taken from Loch Ascog on the hills behind Rothesay's Bogany Point, and from Loch Fad. Bute Estate Office in the High Street grants permits at five shillings for a whole season. The Bute Sailing Club welcomes visitors, and holds regattas for dinghies twice a week from the end of May. Highland Games are held in August. Bute caters for visitors for five months of the year. And in winter her average temperature is thirteen degrees higher than the mainland's.

CHAPTER 4

Mid Argyll: Upper Loch Fyne

Mid Argyll is the district between Loch Fyne, Loch Awe, and Kintyre.

The bare and windy pass of Rest and Be Thankful is the main gate to Argyll's heart: to Dunadd and Inveraray, from which Argyll was ruled in old days, and to Dunoon and Lochgilphead from which it is ruled now. From the broad summit at 860 feet, the road falls through Glen Kinglas in a five-mile zig-zag to Loch Fyne, which pairs with Loch Linnhe as the longest of Scottish sea-lochs—forty miles from the head to the open sea.

This deep penetration of the sea gave Argyll its early importance, when communications were by sea and ship rather than roadless land. Easy passes around the head of Loch Fyne gave access east, north, and west. In consequence, the land between Loch Fyne and Loch Awe drew the first colonization by the Scots and became the heart of their kingdom. A brief sketch of its history is essential to an understanding of what you will see. Historic and prehistoric relics abound like mice in August corn.

The name Argyll is from the Gaelic Earra-ghaidheal (pronounced Er-a-gyl), meaning Coastland of the Gael. In the third century the Scots under Cairbre Riada set up a kingdom in County Antrim called Dalriada ('the portion of Riada'). Around A.D. 220 they first began to colonize Argyll, settling on the flat isthmus of Crinan, which connects Loch Fyne with the Sound of Jura. The base was the natural fortress of Dunadd, which they fortified and made their capital. The new kingdom was likewise named Dalriada, but the settlement was small and not as yet any threat to the Picts, then fully occupied in harassing the Romans, whose power was at its height. The Romans never sought to penetrate Argyll. King Cairbre's arrival was unobstructed.

The real Scottish invasion came later. In A.D. 500, King Erc of the Irish Dalriada died. Under Celtic law the kingship fell to his brother. His three sons, Fergus, Angus and Lorn, thereupon resolved to carve kingdoms of their own out of Alban. They arrived around 503, and they came with a force of several thousand. They came for conquest. Angus took the Argyll islands, notably Islay, which was to be the seat of Kings and Lords of the Isles until 1493. Lorn took the northern part of Argyll, which bears his name to this day. Fergus took Kintyre, Knapdale, and Cowal. On surviving his brothers he united the kingdoms. The Scottish Dalriada now extended from the Firth of Clyde to Ardnamurchan, and was co-extensive with modern Argyll. When the Dalriadan King Kenneth MacAlpin finally overthrew the Picts in 843, the names of Alban and Dalriada died together. Scotland was born.

In the tenth century, the Hebrides and much mainland coast had been seized by Norway. So far as Argyll was concerned, Norse rule ended with the rise of Somerled, the progenitor of Clan Donald and greatest of Scotland's naval chiefs. On succeeding his father as King of Argyll in 1130, he not only drove the Vikings out of Morvern but defeated them at sea. He and his first five successors all held rank as King of the Isles, thereafter as Lord of the Isles in deference to the King of Scots. His grandson, Donald, gave his name to the clan, which became the most powerful of Scottish history. They and the Campbells of Loch Awe supported Robert the Bruce against Edward I of England. Victory at Bannockburn confirmed the MacDonald power throughout Argyll and the Isles, and founded the fortunes of Campbell of Loch Awe. The MacDonalds then fell into a trap as old as their ancient race. Grown too confident in their huge power and tempted to repeated rebellions, they lost all by forfeiture in 1493. The Campbells were able to supplant them as rulers of a large part of Argyll and transferred their headquarters from Loch Awe to Inveraray, Loch Fyne.

Long-running, shapeless hills flank **Loch Fyne**, save where a cluster of mountains rise to 3,000 feet around its head at Beinn Bhuidhe, Beinn Ime, and Beinn an Lochain. Several lesser tops approach or exceed 2,000. All these hills are gentle and grassy. In lower Loch Fyne the containing hills drop to 1000 feet or less, bearing some heather but for the most part still grassy: good ground for cattle and sheep grazing, and thus used from time immemorial. The chief plume of Loch Fyne is the natural wood extending down the coastal strip on both sides. The hill tops are high enough to rise clear of it, and the waters below long enough to stretch far away in

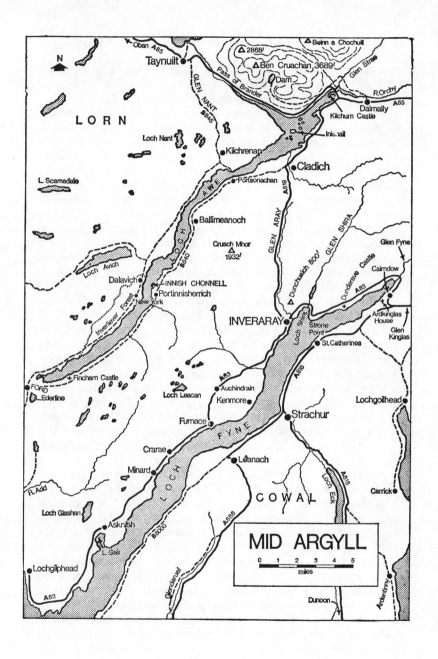

N

Oban A85
Taynuilt
Benn a Chochuill
2868'
Ben Cruachan, 3689'
Dam
Glen Stroe
R.Orchy
A85
Dalmally
Kilchurn Castle
GLEN NANT
B845
Pass of Brander
LORN
Loch Nant
Kilchrenan
Inisnail
Cladich
L.Scamadale
Portsonachan
GLEN ARAY
A819
Ballimeanoch
Cruach Mhor
1932'
GLEN SHIRA
Glen Fyne
Cairndow
A83
Dunderave Castle
Loch Avich
Dalavich
INNISH CHONNELL
Portinnisherrich
New York
Inverliever Forest
B840
LOCH AWE
Duncuaich 800'
Ardkinglas House
Glen Kinglas
INVERARAY
Stone Point
St.Catherines
Loch Shira
FORD
Fincharn Castle
Loch Leacan
A83
Auchindrain
Kenmore
Lochgoilhead
L.Ederline
LOCH FYNE
Furnace
Strachur
Crarae
Leanach
Minard
COWAL
Loch Eck
Carrick
R.Add
A815
A886
A83
Loch Glashan
Asknish
B8000
L.Gair
Lochgilphead
Glendaruel
Dunoon
Ardentinny
A83

MID ARGYLL

0 1 2 3 4 5
miles

slow curves. Wood, water, and mountain combine to enrich much of Argyll (where sheltered) but nowhere does wild land wear so civilized an aspect as upper Loch Fyne.

The Glen Kinglas road sweeps down to Loch Fyneside by-passing Cairndow. You should look for the side-road and turn left to this tiny village, whose white houses are strung along a road facing a stony beach. You have come for Ardkinglas House and gardens, Kilmorich Church, and the old inn. You reach the inn first. When Keats stayed here last century he left behind a memento—his name diamond-scratched on a window-pane of his bedroom. He had walked across the Rest and Be Thankful from Arrochar, hoping to find an inn on the pass, and finding none had continued to Cairndow for breakfast. He must have enjoyed full health, for he wrote from the inn to his brother describing his thirteen-mile walk in terms that showed that he found it no effort. A copy of his letter is held by the innkeeper.

Kilmorich church replaces an early thirteenth-century foundation of the MacNachtans, an ancient family most probably of Pictish descent, who came to Mid Argyll from Loch Tay, and who therefore named the church after Morich, a saint of their native Perthshire diocese. In 1246 they presented it to Inchaffrey Abbey. The old church has long vanished. The new church, built in 1816, is hexagonal with a square tower topped by an elaborately carved parapet, from whose corners four spires rise in Gothic revival style. On the white-washed walls, which are outlined and dressed in grey stone, are set Perpendicular windows in pairs. The building is a fine specimen of a Highland kirk in the unusual 'round' plan, but you will see an even better example at Dalmally, Loch Awe.

Ardkinglas House stands in wooded parkland to the south-west of the village. For more than five hundred years the estate was a Campbell possession extending south-east to Loch Goil and Loch Long. Sir Colin Campbell, the sheriff of Argyll, had his home here in January 1692 when MacIain of Glencoe arrived to take the oath of allegiance before the massacre of his clan. When the Ardkinglas line failed the estate was sold, the larger Loch Fyne part to Sir Andrew Noble in 1905, and the Loch Goil part to Lord Rowallan. The original Ardkinglas Castle, like Dunderave across the loch, would once serve as a useful outpost to Inveraray. But the castle has long since been demolished. The new house, built in 1907, is of creamy, almost honey-coloured sandstone. Its architect was Sir Robert Lorimer, whose works include the Chapel of the

Thistle at St. Giles's Cathedral and the National War Memorial at Edinburgh Castle. In Ardkinglas he built one of the most graceful houses of Argyll.

House and gardens are annually thrown open to the public on Sundays only during April and May under Scotland's Gardens Scheme. Money received goes to charity. The garden does not rival the more famous gardens of Argyll (Crarae, Gigha, and Colonsay), but in itself it is delightful. At the back of the house a stone terrace and lawns face the sea, at the front, broad fields unroll to woodland. Between the house and the main gate, the woodland shrubberies are full of exotic rhododendrons. The larger part of the garden is wild, graced by a lake, by a cherry-orchard where an avenue of twenty-four trees bow hugely blossomed heads, and by massed azaleas, fiery red and yellow, which are the main feature of this and every west coast garden. The best time to visit is the last week of May.

At the farther side of Loch Fyne, four miles down from the head, the tall grey tower of **Dunderave Castle** stands amid a screen of trees. The name is either from Dun da Ramh, the Fort of the Two Oars (there used to be a ferry here) or from Dun an Rudha, the Fort of the Promontory (an ancient dun stands on the point topped by a flagpole). Made famous in *Doom Castle* by the novelist Neil Munro, it wears a pleasingly defiant air, appearing still a 'grim fastness'. Built by the Clan MacNachtan of Glen Shira in 1560 (despite the 1598 carved above the door), it was restored by Sir Robert Lorimer in 1911. The present owner opens it to the public in summer in aid of Scotland's Gardens Scheme and occasionally for other charities. The castle is partially hidden by oak, beech, ash, and sycamore, and is thus easy to miss when travelling up or down the lochside. Above the door in the courtyard are carved these words: *I.M. A.N. Behald the end. Be nocht Vyser nor the Hiest. I Hoip in God.* The first two initials are those of the last Mac-Nachtan to bring a bride to Dunderave and the second two his wife's. The last sentence is the clan's motto from their coat of arms. Within the rooms are fine panelling, hand-moulded ceilings, and antique furniture.

The woods southward down the loch are delightfully shady in summer, better still in spring when beeches are greening or the oaks bursting yellow, best of all in October when they and the hillsides above are blazing red and gold in autumn sun.

Two miles south of Dunderave you round a corner and suddenly find yourself at the edge of Loch Shira. On the opposite shore **Inveraray** sparkles white like scattered quartzite. Small as it is (the population is only 500), the royal burgh of Inveraray is still acknowledged as the capital of Argyll—this for historic and sentimental reasons rather than practical. The name means The Mouth of the Aray. The river flows down a wooded glen behind the town, then zigzags through a wide green strath on which the castle stands.

The foundation of Inveraray was too early for record. There would be a settlement here from the days of the Scots' occupation, for it lay on the natural route from the heart of their kingdom to the Lowlands, and lay too where Glen Aray gave an excellent pass north to Loch Awe. In 1415, Colin Campbell of Loch Awe built a castle close to the present site on the river-bank. Its natural advantage over Loch Awe soon made it the headquarters of the clan. Thenceforward the fate and fortune of Inveraray became one with that of the Campbell family.

The Campbells' attainment of power had been gradual, starting when Gillespic Cambel had won lands at Loch Awe by marriage in the eleventh century. His wife, Aife, claimed descent from the Celtic hero Diarmid, one of Fingal's warriors in the third century. Sir Colin Campbell of Loch Awe added greatly to the family territory. Warlike prowess won him high renown and the name Cailean Mor (the Great Colin). Ever since then the head of Clan Campbell has been known as MacChailein Mor (Son of the Great Colin). Colin's son, Sir Niall was still more the founder of family fortune. He supported Robert the Bruce against all odds and married the king's sister. A grateful brother-in-law hugely increased his estates. In 1457 the chief was raised to an earldom, and the son of the ninth earl to a dukedom in 1701. At the height of Campbell power the chief was the most powerful subject in the kingdom, a despotic ruler supported by four thousand armed clansmen. At that time, it was said, MacChailein Mor would not suffer himself to be announced 'His Grace the Duke of Argyll'. 'Campbell of Argyll' was enough and more weighty.

The second duke, John Campbell, was one of the prime movers in the union of the Parliaments of Scotland and England in 1707. The eleventh duke, Ian Douglas Campbell, became by ill fate the first family victim of the social revolution. On his succession in 1949 crippling death duties forced the sale of vast territories, including the whole of Kintyre, which had been a Campbell possession since the MacDonald forfeiture.

Above Loch Lomond in winter, near Balmaha in Stirlingshire. The loch is Britain's greatest sheet of fresh water (27½ square miles). A glacier valley of 12,000 years ago, it breaches the southern Grampians to give the traveller a strait gate through the Highland Line. In beauty it ranks with Loch Awe and Loch Maree. *Below* a corner of Loch Awe in spring. Twenty-three miles long (only a mile shorter than Lomond), it forms the south-east frontier of Lorn in Argyll. For the angler it is open water, famous for its sea-trout. Even salmon may be taken for no more than the cost of boat-hiring.

The South and North Highland scenes in contrast: *Above* Lochgoilhead in Cowal, Argyll. Loch Goil is a sea loch, but its head lies 31 miles from the open sea at Garroch Head. This channelling of the Atlantic Drift so far inland gives a mild climate, in which exotic plants thrive. *Below* Loch Eriboll in Sutherland, where the land is bare and windswept, sparsely populated, and the rare tree grows low to the ground. This land is very much an Atlantic promontory, with the beauty of moorland hills under wide skies.

By 1743 the old castle had become uninhabitable. The third duke boldly conceived a clean sweep of both castle and town: he would build the new castle on the old site, and transform the environment by moving the town half a mile south to Gallows Foreland, which juts into Loch Fyne at the mouth of Loch Shira. He engaged for this work the outstanding architect Roger Morris, whose clerk of works was William Adam (father of Robert Adam). The work was continued by the fourth and fifth dukes, the latter employing the architect Robert Mylne. Mylne's work was mainly on the castle's interior decoration and the completion of the new town. The whole was thus built between 1744 and 1794. In 1958 the Historic Buildings Council declared that Inveraray was 'an entirety designed to delight the eye from every angle of approach, both by land and water', and should be preserved as a good example of eighteenth-century town planning. A large grant was made to this end, and nearly a hundred of the houses have since been renovated. The work continues.

Approaching from Loch Shira, you see the spacious spread of Strath Aray under the wooded hill of Dunchuaich (800 feet), which bears a watch-tower on its bald top. Castle and town stand apart south of the river, yet are made one entity by the enveloping parkland. You cross the river at the lochside by an elegant double-arch bridge with a high hump, built by Robert Mylne. The old town had extended down the river's south bank from castle to sea, but no trace of it remains. The new Georgian town confronts you between castle grounds and Foreland pier with a great, white-washed triple arch, flanked on the right by the old three-storeyed inn, and on the left by the courthouse, both built by Roger Morris. The old courthouse, now the municipal building, was restored in 1970 and its pink walls made white. The town lies between arch and pier. The archways are an avenue-screen built by Mylne. They give access to a former beechwood avenue running behind the town parallel to the main south road. Until recent years, the beech avenue was one of the sights of Argyll and gave the Mylne arch its *raison d'être*. Planted in 1660, the trees had grown to enormous girth, but were felled during the last war. A re-planting is urgently needed both to justify Mylne's façade and to give some beauty to a now drab road: meantime, a car-park has been made on the plantable ground.

A hundred yards down the avenue, a tall bell-tower of pink granite rises high above the village. The tenth duke built it this century as an addition to the Episcopal church of last century. The church crouches almost unnoticed under its shade. As seen from a distance, the bell-tower appears unduly to dominate the village, whose true focal point should be the original parish church at the head of Main Street—which Mylne designed as the central feature of his town plan. The plan is cruciform, church at centre, Main Street running up to it from the frontal courthouse, circling the church, then shooting south by the lochside. The church displays an unusual combination of white harling, granite, and freestone in a Palladian style quite free of its usually fussy ornamentation. Slender pillars uphold the corners of the roof's tympanum. The three great windows are rounded, each recessed between white square-cut columns. High above the central door, in a big round hole of the tympanum, the church bell swings free. The roof originally bore a slim steeple, which gave the town its focal point, but this was unfortunately taken down during the last war, when it was thought to be endangered by heavy military traffic. There is yet hope of its replacement. The interior was made double, one half to give English services for the castlefolk, the other Gaelic for the townsfolk. The English half only is now used.

The broad main street is uncompromisingly Scottish in character. Near the shore at its seaward end stands an early fifteenth-century cross brought from Iona. The street from there runs to the central church, its houses white-harled tenements severely plain, mostly with shops on the ground floor displaying swing signs in iron-work of excellent design. The row of houses extending south beyond the church are a nineteenth-century addition.

At the north front, to the right-hand side of the inn (Argyll Arms Hotel), another white-washed open arch spans the road through Glen Aray to Loch Awe. Close beside it is the entrance to the castle park. A drive sweeps around the castle to its north-east front, which presents a perfect example of early Gothic revival architecture. The stone is a blue-grey chlorite slate, quarried at Creggans on the far side of the loch. The choice seems peculiar for a Scottish castle. It needs sun to bring out its good quality—a coolness matching well the greensward around. In all other weather its lobster blue is too cold. Two rows of lance-headed windows adorn the front. The uppermost story was added after a serious fire of 1877, and the four round corner-towers were then given their conical spires. Thin clustered columns flank the main doorway, which you approach across a palisaded bridge carried on multiple arches. The severe exterior gives no hint of the richness of decoration within.

On either side of the entrance hall are a dining room and drawing

66

room. The dining room's walls and ceiling are exquisitely painted in huge panels of elaborate floral design around central grisailles, oval in shape, which on the moulded roof and above the doors are circular. All these paintings are the work of an Italian artist, Biago Rebecca. Louis Quinze chairs with splendid tapestry upholstery grace the long table. The drawing room is above all noted for its magnificent French Beauvais tapestries, made in 1770 by Sieur de Menou. The entrance hall leads directly into the armoury hall of a big central tower, from which staircases rise to upper balconies. Far above, a blue ceiling lit by lance-head windows bears the eight coats of arms of the clan. On the walls, and above doors and apses, are displayed in spoked wheel formation muskets, broadswords, targes, and halberds, dating from the fifteenth to eighteenth centuries. Upstairs you can see a bedroom and State Bed, and down below, the old kitchen.

A second drawing room at the south-west side shows another fine example of eighteenth-century décor, in which delicate artwork is combined with the most lavish use of gilt. The walls are overloaded with family paintings and the floors with show-cases, spoiling by congestion one's appreciation of superb rooms as they once would be. In the absence of a gallery, in which might be hung these paintings by Gainsborough, Raeburn, Landseer, Allan Ramsay, and Medina, among many others, one has constantly to remind oneself that since the castle was opened to the public in 1958 the rooms on view are an exhibition. Nobody lives in them. The family makes use of them only on rare occasions. The greater part of the castle—not on view—is still the home of the duke and duchess.

There is no garden worth noting, but the 2,000 acres of wood behind town and castle make a splendid sight as seen from high ground. They were planted in the seventeenth century and have been properly managed ever since. Nearly a hundred acres are re-planted yearly. One silver fir (*Abies pectinata*), 186 feet tall and 21 feet in diameter at shoulder height, is thought to be the largest conifer in Britain. Its age is 285 years. Its fine shape was spoiled in 1964 when one of its twin tops was blasted off in a gale. You can see the tree beside the main road two miles south of Inveraray and opposite Battlefield caravan park.

The arable land around the castle extends north up Glen Aray and Glen Shira. Both are beautifully wooded and carry motor-roads. Glen Aray rises to 675 feet on the pass to Loch Awe. Near the top on the left-hand side, you will see a tall cairn crowning a hillock. This was raised to the memory of the author Neil Munro, who was born at Inveraray in 1864 and died in 1930. His historical novels, *John Splendid*, *The New Road*, and *Doom Castle*, give a lively account of eighteenth-century life in Argyll. **Glen Shira** has two roads, one of them an eight-mile access-road to a big hydro-electric dam at 1,100 feet. This road may not always be open to motor-cars in its upper reaches, in which event, ask permission from the Argyll Estate Office, Inveraray. Rob Roy MacGregor, the notorious outlaw, lived in Glen Shira for eight years at a cottage five miles up, where the Brannie Burn joins the Shira.

The walk up Glen Shira is more enjoyable if the old track up the right bank is taken, and the new tarmac road up the left bank avoided. The two start as one but shortly diverge at the foot of the Dubh Loch. Between gentle hills on either flank, the woodland is almost entirely deciduous—beech, chestnut, sycamore, and ash—with only a few conifers at the Dubh Loch. The meadow-land by the river is broad and lush. In the old days the glen was heavily inhabited; to-day there are only three or four farms. The two roads rejoin at Elrig three miles up. To reach Rob Roy's cottage you must keep a sharp look-out for the side track leading to a wooden bridge over the gorge of the Brannie Burn, which comes in from the right. The track is easy to miss. It lies half a mile beyond a tubular metal gate (with a wooden hut beside it). On crossing the bridge, you come first on a ruined cottage, which is not Rob Roy's—that lies two hundred yards farther and stands on the very edge of the Shira, where a steep bank falling fifty feet to the river is thickly wooded in sycamore and rowan. The walls are tumbled and now stand to only four or five feet. Rob Roy's dirk-handle, carved with his initials, was found this century on a rock ledge by the river, and together with his sporran, found in the cottage when he left it early in the eighteenth century, is exhibited in the armoury hall of Inveraray Castle.

The burgh's population has dropped to its present 500 from its peak of 1,233 in 1841. This has been due in part to the failure of the herring fishing, the amalgamation of crofts into larger farms, and emigration to industrial towns in search of higher income. The tale is the same up and down Loch Fyne. The loch is still famous for its herring, but the industry is now centred at Tarbert and Campbeltown, leaving Inveraray with a burgh crest sadly anachronistic: a netted herring and the motto: *Semper tibi pendeat halec* (May you always have a catch of herring). The pier is still in use. From May to late September passenger steamers call on Tuesdays from the Clyde coast.

Moving five miles down Loch Fyne, you arrive at **Auchindrain,** a farm township dating from 1770. Twenty vernacular buildings with cruck and truss features display a pattern of rural life once typical of the West Highlands. A trust has been formed to restore and furnish the houses in the styles of the eighteenth, mid-nineteenth and early twentieth centuries. The attempt to bring the past alive in this way has the support of the National Musem of Antiquities, Glasgow and Edinburgh universities, the National Trust for Scotland and the Countryside Commission. Part of the new museum was opened in 1967. One mile beyond Auchindrain you cross the **Leacan Water** where the last wolf of Mid Argyll was killed in the eighteenth century by a woman with a spindle. The woman died of shock. Her body was found alongside the spiked wolf at the old bridge.

Argyll has long been famed for two dissimilar products—granite and gardens. At the little village of Furnace beyond Leacan, and again at Crarae three miles farther, you pass huge granite quarries at the roadside. But **Crarae** also has a woodland garden, sited where the river Crarae flows into Loch Fyne, which is one of the three best in the county. The creator of Crarae was Sir George I. Campbell of Succouth. When he succeeded to the estate in 1920 he greatly developed the existing garden. Throughout 33 acres of Glen Crarae he planted numerous unusual conifers—a unique collection to which were added azaleas, exotic rhododendrons, and many rare trees and shrubs. In 1955, Sir George gifted his forest garden to the nation. It is now maintained by the research branch of the Forestry Commission and kept open throughout the year. It is much visited by students of horticulture from all parts of the world.

The best time to visit is in late May or very early June. The approach roads are then alight with new leaf. The sea and the hills are blue and all is gay. The forest garden is entered through the house garden, one mile north of Minard village. Close around the stone house are small lawns; the rest is wild, but wild with a difference. The glen splits the hillside only a short way to the southwest. On both sides paths lead along steep and rocky banks, thick in pink and gold azaleas and rhododendrons blood-red and white. Most surpring is how abundantly they grow on rocky soil. In the farthest upper part of the glen the woodland becomes genuinely wild and the paths rough. A whole day can be spent exploring the grounds and much exercise obtained. It is worth carrying a packed lunch. On the lower southmost ground near the main road there is an avenue of laburnums, where acres of bluebells roll like a sea beneath. This sight is often missed by visitors, although in late May it can be one of the finest around Crarae.

A mile south of **Minard,** the maps mark a 'Minard Castle' standing among woods by the shore: this mansion in Scots Baronial style was in 1966 converted into an hotel. Midway between Minard and Lochgilphead, a bay nearly a mile deep bites into the land at Loch Gair. Little of it can be seen from the main road. You must walk a few hundred yards down to the shore. The loch is beautifully shaped, a circular inlet like an inland lake of southern England. Low, wooded hills cup still water, where in early summer swans paddle with a train of cygnets. The cropped turf close to the shingle beach may be covered in feathery fluff where they preen themselves. A dozen houses, some new and others mellowed by age, stand close to the sea's edge. On the far side of the bay, on the site of a former Campbell castle, the eighteenth century Asknish House is set well back on broad parkland. The clachan is a peaceful backwater seemingly miles from main road traffic.

Not so **Loch Gilp.** Eight miles south, it makes a three-mile inlet with sandy flats that dry out a full mile on the ebb. Set on the great inner curve of the bay, Lochgilphead is the market town and administrative centre for Mid Argyll. Its population hovers around 1,200. The stone-built houses are almost all of them painted stone. They form a square at centre-front with all necessary shops, and from there recede in depth for several hundred yards hillwards. Along the curved sea-front they spread in long line with outward view to the Arran mountains, whose notched crest humps high on the south horizon.

Lochgilphead has a grey look for a West Highland town. Yet the more one sees of it the better one likes it. This cannot be said for its sister village **Ardrishaig,** one and half miles south at outer Loch Gilp. Ardrishaig is plain, drab, and if one turns a critical eye, ugly. It has a good pier but MacBrayne's steamer service has been withdrawn since 1972. In former days Ardrishaig was a busy herring port, but only three fishing boats are now based here. Its centre of interest is the first basin of the Crinan canal, to which ships gain entry by a sea-lock behind the breakwater.

In 1801, **Crinan Canal** was cut nine miles to the Sound of Jura by John Rennie. It allows Clyde shipping to reach the western isles and coast, thus saving an eighty-mile voyage round the stormy Mull of Kintyre. It was not built to take big ships. British Waterways Board control it and make a loss of nearly £10,000 a year. Annual passages number 600 fishing boats, 600 small coasters, including red-funnelled 'puffers', and 1000 yachts of which 80 may pass through the fifteen locks in one summer day. These ships give much life to Ardrishaig and Crinan at either end of the canal, where they lie in the terminal basins before and after passage.

CHAPTER 5

Mid Argyll: Dunadd and Loch Awe

Your westward passage through the Crinan isthmus, whether by boat or road, follows what appears to be a well-ordered Lowland river bordered by its customary lane of leafy trees. On your left lies the Forest of Knapdale, a congestion of hills wooded over their summits, but you are too close under them to see much; on your right the land flattens out on the plain of the Moine Mhor (The Great Moss), which spreads five miles to Kilmartin. The canal ends at the **Crinan** basin.

Tiny as Crinan village is, to Clyde yachtsmen it is the Atlantic Gate, opening on the seas of the Hebrides. Since the first Scots came, the name Dorus Mor, or Great Gate, has in fact been given to the strait off Craignish Point, which projects a black fang at the mouth of Crinan Bay. Low jagged islands lie out to the north-west. The air has a clean tang; the very skies have suddenly become more spacious and the waters wild. The mainland has dropped behind, out of sight and mind. The Hebrides beckon.

I have seen in the basin an eighty-ton yawl tie to the quay. Her professional crew, her burnished brass, her scoured teak deck on which the owner in white flannels and peaked cap sat under an awning to be served cocktails off a silver salver by a white-jacketed steward, seemed like a glimpse of another age. A sight like that is rare nowadays. The bigger ships to-day are the eight-metre cruiser racers. These are Bermudan sloops, whose tall sticks rise high over the village; their crews are young and of both sexes, spare-limbed in blue jeans and bulky above in sweaters. Every movement they make is brisk. They work to time-table, sail in any weather, unhesitatingly head out under lowering skies. They wait here only till the ebb slackens and their ship can knife through the tide-race of Dorus Mor. Alongside them are converted fishing boats and gaff-rigged ketches, some of them fifty years old and still sound, often with elderly crews who have sailed the west coast life-long and care nothing for smart turnout; one can tell the colour of their ship's hull by the paint on their trousers. Clad in woolly bunnets (not 'bonnets', if you please), framed shirts and weathered anoraks, they move on deck as if idle, with a leisurely deliberation. Their ship's hull and sails may (like themselves) appear to be casually patched or painted, but look at their decks instead—clear and clean, a model of order with every rope-end coiled and laid. These are the most experienced seamen in Crinan basin. Among them are lean little sloops, some without auxiliary engines, crewed by keen youngsters, the hard men of the Clyde's dinghy-sailing schools. They have often learned their sailing in boats they have built for themselves from prefabricated kits. Their graduation to west coast cruising has been a test not only of seamanship but of money-management. Sound ships for sale or charter are not cheap. In growing numbers the young have realized that a man gets what he wants if he wants it enough. They have transformed west coast yachting from a preserve of the rich to a recreation for all who will. Even the land-lubbers are here and afloat: families who have chartered a yacht instead of a caravan. They would not know how to hoist a sail, far less rig it. The lowest of the Clyde's low, they motor from port to port. They will not venture out through the Crinan sea-lock, but their decks swarm with eager-eyed children to whom Crinan locks are adventure enough— and in time may lead to greater things. Across this heterogeneous crowd of ships and humanity, the West Highland seamen of the fishing smacks cast irreverent yet not wholly unrespectful eyes. They put their trust in nothing less than an 88 horse-power Kelvin diesel, and to them all this sailing is townsmen's play. But their respect for sail is innate, and so too for sailors. Like all men they delight in the line of a yacht, one of the most beautiful things man makes.

At the time of writing there is a project, for which planning permission has been issued by the county council, to create a marina at Crinan by dredging the old harbour, reclaiming the foreshore, and erecting breakwaters and jetties, thus greatly to improve the existing facilities for yachts.

Overlooking bay and basin, the Mainbrace Hotel stands apart on a rocky promontory. A mile across the mouth of Loch Crinan, **Duntrune Castle** guards the opposite shore (the name is from Dun an t'Sron, Fort of the Point). One of the oldest inhabited castles in Scotland, it was formerly a Campbell seat, until bought in recent years by the Malcolms of Poltalloch. The Malcolms are a small but ancient clan whose land embraces Dunadd, the capital of Dalriada, and all around it a treasury of prehistoric remains without equal on the west seaboard.

Duntrune is thus a private house not normally open to the public, but under the Gardens Scheme it does open for a day each year near the end of May. The garden is small and new. The castle has a keep and curtain-wall dating from the reign of Alexander II in the early thirteenth century. It was last besieged in the Montrose wars of the seventeenth century, when Coll MacDonald of Islay attacked the royalists. He had sent forward his piper as a herald, who was admitted but treacherously seized and thrown into a turret. The garrison laid an ambuscade. When MacDonald approached in his galleys the piper played a pibroch with an urgent warning note. He was cut down where he stood, but MacDonald turned aside. Many years later a skeleton with mutilated hands was discovered under the floor of the hall.

The Moine Mhor and the village of Kilmartin may be reached from Crinan either by way of **Islandadd Bridge**, where the river Add joins inner Loch Crinan, or three miles farther east at Cairnbaan. The **Add bridge** leads direct to the more interesting chambered cairns and sun circle, and the Cairnbaan route to the heart of all, the hill of Dunadd. This latter being also the main road to Kilmartin, you should follow it first. Where it bends leftward to the canal there is a green hillock on the right named Dun Dhomhnuill, on which the MacDonald Lords of the Isles sat to administer justice, surrounded by their court. Their hewn stone chair crowned the top until recent years, when it was destroyed by vandals.

Near the middle of the isthmus, the canal reaches its highest point of 88 feet. A little way farther east is the village and bridge of **Cairnbaan** ('white cairn'), thus named from a mound 12 feet high beside the canal. Flints, bones, a carved slab and a cist were found therein. Two miles north, a tall rocky knoll projects 176 feet from the middle of the Great Moss. This is **Dunadd**. Even without the fortifications built upon it by man, the hill is a natural fort. Its strategic importance is at once made clear when you climb to its summit.

You stand there on short turf humped between outcrops of rock. You look over a sun-smitten plain, dotted with farms and trees, broad marshes and wide fields. These are ringed by the wooded hills of Knapdale and Kilmichael forests, over the top of which peep the horns of Ben Cruachan to the north and the Paps of Jura to the south-west. Beyond the islets peppering the Sound of Jura, you can see the Gulf of Corrievreckan between Jura and Scarba, its notorious whirlpool fallen silent at ten miles' range. Behind you the river Add flows from the hills above Crarae down through the valley of Kilmichael Glassary, then writhes like a python under your feet towards the sea at Crinan. The river is navigable for small craft as far as Kilmichael Glassary (except in dry weather).

There were thus excellent reasons why **Dunadd** should have become the capital of Dalriada. It had been inhabited as a safe region from Stone Age times. The flat approaches exposed any large body of men to full view. Kilmartin Glen to the north gave a good pass to Loch Awe, thence to central and north-east Scotland, or up the west coast to the Great Glen and Inverness; the Crinan isthmus gave a fast route east to Loch Fyne and the Clyde, or south-west down the Sound of Jura to Ireland. The sheltered waterways and hill-passes encouraged trade as well as conquest. More than seventy other forts within a ten-mile radius of Dunadd protected these approaches.

The Irish annalists record that Fergus, Lorn, and Angus sailed up the river Add and landed at the fort of Dunadd, which became the seat of Fergus. According to tradition, he brought with him the stone used by Jacob as a pillow at Bethel. This had long been held at Cashel cathedral in Ireland, where it became known as the Lia Fail (Stone of Destiny) used as the coronation seat of Irish kings. Henceforth it was used thus by Fergus and all subsequent kings of Scotland until its seizure by the English in 1296.

In the seventh and eighth centuries, Dunadd was besieged by Britons and Picts, taken twice but retaken, remaining a seat of Scottish power until the reign of Kenneth MacAlpin. On his conquest of the Picts in 843 he moved his capital to Forteviot and Scone in Perthshire. Dalriada had been a separate kingdom for 345 years, but hereafter seemed a remote region and lost its old importance. The very name fell into disuse and was replaced by Argyll. It has often been asked what became of the Pictish language, of which little trace has ever been found. The simple explanation is that the Picts like the Scots were Celts, and their language probably not dissimilar. For that very reason the Scots' Gaelic would be able to replace and obliterate it.

When you climb the hill you enter the fort by a long gully in the rock, which may once have been roofed. Little trace of the original walls now remains. The hill is divided by rock outcrops into a lower, flattish amphitheatre, which may once have held wooden buildings, and an upper ridge originally walled as a keep. The lower amphitheatre was divided into three forts by walls connecting the rock. Each could be separately defended. Near the upper left-hand side as you ascend, a rude stairway cut into the rock leads up to the summit ridge, which was again divided into three smaller forts forming a triple keep. Several iron spearheads and a sword have been found here, and in the lower amphitheatre numerous quern stones (millstones for grinding corn by hand), pottery, jet ornaments, and bone and iron tools, including combs.

Near the top at centre are three features of great interest. Carved on the stone slabs are the imprint of a human foot, 11 inches long by 4½ wide, a wild boar facing the print, and a basin 10 inches wide by 4 deep. Tradition says that the footprint is that of Fergus, the first king of Dalriada. This most probably is true. At Celtic inaugurations, large stones on which a footprint was cut were customarily used. On Islay they were always used for the inauguration of the Kings and Lords of the Isles, when priests and bishops (of Argyll and the Isles) were present with all chiefs. Clothed in white, the Lord of the Isles would set his foot within the print, thus symbolizing an oath to walk in the steps of his forefathers. It seems certain that the same rite would be held at Dunadd.

The boar's outline is spirited, maybe intended to symbolize courage, a virtue essential to kings. Only two other boars have been found carved on Scottish rock, but rock basins are abundant— normally used as mortars for separating barley from the husk. The Dunadd basin, set close to the footprint, more probably held water for washing the feet, a custom of the time, preceding sacred ceremonies and recorded by Adamnan in the seventh century.

On the close of the Dalriadan period, the Crinan isthmus knew the Vikings, then the Donald Lords of the Isles, and finally came under the sway of the Campbells of Loch Awe. The principal landowners in more recent years have been the Malcolms of Poltalloch. Much surrounding ground has been bought by the Forestry Commission.

The country between Loch Awe and Crinan, being the cradle of Scotland, holds such an immense archaeological wealth—old churches and castles, carved stones, Celtic crosses, sun-circles, standing stones, duns and vitrified forts, chambered cairns, cup and ring marks, and monoliths—that archaeological books fail as yet to give full account.

One area particularly worth a visit is **Nether Largie** at the north edge of the Moss. From Crinan it is best reached across the Islandadd Bridge, thence straight over the Moss four miles to the side-roads east of Stockavulin. On this low farmland south of Kilmartin the prehistoric relics are extensive enough to bear comparison in importance with Avebury and Stonehenge. The principal features of Nether Largie are the South Cairn, which is a Neolithic chambered cairn of 3000–2000 B.C., and a sun-circle at Templewood.

There are several cairns at Nether Largie, but the South Cairn is one of the largest in Britain, 134 feet in diameter. A sepulchral chamber 19 feet long and roofed by great slabs is reached by a tunnel through the side. The floor is clean gravel. This, and two smaller cists, were exposed when the covering stones were removed by local people for wall-building. In such chambers were placed urns containing burnt bodies or bones, and stone coffins holding unburned bodies in a crouching position. They were then roofed with flags, on top of which the enormous cairns were built. At Nether Largie, several burials of different types and periods were distinguished by the evidence of bones, beakers, urns, cists, pottery, and flint arrowheads.

Many of the stones around Nether Largie have cup and ring marks. Cup marks are shallow pits chiselled in the living rock and on standing stones. Some are ringed. They have been found across the world from Scotland to India, but their meaning remains unknown.

The **Templewood stone circle** stands nearby in a field surrounded by well-grown scrub-oak. It dates from the Bronze Age, around 1600 B.C. The main group is a central monolith ringed by eight other standing stones. Five are 8 and 9 feet high, the others 2 feet. A burial chamber lies at centre. The cairn and circle have sunny sites on cut grass, and are preserved (belatedly) as Ancient Monuments by the Ministry of Works.

North of Templewood, the ground rises up in less than a mile to **Kilmartin** village, which marks the start of the five-mile pass to Loch Awe. Kilmartin thus commands the Great Moss. Its church, castle, and a dozen houses are sited along a bend of the main road. Craggy but grassy hills shelter them, for they stand on the flank of the glen with Kilmartin burn flowing below to join the Add.

Chambered cairns of the Bronze Age sprinkle the river's flat bank. The ruins of Kilmartin Castle stand close in to the village on its north side. This sixteenth century tower, probably built by John Carswell, the first rector of Kilmartin, became a Campbell seat. The *Records of Argyll* report here an attempt to murder Colin Campbell. He made his escape through a burning outbuilding, but had to jump into the river to cool his chain mail. The castle is not worthy of close inspection. Kilmartin churchyard is. The church with its square tower is perched on the breast of the hill overlooking Kilmartin Glen where it broadens south to the Great Moss. It was built in 1835 on the site of an older church dating from 1601 and dedicated to St. Martin of Tours. A war memorial arch of ten granite blocks spans the gateway, but the less said of this the better. Immediately within are the two famed Kilmartin crosses.

On the left-hand side of the path, a twelfth-century pillar of greenish slate bears a short-armed cross sculpted and ornamented in traditional Celtic pattern. Of far greater interest and beauty is the cross on the right-hand side. Only the shaft remains, for the arms have been broken off; on its front is carved Christ crucified, on its reverse, Christ in Majesty. He is shown on the front without crown, the face beardless and the head short-haired. The arms (broken) are at right-angles to the body. All these features characterize Celtic art of the tenth century. There are only two known earlier sculptures of Christ carved in relief on the cross, and they show the legs stretched straight, feet separate. At Kilmartin they hang straight, but the feet are crossed, denoting a later conception, now dated to the sixteenth century. The sculpture shows much refinement of feeling in its simple grace.

Elsewhere in the graveyard are many ancient sculptured gravestones, the best of them within a glass-roofed stone building maintained by the Ministry of Works. In an open enclosure are the Poltalloch stones, or gravestones of the Malcolm chiefs. Carved upon them are knights in armour, the straight sword, shears, and other devices.

The Kilmartin Glen passing through the hills to Loch Awe is flat-bottomed and arable land. Near the north end it is flanked by Loch Ederline, where the road runs through an avenue of beech and sycamore. The trees bend over the loch, whose wide fringe of reeds and water-lilies are in morning sun all agleam and glittering against the light. Rolling fields and woods stretch to the hills.

Mid Argyll: Dunadd and Loch Awe

Midway, at the road-junction to Kilmelford and Oban, **Carnassarie Castle** tops a grassy hill to the west side. It is well worth visiting as an excellent example of a sixteenth century fortified house. Square towers with rounded turrets, parapets, and a wall-walk, buttress each end. The walls are punctured by gun-ports. The castle was noted as the home of John Carswell, Bishop of the Isles, who in 1567 printed the first Gaelic book—his translation of Knox's Liturgy. Around 1680 it was owned by Sir Duncan Campbell (who also had the old castle of Asknish on Loch Gair). When Argyll was leading his rebellion of 1685 in support of Monmouth, Carnassarie was besieged and sacked by John Murray, the Marquis of Atholl.

The castle has remarkably fine masonry, a local schist carefully dressed and enriched in detail. Above the main door can still be seen the arms of the Campbell owner—of Argyll and Scotland impaled with his wife's (the earl had married a half-sister of Mary Queen of Scots). On the ground floor are cellars and kitchen, with an open fireplace for roasting a whole ox. At one side of the fire is a circular arched oven for baking bread; at the other, a carved stone head, at whose open mouth a vessel could be filled with water flowing through a stone channel piercing the outer wall.

A spiral stair allows you to climb up to the wall-walk on top of one tower. On the first floor a large withdrawing room has a straight stair down to a wine-cellar. The room formerly opened off a great hall, which has now vanished like the apartments above. The battlements reveal a splendid view over the length and breadth of the wooded glen. The fields around the castle are well kept and cut, shaded by sycamore and ash, and by two Spanish chestnuts at the outer gate.

Kilmartin Glen owes its very being to **Loch Awe,** which in earlier geological times drained south to the Sound of Jura. It thus carved the glen, and when the last glacier withdrew 12,000 years ago it left deposits of gravel and glacial drift, which made the glen fertile and gave the first men well-drained ground for settlement. The first author of all this good, Loch Awe itself, now has two heads, at Ford in the south and Dalmally 23 miles north, where it is fed by the river Orchy. A few miles south of Dalmally, Loch Awe now discharges seven miles west to Loch Etive.

The rivers and burns of Loch Awe and Kilmartin afford good fishing for brown trout and salmon. Much of it is free. The hotel at Ford, and others around Loch Awe at Portsonachan, Ardbrecknish, Dalmally, and **Lochawe** village, are well-known angling resorts.

Loch Awe is open water, famous for its sea-trout. Even salmon may be taken for no more than the incidental costs of boat-hiring and accommodation.

Loch Awe is the south-east frontier of Lorn. Throughout its whole great length, which is less than a mile wide save at Inishail, it ranks with Loch Lomond and Loch Maree as one of the three most beautiful of Scottish freshwater lochs. The south head is enclosed by cone-shaped hills of only a thousand feet, which screen it from wind. There the loch lies very still in quiet bays and backwaters, dyed green by the wooded cones that seem to cast light, not shade, across the water. Plover, duck, and a few oystercatchers may be seen.

The hills bounding the west side of the loch are low for twenty miles. They throw no long shadows; light lingers in the sky after sunset, brightening the water with its own shining yellow. Good roads run down both sides of the loch. Although both are wooded they could hardly be more different: the west coniferous, the east deciduous. The west side is now Forestry Commission ground. Their Inverliever Forest in the south half was bought from the Malcolms of Poltalloch in 1907, and is now the oldest State forest in Scotland. The trees are pine and spruce, mature and thinned, but as one drives through them mile after unchanging mile they cut off all views of the loch and make the road exceedingly monotonous.

Nine miles from Ford there is a new wooden village for forestry workers at Dalavich. A mile farther on, where the river Avich discharges into Loch Awe, a motorable road climbs 300 feet to Loch Avich in the hills above, and so to Kilmelford on the west coast. Inquiries about the state of this road should be made locally before crossing. The maps mark an apparent metropolis at **New York**, three-quarters of a mile south of Dalavich. It comprises a derelict house and pier named from the York Building Company, which after the rising of 1715 acquired confiscated estates to exploit the timber. To the great pleasure of the Scots it went bankrupt.

The road continues north to **Kilchrenan**, where it turns through Glen Nant to Taynuilt and Oban. In Kilchrenan churchyard are ancient carved stones and a block of granite raised in memory of Cailean Mor. The great Sir Colin was ambushed by the Mac-Dougalls of Lorn in 1294, when a sniping archer shot him on the hill-track called the String of Lorn about two miles north of Loch Avich. A big cairn marks the spot. His original tombstone is now built into the east gable of the church.

Rothesay Castle on the island of Bute is one of the most important medieval
castles in Scotland. The main building is a huge circular curtain-wall of
pink and grey sandstone set on a grassy plinth and moated. Four massive drum
towers project from the corners. On the north side, facing Rothesay Bay, the
moat is spanned by a wooden bridge leading into the great fore-tower (*above*).
built by James IV in the 16th century. The main building is 13th century
or earlier, perhaps when Angus, the son of Somerled, became Lord of Bute
after the defeat of the Vikings at sea in 1156.

Above the north end of Loch Fyne, near St. Catherines, Argyll. The longest of Scotland's sea-lochs (41 miles), Loch Fyne was at one time famous for its herring, now caught farther afield. On its shores stand Inveraray, from which the Campbells formerly ruled Argyll, and the fishing port of Tarbert.

Below the west basin of the Crinan Canal, which connects Loch Fyne to the open sea on the Sound of Jura, thus saving small Clyde ships an 80-mile voyage round the Mull of Kintyre. In summer this basin will be packed tight with yachts (80 may pass through in a day). To Clyde yachtsmen this is the Atlantic Gate, and the name Dorus Mor, or Great Gate, is given to the strait off Craignish Point, which projects a low lean finger in the farthest background. The actual point is not seen—the sharp visible point marks the lip of Loch Craignish.

Mid Argyll: Dunadd and Loch Awe

In contrast to the dullness of the west road, the eastern rejoices in natural woods of native variety. Some two miles out of Ford the ruins of **Fincharn Castle** crouch at the water's edge. Dating from the thirteenth century, when it was probably held by the Mac-Dougalls of Lorn, and thereafter by the Campbells of Loch Awe, the remnant is not worth visiting, but it lends an air to a mile of bare shore. You then pass seven miles through the **Wood of Eredine**. The roadsides here are banked deep in foxgloves. In July they glow against the green bracken behind: you thread a road through Elfland. This enchanted wood has two great gaps, the first at Braevallich, facing the deepest stretch of the loch, which plunges from its normal 100 feet to 300, and the second at the tiny village of Portinnisherrich. Note the two islets to north and south. The south has an old chapel, the north, Innis Chonnail, carried on its back the thirteenth-century castle and chief seat of the Campbells of Loch Awe. The ivy-clad ruin is still a substantial tower, only a moat's breadth offshore.

The road holds closely to the loch for eight more miles to Port-sonachan Hotel, which has faced Kilchrenan across the water since the fourteenth century. When Clan Campbell was holding the Loch Awe forts for the crown in 1745, the inn's boat was used for ferrying soldiers across to their barracks at Kilchrenan. The hotel retains the ferry rights to this day. Recent gazetteers, guides, and maps, aver that a ferry still plies across the loch, but in fact there is no such ferry-service.

At **Cladich** you join the main road from Inveraray to Dalmally. On either side of Cladich, high ground allows a clear sight of Ben Cruachan's massive bulk. The bowl of its vast south corrie, circled by the many-peaked crest, is now marred by a concrete dam. When to this we add the pylons and wires, and a big and ugly hutted camp under the eastern corrie at the foot of Glen Strae, we find the formerly magnificent mountain scene despoiled.

Despite this, the lochside between Cladich and Dalmally is one of the finest scenes of its kind in Argyll. It appears at its best when one is moving south from Dalmally rather than north from Cladich, for the wooded capes and islands then prick out against the blue sparkle of the loch. A bird's eye view may be had if you halt on the hill-top half a mile south of the fork where the old Dalmally road joins the shore road. Here, at Achlian, there is a triangulation point 205, which you can reach by crossing a stile.

By contrast with the mild hills of the southern head, this northern end of Loch Awe is ringed by mountains cast on the majestic scale, and set far enough back to be well seen: the eight tops of Ben Cruachan, 3,689 feet, Beinn a Chochuill and Beinn Eunaich, around 3,200 feet, and Beinn Laoigh, 3,708 feet. Between them drive the big rivers of the Strae and Orchy, the latter famous for its salmon. The short, narrow northern head of the loch thus lies pillowed in mountains. The main loch snakes sinuously south. Directly opposite Achlian a mile-wide channel pours west, tapers to a gimlet, and pierces the Pass of Brander at the river Awe. The ancient Gaelic for river was Abh (genitive Abha), hence Loch Abha, later corrupted to Loch Ow and then to Loch Awe.

Across the forking waters below are scattered a dozen islands, wooded in willow, rowan, and birch, with a few pines and much sycamore and ash. Beautiful as they look from this distance, they are even more so at close quarters. You can explore them by hiring a boat from Lochawe village on the far side of the loch near the head. The boat hirer's jetty will be found at the village's west end. In former days, Loch Aweside was much more heavily wooded than now, but much of the natural forest was burned, as elsewhere in the Highlands, to deny the wolf shelter. In the sixteenth century, when wolves were numerous and ravenous, the people of the Highlands often used to bury their dead on islands. Here they are said to have used the large central island of **Inishail**, 'The Isle of Rest'. It swells at centre to a broad hillock, on which stands the ruins of an ancient chapel first mentioned in records of 1257 as dedicated to St. Findoc (one of Columba's followers). Lying on the grass to its east side are two exceptionally fine carved slabs of the fourteenth or fifteenth century. One, probably an altar frontal, shows from left to right two armed soldiers, then Mary holding a chalice towards Christ on the cross, while farther right appears a coat of arms with supporters showing the Somerled galley. The second is a grave-slab showing the Clan Donald straight sword. Several gazetteers state that Inishail once bore a Cistercian nunnery, but there is no good evidence to support that notion. A very small church built on Inishail was in 1736 moved to Cladich, where it was re-erected and still stands by the roadside. It is easy to miss for it looks very much like a grey stone cottage, save for the short open bell-canopy above one gable.

Half a mile north-east of Inishail, **Fraoch Eilean** bears the ruins of a castle hitherto thought to have been built in the thirteenth century by the MacNachtans. Recent research has shown it to be older and more important than earlier surmise had suggested. The island is small—little more than two acres—and especially delightful in spring or early summer when its wild flowers are in bloom: daffodil, wood anemone, primrose, broom, and honeysuckle. The castle, until a few years ago entirely screened by trees, which have now been felled by the owner, Ian Campbell of the old Inverawe family, stands on a crag's brink at the east end. The structure is at several points rather similar to that of Castle Sween in Knapdale, and can now perhaps be dated to the end of the twelfth century. It was almost certainly built by Dughall of Lorn, the son of Somerled, to guard his eastern approaches. By a charter of 1267, granted by Alexander III, the castle passed to the MacNachtans, who, although later allied to the MacDougalls, held it till 1308. In that year the MacDougalls' hostility to Bruce culminated in the battle at the Pass of Brander, as a result of which Bruce gave the castle to Colin, son of his 'beloved Sir Niall Campbell', the son of Cailean Mor. It has remained in Campbell possession to the present day.

The interior of the castle measures 60 feet by 27. It was built as a hall-house and is the only one of Norman period surviving in Scotland. A curtain-wall guards the inland side. Around 1600 the eastern end was built up as a tall tower-house, one gable of which still stands to the original height of four stories. Ospreys nested on top of its chimney as late as 1833, but have not yet returned. The detail of this castle is full of interest.

Fraoch Eilean (which would ordinarily mean Heather Island) has little heather. The name derives instead from a Celtic legend that here grew the berries of eternal youth, guarded by a dragon. Fraoch was the hero who seized the berries and slew the dragon. The story goes that he was set to this quest not by his mistress but by her mother. Her intention not being pure, all went wrong: Fraoch died of his wounds and the berries poisoned the mother.

On the hill of 500 feet, midway along the old road between Achlian and Dalmally, stands a granite monument raised to the memory of Duncan Ban McIntyre (1724–1812), the most celebrated of Gaelic poets. Born in this parish near Bridge of Orchy, where he became a gamekeeper on the Black Mount, he had two passions, mountains and hunting. His great poem, *In Praise of Beinn Dorain*, gives free play to his love and knowledge of hills and the life of the red deer. He was illiterate—but most fully versed in the oral literature of his time. The monument—a round, open-sided temple borne aloft on a massive stepped plinth—should be visited on foot from Dalmally (1½ miles) for its superb view over the most beautiful part of Loch Awe.

Prominently seen from the monument is **Kilchurn Castle** (pronounced Kilhoorn), standing on a spit of land, formerly an island, at the north head of the loch. The name is from Caol a'chuirn, the Strait at the Cairn. The castle was built in 1440 by Sir Colin Campbell of Glen Orchy, who founded the Breadalbane family. Its torn walls stand to full height. From whatever angle it may be seen, the high square keep, flanked by bartizans, seems to rise straight out of the water. Its setting at the foot of great glens and mountains has made it a favourite subject for painters and photographers. During his tour of 1803, Wordsworth wrote his poem on Kilchurn:

> *Child of loud-throated war! the mountain stream*
> *Roars in thy hearing; but thy hour of rest*
> *Is come and thou art silent in thy age,*
> *Save when the winds sweep by . . .*

The castle is easily reached by a walk of half a mile from the main road at the head of the loch. The keep was at first a freestanding tower, the high walls with battlements and turrets extending south being an addition of 1693. In 1740 the Campbells abandoned the castle, reopening it at the 'Forty-five only to house Hanoverian troops. It is now preserved by the Ministry of Works. In the courtyard lies a huge tower-top, blown down in the hurricane that wrecked the Tay Bridge in 1879.

The village of **Dalmally** is set a mile back from Loch Awe at the foot of Glen Orchy. This small but vigorous community is served by the railway line to Oban. It has a good hotel, which has several miles of salmon fishing on the river Orchy. The river's principal source is on the range of the Black Mount, from which it rushes (rather than flows) twelve miles down Glen Orchy from Loch Tulla at the edge of Rannoch Moor. One among its many splendid pools, four miles from Dalmally and frequented by picnickers, is notoriously dangerous, having drowned five adults in recent years. They slip off the fringing rocks and have no chance of life in the raging current.

A few hundred yards north of Dalmally Hotel, an island on the river Orchy carries a small church of exceeding beauty. Set among trees on a hillock, it is the Highland's best example of an eighteenth-

84

century 'round' church, although in fact octagonal with a square tower and spirelets. The stained glass of the west window behind the pulpit epitomizes the rich outdoor colourings of Glen Orchy and Inishail: in the afternoon sun it glows like Loch Awe.

CHAPTER 6

Knapdale

The main body of Argyll, from the shoulder of its Crinan isthmus, shoots south toward Ireland, the longest of Scotland's many arms. From Crinan to the Mull of Kintyre, this peninsula measures fifty-four miles and is never wider than ten. The northern part, almost split off from Kintyre by West Loch Tarbet, is called Knapdale. The name means hill and dale, the word knap implying a protuberant, sharp-sided hill, usually conical and eye-catching although small. With such all Knapdale is heavily endowed. From coast to coast the hills rise and fall in parallel folds: rough moorland that from high ground can look like a choppy sea. The crests and troughs run south-west to north-east and are seen at their pointed best from these angles.

The east coast from Loch Gilp to Tarbet runs twelve miles straight without particular interest. All that is best in Knapdale lies westward. The west coast, split wide and deep along its fault lines by Loch Sween and Loch Caolisport is heavily bayed and spiked. It measures twenty-three miles by rule but treble that in outline. Two roads enter. One from near Crinan strikes south-west down both sides of Loch Sween, the other crosses the middle moors from the east coast to Loch Caolisport, thence around Kilberry Head to the Tarbert isthmus.

If heading for Loch Sween you leave the Crinan Canal at Bellanoch and climb uphill into the **Knapdale Forest.** This forest covers the whole of north-west Knapdale, much of which was sold by the Malcolms of Poltalloch in 1930 to the Forestry Commission. The plantations are of spruce, larch, pine, and Douglas fir. These give way to broad-leaved trees at the head of Loch Coille Bharr, and again at the narrow sea-loch of Caol Scotnish, which is the most northerly of Loch Sween's three heads. Close to Loch Coille Bharr near the Achnamara-Tayvallich road-fork, the Forestry Commission

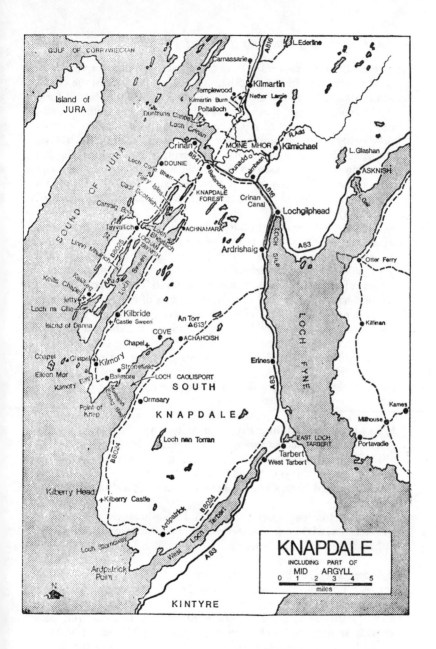

GULF OF CORRYVRECKAN

Island of
JURA

L.Ederline

Carnassarie

Kilmartin
Templewood   Nether Largie
Kilmartin Burn
Poltalloch
Duntrune Castle
Loch Crinan

R.Add

Crinan   MOINE MHOR   Kilmichael

L.Glashan

DOUNIE
Loch Coille Bharr
Fairy Isles
Caol Scotnish
Carsaig Bay

KNAPDALE
FOREST

Ballanoch
Dunadd
Cairnbaan

Crinan
Canal

ASKNISH

Lochgilphead

Tayvallich
Loch a'
Bhealaich
Loch
TAYNEI

ACHNAMARA

A83

Linne Mhuirich
B8025

Loch Sween

Keills Chapel
Keillmore
Jetty
Loch na Cille
Island of Danna

Ardrishaig

LOCH FYNE

Otter Ferry

Kilbride
Castle Sween

An Torr
△613

Kilfinan

COVE
ACHAHOISH
Chapel

Chapel
Eilean Mor
Chapel
Kilmory
Kilmory Bay
Stronefield
Balimore

LOCH CAOLISPORT

SOUTH

KNAPDALE

Erines

A83

Kames

Millhouse

Point of
Knap

Ormsary

Loch nan Torran

Portavadie

B8024

EAST LOCH
TARBERT

Kilberry Head

Kilberry Castle

Tarbert
West Tarbert

Ardpatrick

B8024

Loch Tarbert

Loch Stornoway

West Loch Tarbert

A83

Ardpatrick
Point

N

KINTYRE

KNAPDALE

INCLUDING PART OF
MID ARGYLL

0   1   2   3   4   5
miles

have an information centre from which you can enjoy a variety of forest walks and observe wildlife, or visit a prehistoric stone circle, or a trout hatchery, or climb uphill to get a view of the Paps of Jura. The banks of both lochs are crowded with oak, chestnut, birch, and hazel. The sheets of water running far south from their heads glow richly green, reminding one of the south head of Loch Awe. Caol Scotnish is four miles long. Numerous islets are in spring full of nesting terns. The narrows at the foot broaden out into the main body of Loch Sween, you turn a corner, and **Tayvallich** appears around the sheltered waters of Loch a' Bhealaich (pronounced Veeálaich).

The small village is set in the bay of a greatly shattered peninsula, which from Crinan runs ten miles south to the island of Danna. Tayvallich's bay is matched on the Jura side by Carsaig Bay, and the low pass (bealach) between the two gives name to the village (House of the Pass), which is thus pronounced Tayviállach, stressing the first and third vowels. On the south side of the bay a long arm projects north as a breakwater giving perfect shelter to a score of yachts and as many dinghies lying at moorings. Behind a fringe of jetties lie the houses, several of them new and of good design. At Leachy on the north side is a caravan park and camp site. Tayvallich, delightful in itself, is an excellent centre for exploring the thin peninsulas on either side of Loch Sween, both by car and on foot.

A walk of only three-quarters of a mile leads west to **Carsaig Bay**. It has no sand, but in good contrast to Tayvallich has an open greensward for picnics facing Jura across a four-mile sound. A hill-track continues north along the coast, and you can follow this three miles to the old farmhouse of Dounie. The poet Thomas Campbell lived here when he was tutor to the children of General Napier.

A still better walk goes south from Tayvallich over a low hill to **Lochan Taynish,** a freshwater loch in beautiful woodland. By this unfrequented road the banks on the Tayvallich side are bright with red campion and loud with bees. Across the hill at Lochan Taynish it becomes a shelf between the water's edge and a conical hill of 300 feet, tree-clad to its summit, wooded thickly even on the naked rock of its flank. The deep green water is fringed by reeds and water-lilies, glassily still, yet everywhere rippled by fish and (on your arrival) slashed by duck racing for cover. The scented track is bayed by bluebell patches and where it runs out on marshes at the

88

foot of the loch, whitened by bog-cotton. All the woods around
Tayvallich harbour roe-deer. In the early morning and evening they
may often be seen romping on open fields.

The peninsula on which Tayvallich nestles ends six miles south
in a double point riven by Loch na Cille, which itself is a six-mile
inlet of the Sound of Jura. On your way south you pass the Linne
Mhuirich, a lagoon three miles long with a narrow opening to
Loch Sween. Oysters used to be abundant on Loch Sween,
especially in this lagoon, which had a profitable fishery at the
beginning of the century. In recent years the Scottish Marine
Biological Association proved that oysters planted above the mud-
level flourish; the establishment of a new commercial oyster fishery
has since followed.

The peninsula soon grows exposed as you move south, but as
trees vanish golden broom spreads. An occasional pheasant may be
seen scurrying across the road. At the head of Loch na Cille you
fork left to the tidal island of Danna, to which you cross by a stone
causeway. Herons fish by the shore and dunlins quarter the sands.
Above a foreshore on which ragged robin, bird's-foot trefoil, and
iris run riot, the bare land is farmed. Rocky islands fringing the
south point nearly all carry outcrops like old tooth stumps. The
farthest, **Eilean Mor,** shaped instead like a green anthill, is one of
the most ancient of Scotland's holy islands. Access is difficult, but
a motor-boat may be hired from Crinan Hotel. Near the island's
centre, a twelfth-century chapel with nave and vaulted chancel is
dedicated to St. Carmaig. His original cell, fifteen feet square and
built by his own hands five hundred years earlier (he died in 664),
is sited nearer the south end. On the island's highest point, close
above the cell, a Celtic cross-shaft stands alone upon a grassy
pedestal. One side bears a crucifixion, the other carved foliage. On
the hill north of the church are traces of a beehive cell and other
buildings unknown.

Returning to the head of Loch na Cille, you drive down the west
side of the loch till the road ends at **Keills Chapel,** facing Danna and
Eilean Mor across the water. It has a delightfully open situation,
exposed to wind but saved from the worst blow of storm-seas by a
mile-long point thrusting south-west towards the Paps of Jura and
Islay. The point bristles with slate pinnacles like prehistoric standing
stones. This bit of country has more of a West Highland character
than any other of Knapdale. All is quiet, the road carries little or
no traffic, but the land is alive with colour and music: windy fields

of bog-cotton and ox-eye daisies; flat grassland between the chapel and the old jetty of Keillbeg covered in blue speedwell, yellow iris and buttercup, white clover and daisy, and along the seashore by ragged robin, so thickly that one mistakes it for a carpet of sea pink. Larks sing from early morning to late at night.

The eleventh-century chapel is roofless, but gables and walls are in good order, their stone perfectly laid. It is thought to have been dedicated to St. Columba, who spent some time in Knapdale near the head of Loch Caolisport. Within the walls are a number of fourteenth- and fifteenth-century recumbent slabs carved with wild cats, hounds, sheld-duck, wolves, otters, a fox, a winged horse, a griffin, fish, and the more usual swords, shears, and leafage. Together they form one of the finest collections in Argyll, but are much defaced by weather, for they have not come under the protection of the Ministry of Works. The finest slab of all is the lid of a stone coffin, ornamented with a wealth of delicate detail. Its inscription, hardly decipherable, reads (in translation) *MacNeil caused me to be made*. The MacNeils of Gigha formerly held this land under the Donald Kings and Lords of the Isles.

On a hillock above the chapel, a Celtic cross of blue slate rises ten feet from a circular platform. Sculptured in the twelfth century, it is one of the oldest freestanding crosses of Argyll, almost unique in being carved on one side only. The arms are cut very short with a raised boss at centre, in which a hollow cups three smaller bosses to symbolize the Trinity in Unity. Above, St. Michael treads his dragon; below, Daniel is having his face licked by flanking lions. The shaft is patterned in a key design and spirals.

From the road-end a track leads through the deserted farm of Keillmore to a little bay on the west coast. On its high rocky shore an old stone pier compels attention by the perfection of its construction. No cement has been used. The long narrow stones, exactly cut and laid, have held together unbreached by a century's storms. In former days the pier was used by ferry-boats plying to and from Jura with cattle. Now the pier is brightly yellowed by lichen and sea pink grows thick in the joints. Herons flap heavily by and oystercatchers scream along the shore. In June the bay becomes busy with eider-duck and their trains of young.

A bird sanctuary famous for its nesting duck and swan is the **Fairy Isles** in the central head of Loch Sween. They lie in an inlet of the peninsula dividing Caol Scotnish from the main loch. The only way to reach them is by boat from Tayvallich, a two-mile sail.

If a rowing boat is hired, choose a calm day, for as soon as the bay is cleared a strong current can be met on the ebb from Caol Scotnish. The inlet when reached is a haven of peace and beauty enclosed by woods. There are seven principal islands, some no more than reefs, others wooded and heathery between the crags, or quilted with bluebells. Ashore you may have to tread carefully to avoid crushing the eggs of gulls and oystercatchers.

The neighbourhood of the Fairy Isles can also be reached by walking from the head of Loch Coille Bharr three miles down the peninsula. Entry to the forest is made four and a half miles north of Tayvallich at the right-angled bend nearest the loch. A few hundred yards east of the bend a forestry track leads in where a notice-board invites walkers and prohibits cars. The one-inch map marks the track but not its numerous diversions. The route to the Fairy Isles does not take the first branch to the lochside, which gives a good view, but keeps straight on. The track becomes muddy after rain, but is firm and worth walking in dry weather, especially as a change of scene from the bare ground of Keills and Danna. The conifers give off a heavy aromatic scent. Wood sorrel and garlic spread green in the shade of larch and oak. There is much bird-song.

You ought now to explore the farther side of Loch Sween twelve miles south to the Point of Knap. The head of Loch Sween is a confusing area, for its three long channels are forested and hard to distinguish one from another without much reference to the map. The car-driver must keep his eye on the road. It needs caution, being narrow and twisty with few passing places till you reach Achnamara, a foresty village with two dozen wooden houses. The road straightens. Gradually the woods thin out and you emerge on open country at **Kilbride.** The numerous small birds with white rumps on this stretch are wheatears. When I last passed Kilbride in June I noticed a tiny island a hundred yards offshore covered with roosting eider-drake. I had often wondered where the Loch Sween drakes disappeared to while their duck were with young, and here they were, forty of them packed tight in a 'club'.

A mile beyond Kilbride, **Castle Sween** is maintained by the Ministry of Works as the earliest stone castle in Scotland. It stands by a sandy shore on grassland speckled white and yellow with clover, iris, and buttercup. Ancient ash trees ring its north side. The castle looks best from the high ground to its south, whence it can be seen against the wooded hills of inner Knapdale, and the more spiky and distant hills of Crinan. Its good appearance has been destroyed by an ugly caravan park.

This twelfth-century castle was the first of square Norman build in Celtic Scotland. (The Normans had arrived in large numbers in Scotland around 1124). The Celtic duns and brochs had always been built of close-fitted unmortared stones and made circular, for such a structure is immeasurably stronger than a rectangular against attack by battering-ram. The Norman 'square' castles were, however, mortared, and thus stronger than the old circular forts.

Somerled succeeded his father as King of Argyll around 1130. In 1154 he built Castle Claig on Fraoch Eilean in the Sound of Islay almost exactly like Castle Sween. It seems most probable that he built the latter between 1125 and 1135, for he would then urgently require it as a firm base while he was driving the Vikings out of mainland Argyll. It was occupied and held for him by his Toiseach (Captain) of Knapdale, MacSuidhne Ruadh (Son of the Red Warrior). The name Caisteal Suidhean (pronounced Sweean) or Suidhne means either Castle of the Warriors or else Castle of Suidhne—a dual meaning being probably deliberate as a compliment to one of Somerled's trusted chiefs.

After Somerled, the land was ruled for three hundred years by Clan Donald (which he founded) and by their Kings and Lords of the Isles. At first the castle was the scene of war between Scots and Vikings, then between the Lord of the Isles and the King of Scots. From the fourteenth to the sixteenth centuries the MacNeils of Gigha served as constables, succeeded by the MacMillans. At the first forfeiture of the Lord of the Isles in 1475 the castle was claimed by the Crown and granted in 1481, with much of Knapdale, to Colin Campbell, the first Earl of Argyll. Its downfall came in 1644 at the hands of Alasdair MacDonald, known to history as Young Colkitto, lieutenant to the marquis of Montrose and then fighting for the royalist cause against the Covenanters. He besieged the castle and burnt the Campbells out.

The four walls still stand, buttressed at the middle of each side and at the angles. The north wall has a rectangular keep at its north-east corner (thirteenth century) and a round tower named MacMillan's Tower at its north-west (early fourteenth century). The gateway faces south to the Sound of Jura. In the courtyard, which measures 70 feet by 50, is cut grass and a deep well outside the main keep. The whole ground floor of the keep is a kitchen, with an oven surviving and a waterspout through the wall. MacMillan's Tower abuts the shore, set upon living rock that swells within the walls. You can climb up inside to a high floor pierced by the hole of an oubliette. Prisoners could be dropped down inside to the bottom of a smooth-walled pit, whose only opening is a drain running through the wall to the sea.

Two and a half miles south, near the Point of Knap, the tiny village of Kilmory is widely known for its **chapel of St. Maelrubha** and its fourteenth-century **MacMillan's Cross.** The two have an incongruous site in the centre of the ugliest farm in Argyll, a ramshackle place of rusty corrugated-iron sheds and muddy tracks; apart from which the scene is fair. Green fields slope away for a quarter of a mile to the wide curve of a sandy bay. Several small boats lie on the beach, hauled out for protection, for the bay is much exposed and none may lie at anchor. Each one has lobster creels alongside. The lobsters are fished down the coast to the Point of Knap, and from Eilean Mor and the skerries at the mouth of Loch Sween. On a headland to the west stands the low relic of Dun Fuarlit. It commands a seascape to the island of Gigha and the Paps of Jura, seen to best advantage against an afternoon sun. The sea then holds a brilliant sparkle and the Jura mountains rise black behind—topped when I last saw them by towering jagged clouds.

The chapel has come under the care of the Ministry of Works and is now roofed in glass to protect some thirty engraved stones. The old grey building is like many another, not impressive. But the stones within are most beautiful despite their centuries of weathering. The MacMillan Cross outside stands twelve feet tall. At the intersection of the arms, a large solid circle has been carved with a crucifixion. The Christ has been done with a rude dignity, a unique feature being the Celtic interlacing pattern on the long loin-cloth. Under His outstretched arms are Mary and John. On the shaft, a long straight sword carries on its point a reversed capital P, the meaning of which defies solution. The reverse side bears within the disc an animal biting its own tail. Beneath are a stag seized by hounds and a man raising a long axe. He stands on the inscription, *This is the cross of Alexander MacMillan.*

The road ends a mile farther at **Balimore,** where the last cottage of the coast stands exposed to all winds like a lighthouse on a bluff. A private road continues three miles more to Ellary House on Loch Caolisport, at the other side of the peninsula. In the glen between the two there used to be a village of Stronefield. Last century the landowner evicted the crofters. They battled with the police and gamekeepers and won, but the police returned heavily reinforced and fired the houses. The ruins remain, a scene of abject desolation in a once fertile glen. The fine river falling through it levels out on a grassy strath, and flows on to join the sea at the most beautiful of Argyll's mainland beaches, the Muileann Eiteag Bagh on Loch Caolisport.

To reach these sands from Balimore, walk east across bog to a hill ridge, join a track through a wooded glade, descend past a deserted mill-house to the river, and then stroll on springy turf to the sea. Roe-deer may be seen among the sycamore, birch, and oak. The beach is clean and secluded, facing south to Kilberry Head and Gigha.

There is no through-road from Kilmory to Loch Caolisport. To explore the loch's far side to West Loch Tarbert you have to return to Lochgilphead. Heading north from Kilmory's bare ground to Inner Knapdale, you grow much aware of the transition to woodland, of the growing lushness, the thickening forest, and the ever more powerful scents of vegetation. At Loch Gilp you rejoin the coast road down Loch Fyne. Four miles south, fork right and climb to 634 feet on the watershed of central Knapdale, a land of green hills given to sheep. The descent ends at the wooded head of Loch Caolisport. The mellowed cottages of Achahoish nestle there under the hill of **An Torr.**

An Torr, 613 feet, is crowned by the fort of Caisteal Torr, a stronghold of Conall, fifth king of Dalriada, progenitor of Clan Neil, and kinsman of St. Columba. It has been used as a stone-quarry by local dike-builders for centuries past. Only a fragment remains. But the hill is worth climbing for its superb view down Loch Caolisport to Islay. Adamnan, the seventh-century abbot of Iona, states early in his *Life of St. Columba* that Columba (then named Calum) lived for a while in Alban with King Conall, who ruled Dalriada between 560 and 574. This would appear to precede Columba's voyage from Ireland to Iona in 563, and the supposition makes sense: occupation of the island by a company of monks would have to be negotiated with Dalriada's ruler, especially when it lay so close to his northern frontier with hostile Picts. It may well have been as a result of this visit that Conall made to Columba his gift of Iona. By local tradition, Columba made use of a cave on the west shore of Loch Caolisport near **Cove.** There is every evidence that this could be true. Small as it is, the cave is one of the most remarkable relics of Christianity in Scotland. It lies three miles from Achahoish facing the first bay, which is further identified by the Eilean na h'Uamhaidh (Island of the Cave) at its mouth.

The narrow road around the head of the loch is most beautifully wooded in deciduous trees, for this is a private estate free of the grim grip of the Forestry Commission. Down the lochside the road holds to the shore between the sea's black boulders and fallen crags fringing the wood. Rhododendrons fill the hollows and brown owls nest. Clusters of bluebell and primrose grace any run of grass, even to the water's edge. On turning into the little bay facing Eilean na h'Uamhaidh, you at once see the dark gash of the cave. It lies a hundred yards inland from the road on the face of a crag. A stream alongside falls from a glen above to a clearing in front, where a twelfth-century chapel stands broken of all save one gable and a remnant of wall. Like Caisteal Torr it has been quarried.

The ground between chapel and cave has at one time borne a garden. Red poppy and campion, rose-bush and forget-me-not, speedwell and herb-robert, big yellow iris and biting stonecrop of the white starry kind, these and others still sprout freely from a jungle of fern. Close to the cave are some red rhododendron and white flowering shrubs, and to its left, one tall pine. On the wilder, higher ground, oak, ash, birch, and hazel take command. The burn running through them has a little waterfall lined by iris. Cruising out on the bay are often a couple of wild swan and some shield-duck— gorgeous birds with dark green head and crimson beak, black wing-tips, and a broad orange band across the white breast. Holiday-makers too rarely see them, for in July they migrate to the Bristol Channel and Heligoland.

The cave is high-roofed and twenty yards deep. It is important to know that early this century the floor was excavated three and a half feet and the soil not replaced. On your right as you enter, a round bowl has been cut into the rock at what would formerly have been hand-level. This would be used by the celebrant for washing his hands before mass. Within the cave, a rock platform projects from the right-hand wall. On its top is a drystone altar in good repair. Its stones are flat, neatly set and levelled to a height of approximately three feet by a length of five. You approach it up a strong wooden ladder and may then see a Latin cross, seven inches high, cut into the rock wall about three feet above the mensa. At the right-hand end of the altar, an ambry for holding the sacred vessels has been made within the structure.

Between altar and entrance a second basin has been cut in the rock, this one in the floor of the platform, bigger than the first and fully a foot deep. Some authorities have been sorely perplexed by it, wondering what could be its purpose. It was for washing the feet: Adamnan states explicitly that both hands and feet were washed before celebrating the holy service of the mass. In his day men wore sandals and paid heed to Exodus xxx, 18–21.

The interior of Columba's natural chapel has been granted a permanent blessing of flowers: bluebell and foxglove grow from the inmost rocks, golden saxifrage around the altar's foot, flanked by rose-bush, spleenwort on the roof, herb-robert at the outer cave, and draping the entrance, honeysuckle.

Returning to Achahoish, you go south down the loch's east shore to Kilberry Head, drawing away from woodland to open farmland. At the same time the road goes farther inland and grows monotonous. Directly above Kilberry Head, Kilberry Castle has on public exhibition a collection of sculptured stones, and a carved cross on which Christ is shown contorted. The castle is owned by a branch of the Campbell family and not open to view. Above the front doorway a stone is inscribed: *Plundered and burned by Captain Proby, an English Pirate, 1513. Rebuilt by F.C., 1844.*

The road southward keeps to high ground, now giving spacious views to the Paps of Jura and down the coast of Kintyre, where Gigha seems to float on silvery light. On descending to the bay of Loch Stornoway you pass over the low back of Ardpatrick Point to the quiet woods of West Loch Tarbert. The loch runs ten miles into the land, completely dwarfing its tiny but much more important neighbour of East Loch Tarbert on Loch Fyne. An isthmus only one mile wide divides the two. Apart from the daily steamer to Islay the West Loch is almost empty of shipping. It has no regular fishing apart from one lobsterman, who has to make long voyages. In former days the loch was noted for its oysters. An attempt to revive the industry has been made by the Scottish Marine Biological Association, who planted a quarter of a million oysters in 1956. They were subsequently able to recommend the site but no commercial fishery has yet developed.

At the head of the loch you turn right on to the narrow isthmus, and at this move enter Kintyre.

96

The cross in Kilmartin churchyard, Argyll. This famous cross is of far
greater interest and beauty than any others of Argyll, except possibly the
Kildalton cross of Islay. Only the shaft remains, for the arms have been
broken off. On the front is carved Christ crucified; on the reverse,
Christ in Majesty. He is shown on the front without crown, hair short, face
beardless, and the arms have been at right-angles to the body—features which
characterize Celtic art of the 10th century: but this work may be later. The only
two earlier sculptures of Christ carved in relief on the cross show the legs and feet
separate. Here they hang straight but with feet crossed, which may denote a
concept of the 16th century, at latest.

Above the entrance to the Pass of Brander, Loch Awe, Argyll. The road is a mere ledge, blasted out of the flank of Ben Cruachan, whose slopes plunge into the loch. The pass was the scene of a battle in 1308, when Robert the Bruce defeated the forces of MacDougall of Lorn, and thus won control of Argyll. *Below* Kilchurn Castle, at the north head of Loch Awe. Built in 1440 by Sir Colin Campbell of Glen Orchy, the keep was a free-standing tower, the high walls and turrets extending south being an addition of 1693.

CHAPTER 7

Kintyre

As seen from their own roof, the moors of Kintyre roll forty miles from Tarbert to the Mull, their rounded hills grassed to the tops with only a little heather mixed in. Kintyre holds the best farm land of Argyll for both stock-raising and dairy farming, the latter chiefly in the south. This pastoral fertility is fostered by a mild climate. Snow is rare, fog unknown, and since no high hills draw cloud the rainfall varies between 45 and 55 inches. Kintyre's being so very nearly an island makes it appropriate that the industry next in importance to farming should be fishing, and that, as in the isles, the ports should all be on the east coast, at Tarbert, Carradale, and Campbeltown.

Tarbert lies on the isthmus. Its bay of East Loch Tarbert is small, but an almost perfect haven: three-quarters of a mile long and sharply curved. Several rocky points and two islets guard the passage to the inner bay. Fishing smacks and yachts can lie safe in any weather. Although the isthmus is low and flat, the hills to either side baffle much wind and the town's houses help to fill the gap. The buildings close-packed around the inner harbour are of two and three storeys with shops on the ground floor. The grocery stores are stocked with high-quality goods unusual in a small Highland town with a population of 1,500. Great numbers of yachts call in summer en route to Crinan, for although Tarbert has no canal to the west coast, her position is one of strategic importance by sea and land: the first and only excellent port for a ship northbound from the Sound of Bute; by road a staging point for all men travelling between Glasgow and the isles of Islay, Jura, Gigha, or south Kintyre and the Clyde. Behind the main quay stands the Tarbert Hotel, but most strangely there is no restaurant. Fishermen's cottages line the south front and these and all other houses are clean, neat, and freshly painted. On the hillsides above, sixty or seventy cottages straggle among scrub birch. As specially befits a fishing village, the most prominent building is the church. Its tall tower with short-spired Gothic crown rises from the West Loch Tarbert road, set far enough back to stand aloof yet close enough to be ever-present to the eye.

The busy heart of Tarbert is the south quay where the fishing boats lie, draped with red and yellow buoys and nets, bustling with men and lorries loading and unloading fish-boxes, yet given a more enduring air by the old seamen just sitting around or mending nets. Last century the fleet numbered seventy luggers and 300 men. Their great brown sails made a stirring sight as they left or entered harbour. By 1949 the fleet was down to thirty ships and 200 men, but the value of the fish-landings had reached a peak of £200,000. Now there are twelve ships and 100 men, yet the fishing prospers, for these fast power-boats, equipped with echo-sounders (which guide them to the herring shoals) and all modern gear, sail farther and have greater catching-power than the six-times bigger fleet of last century. Herring, white fish, prawns, and scallops are landed. Succeeding periods of depression and prosperity have characterized west coast fishing, but the Loch Fyne herring, distinguished locally under the name of Glasgow Magistrates, are unlikely to lose their market. A Glasgow Magistrate is big and plump, its flavour delicious when cooked freshly caught, or when kippered at Tarbert under oak-chips.

On the other side of the harbour, the small but famous yacht-yard of Dickie of Tarbert employed a score of men building yachts, fishing boats, and small craft until it closed down in 1967. On a summer weekend there may be as many as eighty Clyde yachts crammed into the inner harbour at night, and the town as busy as a fair, for its distinctive character and varied amenities draw many holiday-makers. A sight most worth seeing in early summer is the garden of Stonefield Castle Hotel, two miles north between road and shore. In the mid nineteenth century, Sir Joseph Dalton Hooker introduced to west Scotland numerous large-leaved rhododendrons from the Himalaya, believing that mild rainy winters would be ideal for growth. He was right. Specimens of the original plants survive to-day at Stonefield among some of the most wonderfully coloured of the genus to be seen in Scotland.

The best point from which to view town and harbour is from **Tarbert Castle** on its 100-foot hillock close to the south. Only a crumbled fifteenth-century keep now stands, perhaps to half its

98

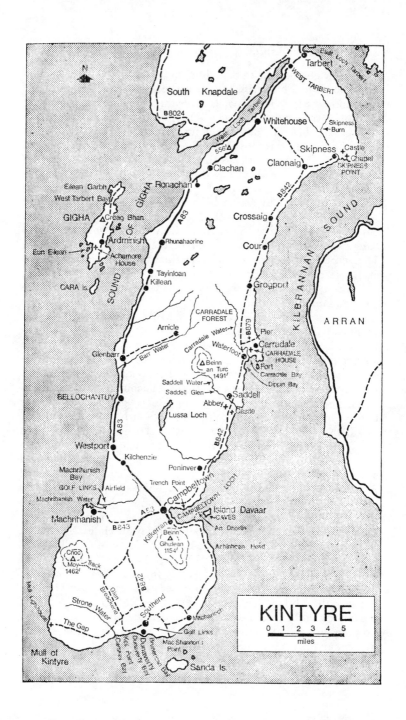

N

South Knapdale

B8024

Tarbert

EAST LOCH TARBERT

WEST TARBERT

WEST LOCH TARBERT

Whitehouse

Skipness
←Burn

556△

Skipness

Castle
Chapel
SKIPNESS
POINT

Clachan

Claonaig

GIGHA
SOUND

Ronachan

B842

Eilean Garbh
West Tarbert Bay

GIGHA

Creag Bhan

Crossaig

△

Ardminish

Cour

Eun Eilean

Achamore
House

Rhunahaorine

SOUND OF GIGHA

CARA Is.

Tayinloan
Killean

Grogport

ARRAN

KILBRANNAN SOUND

CARRADALE
FOREST

Arnicle

Carradale Water→

Waterfoot

Pier

B879

Carradale
CARRADALE
HOUSE

Glenbarr

Barr Water

△ Beinn
an Turc
1491′

Fort
Carradale Bay
Dippin Bay

Saddell Water→
Saddell Glen→

Saddell

BELLOCHANTUY

Abbey
Castle

Lussa Loch

A83

B842

Westport

Kilchenzie

Peninver

Machrihanish
Bay
GOLF LINKS Airfield

Trench Point

CAMPBELTOWN LOCH

Machrihanish Water

CAMPBELTOWN

Machrihanish

A83

Island Davaar
CAVES

B843

Kilkerran

An Dhorlin

B842

Beinn
Ghuilean
1154′

Ardnacross Head

Cnoc
Moy
1462′

△

Track

Strone Water

Glen Breakerie

Southend

The Gap

Mull of Kintyre

Machrihanish

MACHRIHANISH

Golf Links

Brunerican Bay
Dunaverty Bay
Keil Point
Carskey Bay

Mac Shannon's
Point

Sanda Is.

KINTYRE

0 1 2 3 4 5
miles

original height of four storeys, but the ivy-covered stone lends a romantic air to a brisk village. The castle was once of large size, for apart from the keep its low walls cover the whole hill-top. The floors are now grass-covered and close-cropped by sheep, leaving short and springy turf. The date of the first foundation is too early to be known, but there is record that Selbach, the King of Lorn, burnt it in 712. In the thirteenth century its walls enclosed a square of 120 feet. In 1326 Robert the Bruce made repairs and added a courtyard of 300 feet by 240 strengthened by drum towers. Within the more ancient fortress he built a hall-house. Two years later he made Tarbert a burgh with sheriffdom (the first in Argyll and forty-eight years before Inveraray). This was the first attempt by a King of Scots at penetration of Kintyre, then in Clan Donald hands. The accounts for repairing and extending the castle have survived in the oldest Exchequer Rolls: it cost £511. There is no later record of Tarbert as a burgh. Like Kilmun it failed to develop and the creation lapsed.

At the time that Bruce occupied the castle and was displaying his strength to the Argyll chiefs, he 'sailed' in his galley across the isthmus to West Loch Tarbert. Tree trunks were used as rollers. He was by no means the first or last to make such a crossing. One better known was made in 1093 by King Magnus Barefoot, then aged twenty. His invasion of the west coast caught Malcolm III, the King of Scots, mounting an attack on England. This was the Malcolm whose father, Duncan, had been slain by MacBeth in 1040, and who killed MacBeth in battle seventeen years later. To be free of this Norse threat he agreed that Norway retain the Hebrides, on condition that Norse rule remain purely insular and be confined to land around which a ship could sail. Magnus agreed. But he wanted Kintyre ('Better land', said he, 'than the best of the Hebrides.') So he had his galley dragged across the isthmus while he sat at the tiller. No immediate attempt could be made to reverse the seizure, for Malcolm was treacherously killed at Alnwick in November. But twelve years later a son was born to the King of Argyll and his name was Somerled. The days of Norse rule were then numbered. Pennant in his *Tour in Scotland* (1771–75) records that vessels of nine or ten tons were drawn by horses across the isthmus to avoid the perils of the Mull of Kintyre. This sensible custom prevailed until the cutting of the Crinan Canal in 1801. It might well be asked why no canal was cut at Tarbert. James Watt had surveyed the ground in 1770 and pronounced a cut feasible. Sixty years later Henry Bell estimated the cost of a straight cut through rock without need of locks at £90,000 Parliament considered, approved, and a company was formed, but this procedure had taken fifteen years: a money crisis had smitten the nation—costs had doubled and the Crinan Canal had been cut instead.

There is a daily bus service from Glasgow to Campbeltown but the steamer sailing from Gourock is now on Fridays in summer only.

The main road down Kintyre goes by the west coast. The east coast road, which branches off at Whitehouse on West Loch Tarbert, is by comparison narrow and slow, but is scenically the better of the two, both in its villages and the panorama of the Arran hills seen across Kilbrannan Sound. You take this road across the moors to Cloanaig, the first tiny village on the sound, and here turn left up a side-road to **Skipness,** two and a half miles north on a rocky coast. The name Skipness is from the Old Norse Skipa-nes, meaning Ship Point. The village lies in a wide bay bounded by Skipness Point, which marks the entrance to Kilbrannan Sound.

From the hills behind, Skipness Burn pours down a wooded glen, then swings west parallel to a shingly beach. The houses are sited along the inland bank of the burn, from which they look across the sound to Loch Ranza on the Arran shore. Crofting at Skipness died out a hundred years ago, and herring fishing at the close of the nineteenth century. The several farms now engaged in stock-raising lie out of sight behind the village, which is exceedingly quiet and has a deserted air. The row of small, stone-built cottages at the centre were built by a former estate owner. There is no hotel. One or two houses provide bed and breakfast for summer visitors.

Where the burn curves north into its glen it is crossed by a bridge leading to Skipness House, Castle, Chapel, and Point. The house and castle stand a few hundred yards apart on open fields at the seaward fringe of woodland. The house has a walled garden with azalea and rhododendron, which in August is open to the public under the Gardens Scheme. The old castle of square Norman build is in a very good state of preservation, in so far as the walls and keep stand to full height. The structure is of local mica-schist with red sandstone dressings from Arran. It forms a rectangle measuring 40 yards by 27 with three projecting towers and a keep. The castle began as a hall-house in what is now the north-west corner, built around 1220 when Donald of Islay was King of the Isles and Kintyre. The curtain-walls and main keep were added around 1300 and 1500 respectively. The first recorded holder was one Dufgal in 1247, when he presented his chapel of St. Columba to Paisley Abbey. A wall of this chapel is now part of the castle's south curtain. The last holder was Campbell of Argyll from 1499 till his family abandoned the castle around 1700. It has remained in such good state for seven hundred years because it never had to withstand a major siege, was lucky enough to escape the attention of Murray of Atholl in 1685, and was never used as a quarry.

Behind the castle, open farmland sweeps up to bare but grassy hills. The seaward view to Arran and Bute has for its foreground a broad field on which an ancient ruined chapel, dedicated to St. Brendan, stands beside a shingle beach. This fine chapel is without the archaeological interest of ancient crosses and engraved slabs that embellish Kilmory Knap and Keills, but has in itself a beauty that the former lack. It was built around 1261 to compensate Paisley Abbey when the smaller St. Columba's Chapel was demolished to make way for the castle's curtain-walls. It is a much larger building, 82 feet long, having pointed windows and a two-light window on the eastern side in Early English style.

Walking along the shore to Skipness Point, you find a sandy beach backed by a stretch of true machair, bearing clover, daisies, and bird's-foot trefoil. Many eider duck swim offshore in June. Since the beach is exposed the ducklings are often driven ashore by breaking waves. They are then unable to paddle out against the chop, which tumbles them head over heels till they learn to drive into the waves instead of trying to ride the crests. Another enjoyable walk from Skipness Burn goes two miles north-east by road across moorland to the old pier-site facing Bute. There used to be a steamer service to Skipness, but the pier has long since been abandoned and washed away by storm. The village is now served by a bus from Campbeltown calling daily in summer and thrice weekly in winter.

The coast southward from Skipness to Campbeltown is throughout flanked by hill-farms, for the most part green and open, patched with hay and corn and dotted with cattle. The hilly road swoops up and down between wooded glens, and falls away to bays at Crossaig, Cour, and Grogport. At Grogport you enter Carradale Forest. At this point you climb steeply away from the sea to nearly 300 feet on a bare hill, then drop to the long strath of **Carradale Water**. This river is the biggest of Kintyre and one of the best salmon rivers of Argyll. The strath is wooded in oak, ash, birch, and chestnut, and above all with sycamore and lime, which together form short successive avenues. Descending into the strath in a June day one can see the opposite hillside reddened by rhododendron as though by heather.

The river winds tortuously down to the west side of **Carradale Bay,** whose great sandy beach is flanked eastward by a stubby peninsula. The river's south-facing outlet, named Waterfoot, forms a tidal harbour still used by small boats, but not by the fishing fleet, whose new harbour was built in 1959 to the north of the peninsula. The main south road by-passes Carradale. To enter the village, fork east at the lower strath and drive across the back of Carradale Bay between the rhododendron hedges and lime-trees of Carradale House, descending finally to the north port.

The village clusters on a hillside amphitheatre circling the bay. Many of the houses are new, mostly small, commanding a splendid view of the Arran mountains. The harbour faces north, its quay a semi-circular breakwater of concrete and iron. It gives complete shelter to fourteen modern fishing boats, whose main fishing grounds are in Kilbrannan Sound for herring and mackerel, and off Ailsa Craig for whitefish; but the boats often sail as far as Barra Head and the Minch. Herring fishing is the most important industry. A score of farms raise beef cattle and sheep, and keep dairy herds whose milk goes to Campbeltown creamery. The biggest landowner is the Forestry Commission, employing fifty or sixty men. Many of the people still speak Gaelic.

Carradale has several sandy beaches. The biggest and best strand of Kintyre's east coast is the main bay, which must be approached from either side of Carradale House. The eastern approach is by a side-road half a mile short of the pier; the more usual is the western. Starting from the main road-fork, go two hundred yards east then turn down a track through the grounds of Carradale House to the shore. Camping and caravanning by the shore are restricted. Permission must first be asked from the gamekeeper, whose cottage is the first on the left down the track.

The sands of Carradale Bay are three-quarters of a mile long, backed by machair spreading several hundred yards inland to Carradale House. As it leaves the shore, the machair becomes covered in golden whin and rhododendron. The house has a most distinctive architecture. Its numerous slated spires rise out of white walls that positively sparkle against the wooded hills behind. From its front, an avenue of rhododendrons leads to the beach. The gardens are open to the public daily from 1st April to 30th September.

On the outer east side of Carradale Bay, the peninsula ends at a rocky tidal island, which is the true Carradale Point, accessible only at low water. On its top at 133 feet is a circular vitrified fort, which is the best example of its kind on the Argyll coast. Fifty of these forts have been discovered in Scotland (none in England). They were built during the mid-British Iron Age, and the stones of the walls have been fused by heat. At Carradale the fort measures 167 yards (as paced out by myself) around the top of the rampart, and the vitrifaction is continuous. The site had high strategic value. It commanded the Kintyre coast south to Davaar Island off Campbeltown Loch and the whole wide entrance to Kilbrannan Sound.

Some archaeologists have held that the vitrified duns of Scotland were caused accidentally when attackers set fire to wooden supports in the walls. Others say that this notion, which can be conceived in an armchair from particular instances, is quite discredited by wider evidence in the field. Modern experiments show that vitrifaction is caused by a fusion of siliceous rock-rubble when peat, kelp, and wood, in which sand and soda are present, are burned with rubble in a strong wind. They form a slag-like cement. Rock fragments were thus aggregated on the duns to form ramparts that could not be breached in attacks. The uniform strengthening of ramparts along the top edges of defensive slopes like that at Carradale, show that vitrifaction was deliberate. Continuous, double, and concentric vitrified ramparts are found in other parts of Scotland.

If you look due west across Carradale Bay you see the highest hill of Kintyre, Beinn an Turc, rising to 1,491 feet behind Dippin Bay. Its name means Mountain of the Boar. On this hill the Fingalian hero Diarmid fought and slew a huge wild boar in the third century, hence the boar's head on Campbell of Argyll's coat of arms. The Campbells' descent from Diarmid may be questioned by their ill-wishers, but there is no reason to doubt the slaying of a boar. Wild boar were common in the Scottish oak woods up to the fourteenth century and were much hunted. They survived in Argyll till the end of the seventeenth centuyr.

Four miles south of Carradale the road dips deep into **Saddell Glen**. The village of Saddell buried in its wood is tiny but celebrated. On Somerled's death at Renfrew in 1164, his body was carried to Saddell and laid to rest at the old chapel. Here, on the south side of the river, his son Reginald, King of the Isles, built and endowed a Cistercian monastery in memory of his father, the last Celtic King of Argyll and the only Scot able to defeat the Vikings in their own element, the sea itself. The abbey's site at the north edge of the wood is well-chosen, but of the building itself little remains. Its form was a cross, lying west to east, 136 feet long by 24 broad, and in the height of its side walls 20 feet. In the chancel, one of the recumbent tombstones with Celtic carvings is declared, by traditional account only, to be Somerled's. For several hundred years Saddell Abbey ranked as one of the three principal strongholds of religious power on the Argyll mainland, as important for Kintyre as Kilmun for Cowal and Ardchattan for Lorn.

Half a mile south-east of the abbey, at the mouth of Saddell Water beside the shore, stands Saddell Castle, built in 1508 by David Hamilton, Bishop of Argyll. It has since been restored. The castle is an oblong keep 51 feet high with machicolated parapets. Carved above the door is the Galley of Somerled, the symbol of sea-power that appears on all Clan Donald coats of arms.

Beyond Saddell the forest diminishes as you move south, the hills falling lower, the fields growing lusher, the farmland richer, until you turn into Campbeltown Loch and top Trench Point. The grey town of **Campbeltown** is suddenly set before you. It would be unjust to call it ugly, but certainly it is not fair. Campbeltown is no more hideous to the eye than the grunt of a pig to the ear. After one's first start of dismay one begins to think it not unpleasing, then to like it not badly, and at the last to find positive merit where none had seemed to be. Were it home, you would affectionately call it 'The Wee Toon' and be arriving with joy. From the hill of Trench Point you see Campbeltown Loch punch two and a half miles into the land. Like Tarbert Bay on a bigger scale, it takes a strong curve to form an inner haven; the mouth, too, is screened by the Island of Davaar and its great shoal of An Dhorlin, which together shoot out a mile from the south lip. The town arches thickly round the inmost bay, spreading two broad wings of housing development across the hillsides to left and right. At the centre front is a quadrangular harbour, then the main bulk of the town from which a few towers and spires prick out. Green hills swell behind to the shapeless hulk of Beinn Ghuilean, 1,154 feet. The lower slopes to the far right and left are wooded residential districts. Out on the bay, Davaar (misspelt as Davarr on the O.S. map) humps a green and brown back in the exact hue and pattern of Army camouflage cloth.

Campbeltown is a royal burgh with a population of 6,500. It looks isolated on the map, so close to the end of a very long peninsula, but communications are good. The daily air service (twice daily in summer) by B.E.A. from Glasgow takes 40 minutes to Machrihanish airport on the west coast, whence the journey to Campbeltown is 2½ miles by road. There is a twice daily bus service to and from Glasgow by way of Loch Lomond and Inveraray. The old daily steamer service from the Clyde has been withdrawn, and Campbeltown's last sea-links are a twice daily car-ferry to Red Bay in Antrim, and a steamer to Largs in Ayrshire on summer week-ends.

For the present, you enter from Trench Point by the suburb of Dalintober, which was formerly separated from Campbeltown by a deep inlet called the Mussel Ebb. This was filled in last century to form the Kinloch Park of 24 acres, on whose green sweep is set a war memorial, public tennis courts, and a line of trees on its far side. You pass its front along the esplanade and arrive at the quadrangular harbour. Its broad nearer wall is called the Old Quay, the farther the New Quay. Directly behind the Old Quay stands Campbeltown Cross, a carved Celtic cross of the fifteenth century, whose history is unknown. By long custom the citizens welcome in the New Year before it and all funeral processions must be routed to pass by it. From this central point of the sea-front, Main Street runs a mile uphill and all other streets radiate off it to form the mass of the town. Half-way up Main Street stands the grey-painted town hall. The old cross stood in front of it till the last war, when it was taken down for safety's sake and later set up on its present site.

Campbeltown Loch is not like Rothesay Bay busy with the comings and goings of passengers steamers, but very much busier with fishing boats, of which thirty-three are based on the town and hunt the same grounds as the Carradale boats. They do not, however, land their catches here, but carry them straight to Tarbet and Ayr. One's first impressions are of an active harbour committed to sea-trades, and of numerous town shops well-stocked and catering for all normal human wants, for they serve a large and relatively prosperous hinterland. This swift impression gives the key to Campbeltown's character and one's growing regard for it. It is not basically a holiday resort, but part of a wide countryside from which it cannot be divorced, and for which it is the business centre, port, market, and capital. The more important trades of Campbeltown district, apart from herring and white fishing, are farming, organized to a high standard of efficiency on pasture grazed densely by dairy cattle and sheep; a creamery processing 4½ million gallons of milk a year from 162 farms; and two distilleries. In the nineteenth century Campbeltown had thirty-four distilleries, and in any one year might

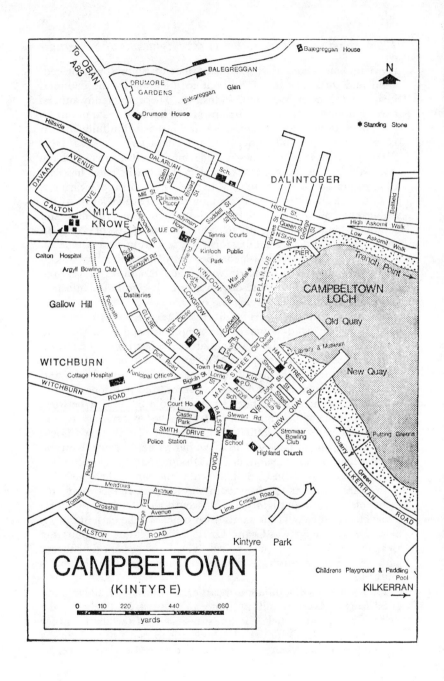

CAMPBELTOWN
(KINTYRE)

0   110   220   440   660
yards

have 6 million gallons of whisky stored in bond. Ships, it was alleged, could find their way to the harbour in thick fog by the bouquet. Such are the most important industries. There are many others. The main point is that Campbeltown is a Highland town not at all dependent on summer visitors for life and business, but fully alive in its own right and wholly independent in character.

The town's social activities include music and drama, and the more athletic musical exercise of piping. The Gaelic choir has won a big reputation at the Gaelic Mod and any chance of hearing a performance should be seized. Among the recreations open to the visitor are golf at the famous sand-dunes of Machrihanish and Southend, tennis, bowling, dinghy-sailing at the regattas of Campbeltown Sailing Club, and angling for trout, seat trout, and salmon on many small rivers and hill-lochs. Several of the latter have been stocked during the last decade with many thousands of yearling trout. The fees are small and details may be had from the information office in Hall Street facing the quay.

The unpretentious museum in Hall Street deserves a visit. It exhibits all the wild fauna of the neighbourhood from stoats to great northern divers; shows in miniature the herring drift nets and ring nets used by the fleet; and displays the weapons and tools of the people through the ages from bone and flint arrowheads and early coins to spinning implements, querns, and millstones.

South Kintyre was inhabited in the middle Stone Age between 7000 and 5000 B.C. When the first Scots began arriving around A.D. 250, some of them settled at the head of Campbeltown Loch. It should be noted, however, that the old name for south Kintyre, Dalruadhain, is not a synonym for Dalriada, and that local guide-book writers who claim Campbeltown as the site of the Dalriadan capital are mistaken. Dalruadhain means 'The red portion', for the whole of south-east Kintyre is red sandstone, which crops out on all its cliffs and colours the sands of its beaches. The earliest known name for the village was Ceann Loch Chille Chiaran, meaning the Head of the Loch of Ciaran's Cell. This later became Lochhead. The earlier name survives as Kilkerran, now given to the loch's south side.

Three quarters of a mile south-east of the Old Quay, the remains of **Kilkerran Castle,** built by James IV in 1498, lie derelict by the shore. Ciaran, often spelt Kieran, was a saint of the sixth century who had been St. Columba's boyhood friend and tutor. Columba was only eighteen when Ciaran died at the age of thirty-three. So highly did Columba think of him that he carried with him on his later travels a little earth from his friend's grave, which he used to found and sanctify two chapels. The first was at or near the present Kilkerran. This was his first outpost on Scottish mainland soil, founded on his way to visit the King of Scots at Dunadd. He then returned to Ireland to gather his twelve brothers. On their voyage to Iona he founded the second chapel at Kilchiaran Bay on the Rhinns of Islay, their first port of call in the Hebrides. St. Ciaran's cell near Campbeltown is (traditionally) a cave at Auchinhoan Head, three and a half miles down the coast from the castle. There are several caves on this stretch of coast. St. Ciaran's has a stone altar and water basin.

In the eleventh and twelfth centuries, Kintyre fell under Norse rule, thereafter under Somerled and the Clan Donald lords until the forfeiture of 1493. A hundred years later the king granted Kintyre to Campbell of Argyll. The seventh earl made Lochhead a burgh in 1609; in 1667 it received its first charter and its new name of Campbeltown in honour of its sponsor. Promotion to a royal burgh came in 1700. Thereafter trade increased to its climax at the close of last century, when the fishing fleet had more than six hundred boats, the distilleries prospered, and a shipyard employing several hundred men built boats up to 4000 tons gross. The depressions following two world wars closed the yard and curtailed other industries, but the town has recovered. The shipyard has been rebuilt and an industrial estate opened with four factories.

Davaar Island, which is so important to the harbour, is grazed but no longer inhabited. Its north point carries a lighthouse. On its south coast are several caves, one of them famous for its wall-painting of Christ crucified. This was done by the artist Alexander MacKinnon, in secret in 1887. Its discovery made a great stir and has drawn thousands of visitors. MacKinnon painted the crucifixion when he was thirty-three. In 1934 he returned at the age of eighty to retouch it. Further retouching since his death has been done by a local artist. Davaar can be reached on foot on the ebb, for it is a tidal island linked to the mainland by a shingle bank called the Dhorlin. You approach it along the Kilkerran road, two miles from the Old Quay.

As you pass the New Quay, you see riding at moorings the Campbeltown lifeboat, *City of Glasgow II*;. This boat and its predecessors have a record of service eminent throughout the Scottish coast. The Mull of Kintyre is notoriously storm-harried. All through history ships have split, or foundered, or found themselves driven by gale winds and huge seas toward a lee shore of 300-foot cliffs. The Campbeltown lifeboat crews have been rescuing them for the last hundred years. Incongruously to such thoughts, one notices along the Killerran road that nearly ever house has palm trees in its garden.

The Dhorlin is three-quarters of a mile long, curling from north to east. No attempt should be made to cross by wading at high water, for the crest can easily be lost. It is best to go at low tide, or whenever the shingle emerges on the ebb. The walk out to the caves requires a leisurely two hours. Sheld-duck, oystercatchers, terns, and gulls will be seen on the sands at the island side. A grassy track runs south-east to join a shingle track around the base of the south cliffs, on which there are seven caves. The cave with the painting is the fifth. Twenty yards in, it is joined by a tunnel of the fourth cave. The roof is sixty feet high. Since it faces south-east it gets sun, allowing the crevices to grow foxgloves, white biting stonecrop, and several other plants. The painting has been done life-size on the smooth back of an alcove in the left-hand wall. The colours are chiefly blue and white and the work competent, being especially good at the face and eyes. At the lower right-hand side appears the face of a cherub.

When Clan Donald held Kintyre, Alexander, the third Lord of the Isles, granted Davaar around 1440 to the monks of Saddell Abbey. The artist's choice of the island for his painting is thus historically appropriate. When you look out from its shore you see the green flank of Beinn Ghuilean lifting gently to 1,154 feet. It too has a cave, the Piper's Cave high up on its shoulder. The legendary piper had been thwarted in love. With a dog at his heels he marched into the cave piping a coronach, in search of hell. He was never seen again, but the dog came out of a cave seven miles away at Southend with its coat singed off. This same story is told of caves in the Argyll islands of Islay, Colonsay, and Mull, and even of Smoo Cave near Cape Wrath.

Campbeltown Bay on the east coast is matched on the west by the **Bay of Machrihanish.** The plain between, four a a half miles wide, is called the Laggan, the narrowest part of south Kintyre and once a peat-moss, now reclaimed by drainage to become good farmland. The Machrihanish beach is the longest strand of Argyll's mainland. It runs four miles from north to south, where it curves west to form a reversed L. The airport at the back of the dunes was described, in the first edition of this guide, as a Royal Air

Force slum, which had been left derelict after the last world war. Since 1968 the rusty Nissen huts and corrugated iron sheds have been swept away, replaced at a cost of £2m. by a NATO air base with administrative buildings and modern housing. Huge oil tanks have also been dug for NATO into Campbeltown's south slopes.

Proceeding then to Machrihanish, you approach the village by way of a rubbish dump and the Argyll colliery. The colliery, which used to employ 250 men, closed down in 1967. Seventy-five years ago the village was named The Pans, because salt was manufactured by evaporation of sea-water during the seventeenth and eighteenth centuries. Now named Machrihanish from a farm to its east, it is small and sadly wanting in character: it might probably not be there at all but for the golf course, which dates from 1876 and has won international renown. A full score of villas were thus built towards the end of last century for letting to summer visitors. In winter they lie empty. A few council houses have since been added, and several of the villas converted to private hotels. The one big hotel sits at the west end facing the south bay and the start of the golf course.

The moment you step on to these four miles of sand, or on to the golf course, Machrihanish is transformed. The beach is broad, the waves crash in green; as seen against the sun they spread a sheen of mussel-blue far up the yellow sands. At noon the islands of Islay, Jura, and Gigha stretch their faded blue along the horizon, but in the evening stand out black against the sunset. A broad belt of marram fringes the beach and behind it rolls the great machair, where the golf course lies on a perfect combination of dunes and springy turf. Larks are everywhere: this is their country and the golfer secondary. The houses of Machrihanish look well from the links, and the NATO buildings are unobtrusive behind the dunes. Your whole world is fair to see.

For the sunbather and swimmer the best part of the beach is the farther, north end at **Westport.** It is reached by the main west road from Campbeltown. Rocks guard the north end and the dunes rise high, breached by gullies opening on to golden sands. These gullies give excellent shelter from wind. You can lie there in comfort and listen to the larks and the sea. No caravans or tents are allowed at Westport and this has been its salvation. Campers and caravanners have a choice of suitable sites to the north, where grassy flats occur at intervals between the main road and the rocky shore. It is one of the attractions of Kintyre that its sand-beaches and roads are uncrowded even in high summer compared to those of the Highlands proper. In May, June, and September the beaches are almost empty. This is true even of Southend, which draws more visitors than Machrihanish.

From Campbeltown to **Southend** is ten miles, first across the flat plain then over low hills where the fields are richly yellowed by buttercups, and finally down the long Conie Glen to the south coast. In this region dairy farms flourish. Southend is a small, plain village of friendly people half a mile in from the shore. In 1830 it had a population of more than 2,000, now fallen to 500 by emigration and the amalgamation of crofts into large farms. The changes have transformed the life of the people from a low to a high standard of living.

Below Southend the coast is gouged by three big bays divided by rocky points. The sands are red, for the rock is red sandstone. From east to west they are named Brunerican, which receives the Conie Water and on its dunes carries the golf course; Dunaverty, with a camp and caravan site on the grass field above; and Carskey, which receives the outflow of two rivers, the Breackerie and Strone, beyond which the land hardens westward, rising in rock and hill to the Mull.

Between the first two bays, **Dunaverty Point** rears up in a bold headland, a great grassy crag split off from the mainland as if by cleaver of the gods. From its top you look out to the island of Sanda, two miles offshore, and beyond to Ireland. The blue Antrim hills are seventeen miles away, but look surprisingly close. The great cleft of the headland shelters an old boathouse, pier, and jetty. Southend once had an important fishing industry, but the only fishing now is for lobster and salmon, each by one man operating from Dunaverty. On the Brunerican Bay side, salmon can be readily netted at the mouth of Conie Water. Lobster are caught along the rocky coast, which starts at MacShannon's Point on the bay's far side, and from the shelves of Sanda's many reefs and skerries.

On top of Dunaverty Rock there once stood a proud fortress of the Lords of the Isles. Scarcely a trace remains. Built in the thirteenth century on the site of an old dun, Dunaverty Castle was only less important than Dunyvaig on Islay, which guarded Clan Donald's fleet. In 1306, Angus II, the fifth King of the Isles, sheltered Bruce at Dunaverty during his adversity, and when the English fleet closed in shipped him across the North Channel to Ireland. The English siege of the castle was repulsed. Throughout the War of

West coast fishing ports. *Above* Tarbert on the Kintyre isthmus, with a
population of 1500, a fleet of 12 ships, and an annual catch of £200,000.
Below Oban on the Firth of Lorn. Population 7,000, fleet of 70, annual catch
over £700,000. Oban is also the region's main touring centre: nearly 40
hotels stand in a phalanx facing the harbour and its three piers, from which
steamers sail to the isles.

Above Ben Cruachan viewed across Loch Etive from North Connel (five miles from Oban). *Below* Castle Stalker on Loch Laich, a bay on the Appin coast of Loch Linnhe. It was built in the 13th century by the MacDougall Lords of Lorn, but after Bannockburn it was owned by the Stewarts. The keep stands four storeys high with crow-stepped gables.

Independence, Angus gave Bruce more powerful support than any other man save Sir James Douglas. Two hundred years later, when the House of Islay's great services to Scotland were forgotten, wrongs remembered, and Kintyre was forfeited, King James IV descended on Tarbert to repair and garrison the royal castle. He then took a hasty decision to translate his *de jure* claim on Kintyre into a *de facto* possession, sailed down to the South End, and seized and garrisoned Dunaverty. Sir John of Islay, Chief of Clan Donald, who had been led by the king to think him his friend, bitterly resented the action. Before the king's ship could round MacShannon's Point on the homeward voyage, Sir John had stormed and re-taken the castle, and in full view of the king hanged the governor from the battlements.

Kintyre became Campbell country in 1607, but no Pax Campbellica blessed Dunaverty. During the wars of Montrose, the castle was seized for the royalists in 1647 by Sir Alexander MacDonald. On the approach of the Covenanters under General Leslie he withdrew to Ireland, but left behind a garrison of his three hundred best men. The siege was lengthy, and having no proper water-supply the defenders at last surrendered. At the exhortation of a presbyterian minister named John Neave, the whole three hundred were massacred and the castle razed.

The finest bay of the south coast is not at Southend, but three miles east at **Macharioch**. Access is through Macharioch farm, whose owner allows camping and caravanning, restricted to give privacy. From flat fields you drop down a steep bank to the sandy beach, which is separated into secluded coves by sandstone crags. Your outlook is not to Ireland but east to the Ayrshire coast and to Ailsa Craig. Seen from here the latter is of perfect symmetry like a fairy knoll floating on the sea, for it looks white when the sun touches it, both from its pale rock and its grassy bonnet covered with the excreta of ten thousand gannets.

Round the corner to the south, the island of Sanda has a lighthouse built in 1950 and a ruined chapel dedicated to St. Ninian. Another old chapel, more easily reached, is that of **Keil** between Dunaverty Bay and Carskey. The coast road from Southend here comes down to the sea's edge, passing on the right first the Keil hotel, then the ruins of Keil school (burned down in 1924). Both are named from the ruined chapel (Cill), which appears just before the road goes beneath tall cliffs of red sandstone. The ruin itself is of small interest, apart from skull and cross-bone carvings on slabs, but an outcropping crag beside it has a flat top on which are carved two footprints, allegedly marking the spot where St. Columba stood on his first arrival in Dalriada. A date inscribed beside them appears to read 564, and if so it is in error. The sharp edges to all these carvings betray them as relatively recent. It is possible that Columba came here on his voyage north to meet King Conall in Knapdale, and that would be shortly before his voyage of 563 to Iona. The chapel is undeniably ancient and deserving of the reverence in which it is held locally—an open-air service is held beside it in the early summer of each year. Two hundred yards to its west, the tall red cliffs are pitted along their base by caves—wet, muddy, and not worth attention. Fulmars nest on the face above.

Caves more worthy of exploration honeycomb the seaward flank of **Cnoc Moy**, 1,462 feet, on the west coast between the Mull and Machrihanish. They are festooned with stalactites. To reach them, turn the corner to Carskey Bay, then drive north up Glen Breackerie, from whose head a track leads to the sea under Cnoc Moy.

Kintyre must not be left without an excursion to the **Mull**. It is mountainous country scourged by gale and quite unlike the rest of the peninsula. The road west from Carskey rises steeply and twistingly to 750 feet, then more gradually, four miles in all, to a pass called The Gap at 1,150 feet. Cars must there be left behind. The road surface remains excellent, but there are no passing places and the gradients between the hairpin bends are extraordinarily steep. A notice warns that descent on wheels is dangerous and prohibited. You therefore walk a mile down a craggy and heathery hillside and drop 850 feet to reach the lighthouse. The walk is all pleasure for the view has an exhilarating immensity. The coast of Ireland, now only twelve miles away, fills the horizon, no longer distant blue as from Dunaverty, but green and clear. The fields and farmlands look just like those of Kintyre itself. Trees and houses can be seen distinctly, especially the lighthouse on the nearer Rathlin Island.

The Mull lighthouse springs from the cliff-top at 300 feet, around it a ring of grass cropped by sheep and busy with chack-chacking wheatears. Ravens soar over the cliff, whose edge slopes too steeply to allow you a glimpse of the vertical face. The lighthouse was built in 1788 and repaired by the Stevensons in 1820. Its light is visible at twenty-four miles' range. Visitors are admitted at the keeper's discretion and conducted round if they arrive between 1 p.m. and one hour before sunset.

The main road north from Campbeltown to Tarbert crosses the

Laggan to Westport and then holds closely to the west coast, rising and swooping across the spurs and rivers that fall from the central hills to the sea. At Bellochantuy (pronounced Balloch-an-tee), four miles north of Westport, the bay has a fine sweep of sand, but is exposed through lack of dunes behind. A little farther the road turns inland for nearly a mile to the woods of Barr Water, which shelter Glenbarr, the most pleasing small village of south Kintyre. On rejoining the coast you may find it dull country, but the seascape will draw all your attention. Islay, once the most important of all Scottish islands, and still one of the more beautiful, is now clear in outline, although farther off than Ireland from the Mull. Much closer at hand—just three miles offshore—Gigha lifts a long humpy back like a sea-serpent. A smaller island off its south end is named Cara from the Norse Karöe meaning Coffin Island, which exactly describes its shape. It is bare and uninhabited, but **Gigha**, which from a distance looks no better, is in fact the most fertile and productive of Scottish islands in relation to size.

Gigha may be reached from West Loch Tarbert by daily steamer, but more conveniently for a day-visit by passenger-ferry from Tayinloan, which faces Gigha's only village of Ardminish directly across the sound. At least one full day should be devoted to Gigha, if only properly to enjoy its famous garden, and two more to explore the island, although it measures only six miles by one and a half.

The name is pronounced Geea with the G hard, deriving from the Norse Gudey, meaning Good Island or God Island. A backbone of rock runs down its centre, rising to 331 feet on Creag Bhan at the north end, but the flanks spread out on rich fields nourishing a dozen dairy farms, which supply a thousand gallons of milk a day to the creamery at Achamore, mostly for cheese-making. The population of 190 is well spread across the island.

Both ends and both sides of Gigha are indented by a score of rocky bays, many of them sandy and some on the west side bird sanctuaries. Eun Eilean Bay (Bird Island Bay) to the south-west has black-throated diver, eider, fulmar, sheld-duck, and numerous others among its dozen islets and jagged points. Tarbert Bay at the north-west end has a strand linking Gigha to Eilean Garbh, one vast gullery with guillemot and eider nesting on the western ledges.

The hill-ridge in June is a wild garden, even the rock being tight-packed with a dwarf whin scented like honey. Sir James Horlick's garden at **Achamore House** lies a mile south of the jetty. Starting from scratch in 1945, he has in twenty years created a garden fit to rank with Colonsay and Inverewe, and to surpass them in woodland beauty. This astonishingly fast work was made possible only through the natural advantages of the site. The garden is set on a raised beach deposit. The soil is a sandy, lime-free loam. The spinal hills screen the land from westerly winds, the Kintyre hills less effectively from easterly. The climate is mild and soft, so that palms grow by the roadside at Ardminish. Most importantly, two large plantations, mostly deciduous trees, were made at Achamore House at the end of last century. Sir James was able to use these as cover in planning his garden.

The broad drive by which you enter presents in May and June a fireworks display of red and orange azaleas. The bushes are massed on the curving lawns, but with space between clumps to let the colour blaze against cool green. The main attraction of the garden, the point that distinguishes it from Crarae and others of the west coast, is the woodland of broad-leaved trees penetrated by winding paths that bring one to unexpected clearings, cunningly placed to let the sun flood through on to laburnums and flame-trees (*Embothrium longifolium*) or to massed beds of primula candelabra, daffodils or lilies. In the remote and wilder parts are banks of bluebells. Spring, summer, and autumn there are plants and shrubs to give colour in mass. Rare tropical shrubs flourish, and the more exotic rhododendrons. In 1962 Sir James made a gift of his valuable plant collection to the National Trust for Scotland, who are carrying out a propagation programme to establish many of the Gigha plants in the Trust's own gardens at Inverewe, Brodick, Culzean, and elsewhere. This does not mean that the Gigha garden is Trust property. It is open to the public daily from dawn to dusk between 1st April and 30th September.

The ferry-boat crosses the three-mile sound from Tayinloan in half an hour or less according to weather.

Continuing north up Kintyre, you pass through a wooded glen at Ronachan between banks of rhododendron. Here the road turns to the village of Clachan and climbs 400 feet. At the top, a hillock of 556 feet beside the road gives one of Kintyre's better views, and the best of all of West Loch Tarbert. Its shining channel pierces deep into wooded and knobbly hills. The rolling moors of Kintyre, you suddenly realize, are behind you. In front waits the Knapdale hill-chop. You side-step to the east coast and pass through to Crinan, bound now for Lorn.

CHAPTER 8

Nether Lorn

The name Lorn was given to the kingdom taken by Lorn, the son of
Erc, around A.D. 500. It includes all the land between Loch Awe
and the Firth of Lorn. Loch Leven is the northern boundary, and
the Bealach Mor, the Great Pass, at the head of Loch Craignish,
the southern. Between stretches forty miles of wild coast with Oban
at centre as chief town and heart of all. To Oban's south, Nether
Lorn is a hilly plateau rarely more than 1,200 feet high, split inland
by glens, rivers, and lochs, and along its periphery shattered into
points, peninsulas, and an archipelago of twenty or thirty islands,
not counting two hundred skerries, some of bare rock, some with
grassy and even flowery pasture for sheep and cattle, but all of
peculiar beauty. The principal islands are Seil, Luing, Scarba, and
the Isles of the Sea. In their narrow straits run notorious tide-races,
notably the Grey Dog and the Corrievreckan to north and south of
Scarba, the Fladda Narrows at the Sound of Luing, and the Dorus
Mor off Craignish Point. The two latter lie on the normal coastal
passage. Small boats and yachts have to time their arrival for fair
tide or slack water, otherwise they cannot get through against the
current.

The mainland districts of Nether Lorn are Kilbrandon, Kilninver,
Kilmelford, and the peninsula of Craignish. Approaching from the
Crinan isthmus through Kilmartin, you enter **Craignish** from the
crest of the Bealach Mor at 546 feet. The steep descent gives the
finest views to be had of Loch Craignish on the peninsula's near
side. Broad as the loch is and six miles long, it seems choked with
islands, a dozen at least, large and small. All are grassy, the three
bigger ones wooded. Green flats grazed by cattle spread out at the
loch's head behind a shingle shore. Down the far side, farmland
slopes up to low hills, which in July are yellowed by hay, but south-

ward toward Craignish Point bare at all times. If you turn down the
by-road on that side you are led through the tiny village of Ardfern,
and two miles beyond it pass from the east coast of the peninsula to
the west at Loch Beag. At the head of this inlet stands Craignish
Castle, originally a simple keep held by the MacDougalls, then for
many centuries the chief seat of the Campbells of Craignish. It is
now part of a modern mansion held in other hands. The grounds
are opened to the public in May and June under Scotland's Gardens
Scheme. The rhododendron garden was laid out by Osgood
MacKenzie, famous for his creation of Inverewe Gardens, Wester
Ross, between 1862 and 1922. The first fort on the site of Craignish
is said to have been built in the twelfth century, but the first record
of it is in 1414. The present keep is sixteenth century. In 1647, when
Sir Alexander MacDonald sacked Castle Sween and took Dunaverty,
he also attacked Craignish, which withstood his siege for three
weeks.

The road ends at a derelict pier at the mouth of Loch Beag. An
easy, mile-long walk southward over the moor brings you to
Craignish Point on the Dorus Mor. The Great Gate is the strait
between the point and the island of Garbh Reisa. At mid-tide,
when the current races through at eight knots, the surface takes a
sullen swirl and becomes patterned with boiling eddies, or if setting
against strong wind is whitened by a fierce chop. Menacing as it
looks, the race is safe for a ship passing through with the tide, and
so too are the Fladda Narrows off Luing. But this rule does not hold
for Corrievreckan.

Looking west from Craignish Point, you can see the Gulf of
Corrievreckan between Scarba and Jura four miles away. The
correct name is Coire Bhreacain, Gaelic for Speckled Corrie, named
thus from its streaky overfalls. The strait is a mile wide by two miles
long. On this coast the flood sets north up the Sound of Jura, then
drives west at nine knots through the Gulf where it strikes a submerged rock pyramid. The upsurge causes a huge whirlpool in
which small ships have been lost. In a westerly wind, which blows
against the flood, the roar of the great race can be heard from
Craignish. In a gale it can be heard along twenty miles of the Lorn-
to-Knapdale coast. The race cannot be seen from the point (you
can go to its brink on Scarba), but by climbing the hill of 193 feet
behind the point you can, if the tide is flooding, see the white
tumult of the Jura race where it speeds on approaching the entrance.
Ships with less driving power than the race, and all ships under sail,

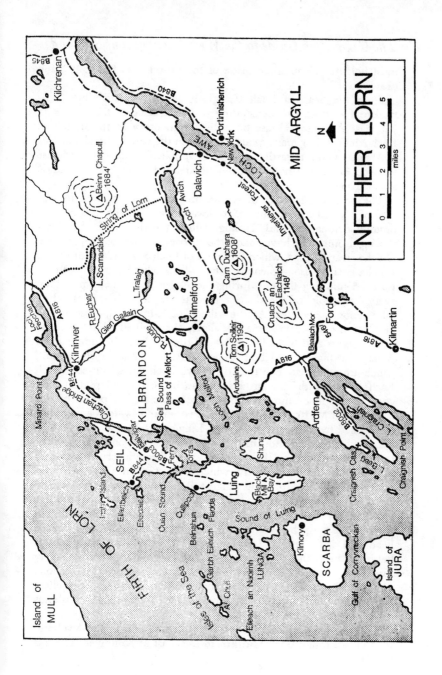

NETHER LORN

N

0 1 2 3 4 5 miles

Island of MULL

Kilchrenan

B845

B840

Portinnisherrich

New York

LOCH AWE

MID ARGYLL

Inverliever Forest

Beinn Chapull 1684'

String of Lorn

L.Scamadale

Loch Avich

Dalavich

Cam Duchara 1608'

Kilmelford

Cruach an Eachlaich 1148'

Tom Soilleir 1199'

Ford

Kilmartin

A816

Bealach Mor

Loch Feochan

Minard Point

A816

Kilninver

R.Euchar

Glen Gallain

L.Tralaig

R.Oude

Pass of Melfort

Sound of Melfort

Arduaine

Ford

A816

Ardfern

B8002

Loch Craignish

A816

KILBRANDON

B844

Clachan Bridge

SEIL

Balvicar

Ferry

Seil Sound

Loch Melfort

Ellanbeich

Ellenabeich

Easdale

Cuan Sound

Torsa

Shuna

Black Mill Bay

Craignish Cas.

Craignish Point

FIRTH OF LORN

Belnahua

Cullipool

Garbh Eileach

Fladda

Luing

Sound of Luing

Kilmory

SCARBA

Gulf of Corryvreckan

Isles of the Sea

Eileach an Naoimh

A'Chuli

LUNGA

Island of JURA

must hold to the mainland side of the nearer isles to avoid being drawn to it.

From the head of Loch Craignish you enter north into **Kilmelford** district. On descending from the back of the peninsula you pass Arduaine House on a big promontory at the mouth of Loch Melfort. For many years it has been the seat of the Campbells of Arduaine and its garden open to the public, but in 1966 the house was converted to a hotel and much extended. It looks over island-studded seas.

The principal features of Kilmelford are its lochs, both its sea-loch of Melfort and a score of freshwater lochs on the hills behind, notably Scamadale and Tralaig, which together with the rivers flowing from them have made the district a fisherman's paradise. On the river Euchar, which flows out of Loch Scamadale into Loch Feochan, there is a splendid salmon-leap where big fish can be watched jumping the fall during the August run. In former days, every household of the district used to lay in a barrel of salted salmon for the winter. At the village of Kilmelford, close to the head of the sea-loch named Melfort, the Cuilfail Hotel has the fishing rights and boats for several of the hill lochs including Loch Avich, the biggest and best known—although not for its salmon, which are unable to leap the falls above Loch Awe. You can reach Loch Avich by driving up a side-road on to the hill plateau and crossing the moorland watershed. From the higher points of this road **Loch Melfort** looks like a vast inland water, apparently landlocked by the islands of Tarsa, Luing, and Shuna.

Loch Melfort has no sandy bays but offers a good walk by the track along its north (Kilbrandon) shore through scrub birch and ash. Sea-trout will rise to fly, which is unusual in a sea-loch, and give good sport in July and August. The main road north rises to the Pass of Melfort. In its deep ravine the cataracting Oude has knifed its way south through a mass of andesite. An old road runs through the gorge below the new road and is worth walking from the head of Loch Melfort. It presents the kind of wild track almost banished from the Highlands by road 'improvements' and rarely seen now except in nineteenth-century romantic prints. You look down southward upon tree-tops that seem to fill the broad Melfort corrie with fluff; beyond and below which, a rabble of islands spread across the great bay.

The new north road crosses the river Oude at a higher level and then falls through **Glen Gallain** to the coast at Kilninver. There is much wild thyme by the road. When the sun warms a clump it yields up a delicate and fragrant scent like lavender, but sharper as though mixed with a tang of bog-myrtle. The leaf is tiny and tongue-shaped, the flower purple like ling heather. The river Gallain joins the sea at the long inlet of Loch Feochan, which bounds Nether Lorn. Just before reaching it, you come to a road-fork at Kilninver, and bound now for Seil and Luing, turn left into Kilbrandon.

Kilbrandon is a huge headland, four miles wide by six long. From the middle of its west coast it shoots southward the ten-mile 'penin-sula' of Seil and Luing. What might have been its two isthmuses are narrow, sea-flooded channels. The first is the **Clachan Sound**, only seventy feet wide, by which you cross to the island of Seil. The high-humped bridge that spans it is known as 'the bridge across the Atlantic'. It was built in 1792 from plans by Thomas Telford. Its single stone arch lifts forty feet above the bed of the sound, allowing vessels of forty tons to pass under at high tide. On rare occasions whales have been trapped in the sound. They try to force a passage and stick where the water shallows, for they have no room to turn and cannot reverse. The biggest whale thus caught was in 1835. It measured 78 feet, with a lower jaw 21 feet long. Two years later, a school of 192 pilot whales stranded at the same place, but the largest was only 26 feet. The other south wall of the bridge is in summer purpled by fairy foxglove (*erinus alpinus*).

The islands of Seil and Luing, and their outliers of Easdale, Shuna, Torsa, Belnahua, and many others, are collectively known as the **Slate Islands**. Their pre-Cambrian rock is (like gneiss) one of the oldest known and too early to carry fossils. The prosperity of Kilbrandon was for the last two hundred years bound up with the islands' slate quarries, which gave highly skilled employment to several hundred men. This industry has totally collapsed. One by one the quarries have closed down, at first through a catastrophic inflooding of the sea at Easdale, where 240 men lost their jobs, then by a loss of markets through rising freight charges and the competi-tion of cheaper and lighter roofing materials, and finally, by the growing shortage of skilled men. In 1965 the only quarry remaining active was at Balvicar on Seil, and that too has recently closed.

The people live by farming, lobster-fishing, tool-making at Easdale, and lorry-driving. In 1950, Brittany oysters were laid experimentally in Seil Sound, and those in Balvicar Bay produced the second largest among all West Highland layings. In spite of local interest, no fishery has yet been established. At Balvicar the road again forks, one branch toward Luing and the other eastward to Easdale. The name Easdale is generally applied both to the island and to the village of Ellanbeich facing it on a bay of the Seil shore. You descend on Easdale by a steep hill, on which a knoll (with an indicator) gives wide views to the Isles of the Sea, Scarba and Lunga and the Fladda lighthouse. On a clear day you can see Colonsay and Oronsay.

Ellanbeich sits on the shore of Easdale Sound, whose channel, 150 yards wide, is partially filled with slate debris and may be crossed by passenger ferry to Easdale Island. Adjoining the old stone pier are three long, unbroken, and parallel rows of cottages, all of the typical fishing or mining kind: of two rooms, roofs slated but sagging, walls short and white-washed, windows and doors picked out in green, blue, red, and yellow. Another half-dozen cottages, semi-circling the pier, have now become shops selling handicraft goods to tourists. These and several small cafés and a hotel cater for the daily bus-tours from Oban. Motor-boats cruise in settled weather around the neighbouring isles, and as far afield as Loch Melfort and Loch Spelve in Mull. Near at hand are the deserted and desolate quarries of Easdale Island. The best of this country is to be seen from the cliff-tops behind Ellanbeich: the isles of the Firth of Lorn line the horizon and the great bluffs of the Ross of Mull recede far westward into the shining Atlantic. At the south end of the village, the garden of An Cala House is open to the public from April to the end of September.

Returning to Balvicar you turn south to Luing. Half-way there you pass Ballachuan Loch, seen below on your left, and facing it across the main road on your right, **Kilbrandon** Parish Church. The church and parish are named Kilbrandon after St. Brendan of Clonfert in Galway. He made repeated visits to Lorn in the sixth century, establishing a monastery on the Isles of the Sea in 542 (twenty-one years before St. Columba came to Iona) and a few years later a church (or cell) underneath the site of the church in which you stand. He died at a great age in 577. This whole western seaboard of Argyll was Christian country before Columba arrived on his tough mission of converting the Picts.

The church itself is of small interest architecturally, but it contains some admirable modern stained glass in a series of five windows by Douglas Strachan. Three on the east wall seem most appropriate to an island parish—they illustrate scenes from the Sea of Galilee. The central window is perhaps the best example of Dr Strachan's work. A ship lies helpless in wild seas, sails torn, rudder smashed. Lightning flashes down the length of the window. Leviathan towers over ship and crew. The portrayal in glowing colour of the storm's sweep, the crew's terror, and Christ's self-possession, has a lively drama unique in Highland stained glass.

Many renowned and some infamous men have their burial ground in Kilbrandon churchyard, among them the Campbells of Cawdor (or Calder). In their origin they gave rise to the much quoted and frequently misinterpreted words, 'It's a far cry to Lochow' (Lochow was the early spelling of Loch Awe). In 1499 Muriel of Calder, heiress of the ancient family of Calder in Nairn-shire, had the misfortune to become the ward of Archibald Campbell, the second earl of Argyll. He planned to win her lands by marrying her to his son John. She was four years old and her mother hostile to Argyll's proposal, so he commissioned Campbell of Inverliever to kidnap her. The girl was successfully abducted from her uncle's home at Kilravock Castle (pronounced Kilrawk) in Nairn. Her kinsmen pursued and overtook the Campbells at the head of Strathnairn. Inverliever sent the girl on with a small party while he faced about and fought a rearguard action. In the bitter fight en-suing, when the day's fortune hung in the balance and no word could reach nor help could come from distant clansmen, his situa-tion wrung from Inverliever 'It's a far cry to Lochow'.

He escaped with heavy losses. Ten years later the young heiress suffered a forced marriage to Sir John Campbell at Inveraray, the Cawdor branch of the Campbells was formed, and their claim to grace staked on thrice holy ground, at Kilbrandon.

The **Cuan Sound** between Seil and Luing is two hundred yards wide and the spring tides go through at nine miles per hour. A free car ferry gives continuous daily service between 8 a.m. and noon and 1 p.m. and 6, thereafter till midnight but not for cars and not free of charge. Luing is a green, rough island, five and a half miles long by one and a half broad, much more fertile than Seil in its south half but sparsely populated—200 as against Seil's 500. Until the last war Luing had fine dairy herds supplying the whole island with milk and exporting 90 gallons a day to the Oban creamery. The island has since been bought by farmers who have closed the dairy farms and are instead running a cattle ranch for stock-raising.

The principal village is **Cullipool** on the north-west coast. As you enter you pass a string of detached white cottages facing a rocky shore, followed by a quarter mile gap to the old village beside the slate quarries. The Cullipool quarry, first opened in the late nineteenth century, became the most important in the West Highlands and employed 150 men producing around 15,000 slates a week. It closed down in 1965, and since then there has settled on Cullipool a cloud of deadness and desolation. The quarries of course were always ugly, but they gave men an active life in skilled work—and they have made their own contribution to beauty elsewhere. When Iona Cathedral was being rebuilt, it was seen that the broken slates of the ruin had rust-coloured pitmarks, revealing Seil or Luing as their source. Some of the rock there is peppered with yellow crystals and iron pyrites, which weather out from the slate as seen at Iona. The new slates were therefore chosen from the Cullipool quarry.

No west coast passage is so splendidly endowed with islands as the **Sound of Luing**. They swarm upon it like bees on a branch. To distinguish one from another is difficult at first, but you will want to know the more important. Take your stance midway between the north and south villages, and as reference point use the white Fladda lighthouse, which stands on a skerry a mile offshore. The light is now automatic, serviced by one of Cullipool's lobster-fishermen. The house attached to the tower lies empty. The farthest island behind the light is Eileach an Naoimh, the Holy Isle of the four Isles of the Sea. Behind the light to its right is Garbh Eileach with trees on its north end. In front of it and much closer rises the hump of Belnahua, so deeply quarried for its slate that the back of the island broke and the workings had to be abandoned. Immediately to Fladda's left is Dubh Sgeir, the Black Skerry, with a beacon. The main sea-passage goes between the two. Filling the gap between the two lights are the Eileans Dubh Beag and Dubh Mor, with an exceedingly narrow but navigable channel between. Well to their left, the apparent green north point of Scarba is in fact Lunga, separated from the round mountain of Scarba by the invisible race of the Grey Dog.

These are the most treacherous seas and complicated channels of the west coast. Many ships have been wrecked. Do not be deceived by watching the lobster-fishermen, at least four of whom set their creels amidst the isles and reefs, and seem to come and go with careless freedom even in threatening weather. They have such an intimate knowledge of the tides and races, and the numerous local peculiarities of these at different hours, that they go safely where others would drown. At Fraoich Eilean, close inshore, they have one of the larger lobster ponds of the west coast. Lobsters are stored as caught and refished to suit the market.

The lobster-fisherman who live at South Cullipool will ferry out to the Holy Isle anyone who wishes to visit the monastery. The voyage out is six and a half miles and a calm day must be chosen. The ruins (dated ninth century) are the most ancient ecclesiastical remains extant in Scotland, and the island is one of the most delightful of all Argyll. Apart from which the sail is worth making for its own sake. You go out through long low islands craggily towered, threading your way between skerries by narrow channels where Atlantic grey seals bask on the rocks or swim nose up to inspect you. Oyster-catchers and gulls scream in the straits and guillemots dive in the open seas between. There are four **Isles of the Sea,** green and hummocky, all with arched backs and outcropping rock. They lie on the Firth of Lorn in line astern, each with high cliffs to the west. Their name derives from the ancient Gaelic used by St. Columba and Adamnan, who called them Hinba (pronounced Eenba). *In* meant Island, *Ba* Sea, and H indicated the plural, hence Isles of the Sea. The latter name has lasted to the present day, but the O.S. maps misguidedly name them Garvellachs, after the largest island, Garbh Eileach. St. Columba's *Hinba* was the islet-sanctuary to which he used to withdraw at intervals for prayer and contemplation, and which became as dear to him as Iona. It can now be certainly identified as the Eileach an Naoimh.

As you approach them, the smallest and most northerly is **Dun Chonnuill.** On top of one of its rocky heights is set the fort of Conall Cearnach, an Ulster hero of the first century. Its remains (presumably rebuilt when the MacDougalls held it in the thirteenth century or when MacLean of Duart was given it by Robert III around 1400) can still be seen if one lands, but landing is difficult even in fine weather. The big island next to it is **Garbh Eileach.** It was once inhabited and is still grazed by sheep and cattle ferried out from Luing. On its south side there is a shepherd's house in good condition, and a burial ground called Cladh Dhuban with rough, unsculpted gravestones. It is thought to have been named from a king of Scots, or from one of several princes, called Duban. Very close to Garbh Eileach's south-west end is **A' Chuli** or Cuil-i-Breannan, the Retreat of St. Brendan. It once held a cell or chapel allegedly used by St. Brendan, but no trace remains.

Eileach an Naoimh, pronounced Noo, is the last of the four. There may at first appear to be more islands, because several tiny skerries stand clear against the sky to look bigger than they are. The word Eileach does not mean Islet (as several Celtic scholars have thought), but is a spelling of Aileach, which means Rocky Mound. Eileach an Naoimh thus means Rock of the Saint(s). The monastic buildings are now in the care of the Ministry of Works. They are set low down on the south-east slope of the highest hill, Dun Bhreanain, 252 feet, in a green hollow. You enter a creek behind a screen of seven skerries and land near St. Columba's well, where a spring runs into a basin overgrown with water cress.

The monastery site is spacious. The chapel walls, 3 feet thick, measure approximately 22 feet by 12 feet. Within is only one carved slab, indecipherable. Beyond the chapel stands a small stone building with a stone oven set over a fireplace and flue—probably a kiln for drying corn. Lower down nearer the shore are two circular beehive cells built as one semi-detached structure, forming a figure-of-eight with communicating passage. One has been rebuilt by the Ministry of Works to a roof-height of ten feet, but left with half the roof unfinished so that one can see how the arch is formed by the overlapping of the flat stones. Between the hives and the shore stands a natural rock pulpit.

To the south of the chapel lies the monastery building. Only low walls remain. Adjoining it again to the south is a former herb garden and a graveyard with slabs upended, one of which bears a simple cross. When Dr. MacCulloch rediscovered the monastery in 1824 he found some of the tombs carved with ships, arms, and cognizances of the Clans Donald, Lean, Kinnon, and others. He spoke too of ornamented stones and crosses. All these have disappeared in the hands of thieving visitors. The Luing men have record early this century of one good stone, raised and cleaned and replaced at the head of a grave, and which vanished off the island inside a year. We plead that nothing more be stolen.

A little hill rises southward from the monastic hollow. When you breast the top you find a gravestone said to be that of Eithne, St. Columba's mother, Princess of Leinster. It is an upended slate slab barely two feet high, roughly incised with a cross.

When I last visited Eileach an Naoimh, in June 1965, there had been no sheep or cattle on the island for three months, the grass was lush and packed with more flowers than I have ever seen on a Hebridean island. Honeysuckle sprouted from the crags, yellow iris filled the hollows, among the grass were meadow-sweet, spring cinque-foil, orchid, scarlet pimpernel, primrose, blue pansy—

within half an hour I had counted and listed fifty different kinds of flowers, most of them in bloom. A corncrake was noisily busy among them, and larks on the upper slopes.

The island is a mile long. A boggy and rocky walk may be enjoyed along the shore to the north point. Near it you pass under a magnificent sandstone arch called A'Chlarsach, or the Harp. The rock-curtain through which the bore has been made was formed when the sea was higher than now, or the land lower—depressed by polar ice, after the melting of which the land slowly 'sprang' back to its present position. You should return along the top of the island's high spine, which gives excellent walking. On its west side the cliffs fall nearly sheer to a continuous rock platform at sea-level; the east side slopes gently. The crest is often narrow but always grassy and flowered to the brink. On my last visit the sea was peacock-blue and Lorn's throng of islands fringed by foam. At the far inland boundary, the twin horns of Ben Cruachan stood high and spiky on the sky.

Among the neighbouring isles **Scarba has the most imposing** presence. You reach it from Luing by driving south to Black Mill Bay, whence another lobsterman will ferry you across to the northeast shore under the woods of Kilmory. The island is a round mountain lifting steeply out of the sea to 1,470 feet. A few cattle and sheep and a herd of red deer are grazed by the owner, who until recently (Scarba is for sale at the time of writing) had a herdsman-keeper at Kilmory Lodge. To north and west the shores are ringed high by rock. Seals are normally seen basking along the east shore, more especially on Lunga.

From Kilmory, a foot-track goes south down the coast at a height of 400 feet, then heads west high alongside the Gulf of Corrievreckan. A three-mile walk from Kilmory will bring you opposite the great **whirlpool**, which can be clearly seen two hundred yards offshore. Locally it is called the Cailleach (the Hag). Make a steep descent on heather to the rocky edge of the strait. There is no beach, only riven rock cleft by guts. When the tide floods east to west the gulf is in uproar and the whirl never absent save for one hour at high and low water. If a strong westerly wind should blow against a spring flood the breakers at the overfall may be twenty feet high and spout as high as the mast of a ship. Both shores are savagely wild. On the Jura side, the hill ridges falling seaward recede one behind the other in claws and bays and capes, all black on white water.

One may often hear the story, taken from Adamnan's *Life of*

St. Columba, that the gulf is named after Brecan, the son of a king of Norway, who foundered in the whirlpool with his fleet of fifty boats. But Adamnan's *Charybdis Brecani* expressly refers to the tide-race between Rathlin and the coast of Antrim.

If you find clear weather, climb to the summit of Cruach Scarba. The Firth of Lorn, from its wide mouth between Jura and the Ross of Mull, stretches sixty miles inland, changing its name to Loch Linnhe off the Appin coast. Its upper waters are of course invisible, but the line carries the eye to the vast Highland fault that splits Scotland by way of the Great Glen to Inverness.

When you return to the mainland over the Clachan Bridge, drive north through Kilninver to **Loch Feochan**. In its four-mile length this narrow sea-loch takes three bends between the hills; being thus well sheltered it is much favoured by wild swans, of which I have counted thirty together. One mile beyond Kilninver, a natural rock pier by the shore is known as Creag na Marbh, the Rock of the Dead. At this rock the royal galleys used to wait to carry the dead kings of Scots to Iona. Most of the kings had been buried there from Fergus onward, and the custom continued for a long time after the capital had been removed from Dalriada to Forteviot and Scone. It was during this latter period that the Creag na Marbh was used and named. From Fergus to James VI, who was the last king of Scots to live in Scotland, sixty-three kings had succeeded each other in one thousand one hundred years. Of these, forty-eight lie in the Reilig Orain of Iona.

You round the head of the loch and in four miles reach Oban.

CHAPTER 9

Mid Lorn

Oban is the capital of Lorn. If you approach from Glasgow or Edinburgh your routes by road or rail meet first at **Crianlarich** in Perthshire. Crianlarich is a hub whose road and rail spokes radiate east to Stirling, west to Oban, south to the Clyde, and north to Fort William. It has assumed new importance since the opening in 1965 of the giant pulp mill at Fort William, for which its railway station has become a collecting point and loading depot. Vast quantities of timber, arriving by road from the forests of Argyll and Perthshire, are carried north by rail.

The little village of Crianlarich, at 500 feet in **Strath Fillan**, gives small hint of this activity in its backyard. Strath Fillan is a broad and open valley, especially lovely along the five miles of its river between Crianlarich and Tyndrum. The biggest mountains of the Southern Highlands surround it, yet lean far enough back to give open skies. Three miles to its south-east, Ben More and Stobinian, both exceeding 3,800 feet, are the highest mountains in Britain south of Strathtay. Southward, a range of five mountains rise to 3,428 feet on Cruach Ardrain. Four miles west stand Beinn Oss and Dubhchraig (pronounced Doochray), and behind them both Beinn Laoigh (pronounced Lui), 3,708 feet. Laoigh's spired peak, sculpted underneath by an eastern corrie, is the most shapely mountain in Perthshire, best seen midway up the strath at the Dail Righ, or King's Field, where a track to Coninish farm forks from the main road. The track gives easy access to the mountain, which in winter offers excellent snow-climbing in its eastern corrie at 3,000 feet. The tiny stream that issues out of this corrie becomes in due course the mightiest of Scotland's rivers, changing its name the while from Rund to Coninish, Fillan, Dochart, and at last to Tay.

The mountains around draw hill-walkers at all seasons of the year. They are bare rugged mountains, but like all in the Southern

Highlands, grassy and heavily grazed by sheep. Good angling may be had on lochs and rivers. The hotels at Crianlarich and Tyndrum cater for all-comers, but especially fishermen in summer and skiers in winter. Your first link with Lorn, an indirect and historical link, comes in Strath Fillan when you turn a sharp corner and cross the bridge over the river. Between the bridge and the Coninish track the flat ground on your left is Dail Righ. Robert the Bruce, on his defeat by the English at Methven in 1306, retreated west through Perthshire to seek refuge with Campbell of Loch Awe. In Strath Fillan he had to pass through the hostile territory of John Mac-Dougall, Lord of Lorn, who attacked him at Dail Righ and routed his small force. Bruce escaped south down the strath only to be waylaid at Loch Dochart by three MacDougall scouts. He probably wore armour for he killed them all, but left his brooch, which had bound his cloak, in the dying grasp of the last man. The brooch has since been known as the Brooch of Lorn, and remained the Mac-Dougall's prized possession for 341 years. Its subsequent history, how it disappeared, and how it returned to MacDougall hands 178 years later, will be told when we come to Oban.

The MacDougall's hostility to Bruce needs some explaining. Somerled in 1150 had given the Lordship of Lorn to his son Dughall, from whom Clan Dougall descended. John of Lorn had at least eight castles around the Lorn coast, and controlled several more including those of eastern Loch Awe. In 1306 Bruce had the full and active support of Angus, King of the Isles, with whom the Lord of Lorn might in normal course have been in alliance. Unfortunately MacDougall had married the daughter of the Red Comyn, John of Badenoch, whom Bruce had killed with his dagger in January 1306 before the high altar of Greyfriars Church at Dumfries.

Immediately on leaving Tyndrum, the Oban road and railway enter Argyll and Lorn. They sweep westward down Glen Lochy to Strath Orchy and Dalmally, then round the head of Loch Awe on to the slopes of Ben Cruachan. You are now in Mid Lorn and on one of the most popular tourist routes of the West Highlands. Half a mile down the loch you pass through the little village of **Lochawe,** It has two hotels by the roadside, but is otherwise largely hidden, for several of its best-sited houses are down on the shore or set well back above the road. At the west end, boats may be hired for enjoyment of the loch's free fishing, or for exploring the islands. As on almost all the big Highland lochs, the beauty of the shores and islands and surrounding mountain country is seen to far greater advantage from the water than from any other position.

More than half a mile beyond Loch Awe Hotel, the **Kirk of St. Conan** sits amid the lochside woods. Like the island of Innis Chonain a mile farther along the shore, it is named from Conan, a saint of the sixth century and disciple of St. Columba. The kirk has been built on the site of an early St. Conan's chapel, fragments of which survive in the grounds as low stone walls. The new church was designed and raised between 1881 and 1930 by Douglas Walter Campbell of Innis Chonain. He used granite from Ben Cruachan and built mainly in a spacious Norman or Romanesque style, at once dignified and draughty, but he added to this a variety of different styles. One of his two towers is Saxon, the other from Picardy. Unlike the simple Dalmally Church in the same Parish St. Conan's fails to fit its environment. Both have beauty, but St. Conan's is a curio, an example of excellence misplaced. The architect appears to have strained too much after grandiose effects. In the south transept, Robert the Bruce lies in effigy on a great stone pediment, in the side of which an ivory casket holds a splinter of bone from his skeleton (the rest of Bruce is in Dunfermline Abbey). The oak roof is of timber from the old warships *Duke of Wellington* and *Caledonia*. Two candlesticks come from Christ Church, Oxford, Dolphin chairs from Venice, and carved pieces of reredos from Eton Chapel. There are several other oddities. The church is much visited in summer by tourists.

From Innis Chonain, Loch Awe tapers four miles west into the Pass of Brander, thinning to a river that flows four miles into Loch Etive. Although a sea-loch, Loch Etive is almost as much an inland water as Loch Awe. It winds eighteen miles into the mountains of Lorn, moating the far side of **Ben Cruachan** as Loch Awe moats the south and east. Cruachan thus towers above Mid Lorn like a natural dun of fabulous size, eighteen miles in circumference and 3,689 feet high. There are twenty-eight higher mountains in Scotland. Encouraged by this thought, and if you have the will and the weather, you should traverse all of its eight tops: between them they reveal the whole of Lorn in a series of splendid panoramas. The quickest route of ascent goes by the North of Scotland Hydro-Electric Board's new road starting near the Kirk of St. Conan and rising in three miles to the dam at 1,200 feet in the great south corrie. From there you can strike east to the first peak, or else cross the dam and go straight to the summit by its south ridge.

The construction of **the dam,** and more especially of the underground galleries, tunnels, pipes, and vast machine-hall hewn out of
the mountain's granite heart, are one of the greater feats of modern
engineering in Britain. The dam itself is 1,000 feet long and 150 high,
but although eye-catching, it is not one of the scheme's marvels:
these are hidden below at a cost of twenty-four million pounds.
The Cruachan scheme was opened in 1965 as a pumped storage
station, the second biggest of its kind in the world (the biggest is in
Luxembourg). Its four generating turbines have a capacity of
400 megawatts and an average yearly output of 450 million units
(more than the nuclear power station at Hunterston in Ayrshire)
and they are reversible—they can drive the water back up the
mountain into the reservoir behind the dam. They do this by way of
two steep shafts, each 16 feet wide, which have been blasted through
solid rock. There is no way of storing electricity in great amounts
except by using it thus to rebuild a potential water-power. Thus the
Hunterston station, which uses nuclear fuel and cannot be switched
off when demand falls at night or at week-ends, then feeds its electricity to the reversed turbines at Cruachan. Energy that would
otherwise go to waste is stored in the Cruachan corrie as water,
available at a few minutes' notice to meet any demand.

Permission for cars to visit the dam is not normally given—
although the road is good with passing places. Visitors must go on
foot. But summer visitors to Oban may join a bus tour, run by
Highland Omnibuses Ltd, to both the dam and power station,
with conducted access through the tunnel to the machine
hall.

Returning to the lochside, you begin to enter the **Pass of
Brander.** The loch greatly narrows; on both sides the hill-flanks
steepen, become craggy, on the far side lined by broken cliffs. On
the Cruachan side the crags are thickly grown with trees. A most
formidable pass this must have been before the road was blasted
out of the hill-flank. To-day it still seems a little oppressive, being so
narrowly enclosed. The loch formerly ended and the river Awe
began between twin rocks called the Rocks of Brander, but these
have vanished with the building of a small dam across the outflow.

The pass was the scene of Bruce's revenge on the MacDougalls.
In 1308, he and Sir James Douglas fought a series of campaigns in
Argyll to break the power of turbulent chiefs. To halt his advance
into Lorn the MacDougalls, watched by their ailing chief from a
galley on the loch, tried to ambush Bruce from the hill-ground

above the defile. Bruce had anticipated a manœuvre so obvious. When his scouts had reported, he sent Sir James Douglas up the mountain with a company of archers to outflank the enemy from higher ground. He then led his men through the pass. It was an act of courage despite the precautions. The MacDougalls thought him trapped and began to roll down huge boulders. Bruce swiftly countered. His lightest armed men attacked uphill while Douglas drove down from above and the side. The MacDougalls were routed and lost many dead. Bruce went on to besiege and take Dunstaffnage Castle at Loch Etive. The MacDougalls thus lost a great part of their territory, which Bruce gave to Campbell of Loch Awe.

The dam across the river Awe has not much changed the level of the loch. A tunnel taps the water to feed a power-house at Bonawe on Loch Etiveside. Instead of a fish-ladder, the dam has an electric lift, which every three hours carries the incoming salmon and sea-trout 30 feet up to the top, where they are released into the loch. You may walk on to the dam, but unfortunately cannot see the lift operating.

Lower down, you cross the river at Bridge of Awe and soon enter Taynuilt village at the foot of **Glen Nant**. You can drive up Glen Nant to the watershed at 500 feet, then down to Kilchrenan on Loch Awe (see page 80). Less than two miles up the wooded nearer side there is a well-known picnic site at the **Tailor's Leap**. The tailor (according to tradition) had an illicit still at the nearby tributary burn, where it plunges over a forty-foot waterfall into the Nant. He made his leap across the Nant when pursued by excisemen.

In **Taynuilt village**, on a hillock behind the church of Muckairn (which faces Taynuilt Hotel), there stands a monument unique in the Highlands—the first in Britain raised to Lord Nelson. Its presence here seems doubly strange when one remembers that Highland people of the time were more attached to the Auld Alliance with France than to the new one with England. The chain of cause and effect leading to its erection starts with the devastation of English woodland by iron-smelters in the sixteenth century. Queen Elizabeth took alarm. Oak was needed for ship-building. She forbade further felling and the iron-smelters moved to Scotland, later causing immense destruction to the great woods at Speyside. The Taynuilt region was then heavily forested in oak and beech. In the eighteenth century, Bonawe and Taynuilt became an important centre of the industry, importing ore from England and employing large numbers of Lancashire workmen. When news of Nelson's victory and death at Trafalgar broke in October 1805, the Englishmen at Taynuilt at once raised a large standing stone, which was of unknown age and had long been fallen, and set it on edge in his honour. It thus precedes his column in Trafalgar Square by thirty-seven years, and bears the inscription: *To the memory of Lord Nelson: this stone was erected by the Lorn Furnace workmen in 1805.* A few years later, the introduction of blast furnaces ended the Highland industry.

From Taynuilt, two side-roads lead down to **Loch Etive** at Airds Bay. The old furnace, called a 'bloomery', still stands by the shore and has now become an industrial monument under the care of the Ministry of Works. On the far side of the loch you see the coast of Benderloch, defaced by the Bonawe granite quarry. The loch narrows here to 400 yards and is crossed by a car-ferry giving access to Benderloch and Appin. At the Bonawe Narrows the roads up the two sides of Loch Etive come to an end. A new road is unfortunately planned for the upper reach of ten miles, which at present is served by footpaths and motor-boats. The very best way to see Loch Etive as a whole, including the twelve great mountains that stand around its upper reach, is to sail up the loch from Achnacloich, three miles west of Taynuilt (and seven north of Oban). There is a railway station, camp-site, and pier at this little bay, and a motor-vessel, *Etive Shearwater*, which every forenoon sails to the head of the loch. Its complement is 130 passengers and meals are served aboard. I strongly recommend the cruise, which takes six hours.

The loch stretches far into the roadless hills of the Blackmount Forest, introducing you to a remote and magnificent mountain landscape that you can see no other way unless you are a mountaineer or long-distance walker, and then not so well. Eagles soar above the crags, and although you will have to be lucky to observe these you are certain to see the seals around Airds Point and red deer grazing by the birch and alder groves. Loch Etiveside was the homeland of Deirdre—Deirdre of the Sorrows, as she is commonly called. Her story has so often been misstated in differing versions, and her early years wrongly set in Ireland, that the simple story of her tragedy needs to be retold. Her name, Deirdre NicCruithnigh, has been frequently mistranslated as Daughter of the Musician (from Cruitear, a musician or harpist). Cruithnigh is in fact the

ancient name for the Picts who occupied Loch Etiveside and also
part of Northern Ireland. Deirdre's name simply indicates that she
was Daughter of the Picts. Her father was King of Picts in the first
century. While she was still a young girl he betrothed her to
Conchobar, King of Ulster, who was to fetch her over to Ireland
when she was eighteen.

She spent her girlhood at Loch Etive in the company of three
fine lads of her own age, the sons of Uisneach. Her closest friend of
these three was Naoise, but their association was a boy-and-girl
idyll—all three of the lads loving her deeply and she them. Brought
up as they were under the strict supervision given to a daughter of
the Pictish royal house, there was no question of love-making in the
full sense. The boys hunted for sport and food, bringing to Deirdre
the flesh of deer, fish, and badger; they would picnic by the side of
Deirdre's waterfall in Glen Etive, or in her House of the Sun (Tigh
Grianach), or in Naoise's wood—the Coille Naoise in the bay
between Achnacloich and Airds Point.

After ten happy years spent by the young folk in the land of the
Cruithnigh, the day came when Conchobar's men arrived to claim
the princess. The pain of parting was more than Deirdre would
endure. She refused to leave without her three friends, and Conchobar's headman had finally to pledge the word of his king to a 'safe
conduct' for the sons of Uisneach. On the seaway to Ireland,
Deirdre composed and sang her lovely song of seven or eight verses,
her *Farewell to Alban*. It has survived through the centuries for one
reason—its most powerful expression of a universal experience,
sorrow on leaving a homeland.

Deirdre could not in the end give up her love of the three youths
to marry Conchobar. The furious king had the brothers killed, and
not long afterwards Deirdre died of a broken heart. The Druids of
Ulster granted her dying wish: they opened the grave of the three
brothers and laid her to rest beside them.

Dun MhicUisneachan, the Fort of the Sons of Uisneach, is sited at
Ledaig on the Benderloch shore of outer Loch Etive.

Seven miles west of Taynuilt, at Connel, Loch Etive has another
and better-known narrows at the **Falls of Lora**, just one mile from
the open sea. The falls are in fact rapids, caused by the outflow
cascading across a ledge of rock at ebb-tide. The name is from
Laoighre, an early Celtic hero. The loch is here crossed by road
carried on a cantilever bridge. Ships may sail under at high water,
provided that mast height does not exceed forty-five feet. On the

far side at North Connel an airstrip was opened in 1967. Loganair run a week-end service from Glasgow from May to October—flight time 30 minutes. The aircraft fly on to Mull after a 15-minute halt. The railway line that formerly crossed the bridge to serve the Lorn coast to Ballachulish on Loch Leven, was closed in 1966.

The Oban road holds to the Etive shore as far as the last bay at Dunstaffnage, where a new housing-scheme called Dunbeg has recently arisen. The bay is much used by cruising yachts as one of the safer anchorages of the Lorn coast. Eilean Mor screens it to seaward and the mainland juts out a guarding arm. On the top of this point, the famous castle of **Dunstaffnage** rises like a huge grey-green boulder out of a tree-covered hill. The curtain-walls, 10 feet thick and 60 feet high between round towers that buttress the corners, are hardly beautiful, but they are an exceptionally well-preserved example of a thirteenth-century castle of enceinte. Its builder was Ewen of Lorn, a descendant of Somerled's eldest son Dughall. He named it Dun Stamh Neas (pronounced Dunstavnish), Fort of the Seaweed Point. Long before his time, the prehistoric fort of Dunbeg had been sited on a green knoll at the head of the bay, and according to tradition became a seat of the Dalriadic kings, who had latterly kept the Stone of Destiny there before removing it to Scone for the coronation of Kenneth MacAlpine in 844.

Dunstaffnage Castle was taken from John MacDougall of Lorn by Bruce in 1308. Campbell of Loch Awe became the hereditary keeper, and his hereditary constable has ever since been known as Captain of Dunstaffnage. In 1652 the castle was garrisoned by Cromwell's troops and in 1685, when the Earl of Argyll rebelled, it was burnt by Atholl. Later it was repaired and held by Argyll for the Hanoverians in 1716 and 1745. When Flora MacDonald was arrested in Skye for aiding the escape of Prince Charles Edward, she was taken aboard H.M.S. *Furnace* to Dunstaffnage and held there for ten days before continuing to London. A great fire destoyed the domestic part of the castle in 1810.

The interior has long been a desolate scene, the courtyard forlorn and the old house ruinous. In recent years the Ministry of Works began its renovation. They are still at work at the time of writing, but already a great change for the better has been made. The castle can be visited during normal working hours. A hundred and fifty yards to the south-west of the castle, a ruinous chapel of the thirteenth century still has graceful lancet windows in Early English style and several unusual refinements of detail. Dalriadic kings are said to be buried in the vault. In this chapel was celebrated, if one dare use such a word of a tragedy, a marriage unique in Highland history. In 1386, the Lordship of Lorn had passed by marriage from the MacDougalls to the Stewarts. Seventy-five years later, history looked like repeating itself when Sir John Stewart, Lord of Lorn, found himself with three daughters and no male heir. All three girls married Campbells, one of whom was Colin, the ruthless first Earl of Argyll. Sir John was determined that Argyll would not win the lordship. He had one illegitimate son, Dugald, aged eighteen. Being now a widower and anxious to legitimize the boy, he determined to marry again. In 1463 he summoned Dugald and his mother from Loch Earn to Dunstaffnage. On December 20th, the bridal party came out of the castle and walked across the grass to the wooded chapel. Among the crowd of guests and followers standing there were many disappointed and envious men: the Campbell chiefs: Walter Stewart, brother to Sir John but a mean, unscrupulous man, who had already been plotting with Campbell of Argyll (the document in proof is in Register House, Edinburgh, dated 1462) for the division of Lorn between them; and Alan, second son of MacDougall, apparently maddened by envy at thought of ancestral land lost, and now a blind tool in the hands of Argyll and Walter Stewart.

As the bride and bridegroom approached the chapel, Alan MacDougall sprang at them with drawn dagger and struck hard at Sir John Stewart. He fell mortally wounded at the chapel's door. The company stood shocked and Alan escaped. Dugald had moved to pursue, but was stopped by the self-possessed priest, who urged them all to defeat the murder and clinch the marriage at once. Sir John grasped what was said. The priest helping him, he pushed the ring on to his bride's finger and died.

From that day, no man in Lorn would follow any but Dugald Stewart, except the MacDougalls. He met them in battle at Bridge of Orchy soon after the murder, when their loss in men was so great that they never again recovered strength in Argyll. But the action proved indecisive. In Edinburgh, the law dealt Dugald cards from a stacked hand: Campbell of Argyll was Justiciary of Scotland, King James III but a boy of twelve. With Campbell's aid, Walter Stewart made good a bad claim to the land of Lorn. Dugald was compelled to surrender all save Appin, of which he became the first chief. Walter then made over Lorn to the Earl of Argyll, retaining for himself only the jackal's share of minor Stewart possessions. And such is the way in which the House of Argyll now has the Lordship of Lorn among its numerous titles.

Behind Dunstaffnage, the road turns three miles south to Oban.

CHAPTER 10

Oban

'The Small Creek', such is the English of the Gaelic name under which **Oban** hides its diminished head. The harbour is the best of the Highland seaboard, the town the unrivalled centre for West Highland touring, and this more by reason of its 'small creek' than its focal point in the Lorn road-system. The roads indeed offer many a fine tour—out through Nether Lorn or the Pass of Brander, then around Loch Awe or Loch Fyne; or north to Glencoe and back by Strath Orchy; these plus a score of variations. But when you stand by the Oban sea-front it is no longer the roads but the channelled isles that call to you: the Firth of Lorn and the Sound of Mull, the Lynn of Lorn and Loch Linnhe, the open sea-ways to Mull and Lismore, Staffa and Iona, Coll and Tiree, or even to Barra and South Uist in the Outer Hebrides. All the means are here. The red-funnelled steamers jostle at the two piers, near them the motor-launches, bound for the inner isles, or on hire for any goal you choose along the Lorn coast. You can take your car by ferry to Mull and Morvern, and travel on to Ardgour, Moidart, and Ardnamurchan. At Oban you have constant awareness of these sea-ways opening out before you—that exploratory adventure is yours if you choose, and that is the greater part of Oban's allure.

The town is ringed by low wooded hills, whose upper slopes are heavily peppered with big houses. Its bay, a mile deep by half a mile wide, is almost landlocked by the island of Kerrera (accent on last syllable). Kerrera's four-mile length bars the outer bay with green hills, above which the mountains of Mull swell high across the Firth of Lorn. Kerrera, with its winking lighthouse at the north end, makes what would be a small and exposed bay into a spacious harbour entered by north and south channels. The close ring of hills behind, and the bay's strong arms knuckled by the rock of Dunollie

Castle at the north end, and by the Dungallon bluff at the south, complete the shelter.

On the flat ground of Gleann Sheileach to the south, by which the railway line enters, the town first developed from a cluster of thatched cottages in the eighteenth century. As you see it to-day it looks a handsome Victorian town. New as it is, Oban has been inhabited for eight or nine thousand years. In the period 1869 to 1894, when the new town was rising and quarrymen working on a stretch of low cliff, where George Street now runs north to south, seven caves were discovered with remains of Azilian man (6000 B.C.). These Middle Stone Age people had migrated from Europe after Britain became an island. Their caves were sited along the edge of a raised beach and occupied when the shore-line was fifty feet higher than now. The present beach is a hundred yards to its west. In the most rewarding cave, named MacArthur's after the discoverer, were found two human skulls, a score of flints, three stone hammers, harpoons of deer-horn, and implements of horn and bone. Azilian man was a hunter and had not reached the pastoral stage.

A natural gateway to the west, Oban began to grow in the early nineteenth century, doubling its population from 600 to 1,500 as ship-building and farming developed. The town was created a burgh in 1811, town planning was undertaken, piers built, sailings to the Western Isles and Lorn coast were greatly extended, but more than by all these the new Oban was made by the arrival of steamboats around 1850 and then of the railway in 1880. The population has steadily grown since to its present 7,000. In 1967 an airport was opened at North Connel (5 miles) providing a week-end summer service to Glasgow. Oban draws most wealth from the tourist trade, but with seven lean months in twelve that would not be enough to keep the whole community. The harbour ties with Mallaig as the busiest fishing port of the west coast with a fleet of seventy ships; in 1971 the value of the catch was over £1m. Other local industries range from a tweed mill and whisky distillery to a factory at Barcaldine for processing seaweed.

Oban has three piers. You will find the yachts and dinghies at the South Pier along the Dungallon shore. To the Railway Pier a few hundred yards to its north come the fishing boats, usually a dozen or fourteen at any one time, and the car ferry for Mull. To the North Pier at the town's centre, come the ferries for Colonsay, Barra, Lochboisdale (South Uist) and excursion steamers, and along the sea-wall of the Corran Esplanade, which runs from the North Pier

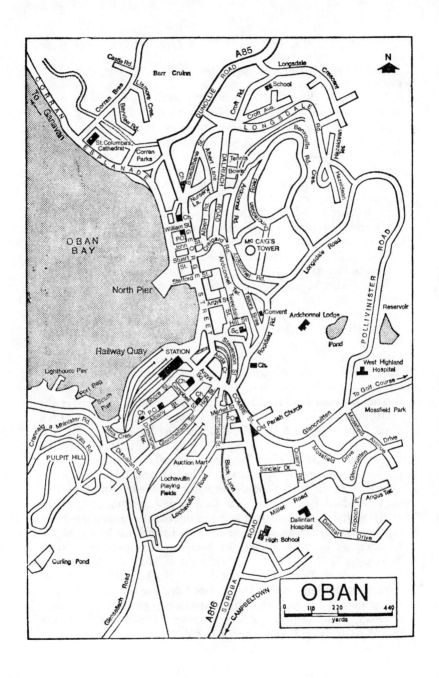

toward Dunollie, you will find the small boats for hire or for local cruises.

Standing at Oban's piers, facing the town, you have only to lift your head to be affronted by McCaig's Folly. This round tower squats on top of a wooded hill directly above the town's centre and North Pier. Its arcaded tiers are a miniature of the Colosseum of Rome, save that the latter's plan is oval with its window-arches round-headed, McCaig's a circle with windows pointed. The stone is local granite, for which McCaig be praised; his structure wholly out of harmony with all else in Oban. Its effect is damnable, if one feels in damning mood. The town council floodlight it at night, and this by accident of an inspired effrontery is happily spectacular: it is then divorced from the town below, and standing thus alone it crowns its hill like a halo. As seen by day it might grace the site of Nero's Golden House in Rome, but on Oban it sits like an incubus.

John Stuart McCaig was an Oban banker. He raised the tower between 1890 and 1900 with the good intention of aiding unemployed masons and as a personal memorial. The work was abandoned when the walls were completed. In 1970, its interior wilderness was transformed into a garden with shrubberies. It can easily be reached from George Street by way of Craigard Road. The view to Mull through the seaward arches alone justifies the climb.

The best viewpoint in Oban is the top of **Pulpit Hill** above the south harbour. To reach it, follow George Street south to Argyll Square, then carry on straight along Albany Street to its end, and turn right on to a road spiralling widely up the hill. Oban from here looks every inch a West Highland capital. Its rather massive solidity is lightened by the sparkle on the bay, which just before and after sunset can blind the eye with its ripple of wind and tide. The skies over Mull and Morvern can then be delicately tinted in subtle hues, or crudely in primary colours, and even if storm-clouded can quicken us. Far out through the narrow channel, the long island of Lismore lies prostrate under the Morven hills. As soon as dusk falls across Loch Linnhe and the Sound of Mull, lights prick out and flash from Duart Point and Lady's Rock, and from remote skerries, reminding us that the seas of Lorn are not only the wild wastes they now appear, but highways closely guarded by the men of Oban, whose keepers under the Northern Lighthouse Board are spread as far afield as Skerryvore, sixty miles out on the black Atlantic.

Below Pulpit Hill on its west side, Dungallon Park is the home of the Oban Sailing Club and the Water Ski Club. Both welcome visitors. Many yachts come from the Clyde for the Oban Regatta, which is held during the first week of August. The water ski-ing is open to everyone.

There are two other parks, Mossfield to the east of the town and Corran to the north. Mossfield is reached from Argyll Square through Crombie Street to Glencruitten Road. The park has a fine playing field for football and shinty—the latter a Highland game like hockey, but faster and allowing a full swing of the stick— and for the Highland games held during the second week of September. Beside the field is the Glencruitten golf course, its woods and low hills flanking the greens and fairways. The Corran Park is a small one at the waterfront, half-way along the esplanade beyond the North Pier. A pipe-band plays in this park thrice weekly. A new town hall was opened here in 1965. The architectural style is modern, spacious within and simple throughout, although several different materials have been used for exterior facings. It is far enough along the epslanade and sufficiently isolated not to clash with the town's older buildings. It won the Civic Trust award in 1965 for environmental design. The landscaping is appropriately uncluttered—a broad grass lawn, a screened terrace, a few seats, and the detail done with taste. The hall has a full stage and seats a thousand. The restaurant at the front is the best in Oban, supplying at least in part a lack that afflicts this and every other West Highland town, where a good dinner is hard to find outside one of the bigger hotels. Upstairs the hall has a library, reading room, and space for a museum, which is yet to be, for the exhibits that ought to be here are dispersed through other museums. The hall is used as a conference centre by organizations from all parts of the country, and for Oban's dances and concerts.

A couple of hundred yards farther along the esplanade is the pink granite cathedral of St. Columba, in the Roman Catholic diocese of Argyll and the Isles. It was the work of Sir Giles Gilbert Scott, the architect of Liverpool Cathedral. The Oban cathedral is one of the few in the world built entirely of granite, and is small of its kind, having a tall tower but no transepts.

Corran in Gaelic means a curved shore. The curve ends near the cathedral, and the Corran Esplanade soon merges into the Ganavan Road, at the far end of which lie Ganavan sands. Half-way there you pass between the shore and the great rock on which **Dunollie**

Castle is poised over the sea. The seaward wall is wholly cased in
ivy, no stone showing. A few hundred yards short of it, on the right-
hand side of the road, a tall rock pillar is called the Clach a'Choin,
or the Dog Stone. Its rock is a conglomerate known as pudding-
stone, eroded out by the sea when the land was lower than now. To
this great pillar Fingal used to tie his legendary hunting-dog, Bran,
presumably when calling at Dunollie in the third century. More
likely it was the site of the castle's kennels. When the fort was built
is not known, but the first records are of three burnings to the
ground between 685 and 700. In the second of these the King of
Lorn, Ainfcellach, was carried off a prisoner to Ireland; in the
third, his brother Selbach, King of Dalriada, fully avenged him and
then built the fourth fort in 713.

The existing castle is of disputed date, not later than the fifteenth
century and not earlier than the twelfth. Much of it could have been
built by Somerled's eldest son Dughall when he received the lordship of Lorn in the twelfth century, for his family were the earliest
western exponents of its style. The Galley of Lorn, which appears on
the MacDougalls' coat of arms, was taken from the Great Seal of
Somerled. In every instance where a galley appears on armorial
bearings it has either been inherited by families of that descent, or
has been borrowed by other families originally vassals of the Lords
of the Isles. You reach the castle from its north side and climb steeply
up from a small wooded glen, in fact the outer garden of an adjoining
mansion-house in which the MacDougall chief now lives. The
Brooch of Lorn has been held here since 1825, the year of its
recovery.

The castle is set on the brink of a crag nearly seventy feet high.
Of the former enceinte, only the north and east curtain-walls still
stand, with the keep set diagonally in their angle—an unusual
arrangement. This ivy-clad keep is more or less intact, although no
longer turreted and battlemented to its original fifty feet. The castle
has two gateways. The north gate, most unfortunately now filled in
and blocked, took a sharp zig-zag through the wall to give an easily
defended entry. The east gate is straight, and by that you can still
enter the old yard. The castle has been of immense strength. These
ten-foot thick walls topping such precipitous rock were well-nigh
impregnable, as was proven when Dunollie successfully withstood
the siege of General Leslie's covenanters in 1647. Again, in the
Rising of 1715, when the chief was out for the Old Pretender, his
wife held Dunollie against the full force of the Argyll Militia. Their

Early morning at Loch Rannoch, Perthshire, at the far eastern boundary of
Rannoch Moor, which spreads sixteen miles west to Kingshouse, Glen Coe.

Above Glen Coe from its north side looking south-west towards the Three Sisters: Beinn Fhada extreme left, Gearr Aonach the squat dark tower, and Aonach Dubh extreme right. The snowy peak is Stob Coire nam Lochan, 3,657 feet.
Below Kingshouse, the oldest inn in Scotland, sits on the bank of the river Etive at the west edge of Rannoch Moor. To its extreme right, Glen Coe falls away to the sea. The hill behind is Sron na Creise. The skiing slopes of Meall a' Bhuiridh lie a mile to its left (out of sight).

land was forfeited that year, but restored in 1745 for 'loyalty to the Crown'.

The Ganavan road ends a mile farther north at the Ganavan sands. The shallow bay is screened between the cliffs of Ganavan Hill and the lower woods of Dunollie. This being Oban's only sandy beach, its environment has all the usual trappings of a small seaside place.

On the other side of Oban, among the hills to its south-east, **Loch Nell** (from Loch nan Eala, the Loch of the Swans) is the source of Oban's water-supply. It gives sea-trout fishing and boats may be hired. Information about the fishing here and on Loch Awe and Loch Etive and smaller hill-lochs, may be had from Oban's information bureau in Albany Street. Advice on the best sea-fishing banks is better obtained from the boat-hirers on the esplanade.

From the esplanade, motor-boat excursions are run to the island of **Kerrera**, which bears near its south point the MacDougalls' second stronghold, Gylen Castle. You can also reach it more conveniently by driving from Argyll Square and Albany Street rather less than two miles down the Gallanach coast-road, then by ferry across the sound. The island has good green pasture grazed by livestock. In itself it has small beauty, but a splendid view of the Lorn coast can be had from its highest hill, 617 feet, between the ferry and the castle. Your walk southward along the shore to Gylen farm, then across the hill to the castle, is scented with the bloom of honeysuckle, meadow-sweet, and wild roses, and on the hill-track by clumps of wild thyme. Just before reaching the farm, you pass Horse Shoe Bay, which is the packing station for the Lorn lobster industry. The rafts floating on the surface may each hold as many as a thousand lobsters, brought here from the storage pond at Cullipool to be sent to market.

Gylen Castle has a wild site on a rock pillar jutting up from the sea's edge. The rocks that jag the foreshore made attack from seaward impossible. The name is from the Gaelic Caisteal nan Geimhlean, meaning Castle of the Fountains, for its two towers, only one of which now stands tall, were built beside natural springs. The castle dates from 1587, but there may have been an earlier fort on Kerrera, for the island was invested in July 1249 by Alexander II. He came to enforce his suzerainty on Ewen of Lorn, who paid homage to Norway, and anchored his fleet in Horse Shoe Bay. He spent that night aboard ship, and next morning told his nobles that St. Columba had appeared to him in a dream and commanded his return. They urged him to pay heed, but Alexander refused, landed, and was at once stricken with an illness of which he died before he could be taken off the island. The place of his death has been named Dalrigh (King's Field,) close beside the farm.

Some years later, King Hakon sheltered his fleet in Horse Shoe Bay on his voyage to Largs. In the Covenanting wars of 1647, Gylen was besieged by a detachment of General Leslie's army at the instigation of Argyll. The castle was captured and burnt, and then, at the exhortation of that Protestant minister John Neave, of evil repute, the MacDougall defenders were slaughtered, their crime loyalty to their king. The Brooch of Lorn, which had been held at the castle, was taken as loot by one of Leslie's officers, Campbell of Inverawe. No news of the brooch's fate escaped to the MacDougalls at Dunollie—there were no survivors. For nearly two centuries they believed it destroyed. In 1822, it came into the hands of Campbell of Bragleen, a descendant of Inverawe. On Bragleen's death the brooch passed to one of his trustees, General Sir Duncan Campbell of Lochnell, who by agreement with the family presented it to his neighbour, MacDougall of Dunollie, at a county gathering in 1825.

The Brooch of Lorn is a Celtic silver disc four and a half inches in diameter, ornamented with filigree and shaped to a dome at centre. The dome is crowned with a large rock-crystal whose heart holds a fiery glow, and is circled by eight jewelled obelisks. The dome can be unscrewed to disclose a cavity, hence the brooch is classed as a reliquary—an unusually early example if indeed Bruce's.

More than any other Scottish resort, Oban by day appears to be a town of hotels. They stand in phalanx of forty abreast along the waterfront, of every size from 130-bedroom to 8, and from four star grade to zero. In the quality of meals served the half-dozen best are much at the same level, which is not a notably high level if comparison be made with Scotland's bigger cities, and which varies from year to year as chefs and staff come and go. The hotels at night lose their command of the sea-front to the rail-head pier. Fishing boats swarm around the quay, unloading their catch in a blaze of light and activity, derricks swinging from ship to quayside, where waiting lorries take aboard the boxed fish. The harbour, not the town, then gives Oban its heart, alive like the Dunollie crystal.

Big steamers alongside both piers prepare for to-morrow's sailings to Barra and South Uist, and to the isles of Argyll. One of the nearer islands most worth visiting, especially if you would like to spend a day walking on it, is Lismore on Loch Linnhe. But that lies in Appin, to which we now move north.

CHAPTER 11

Upper Lorn

Upper Lorn is pierced deeply by three sea-lochs. Loch Etive gives it a south coast, Loch Creran pinches into its middle, and Loch Leven bounds the north. Two big peninsulas are thus formed: Benderloch between Loch Etive and Loch Creran, and Appin between Loch Creran and Loch Linnhe. The interior, which includes Glen Coe, is packed tight with high mountains, and is thus uninhabited, except where penetrated by its three great glens, the Etive, Coe, and Creran. The people live on the coastal fringes.

BENDERLOCH

You enter Benderloch from Oban across Connel Bridge. The bridge carried both road and rail until 1966, when the closure of the railway-line forced abandonment of road-tolls. These tolls at the bridge had for long been a most iniquitous exaction on the trade and life of Lorn. A much freer flow of traffic will result when the bridges at Connel and Loch Creran, and other parts of the old railway track, are incorporated in the new road-improvement now planned for the Benderloch coast.

Benderloch projects into the Lynn of Lorn, a flat western peninsula carved into nine bays. The beaches are stony, but the nearest, the Tralee beach of Ardmucknish Bay, has the best sand of Upper Lorn. You approach it from Connel across wide flats to Ledaig, where there are good camping and caravan sites and a well-stocked shop close-by at New Selma. Here you turn left to the beach. On the ground behind it—the common grazing of the Keil crofters— a large and well-equipped caravan and camping park enjoys a nearly complete monopoly of the sands. At the south end of the beach, near the old railway station, a grassy hillock bears on its top the faint trace of **Dun Mhic Uisneachan**, the Fort of the Sons of Uisneach.

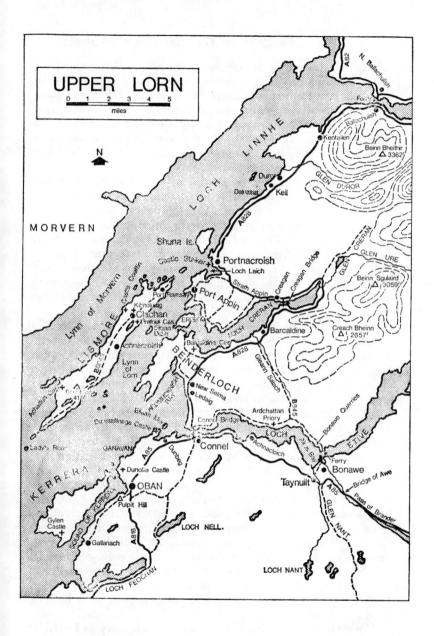

UPPER LORN

0 1 2 3 4 5
miles

N

MORVERN

LOCH LINNHE

A82

N. Ballachulish

Fort

Ballachulish

Kentallen

Beinn Bheithir
△ 3362'

GLEN DUROR

Duror

Dalnatrat

Keil

A828

Shuna Is.

Castle Stalker

Portnacroish

Loch Laich

GLEN CRERAN

GLEN URE

Creagan

Creagan Bridge

Beinn Sgulaird
△ 3059'

Lynn of Morvern

LISMORE

Castle Coeffin

Port Ramsay

Port Appin

Strath Appin

LOCH CRERAN

Kilmoluag

Clachan

Tirefour Cas.

Stean Dubh

ERISKA

Barcaldine

Creach Bheinn
△ 2657'

Achnacroish

Lynn of Lorn

Barcaldine Cas.

A828

BENDERLOCH

Glearn Salach

B845

New Selma

Ledaig

Ardchattan Priory

Bonawe Quarries

Bendurran Cas.

Eilean Munde

Dunstaffnage Castle

Connel Bridge

Airds Bay

LOCH

Achnacloich

Ferry

GANAVAN

A85

Dunbeg

Connel

Bonawe

ETIVE

Bridge of Awe

Lady's Rock

KERRERA

Dunollie Castle

OBAN

Taynuilt

A85

Pass of Brander

SOUND OF KERRERA

Pulpit Hill

△

GLEN NANT

Gylen Castle

A816

Gallanach

LOCH NELL.

LOCH NANT

LOCH FEOCHAN

Some historians consider the fort to have been Beregonium, the seat of Pictish kings, and it was so named by George Buchanan (sixteenth century) in his Latin *History of Scotland*. Support is given to the notion by the local tradition that Pictish kings were buried on the island of Lismore, which lies only one and a half miles off the Benderloch coast. Beregonium, like the Scots' fort on Dunadd, was a multiple structure incorporating several forts on the one hill. The upper fort was vitrified.

The roads going farther out from Keil into the peninsula are bad and narrow. You should avoid them unless on foot, when they can be enjoyed. The lanes are lined with blackthorn and alder; foxgloves grow in the woods. Most of the open ground is farmed, but in parts marshy. On the Loch Creran shore, Barcaldine Castle, to which you can drive, was built in the sixteenth century by Sir Duncan Campbell of Glenorchy. Long ruinous it was restored early this century and retains the old bottle-neck dungeon, banqueting hall, and spiral staircase. Neither castle nor garden are open to the public.

The interior of Benderloch can be explored if you first drive two and a half miles east by Loch Creranside to **Barcaldine forest**. This is only one of several estates in Upper Lorn purchased by the Forestry Commission. Others are at Duror, Ballachulish, and Glen Coe. The Barcaldine forest is planted across the hillslopes to either side of **Gleann Salach**, which splits Benderloch north to south, thus giving a hill-pass from Loch Creran to Loch Etive. Your ascent by road leads through a splendid avenue of overhanging birches, for which there is need to be thankful—the Forestry Commission officers usually fell birches. The road emerges on to the bare summit of the pass. Loch Etive winds 500 feet below. On its farther side Taynuilt and Bonawe lie on a green hillsward, open yet woody, from which Ben Cruachan lifts in one sweep of 3,600 feet. The Bonawe quarry, to which you now steeply descend, seems all the more squalid. Grey granite tenements flank it, some empty but all unsightly. The quarries have been worked for more than a hundred years, at one time employing 300 men and now only 50 or 60. In Benderloch there are no large sheep farms. The low ground is cultivated only along the shores of Loch Etive and Loch Creran. On high ground, cattle, sheep, and red deer may often be seen grazing together.

The shore road running back west from the quarry to Ledaig is bordered by honeysuckle and trees in variety. A mile from Gleann

Salach you pass **Ardchattan Priory**, one of the more famous houses of Lorn. Although now a privately-owned house, it is built on the site of, and still incorporates, an ancient monastery founded in 1230 by Duncan MacDougall, Lord of Lorn, for the Valliscaulian Order. The dedication is to St. Cattan. In 1309, at the conclusion of his campaign in Lorn, Bruce held at the priory the last national council at which speech was in Gaelic. The priory brought great benefits to the life of Lorn in an active life of several centuries, which ended at the Reformation, when the lands were divided among lay proprietors. The act of Cromwell's troops, who burned the building in 1654, was blind vandalism. The remains are open to the public as an ancient monument. They show fine examples of First Pointed work, an eleventh-century cross slab, a carved coffin lid, and several carved stones.

Five miles west you rejoin the main coast road and so return to Barcaldine on the shore of Loch Creran. The big factory there on the left-hand side of the road processes seaweed, which is collected by the crofters of the Outer Hebrides, dried and milled to a fine grain, then sent to Barcaldine for further reduction. The product is a chemical used for stabilizing pulps and liquids, like jellies, ices, and puddings, and for the manufacture of textiles, pottery, and paper.

APPIN

Loch Creran runs nine miles into the hills in three big twists. At the last twist it narrows to 150 yards and is there crossed by the Creagan railway bridge. When its conversion to a motor-road is finally made, one will be able to enter direct into Appin and be saved a dull detour of five and a half miles round the head of the loch. From the head one can visit **Glen Creran**, either to climb one of the *Munros* that tower above its six-mile strath, or to walk across the passes to Glen Coe or Glen Etive.

Glen Creran forks three miles from the sea. The left-hand fork screws deeply into the Appin hills and carries a track over its north ridge to Ballachulish, near Glen Coe. The right-hand fork is **Glen Ure**. The big house at its foot was once the home of Colin Campbell, better known as the Red Fox of the Appin murder mystery (see page 159). The glen, wooded in oak and birch, mounts east to a saddle at 800 feet between Beinn Fhionnlaidh on one side and Beinn Sgulaird on the other, both over 3,000 feet. Rough moorland then falls away to Kinlochetive. Across the broad flats of lower Glen

Etive tower the jagged peaks of the Black Mount, a thicket of mountains nine miles deep screening the Moor of Rannoch.

From the north shore of Loch Creran you enter **Strath Appin**, whose broad valley cuts across the Appin peninsula to Loch Linnhe. Its Loch Creran shore takes a side-road rounding the tip of the much-bayed peninsula to Port Appin on the far side, thence to rejoin the main road. The bays are well-sheltered, for the mouth of Loch Creran is almost closed by the island of Eriska, and then barred farther out by the north end of Lismore. Looking south from the shore you see across the loch the forested mountains of Barcaldine rising to over 2,000 feet. Delightful as the scene may be, the road is bad and narrow. Motorists should avoid it and go straight through Strath Appin to the west side. The coast here is bitten deep by Loch Laich, which almost makes Strath Appin an isthmus. The road splits at the back of the bay, the main road continuing north to Portnacroish at the outer arm, where Castle Stalker is perched on a tiny island, and the left-hand fork running west to Port Appin, from which a ferry plies to Lismore.

Castle Stalker is by far the best-sited castle of the Lorn coast, as romantic in its history as Dunollie, Gylen, or Dunstaffnage, and more beautifully set among sea-lapped mountains. Its tiny rock, capped by turf, lies close inshore but tantalisingly out of reach unless one can borrow a boat at Portnacroish or Port Appin. The castle on its top is a rectangular keep, which in sunshine turns a mellow sandstone colour. Behind and to its left-hand side, the Appin shore across Loch Laich is patterned in bays and points, which balance the blue Morvern hills rising over the green back of Lismore. When the sun lifts to the south, the isles and capes stand black on a silver race, but earlier in the day the tawny stone of the old keep is reflected across blue-green sea till its battlements mingle with the seaweed near one's feet.

The castle's correct name is Stalcair, the Castle of the Hunter. It was built in the thirteenth century by the MacDougalls, but after Bannockburn was owned in 1320 by Sir John Stewart, who acquired the Lordship of Lorn. In 1450, Duncan Stewart of Appin repaired it as a hunting seat for his kinsman James IV. When Sir John Stewart, Lord of Lorn, was murdered by Alan MacDougall on his wedding day at Dunstaffnage (see page 137), his son Dugald Stewart came to live in Caisteal Stalcair after the battle of Bridge of Orchy. Five years later, Dugald had a full revenge on his father's murderer. In the graveyard of the Episcopal church at Portnacroish, a granite stone on a crag carries the inscription: *1468. Above this spot was fought the bloody battle of Stalc, in which many hundreds fell, when the Stewarts and the MacLarens, their allies, in defence of Dugald, Chief of Appin, son of Sir John Stewart, Lord of Lorn and Innermeath, defeated the combined forces of the MacDougalls and the MacFarlanes.* The murderer was among the killed. Dugald lost the Lordship of Lorn to the guile of Argyll, but he ruled Appin for thirty-four years. When the rest of Lorn fell to the hated Campbells, the people left the country in such numbers that the event became known as Imeach Mor, the Great Flitting of Lorn.

The landing place at Eilean Stalcair is a tiny inlet on the south-east side. One climbs the rock above on roughly-hewn steps and walks over splendid turf to the castle's main gate. The keep stands four storeys high with crow-stepped gables pointing at the sky. The gateway is not on the ground floor but the first floor, which one gains by an outside stone stairway. This is guarded by a protuberant parapet on the battlements pierced by holes for pouring boiling oil or molten lead on the heads of the unwelcome. The first floor hall, roughly thirty feet by twenty, has a fireplace and stone seats. In its north-west angle a black pit for prisoners plunges into the island's rock. The walls, nine feet thick, have a spiral staircase leading to the second floor. The fourth floor has been a later addition with dormer windows. On the ground floor are vaulted chambers reached by a door in the east wall.

The Stewarts temporarily lost the castle in 1689 when the young chief Duncan, the King's hereditary keeper, exchanged it during a carousel for an eight-oared birlinn (galley) offered by Campbell of Airds. Next day Campbell was sufficiently grasping to hold the now sober and appalled Duncan to his drunken word. He took possession. The Stewart clan were then out at the battle of Killicrankie, fighting, under Graham of Claverhouse, Viscount Dundee, for the restoration of James II against an English army of William of Orange. On the Jacobite victory, Stewart of Ardsheal, the clan's leader in the battle, returned hot-foot to Lorn and threw the Campbells out of Castle Stalcair, which he held anew for King James. But the death of Graham at Killicrankie had left the Highland army without a general. It broke up, and Argyll seized his heaven-sent opportunity. His father had been beheaded four years earlier for his part in the Monmouth rebellion, and estates and titles forfeited. Archibald the son and heir, destined to be tenth earl and first duke, now restored the family fortunes by vigorous support of the Dutchman. His men were soon at the door of Castle Stalcair. The Stewarts held out for nearly a year and when forced to surrender won good terms but lost the castle. In the Rising of 1745, Argyll garrisoned the castle with Hanovarian troops. The estate was sold by the Campbells in the mid-nineteenth century, but in 1908 the castle returned to Stewart possession by purchase. In 1966 it was sold yet again. The new owner has re-roofed it and plans to make it his home after a ten-year renovation.

The rocky points of the Appin shore, which give Castle Stalcair such a good background as seen from Portnacroish, shelter the bays of Port Appin on the Lynn of Lorn. The little village, with its hotel and white-washed houses, is wooded and sheltered and yet open to the sea and isles of Loch Linnhe. At Airds Bay (the south bay) there is a natural arch on the west point. From the jetty on the north bay a motor-launch plies to the north end of **Lismore**. The ferry is not continuous, but sails on call as often as wanted for a small fare. The ferryman's house is in Port Appin.

The Appin ferry is the easiest way to reach Lismore, for the sea-passage is only three-quarters of a mile as against six from Oban, but it is not necessarily the best way. One lands at the north tip of an island ten miles long by one mile wide, with no public transport or shelter in wet weather. Lismore cannot be fully seen on a one-day visit from Port Appin. The better alternative is to sail from Oban to Achnacroish at the island's centre, and from there to explore the southern two-thirds. On the second day, cross from Port Appin to explore the northern third. Lismore may be walked from end to end in one day from Oban by using the north ferry for return to the mainland, provided that road transport can be arranged from Port Appin.

Like so many of the inhabited isles, Lismore looks uninteresting from afar—low and bare and dull. On landing, you will find it to be one of the more delightful islands. It is served twice a day from Oban by the R.M.S. *Loch Toscaig*, a converted fishing boat sailing morning and afternoon. The sail out past Dunollie is worth making for its own sake. Dunstaffnage appears on its point with Ben Cruachan rising behind, and before reaching the pier at Achnacroish the summit of Ben Nevis is seen at the head of Loch Linnhe. The farther you sail the more splendid does the view of the Argyll mountains become; even so, it is surpassed by that from the spine of Lismore itself.

The island has a population of 140 and is traversed lengthwise by one road, which holds to the centre line except at the two ends. It is an outstanding feature of Lismore that the land is heavily furrowed by shallow troughs or hollows running lengthwise (the road follows one of them) thus giving an abundance of sheltered grazings, fields, and farms, and allowing the growth of trees, commonly ash and sycamore, as additional shelter-belts. The ground carries more trees than would seem possible from a distance, for they are hidden by invisible ribs and hillocks. The north point is more openly wooded. Cattle and sheep graze on the grasslands, which cover almost the whole island. Cattle are abundant and bred for sale rather than dairy-farming. The numerous farms spreading down the length from farthest north to south lie well off the centre line, from which they are reached by metalled side-roads. The bulk of the population live in the north half: it is better ground and less exposed. Achnacroish has the pier and post office, but few houses. The main 'centres of population' are the high road, and Port Ramsay in the north-west bay, which can boast a row of twelve cottages. The greater part of Lismore is owned by the duke of Argyll. The farmers are his tenants.

Lismore in Gaelic means the Great Garden, and is the meaning generally accepted. But the word Lios from which it derives also means a residence or palace, a fortified place, and an enclosure. By happy chance all four meanings apply. The island has an ancient monastic site at Kilmoluaig, which would certainly be enclosed and have a garden, and on this site a cathedral was later built for the bishopric of Argyll. Lismore has also three castles and several duns. The castles are Tirefour, a tall galleried broch on the east coast opposite Eilean Dubh; Castle Coeffin, a total ruin on the west coast opposite Tirefour; and Achadun Castle, built in the thirteenth century as the bishop's palace on the south-west coast. The early Kings and later Lords of Lorn would probably build and certainly need these castles to guard their sea-approach. Achadun, incidentally, has a gush of water from its rocks—the only running water known to me on Lismore. The people's water-supply is from wells and springs. The rock is in main part limestone, giving a fertile soil rich in wild flowers and the best grazing in Appin. This alone would support the name Garden.

When you climb from the pier on to the main central road, and turn north, you will find the air heavily scented by meadow-sweet, which grows in thick banks alongside. In the moister troughs are wide columns of yellow monkey-flower and iris. Farther on towards the north, primrose is abundant among red and white clover, pink and white orchid, dog-rose, and cushions of wild thyme. In the hollows are much hawthorn and elderberry; corncrakes rattle among the hay, and everywhere on open ground larks sing. There is no sand down by the shore, which is clean and rocky, with several deep-water bays of small size. The eastern islets are noisy with gulleries.

The two-room cottages along this road are painted white with windows and doors in gay colours, all with little gardens full of flowers. About one third of the way to the north point you pass a grocer's store at Clachan, and a little way beyond, on the left-hand side of the road, find the cathedral church of **Kilmoluaig**. It dates from the thirteenth century and is still in use, but not as a cathedral. Measuring only 60 feet by 20, it no longer has a tower and nave: their foundations lie to the west of the present building. St. Moluaig, to whom the cathedral and the church were dedicated, came to Lismore between 561 and 564, at the very time of St. Columba's arrival on Iona. The two worked independently. Using Lismore as his base, Moluaig founded monasteries at Lismore, Rosemarkie (Ross), and Mortlach (Banffshire), all of which became bishops' sees. On his death in 592, his body was brought to Lismore and buried in the churchyard. His pastoral staff is still in possession of the Livingstone family as hereditary keepers for the parish, and is at present held for safety's sake in the vaults of Inveraray Castle. It is a plain thorn stick three feet long and curved slightly at one end.

The cathedral was founded around 1200 because the then bishop of Dunkeld and Argyll had no Gaelic. The lack made his administration of Argyll near to impossible. The Pope granted his petition that Argyll be severed from his diocese. A small cathedral was built on Lismore and made the centre of the new diocese of Argyll. But the roving spirit that moved St. Moluaig was now on the wane. Only forty-nine years later the Pope had to grant another petition—that the bishop's seat be moved to a more convenient centre, accessible without need to cross stormy seas.

The old cathedral was burnt to the ground at the Reformation. The present building is the choir. In 1749 it was given a roof and nine feet were taken off the height of the original walls. As seen now it is a plain parish kirk, with round-headed windows and short open bell-tower.

The road running southward down the island from the central road-fork penetrates still quieter, less inhabited land. After the first two miles the tarmac ends and a firm, grassy track continues in a long furrow under the lee of the island's rising back. You pass two lochs fringed by reeds, which like the cornfields farther back along the road whisper in the wind. Lime trees and chestnut grow in one eastern bay and the scent of honeysuckle rises dominant from a profusion of flowers. On this low sheltered ground you must pay for your pleasures by losing the outward views that are the greater reward of a short visit to Lismore. For these you should climb on to the island's spine. To win the best of both worlds in exploring the south half, your better way is to move on to the main ridge before reaching the end of the tarmac, and to follow the ridge over its highest point of Barr More, 417 feet, then to continue down to the south end and return by the track.

This southward ridge-walk is the best of its kind on the west coast of Scotland. As you rise on to it, the farmfields below are patterned brightly in colour from the pink of seeded hay to the dark green of potato. They stretch out between the channels of the Lynn of Lorn and the Lynn of Morvern, which unite ahead into a firth opening wide to the Atlantic, and astern into Loch Linnhe's deep bore. At the top of Barr More the skyscape is vast, and made so not by its emptiness, but by the throng of high and pointed hills lifting out of glittering seas and islands. Nowhere else on the Highland coast can you enjoy a view of the mountainous mainland to equal this one. Surrounding you are the highest mountains of Lorn, Appin, Lochaber, Ardgour, Morvern, and Mull. They rise darkly blue and shadowed by each other even in sun, a great congregation of peaks, yet many of them of shape so distinctive that you will want to know what they are. Granted the aid of a map it is still hard to name them. A few indications will help:

In Ardgour, slightly to the east of true north, the highest peak is **Garbh Bheinn**. In Lochaber to the north-east the highest and farthest is **Ben Nevis**. In front of it, within the bounds of Appin, the double-headed and most shapely summit is **Beinn Bheithir** (pronounced Vare). Much closer to the east, and slightly north of east, are the twin Glen Creran hills of **Beinn Fhionnlaidh** and **Sgulaird**. South of east, **Ben Cruachan** stands pre-eminent. Southward down the Firth of Lorn, you look to the Isles of the Sea, Scarba, and the Paps of Jura. On Mull to your west-south-west the highest point is **Ben More**.

When you walk down to the south end of Lismore's spine you overlook a lighthouse on a spray of islets, and can see beyond them a lonely skerry called Lady's Rock, which at high tide is submerged.

It carries a white beacon and lies one mile off Duart Castle on the Mull coast. The castle is the ancient seat of the MacLeans of Duart, held for them to-day by Sir Charles, the Chief Scout, and in former days by chiefs of lesser virtue, of which Lady's Rock is a permanent reminder. In 1523, Lachlan MacLean of Duart resolved, no doubt for what seemed to him good cause, that he must be rid of his wife. He had to move at once boldly yet circumspectly, for her maiden name was Lady Catherine Campbell, sister of the earl of Argyll. One night he tied her up and rowed her out to Lady's Rock, and there marooned her at low tide. When he looked out next morning from Duart the rock was swept bare as planned. He at once sent messengers to Inveraray Castle, conveying to MacChailein Mor the sad news of his sister's death, and expressing a reverent wish to bring her body to Inveraray for burial among her ancestors.

The high relish with which Campbell must have accepted the proposal was soon to be made plain. A day or two later MacLean with a large retinue of his kinsmen arrived at Inveraray Castle with the coffin. The mourning widower was at once ushered into the great dining hall, that he might be refreshed after his harrowing journey, and there, waiting for him at the head of the table, sat his wife. She had been rescued from the skerry shortly before high tide by a passing boat's crew from Tayvallich. No word of this was said at the dinner table either by MacChailein Mor or his sister. The state of mind in which their guest was obliged to eat his meal must have caused his hosts immense satisfaction. To prolong it further, they allowed him to make his escape. After a discreet interval, his wife's brother, Sir John Campbell of Calder, murdered him in his bed in Edinburgh.

Returning to Portnacroish, you move up the wooded coast of Appin, originally named as the 'abbey land' of Lismore, and pass through the small villages of **Duror** and **Kentallen** on the shore of Beinn Bheithir. The mountain's two shapely tops rise to nearly 3,300 feet above the mouth of Loch Leven, which here drives ten miles inland to divide Appin from Lochaber. On the mountain's north side the **Ballachulish Narrows** are crossed by ferry, saving —if one is bound for Fort William—a detour of eighteen miles round the head of the loch.

Duror, Kentallen, and Ballachulish are all linked in the Appin murder, which Stevenson made known to a wide public in *Kidnapped*. At the close of the 'Forty-five, the Stewart lands were forfeited. Colin Campbell of Glenure, known as the Red Fox, was made government factor in Appin. He began to evict Stewarts from the better land and to replace them with men of Campbell blood. Among those evicted was James Stewart of the Glens, who lost his farm in Glen Duror. In May 1752, the Red Fox made another descent on Appin to enforce new evictions. He came from Fort William with several mounted men, crossed the Ballachulish ferry, and took the old road through Kentallen. There he was twice shot from a holly tree on the hillside. He fell dead from his horse while his attacker made his escape unseen. When the news reached Duror, James of the Glens was sowing oats on his bit of land at Acharn. Suspicion had fallen (incorrectly, it is said) on Alan Breac Stewart, but since he could not be found, James of the Glens was arrested instead and without warrant. His trial at Inveraray has become the Highlands' most notorious case of legal injustice. It was heard before the duke of Argyll as Lord Justice General of Scotland, and a packed jury of whom eleven were Campbells chosen by their chief. There was no good evidence against James. A score of men had better cause than he to kill Campbell of Glenure. But here was a bird in the hand—so they hanged him at Ballachulish.

The mountain slopes of Appin are heavily wooded with conifers around Duror, and again on Beinn Bheithir's north side above Loch Leven. On rounding the mountain's west flank you suddenly see the Pap of Glencoe. It rears up in a dark cone six miles east. Then you arrive at Ballachulish Hotel with its ferry and garage alongside. Immediately east of the hotel stands the wooded hillock on which James of the Glens was hanged. A footpath winds up from a big sycamore tree. The top has a clear view across the five-mile sheet of Loch Linnhe to Garbh Bheinn of Ardgour, always pre-eminent among its large attendant train of lesser peaks, for it is given a noble lift by a great rock buttress under the summit. When the sun is setting behind these Ardgour hills they become an ebony screen, dividing a burning sea from sky. By your side on the hill-top stands an inelegant monument. A square block of grey granite is topped by a round collar bearing a white quartzite boulder. Inscribed on the granite are these words: *In memory of James Stewart of Acharn, who was executed on this spot on 8th November 1752 for a crime of which he was not guilty.*

The Campbells hanged him at sunset. When he was dead they strung the body in chains from the gallows, and there it swung for two months under guard till the picked bones dropped off. Then they wired the skeleton and re-hung it. Later in the year, the gibbet was cast into Loch Linnhe, and eventually drifting south to Bonawe was salvaged to help build a bridge. The identity of the true murderer, known to the leading Stewarts of the time, has for motives of clan loyalty been held to the present day as a family secret.

The strait of Ballachulish is only two hundred yards wide. Another hotel faces you on the far side at North Ballachulish. The car-ferry has recently been replaced by a concrete suspension bridge. There had long been a demand for a bridge here, for long queues of cars formed at both sides at the height of summer. If half an hour or so is not of any consequence you may drive round the loch by Kinlochleven. Moving east from the ferry, you enter Ballachulish proper, a long straggling village without any pleasing character and greatly marred by huge heaps of debris from its old slate quarries. These were opened in 1694, two years after the massacre of Glen Coe, and closed only in recent years, now to lie derelict.

For the present, I omit Glen Coe and pass on eastward to **Kinlochleven**. The township is the ugliest on two thousand miles of Highland coast, this through an industry of high social value employing nearly a thousand men and women. Hydro-electric power for the factory is supplied from the huge Blackwater reservoir, sited four miles east in the hills behind Rannoch Moor. In fine weather, the journey around the head of Loch Leven is rewarding in its own right. Kinlochleven nestles at the foot of the Mamore Forest, a range of spiry mountains seen well from the high road of approach. The mountain scale is great enough to absorb the town into itself, so that (as long as one is not in the town) wood, loch, and mountain wholly dominate the scene, the town shrinking to merely wart-like dimension. High above its north side, **Mamore Lodge** is one of the more splendidly sited houses of the West Highlands. It perches 600 feet up on the flank of Am Bodach, 3,382 feet, close to the old military road linking Kinlochleven with Fort William. Formerly a shooting lodge, used by King Edward VII, its site gives access along the old deer-stalking tracks and disused roads that range sixty miles and more across the Mamore Forest to Glen Nevis, Loch Treig, Glen Spean, Blackwater, and Fort William. Most wonderful panoramas of loch and mountain are enjoyed from the heights, and frequent sightings of the red deer herds.

Your road out of Kinlochleven to North Ballachulish holds closely to the north shore of the loch, granting ever-changing views across wood and water to the Appin mountains, and more especially, towards the end, to the wide and toothy jaws of Glen Coe.

Iona. *Above* the 13th century Nunnery of St. Mary, built by Ragnall, King of the Isles (the son of Somerled). The stone is pink granite varied with black schist and creamy sandstone. The low walls, rising and falling between tall pointed gables, have become a natural rock garden. The ruin is perhaps the most beautiful of the whole seaboard. *Below* the central farmlands above the west coast of Iona, which is lined with sandy beaches.

Far left
The 10th century Celtic cross
of St. Martin, which stands
outside the west door of
Iona cathedral.
Left
The shaft of an ancient Celtic
cross inside the chapel of
Pennygowan, Mull. The front shows
interlacing flowers above a galley
under sail (the Lords of the
Isles' symbol of sea-power); the
reverse side shows the Virgin and
Child. In this chapel one of the
early MacLeans of Duart and his
wife practised black magic.
Below
Fingal's Cave at the south point
of the island of Staffa (the
Norse for stave, for the Norsemen
built their houses of tree-trunks
set vertically, like the cave's
black basaltic columns). The name
Fingal is from a 3rd century
Irish hero, called by the Scots
Fionn na Ghal (Chief of Valour),
who defended the Hebrides against
Viking pirates.

CHAPTER 12

Glen Coe

Glen Coe is not usually approached along the Appin coast unless by people centred on Oban. The direct route from the Lowlands goes through Tyndrum over the Moor of Rannoch. At the top of the steep pass above Tyndrum, road and rail leave Perthshire to enter Argyll, and to fall at a long gentle incline to Bridge of Orchy. The main feature of this passage is the magnificent sweep of Beinn Dorain, 3,524 feet, to the east of the road; from summit to foot the slope takes an uninterrupted curve like the leech of a sail.

Bridge of Orchy Hotel is a centre for fishing, ski-ing, mountaineering, and stalking. From Loch Tulla, which lies only a mile to the north, the river Orchy flows down Glen Orchy south-west to Loch Awe. Loch Tulla in turn is fed from the great basin of Loch Dochard at the heart of a huge mountain range to the west known as the Blackmount Forest and comprising the whole massif between Rannoch Moor and Glen Etive. Loch Dochard is thus ringed by a twenty-two-mile horse-shoe and kept filled by the score of burns flowing off it. As seen from the east shore of Loch Tulla, which offers a foreground of sandy beach, the farthest mountains, Ben Starav, 3,541 feet, and Stob Cor' an Albannaich, 3,425 feet, are wedge-shaped and pointed; the nearer, Stob Ghabhar (pronounced Gowr), 3,565 feet, and Stob a Choire Odhair (pronounced Corrour), 3,058 feet, are sculpted by deep corries. At the south-west end of Loch Tulla, the woods of Scots pine are remnants of the old Caledonian forest.

Loch Dochard may be reached by following the old Glen Coe road, which strikes left from Bridge of Orchy. It is open to cars as far as Forest Lodge at the west end of Loch Tulla. Duncan Ban McIntyre, the Gaelic bard, was born nearby at Inveroran. From the lodge, a good track leads west to Loch Dochard through one of the finest deer forests and mountain scenes in the West Highlands. The track continues south-west to Glen Kinglass, thence to Loch Etive and Kinlochetive. This twenty-mile walk through the **Black Mount** is recommended if transport can be arranged at the far end.

The name Black Mount was originally and is strictly applied only to the high-swelling ground to the north, between Rannoch Moor and the Corrie Ba of the Clachlet massif to its west. The old Glen Coe road from Bridge of Orchy traversed the very centre of the Black Mount, reaching 1,450 feet on the shoulder of Meall a' Bhuiridh before the final drop to Glen Coe. It is a most exposed situation in winter and the road used to be blocked by snow for long periods. It is still a right-of-way and gives a most enjoyable walk of eight miles from Forest Lodge. The new road, opened in 1935, is scarcely less exposed but holds to lower ground at a maximum height of 1,143 feet. It too is often blocked but rarely for more than a few hours in blizzard: Argyll District Council maintains a most efficient snow-plough team.

At the top of the Black Mount pass you emerge on to the Moor of Rannoch. Road and rail have now parted, the railway swinging far eastward to the other side of the moor, bound for Fort William and Mallaig, and for part of the way borne on ground so boggy that the line is carried on floating brushwood, at another part roofed to keep the track open in blizzard. The road holds to long flats under the mountains between Loch Ba and Lochan na h'Achlaise. Your eyes at first are drawn to the depths of Corrie Ba on your left. This gigantic corrie of Clachlet, 3,600 feet, is the biggest in Scotland, exceeding in size even the famous Garbh Choire of Braeriach in the Cairngorms. It lies deep and dusky behind a foreground of sparkling lochans, whose surface is flecked by reeds and rocks and bog-cotton. To its left, the high head of Stob Ghabhar is poised like a lizard's over the lochan of its uppermost hollow, to which dark cliffs plunge from the summit.

Rannoch Moor, 1,000 feet above the sea, is a vast triangle whose points are Loch Tulla, Loch Rannoch, and Kingshouse Inn, and whose sides enclose an area of 56 square miles. In foul weather there is no place more desolate in all Scotland. Much of it is so level that one can walk ten miles in a straight line without gaining or losing more than 50 feet. It undulates, none the less, between 550 feet at Loch Tulla and 1,795 feet on small hills near Loch Laidon. It sends its rivers to both the west and east coasts: to the Atlantic by way of the rivers Etive and Orchy, to the North Sea by way of its main drainage line, the river Ba, which falls from Clachlet to Loch Ba,

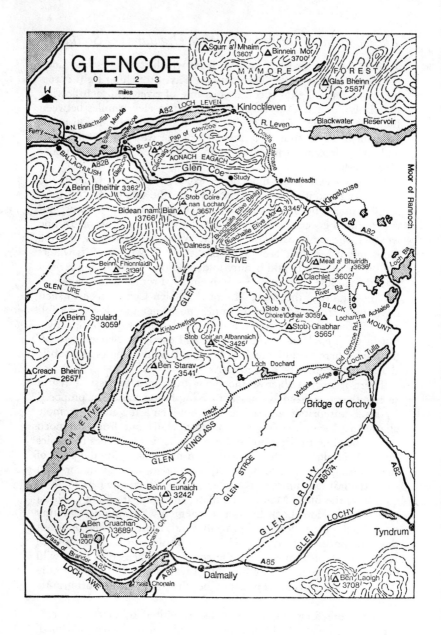

GLENCOE

0 1 2 3
miles

W

Sgurr a' Mhaim 3601'
Binnein Mor 3700'
MAMORE FOREST
Glas Bheinn 2587'

A82 LOCH LEVEN
Kinlochleven
R. Leven
Blackwater Reservoir

Ferry
N. Ballachulish
BALLACHULISH
A828
Eilean Munde
Br. of Coe
Clachaig
Pap of Glencoe
AONACH EAGACH
Glen Coe
Study
Altnafeadh
Devil's Staircase

Kingshouse

Beinn (Bheithir 3362'

Stob Coire nan Lochan 3657'
Bidean nam Bian 3766'
Buachaille Etive Beag
Buachaille Etive Mor 3345'

A82
Loch Ba
Moor of Rannoch

Dalness
ETIVE

Beinn Fhionnlaidh 3139'

Meall a' Bhuiridh 3636'
Clachlet 3602'
River Ba

GLEN URE

GLEN

Stob a Choire Odhair 3058'
Stob Ghabhar 3565'
BLACK
Lochan na Achlaise

Beinn Sgulaird 3059'

Kinlochetive

Stob Coir' an Albannaich 3425'

MOUNT
Old Glencoe Rd.
Loch Tulla

Creach Bheinn 2657'

Ben Starav 3541'

Loch Dochard
Victoria Bridge

Bridge of Orchy

track

LOCH ETIVE

GLEN KINGLASS

GLEN STROE

GLEN ORCHY
B8074

A82

Beinn Eunaich 3242'

GLEN LOCHY

Tyndrum

Ben Cruachan 3689'
Dam 1200'
St. Conan's Ch.
Pass of Brander A85

LOCH AWE
A819
Chonain
Dalmally
A85

Ben Laoigh 3708'

flowing thence into Loch Laidon, from which it empties into Loch Rannoch, and so to the Tummel and Tay. Stretching right across the moor there is thus a continuous line of river and loch flowing sluggishly, for the level drops only 57 feet in eleven miles between Loch Ba and the railway bridge near Rannoch station. On a hot June day it is possible to swim most of the way across the moor, and on a freezing winter's day to skate over it (feats actually accomplished).

In clear weather the moor gives excellent if rough walking. Its legendary reputation for bog derives from the tale of the 'floating' railway line. The bog is there in the shape of countless tarns, but the ground between is wide and dry, for the tarns drain it. In fine weather one can cross with dry feet. Were its lochans all tiny the moor might resemble a cratered battlefield but a few of its waters are broad enough to add beauty to desolation. An excursion far out into the middle is strongly recommended. From nowhere else can the mountains of the Black Mount and Glen Coe be seen to such advantage, free of all foreshortening, no longer too close for a full appreciation of shapes, which are seen at last in proper perspective, full in stature, clean-carved by glen and corrie, yet far enough off for atmosphere to clothe their hollows in the dusky blues and subtle shades that cannot be seen nearer.

There is no road across the moor from east to west. I regret to say that one from Rannoch to Kingshouse has been proposed by local authorities and if made would end the moor's remote character. Meantime, only a footpath leads out from Rannoch station heading to Kingshouse thirteen miles west. It goes two miles up Loch Laidonside, then nearly seven miles alongside the poles of the electric-power line to Black Corries Lodge, where a motor-road eases the last four miles to Kingshouse Inn. By far the best route in goes from the Black Mount road along the south shores of Loch Ba and Loch Laidon. Loch Laidon is indented with innumerable tiny bays filled with a clean and gravelly sand, most tempting on a hot day; the northern shore, by which one returns to Kinghouse from Rannoch, is pleasanter than the southern. There one finds wild flowers by the path, a little bay full of waterlilies, and about a mile down the loch the best of its sandy beaches, backed by short granite crags.

In the breeding season the lochs are visited by black- and red-throated divers, which behave like submarines when alarmed, submerging until only the head and neck remain above water.

Wild swan fly in, and duck come down among the heather. In the wide mosses farther away from the lochs, greenshanks take cover. There are few peat-hags, but where they are seen they still expose the bare bones of the Old Wood of Caledon. Were it not for the hungry deer there is every reason to believe that the natural forest might grow back again, for the small islands out on the lochs are well-wooded with birch, rowan, and pine.

The Wood of Caledon[1] formerly extended from Glen Coe to Braemar, and from Glen Lyon to Glen Affric. It harboured brown bear, wild boar, wolf, mosquito, and brigand. Its destruction by fire and felling occurred in two main phases, first between the ninth and twelfth centuries, when invading Vikings and warring clans set the woods alight to cover retreat, smoke out refugees, halt or destroy enemies, and who felled to get ship-timber; and second between the fifteenth and eighteenth centuries, when the English and Scots felled for iron-smelting, the Highlanders burned and felled to kill wolves and brigands, and the army commanders to destroy rebels. The more recent needs of the two world wars completed that destruction. Remnants of this once vast forest can be seen at Loch Tulla, and at the Black Wood of Rannoch.

At the north-west side of the moor, your road sweeps round the east flank of Meall a'Bhuiridh, and there at last springs the dark tower of **Buachaille Etive Mor** at the gate of Glen Coe. The Buachaille, 3,345 feet, stands in the angle between Glen Coe and Glen Etive. The name means the Great Herdsman of Etive, for its main ridge flanks that glen for four miles to Dalness, and there has always been good cattle-grazing in lower Glen Etive (until its acquisition by the Forestry Commission). The summit peak at the north end presents to the Moor of Rannoch a clean, pointed wall of rock. The mountain is the most popular rock-climbing centre in Scotland, just two hours' car-run from Glasgow. The rock is a rough rhyolite.

The mountain is seen to greatest effect from the first big bend of the road beyond the Glen Etive road-fork. From there, the famous **Crowberry Tower** can be seen projecting close under the summit. The ridge plunging seven hundred feet from the tower is the best-known rock-climb in Scotland, and the big gully to its immediate right is one of the better ice-climbs. In the early morning a memorable view is to be had from Kingshouse, which is Scotland's oldest inn, now fully modernized, situated on the river Etive a short way

[1]See *The Highlands and Islands* by F. Fraser Darling and J. Morton Boyd, 1965.

off the new road. The sun's rays stretch level across the moor and flood-light the great cone of rock, suffusing it with fiery pink in winter when snow-clad.

Facing Buachaille across Glen Etive is Clachlet. Its nearer top, Sron na Creise, presents to Kingshouse a formidable-looking wall, a mile to the left of which rises the summit of the massif, **Meall a' Bhuiridh** (pronounced Mellavoory), 3,636 feet. Its upper slopes are the principal ski-ing grounds of West Scotland. The Scottish Ski Club set up a ski-tow on the north slopes facing Kingshouse, and this tow has been taken over and improved by the White Corries Company, who have added a chairlift on the lower slopes. Access is had by the old Black Mount road from Kingshouse road-end, from which a new road has been made to the foot of the chairlift. The lift goes to the 'plateau' at 2,250 feet, and then the tow takes over on the last 1,350, where the best ski-slopes lie. In exceptionally good years, ski-ing has been possible on the upper slopes as late as the end of June, giving a seven months' season. The chairlift is run during the summer in fine weather to carry tourists up to the plateau.

Glen Etive is ten miles long. The river Etive rises on the Black Corries of Rannoch Moor and flows into the glen between the Buachaille and Clachlet. Its waters are brown compared to the clear Coe, but in summer are warmer after their passage over the flat moor. Although without waterfalls of note, the river throughout its course has carved a series of splendid pools, the deepest and longest of these being nine miles down the glen at Coileitir. The scene from the bridge there has a foreground of river-gorge with a woodland strip leading the eye up to the Buachaille Etive Beag soaring behind. This lower half of the glen is by far the better. The upper half is walled as far as Dalness by bare mountain flanks. Below Dalness Lodge the glen widens to a strath. The mountains on each side are set farther back and widely breached by corries and burns. The strath is sunnier, more open and fertile, fringed by trees on the hill-slopes, and ends on the eighteen-mile stretch of Loch Etive. This, although a sea-loch, is almost tideless—an effect of the cataract at the Falls of Lora. The water at the loch's head, where the river Etive pours in, is almost fresh and freezes right across in winter.

The most lovely view in Glen Etive is to be had one and a half miles below Dalness from the south shore of a nameless lochan. You look north across a tiny wooded island to the wide, graceful curve of the Lairig Gartain. It sweeps between the two Buachailles, which are reflected in the blue water at your feet. The way they seem to stand guard over the strath makes clear how they won their names. Deirdre's home was said to be less than two miles up the river from here, on the left bank where grassy slopes face Dalness Lodge. Her grianan, or fold for sunshine, was probably on the slopes of An Grianan, 1,795 feet, west of Kinlochetive.

By long custom, the whole valley from Rannoch Moor to the sea at Loch Leven is called Glen Coe, but in fact the headwaters of the Coe lie about four miles west of Kingshouse. As you travel west from Buachaille you pass the stalker's cottage at Altnafeadh. Behind it, the **Devil's Staircase** can be seen zig-zagging up the hill-slope behind before dropping to Kinlochleven. It is an old military road of 1750, made not by General Wade (who built his Highland roads between 1726 and 1737) but by General Caulfeild. It gives an easy pass of four miles in fine weather, but can be very different in winter. When the Blackwater dam was being made on the far side of the hill in 1905, and an army of navvies were encamped there, many died of cold and exposure on the snow of the Devil's Staircase when walking to and from Kingshouse Inn, their nameless bodies being discovered only when the snows melted in spring. From the slopes of the hill to the left-hand side of the Devil's Staircase rises the infant Coe, a slender thread barely visible save in spate, but soon to slice its way eight miles through the rock of the glen.

A mile to the west of Altnafeadh, a tiny loch on the south side of the road is Lochan na Fola, the Little Loch of Blood, where at Christmas in 1543 several men of the glen killed each other after a quarrel over the division of a Christmas gift of cheese. Above the lochan to its south, the **Buachaille Etive Beag** towers craggily to 3,129 feet, divided from its bigger brother by the Lairig Gartain, but joined to it at the far end, where its own summit lies, by the beautifully curved pass that you admired from lower Glen Etive. As you round the north face you cross the watershed at 1,000 feet and at last travel by the waters of the Coe itself. The little Buachaille is separated again from its still bigger western neighbour, Bidean nam Bian, by the Lairig Eilde, through which a path runs from Dalness in Glen Etive to the Study in Glencoe.

The Study is the true head of the glen. The name is a corruption of the old Scots Stiddie, which means Anvil. The still earlier Gaelic name was a finer one—Innean a' Cheathaich, the Anvil of the Mist. It is a flat-topped rock on the old road, which here rises higher than the new. Immediately below, the Coe plunges through a gorge under a high waterfall of the Allt Lairig Eilde, carving a series of clear green pools down to a confluence called The Meeting of Three Waters. The Study gives that impressive view of the Three Sisters of Glen Coe, which figure in MacCulloch's famous painting in the Glasgow Art Gallery.

Glen Coe is no great beauty. One cannot compare it with Glen Affric or Glen Lyon, which show a rich variety of water and woodland scene. It is bare and bleak, adorned by neither tree nor heather. It is in truth a deep trough. But viewed from the Study it has a wild and ugly majesty. When you lift your eyes from the glen to the mountains towering above, you see an array of rock peaks, packed close, trenched by ravines, of its own kind unrivalled. All other glens seem tame by comparison; they are certainly not so uncompromisingly precipitous. On both flanks the cliffs rise to 3,000 feet from the green flats of Loch Achtriochtan. The whole south side of the glen is walled by the highest mountain of Argyll, Bidean nam Bian, the Peak of the Bens, named thus from its nine tops. The summit, 3,766 feet, may be seen from here between the first and second Sisters as a distant dome, apparently much lower than the nearer, more graceful peak of Stob Coire nan Lochan, which appears above the second Sister's arched back. The Three Sisters are no more than the butt ends of three great spurs of Bidean. They hang over the glen in bulges of black rock, named in descending order Beinn Fhada (the Long Mountain), Gearr Aonach (the Short Ridge), and Aonach Dubh (the Black Ridge). The opposite, north side of the glen is walled by the unbroken flank of the Aonach Eagach (the Notched Ridge), running three miles to Clachaig. Its shattered crest gives a scramble along one of the two narrowest summit ridges on the Scottish mainland (the other is An Teallach in Ross). The climbing over its rocky pinnacles in winter is similar to that of an Alpine ridge.

Move on from the Study through the gorge. The rough bed of the glen falls away to a sudden flattening where Loch Achtriochtan lies at the base of Aonach Dubh. On the right-hand side of the road are some broken walls and one or two birch and sycamore trees. These are all that remain of the old village of Achtriochtan, which was evacuated after a landslide from the Aonach Eagach. The loch is much visited by swans, herons, cormorants, and black-throated divers. By the burns are dippers, grey wagtail, and water-ousel. The most impressive feature of the glen near the loch is the great north cliff of **Aonach Dubh**. On its upper face is the high dark slit of Ossian's Cave. From the nearest grassy ledge below it, entry can be gained by a moderately difficult rock climb of two hundred feet named Ossian's Ladder. The first ascent was made in 1868 by Neil Marquis, a shepherd—the first recorded rock climb in Glen Coe. Ossian, the son of Fingal, was a legendary Gaelic bard of the third century. If he ever made the climb we can at least be certain that he never occupied the cave. The floor is set at an angle of 45 degrees—one can hardly stand upright without handhold, and the vegetation is wet and luxuriant. A metal box at the back contains the names of visitors.

Alongside its three spurs, **Bidean nam Bian** presents to you three great corries. The mountain is one of the most interesting in Scotland, for the structure is complex. One can walk twelve miles on its high ridges. Route-finding is unusually difficult in cloud and the flanks are largely bare rock. No one, however experienced, should set foot on the mountain without map and compass. It ranks second to Ben Nevis as the most dangerous mountain in Scotland. A very great number of accidents, many of them fatal, have occurred on it during the last twenty years, especially in winter.

The summit hides behind outliers and cannot be seen from Glen Coe save from the Study and the Clachaig road-fork. From the latter you look into Coire nam Beith, above whose upper lip Bidean thrusts to the sky twin buttresses. On the right-hand is the Church Door Buttress, on the left the Diamond. They seem dwarfed by the nearer and formidable crags of Stob Coire nam Beith to their right. The lower corrie is walled on the left by a row of triple-tiered buttresses forming the west face of Stob Coire nan Lochan.

For the hill-walker, the best and most interesting route to the summit lies up this corrie. For the less ambitious, the most rewarding excursion on Bidean is the penetration of Coire Gabhail (pronounced Gyle) between the two upper Sisters. It has long been known to mountaineers as the Lost Valley of Bidean, because the upper corrie is invisible from the glen. The Gaelic name means the Corrie of Capture, for the MacDonalds used to hide their plundered cattle in it—they were notoriously a thorn in the flesh of near and distant neighbours. Access is had below the gorge near the Meeting of Three Waters, where a footbridge crosses the Coe. A footpath goes up the bank of the Allt Coire Gabhail where it plummets through a ravine, at first high on the flank among birch trees, which make a lovely sight in spring and autumn. Higher up the path becomes hard to follow among a mass of huge rocks, where the burn vanishes. There are several caves here. Beyond the barrier you break out on to the flat floor of the upper corrie. It stretches half a mile as a meadow encircled by the jagged ridges of Bidean and by great cliffs on either flank. These make it a true mountain sanctuary.

Directly above Clachaig Hotel, **Sgor nam Fiannaidh** (the Peak of the Fiann), 3,168 feet, is split from top to bottom by a chasm called the Clachaig Gully, which has become a famous rock-climb. Fiann was the name given to Fingal's standing army, a detachment of which is said to have occupied lower Glen Coe in the third century. There has long been a tradition in the glen that the Fiann dug four great trenches on the slopes of the Pap of Glen Coe, which is Sgor nam Fiannaidh's north-west top, and threw out earthworks as defence against the Vikings, whom they finally met in battle at Laroch, a mile west of Glencoe village. There is evidence on the ground in support of these traditions. At West Laroch, eleven ancient graves covered by stone slabs, on a site locally known in Gaelic as 'the Ringed Garden' (it used to be ringed by yew trees), are believed to be those of the dead in battle. They could be Viking graves, but proof must await an archaeological dig. Meantime, the long-lost Fiann trenches were re-discovered in 1966 on the open south-west slopes of the Pap at the 500-foot contour (map reference 115586). See also page **257.**

By the river at Clachaig is the National Trust's visitor reception centre (café) from which a path leads through the woods to a knoll.This is the **Signal Rock**, from which MacDonald chiefs used to summon their clan in emergency. Access to the knoll may be had from the main road by a footbridge over the Coe one-third of a mile below the Clachaig road-fork. The Signal Rock was not used by Campbell of Glenlyon for starting the massacre in the early hours of 13th February, 1692. The MacDonalds inhabited the five miles of glen from Achtriochtan to Invercoe and the government troops were billeted over the whole strath. No signal less than a beacon could be seen from end to end, and the essence of the attack was surprise under cover of darkness.

On the west side of the knoll, beside the new road, there once stood the old village of Achnacon. It was burned down at the massacre, and the scattered blackened stones could be seen until recent years. A mile down the road to the left is a big camping and caravan park. Below Clachaig the character of the glen greatly changes. It widens to a strath of green pasture alongside a gently flowing river. On the right-hand bank, woods line the old road to Invercoe, where the village of **Carnoch,** commonly called Glencoe village, spreads south across sunny flats to the new main road. It enjoys a superb view down Loch Leven to the rugged hills of Ardgour. A small museum cottage was opened in the village in 1967.

In Carnoch, at the old Bridge of Coe, a side-road runs up-river a hundred yards to a hillock, on which stands a unique Celtic cross, as slender as a flagpole and as tall, raised *In memory of MacIan, Chief of Glencoe, who fell with his people in the massacre of Glencoe.* He is buried offshore on Eilean Munde, which commands the strath.

The name Glen Coe does not, as Macaulay said in his *History of England*, mean the Glen of Weeping, although his erroneous inter-pretation for long seemed appropriate as a comment on the massacre. The brutality of that slaughter was by no means unique in Scottish history. Numerous others with bigger death-roll had occurred in the past and been 'forgotten'. The three points that have appalled the people of our country for nearly three hundred years are the cold-blooded planning of mass-murder as a matter of public policy by men of responsible position in government, their treacherous abuse of the victims' hospitality as a deliberately chosen means, and the approval of all this by the king, even though not a man of our race.

Glen Coe belonged originally to the MacDougalls as part of their Lordship of Lorn. When Robert the Bruce forfeited their lands he gave Glen Coe to the Lord of the Isles, Angus Og MacDonald of Islay, who gave it to his bastard son, Iain Og Fraoich, Young John of the Heather. From this Iain the MacDonalds of Glen Coe took their name MacIain, and their badge—a bush of heather. When the lands and titles of the Lords of the Isles were forfeited in their own turn by James IV, Glen Coe passed to the Stewarts of Appin, from whom the MacDonald chiefs thereafter held their land.

When the Stewart king, James II and VII, lost the throne to William of Orange in 1689, the clans fought for him at Killie-crankie and won, but lost their cause by Dundee's death. In August 1691, William III proclaimed a pardon for rebels provided that they took an oath of allegiance before 1st January, 1692. In the eyes of MacIain, who is known to have been a man of high honour and integrity, and of other loyal chiefs, such an oath to a Dutch usurper was impossible without the permission of their true king. They sent to James at St. Germain for this permission, which did not reach Glen Coe till 31st December. That same day, MacIain presented himself to Colonel Hill, the Governor of Fort William, only to learn to his dismay that the governor could not administer the oath, which must be made before Campbell of Ardkinglas, the Sheriff of Argyll, at Inveraray. Hill realized that MacIain must now be late in arriving there, so he gave him a signed certificate declaring that he had made verbal acceptance of allegiance before the official expiry date.

MacIain at once set off on that sixty-mile journey. He was delayed by snow, and then detained at Barcaldine in Appin by a small army detachment, and reached Inveraray two days late to find Ardkinglas absent. The oath was not administered till the 6th. The late-dated form of allegiance was then forwarded to Edinburgh together with Hill's certificate, despite which Glencoe's submission was not accepted.

On 7th January, Sir John Dalrymple, the Master of Stair and Secretary of State for Scotland, wrote from London to Sir Thomas Livingstone, the officer commanding the army in Scotland, giving him orders to destroy the clan, adding: 'I hope the soldiers will not trouble the government with prisoners'. By the 9th, Dalrymple had heard of Glencoe's submission. But MacDonald's hereditary foes, the Campbell earls of Argyll and Breadalbane, were in London with the Master of Stair that very month. Breadalbane had already been proposing and Dalrymple planning the massacre a full month and more before the amnesty expired. In one of these early letters, Dalrymple had written, 'The winter is the only season in which we are sure the Highlanders cannot escape us, nor carry their wives, bairns, and cattle to the mountains.' It would seem that Dalrymple was moved by religious prejudice, for in one of his later letters, urging army officers to their bloody parts, he damns the men of Glen Coe as 'all papists' (they were in fact Episcopalian). The Campbells' motives, on the other hand, were political.

On 30th January Dalrymple wrote again to Livingstone: 'I am glad that Glencoe did not come within the time prescribed . . . I think to herry their cattle or burn their houses is but to render them desperate . . . I believe you will be satisfied it were a great advantage to the nation that thieving tribe were rooted out and cut off. It must be quietly done, otherwise they will make shift for both the men and their cattle.' In a letter to the governor of Fort William that same day he wrote: 'Pray, when anything concerning Glencoe is resolved, let it be secret and sudden . . . better not meddle with them than not do it to purpose, to cut off that nest of robbers who have fallen in the mercy of the law now when there is force and opportunity.'

On February 1st, a hundred and twenty men of Argyll's regiment arrived in Glen Coe under Campbell of Glenlyon. He informed the chief's elder son, who came out with men to challenge him, that the garrison of Fort William was overcrowded, and that they must be billeted in the glen. He and his subalterns gave their word of honour that they came with no hostile intention. Young Mac-Donald suspected no ill and gave the soldiers quarters up and down the glen. For two weeks the officers and men were hospitably entertained. The MacDonalds inhabited ten villages between the sea and Loch Achtriochtan. Their houses were thatched cottages, their livestock mainly black cattle, with horses, sheep, and goats. The people grew their own corn.

Every day, Campbell of Glenlyon visited and was warmly welcomed by the chief's younger son, Alexander MacDonald, who was married to his niece, and on the night of the twelfth played cards with the two brothers. A blizzard broke in the early hours of the morning. At five o'clock, while it was still dark, the soldiers fell on their hosts. Men, women, and children were butchered. The old chief, then living in his house in Gleann Leac na Muidhe on the south side of Glen Coe, was shot in the back as he rose from bed and fell back dead in his wife's arms. She was then stripped naked. The soldiers tore the rings off her fingers with their teeth and so ill-used her that she died. Up and down the glen the work of burning and murder went on indiscriminately, for babes and men of eighty were killed or burned alive in the thatched houses. It seems probable that many unwilling soldiers were deliberately inefficient, for out of an adult population of 150 only 40 were killed. The continuing blizzard delayed the arrival from Fort William of eight hundred troops, who were to have crossed the Devil's Staircase to block the upper reaches of the glen. Under cover of the snowstorm, many survivors of both sexes and all ages escaped half naked to the hills. Left thus without food or shelter, they died from exposure in numbers no less than those murdered. Their cattle and horses, about a thousand head, were driven off to Fort William and divided among the garrison's officers.

A month later the Secretary of State was writing, 'This business of Glencoe makes a scurvy noise.' Indeed, his infamy seems destined to live forever. Parliament soon denounced the massacre as 'Murder under Trust'—in Scots law a crime so heinous that it carried the quadruple penalties of hanging, disembowelling, beheading, and quartering. A commission of inquiry was appointed. Breadalbane was declared to have been the Master of Stair's adviser but was never brought to account. The Master of Stair lost his secretaryship but was given a pension and later reinstated. As for Livingstone, he ended up with a peerage and a monument in Westminster Abbey. All three Campbells escaped justice but their name in the West Highlands was execrated for a century.

The MacDonalds resettled the glen and fought twice more for the Stewart kings in the risings of 1715 and 1745. In the peace that followed, their numbers grew until sheep-rearing ushered in the Clearances. Tenants were evicted, cornfields given to grass, the clachans left derelict. By 1820, the clan that men had failed to extirpate by massacre went down before sheep.

CHAPTER 13

Island of Mull

Mull is an island of mountains and rough moorland, of forested glens and headland cliffs, of bare peninsulas and rocky coves, measuring between its farthest points twenty-five miles by twenty. The population is 2,240. All sheltered ports lie on the east coast. Mull differs from most other Hebridean islands in having its west coast deeply indented by sea-lochs, and its east not bleak but woodily green, the latter because only the Sound of Mull, a mile and a half wide by twenty long, separates it from the shelter of Morvern. The shipping line to the mainland is not the short one across the sound to Morvern but eight miles across the Firth of Lorn to Oban. A car-ferry sails from Oban four times daily in summer and twice in winter to Craignure at the south end of the sound, and a steamer three times weekly to Tobermory at the north end. They are met by buses. In summer, additional sailings go right round the island by way of Iona, Staffa, and Tobermory. The car-ferry makes also daily summer sailings from Fishnish to Loch Aline in Morvern. A new luxury hotel was opened at Craignure in 1971.

Your approach from Oban takes you past Lady's Rock (see page **158**) and close under the walls of **Duart Castle** on Mull's south-east coast. The name Duart is from Dubh Ard, the Black Height—a crag on which the castle stands above the shore. It was built by the Kings of the Isles in the thirteenth century. By a charter of 12th July, 1390, signed at Ardtornish Castle on the Morvern shore, Donald, the second Lord of the Isles, granted Duart Castle to Lachlan MacLean, who in 1366 had married his sister. This Lachlan founded the House of Duart. The origin of Clan Lean is from Gillean of the Axe, who distinguished himself against the Vikings at the Battle of Largs. Campbell of Argyll finally broke their power, acquiring south Mull when William of Orange forfeited Sir John MacLean in 1691. Duart Castle then fell into ruin until 1912, when it was bought by Sir Fitzroy MacLean and fully restored. To-day it is the home of Sir Charles Hector Fitzroy Mac-Lean, the twenty-seventh chief of his line, who opens it to the public. The great keep, 63 feet by 46 with walls nearly 15 feet thick was probably built by the first Lachlan around 1390. The courtyard to its east is enclosed by a wall of enceinte, which formed the earlier castle. The design is similar to that of the thirteenth-century Mingary Castle on the coast of Ardnamurchan.

On rounding Duart Point, you see Torosay Castle at the back of Duart Bay. This is a house in Victorian baronial style, set in woodland that steadily thickens along the coast after you land at Craignure and drive north to Tobermory. Nine miles up the coast you pass the foot of Glen Forsa, a mile and a half short of Salen Bay. An air-strip was opened here in 1967, close to Glen Forsa House Hotel. Flying time from Glasgow airport is little more than 55 minutes including the stop at Oban. A week-end service is operated from May to October by Loganair. The air-strip provides an ambulance-service for the new Salen hospital.

By the roadside half a mile east of the Forsa river is the ruined chapel of **Pennygowan,** at which one of the early MacLeans of Duart and his wife practised black magic (they roasted cats to summon the devil). In the ancient graveyard are many recumbent stones, but within the chapel there stands erect the broken shaft of a Celtic cross carved on one side with interlacing flowers above a galley under sail, and on the other with Virgin and Child. These carvings are of singular beauty not seen elsewhere in Mull stone.

The next bay up the coast is **Salen's,** on the narrow isthmus dividing Mull's northern head from its mountainous body. The isthmus is made by Loch na Keal's biting in from the west coast to within two and a half miles of the Sound of Mull. The wooded village of Salen looks out across the wide bay to the Morvern hills. It was founded by Lachlan MacQuarie, 'the father of Australia', who was born in 1761 on the island of Ulva at the mouth of Loch na Keal. On his retirement from the governorship of New South Wales he bought the Salen estate and built the village. He died at his house of Grulin above the shore of Loch na Keal, where his mausoleum draws many Australian visitors.

On the north side of Salen Bay, the ruin of **Aros Castle** stands on a craggy hillock. Like Duart it was built by the Kings of the Isles, but kept before 1308 by MacDougall, the Lord of Lorn. It formed one unit of a planned defence system for the Lorn coast.

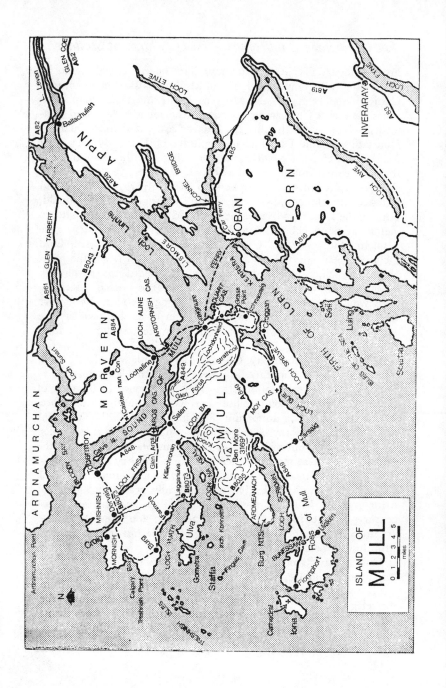

ISLAND OF
MULL

0 1 2 3 4 5
miles

N

From Mingary Castle on Ardnamurchan, beacon signals could be flashed ten miles down the Sound of Mull to Caisteal nan Con (the Castle of the Dogs) on the Morvern coast, and from there three times back and forth across and down the sound to Aros, to Ardtornish Castle at Loch Aline, to Duart Castle, and from Duart to Dunstaffnage and Dunollie at the heart of Lorn. By this early warning system, the MacDougall could know within half an hour that his farthest frontier was threatened, or by reverse process could summon force from the periphery to the centre. After Bruce had forfeited MacDougall, he returned Mull to Angus Og MacDonald, King of the Isles, who by sea and land had contributed so greatly to victory at Bannockburn. And MacDonald, as we have seen, gave Mull to MacLean. Aros Castle was last used in 1608, when Lord Ochiltree held court there as viceroy for James VI. All the great Hebridean chiefs attended, were invited aboard the royal ship *Moon*, ostensibly to hear the Bishop of the Isles preach a sermon, after which they were well-dined and made prisoner. They were taken to Edinburgh and released only after promising to ratify the 1609 Statutes of Iona, which made urgently-needed reforms in their rule of the Hebrides.

At the back of Salen Bay, **Glen Aros** runs inland to Loch Frisa. The glen is heavily forested in pine, spruce, and larch planted in 1925. The Forestry Commission plans to export 8,000 tons of timber a year to the pulp-mill at Fort William, and are therefore, say farmers, gobbling up too much grazing ground to the detriment of a balanced economy. A side-road goes up the south side of Glen Aros and breaks out of it to cross the hill-moors to Dervaig on the north coast. These moors in their greenness are very different from most Highland moorland north of Kintyre. The underlying rock is Tertiary basalt, which gives soil naturally grassy and good for cattle-grazing. Much of the ground's fertility was cast away last century by the move to sheep-farming on too great a scale— accompanied by the exodus not only of cattle but of humans too. Mull lost 85% of her population.

Most of Mull's people live in the northern third, chiefly Salen, Tobermory, and Dervaig. Tobermory as the chief port and capital has 640. The road north from Salen (note the buzzards perching on the telegraph poles) shows eastern Mull at its best, especially from the high ground above Tobermory Bay. Look south down the sound. Its curves of shining water, into which grassy capes thrust from Mull, lead your eye to Ben Cruachan of Lorn. On the Mull shore, the farmlands are seen to be a narrow strip between the sea and hillslopes dark with conifers, but along the roadside there is much natural woodland—oak, ash, and birch—and heather enough to brighten the ditches.

Tobermory, named from Tobar Mhoire, St. Mary's Well, lies in a hilly amphitheatre circling one of the best bays and safest anchorages of the Hebrides. A mile wide and long, the bay is crowded with yachts and small boats, and owes its excellence to Calve Island, which bars it to the south-east. The little town has a distinctly oceanic atmosphere, yet surprisingly is not a fishing port. In 1788 the British Fisheries Society tried unsuccessfully to develop the industry and built the houses along the front. The only fishing now is by a very few men for salmon, lobster, and whelk. Tourism has become the chief money-earner. The steep hillside close around the bay is wooded with sycamore and ringed to a high level by houses; the main street goes round the harbour wall. The eighteenth-century houses have pointed attics on the second or third storeys; their stone walls are painted black, white, cream, or pink, with windows differently framed. All look neat and bright.

Tobermory has good hotels and numerous boarding-houses. Motor-boats can be hired for cruising to the mainland coast. A thrice daily sailing is made five miles across outer Loch Sunart to Mingary in Ardnamurchan. The thrice weekly steamer from Oban continues outward to the islands of Coll, Tiree, Barra, South Uist, and back next day to Tobermory.

In 1588, after the destruction of the Armada, a Spanish ship of unknown name put into Tobermory Bay. In exchange for supplies, the captain lent MacLean of Duart one hundred Spanish soldiers to attack Mingary Castle and to feud with MacLean of Coll. A report leaked out, perhaps from the Spanish troops, that the ship held the Armada's treasure chest of £300,000 in gold coin. By what agency is not certainly known—but most likely under MacLean's orders—someone stole aboard and fired the ship's magazine. With 350 men aboard, she blew up and sank in 11 fathoms 80 yards offshore. Numerous attempts have been made to salvage the treasure. The last determined effort was made in 1955 by the duke of Argyll with help from navy divers. But the galleon has been engulfed by clay and lies under a thirty-foot layer. The only objects recovered have been a few dubloons, gold chain, brass cannon, and silver goblets.

The bleakest, windiest part of Mull is the northern headlands of

Mishnish, Quinish, and Mornish. The road round Mull avoids
them; from Tobermory it rises westward on to grassy moors three
miles inland, then winds like a distiller's worm down to **Dervaig** at
the wooded head of Loch a' Chuinn. Its forty white houses between
heathery hills and the sea are Mull's most beautiful village. The
house of Druimard, half a mile south on the Salen road, has
Scotland's smallest professional theatre, seating sixty people and
presenting, on four days a week in summer, good plays well acted.
The experience is recommended. The company plays to full houses:
you must telephone Dervaig 267 to book a seat. Druimard tea-room
and guest-house is under the same management.

On the west side of Loch a' Chuinn, a side-road runs out to Mull's
finest seascape at **Croig** on the Mornish headland. The jetty on its
half-mile creek used to be the landing point for outer island cattle,
which were then driven to Grass Point near Craignure and re-
embarked for Oban. Rhum, Eigg, Canna, and the Cuillin are
twenty-five to forty miles away but look astonishingly close, for they
tower straight out of the sea. They are framed by the rocky arms of
the creek and by the far-thrusting Ardnamurchan Point.

The next big bay down the coast is **Calgary**. It has the only
shell-sand beach of West Mull, and has it in generous quantity
with most of the desirable trimmings—a sweep of green machair,
wooded hill-slopes, and bold outer cliffs. Emigrants from Calgary
founded and named the Canadian city of Calgary in 1883.

South of Calgary, you cross the back of the Treshnish headland to
Burg on the coast of Loch Tuath—the wide channel between Mull
and Ulva—and there enjoy the most splendid landscape in Mull: this
whole coast is deeply indented by Loch na Keal and Loch Scridain,
and buttressed by cliffs rising to 1,000 feet on the bluffs between.
Mull's highest mountain, Ben More, flanks the inland side, and a
host of islands to seaward. Beyond Ulva and Gometra, the bigger
islands of Loch na Keal are Little Colonsay, Forsa, and Inch
Kenneth close to the huge cliffs lining the Gribun shore. Farther
out to sea are the Treshnish Isles, breeding stations for seabirds
and Atlantic seals. Four miles to their south-east you can see
Staffa, but Fingal's Cave is hidden from you on the other side
facing Iona. The cathedral on Iona looks at fifteen miles' range like
a boulder on a green field. On a headland above Loch Tuath,
half a mile to the south-west of Burg, is the ruin of Dun Asgain
dating from 1 B.C. Its view-point is even better than Burg's.

The road down to Loch Tuath is narrow and twisting, but
180

delightfully wooded. Ulva is now only two hundred yards offshore. Privately owned and farmed, it is not accessible by ferry without permission. On the Mull shore, between Oskamull Farm and Ulva is a grave (date unknown) alleged to be that of Lord Ullin's daughter and the chief of Ulva. According to local tradition they were wrecked while trying to ferry across Loch na Keal from Gribun. The poet Thomas Campbell probably heard the story in 1795, when he had the job of tutor at Sunipol House, a mile and a half north of Calgary.

On rounding the head of Loch na Keal, you pass the Salen isthmus to the woods of Grulin, then move on to narrow flats between Ben More and the sea. **Ben More**, 3,169 feet, is most easily climbed from Dishig, opposite the island of Forsa. The view from the top in fine weather extends from Ireland to the Outer Hebrides. The most westerly slopes of Ben More meet the sea in 800-foot cliffs, which give Loch na Keal its name—Ceal is an old Gaelic word for Cliff. The road edges round them on a ledge, which after heavy rain is littered with fallen stone, and runs out on to the Gribun flats facing **Inch Kenneth**. This island is named from Cainnech, a follower of St. Columba. On its south-east side, an ancient chapel of the First Pointed period has lancet windows deeply splayed, and sculptured slabs and Celtic crosses in the graveyard. There is a tradition that Kings of Scotland have been buried here when seas were too stormy for the crossing to Iona. Perhaps for 'kings' one ought to read 'chiefs'. Boswell and Johnson spent a few nights on Inch Kenneth in 1773 as guests of Sir Alan MacLean, the twenty-second chief of Duart. MacLean took them to visit MacLaine of Loch Buie, who succeeded, where all had failed, in reducing the loquacious doctor to silence by demanding, 'Are you of the Johnstons of Glencroe or of Ardnamurchan?'

The half-dozen houses of **Gribun** village line the road between the hill-cliffs and the seaward fields. Last century a newly married couple came to one of the cottages on their wedding night. A storm broke at midnight, dislodging from the cliff a boulder weighing many thousands of tons. It fell straight on to the cottage, crushing it flat. The lovers were never seen again. You can see this enormous rock poised between the first two cottages on the left, with the old garden wall still standing round it.

The Gribun sea-cliffs to the south have in MacKinnon's Cave perhaps the biggest cave in the Hebrides—much longer than Fingal's, longer, wider, and higher than the famous cave of Eigg.

The Companion Guide to the West Highlands of Scotland

It lies a mile south-west of Balmeanach Farm. You can enter at low tide and will need a torch. Drive to the farm-house, then walk over the fields to their south end, where a small gate at the cliff-top opens to a muddy track descending to the shore. The cave is opposite the southmost of a string of skerries, beyond a cliff-face waterfall. The floor is clean pebble at the long entrance passage, leading to sand in the main chamber, which at one hundred yards marks the half-way point. The cave then turns sharp right to the inmost chamber, where small stalactites hang from a red roof.

At Gribun the road turns inland to cross the huge Ardmeanach headland to its Loch Scridain shore. Loch Scridain, the Loch of the Screes, divides the twenty-mile leg of the Ross of Mull from the main body, and is named from **the Wilderness** on its headland. The Wilderness is a three-mile coastal strip of stone blocks fallen from 1,200-foot sea-cliffs. Its southern half, in the care of the National Trust for Scotland, contains a geological curio. Implanted on the cliff-face is the trunk of a fossil tree 40 feet tall. The rock is Tertiary basalt. The living tree was engulfed by lava-flow fifty million years ago in the Miocene Age. You will have great difficulty in reaching the Wilderness. I advise against trying unless you are a fanatical geologist. The approach-road from the head of Loch Scridain is the worst in Mull—four miles of mud, rock, and potholes on steep hills to Burg cottage. Two exceedingly rough miles must then be walked to the tree, and arrival timed for low water to turn a buttress of the sea-cliff.

The road down the Ross of Mull to Iona has been greatly improved since 1966, for it carries much tourist traffic. The direct route from Craignure is down the Sound of Mull to Loch Spelve, on whose opposite shore are the old slipways on which Duart's war-galleys used to be hauled out. The main road then goes west through the hills by way of Glen More to the Ross, but a side road down Loch Spelve cuts through a forested glen to the south coast at Loch Buie, where it ends.

Loch Buie is a big bay on the Firth of Lorn, open to the south-west and only partially screened by rocky headlands running three miles out. The estate used to be called the Garden of Mull. The ground at its head does look unusually fertile with broad hayfields and thick woodland around Lochbuie House. Between the house and a sandy beach stands the fourteenth-century Moy Castle, the ancient seat of the MacLaines of Lochbuie. Ivy-covered and battlemented, it remains in good preservation but is not open to the

182

public. Off the dining hall it has a dungeon unique in the Highlands
—a pit filled with water to a depth of nine feet from which one
rounded stone emerges at centre. On this the prisoner sat in darkness.

A most pleasant if rough walk from Lochbuie is by the old bridle-
track five miles along the rocky south coast of the Ross to Carsaig.
From this track you can look across the firth to the Isles of the Sea
and Colonsay. The main road down the Ross keeps to the north
coast, for which you must return to Loch Spelve and pass through
Glen More—a typically Highland defile, bleak in the pass and bare
on the western descent. The Ross too is bare, but although hilly is
mostly low moorland with sheltered pockets, of which Carsaig is
one. The south coastline is the most interesting in Mull, continuously
cliffed by basalt, at the west end by granite, and broken by sandy
bays and islets. Two roads from the north coast cross to Carsaig and
Uisken.

Three miles down Loch Scridain, at Pennyghael (where there is
a good restaurant and bar), the first side-road strikes south over the
moor and falls steeply to **Carsaig Bay**. Carsaig is a wooded hollow
with prosperous farms and big houses. Across the bay from the pier
is the Uamh nan Cailleach, the Nun's Cave, where the sandstone
was cut for dressing Iona Abbey in 1500. The bankers on which the
masons chiselled the freestone mouldings that decorate the doorways, pillars, and windows of the abbey are still there, with the
chips still on the floor, as if the masons had left yesterday.

The most interesting excursion, if you are prepared to walk three
and a half miles each way, is to the Carsaig Arches at Malcolm's
Point. Allow two hours to reach them and wear boots, for the route
goes west under the cliffs either on steep grass (where herds of
wild goat can be seen) or along a stony shore. **At Malcolm's
Point**, cliffs of columnar basalt rise 750 feet. Jutting into the sea
from their base, a headland is pierced by an arch 60 feet high and
wide. Its rock columns are inhabited by a large colony of shags.
Beyond the arch is a deep sea-filled cauldron, on whose far side a
chisel-bladed spire rises to 120 feet pierced by a lancet window 73
feet high.

Returning from Carsaig to the north coast road, you arrive
farther west at **Bunessan**, meaning 'At the Foot of the Waterfall'
(which is out of sight up the hill). Bunessan is the principal village of
south Mull and the best centre for exploring the Ross, and Iona too
when all rooms there are taken. Although it has a harbour on a big

and sheltered bay, Bunessan has no fishing industry—any fishing boats seen will have called in from mainland ports. At the west end of the village, a road crosses the moors to Uisken on the south coast. Uisken is a small crofting village with a wide sandy beach, bearing above the foreshore a very heavy crop of meadow cranesbill. A dozen islets close offshore give it much needed protection against the sea. Between Uisken and the Sound of Iona there are several other sandy bays, but these are hard of access for no roads lead in and the moorland is exceptionally rough and boggy.

The road west from Bunessan ends six miles farther on the Sound of Iona. The ferry-point is **Fionnphort** (pronounced Finnafort). A mile short of Fionnphort you pass on the left Loch Poit na h'I, where the monks from Iona Abbey used to fish. It is now the hunting-home of sleek-backed otter. There are no sea-trout—the fishing indeed is not very good—but a few baskets of brown trout are occasionally taken. The islet at its south end has the remains of a crannog, whose low walls are moss-covered. Flocks of wild duck and geese and swans come down in winter. Waterhen breed, mooring their floating nests to rushes—a cradle often violently rocked, for the Ross is notoriously windy. The moorings normally hold till snapped by autumn gales, when the old nests can be seen cast up on the shores.

Iona lies one mile off Fionnphort. A continuous daily ferry-service (passengers only) makes access easy. In summer a thrice-weekly steamer sails from Oban. Had Iona never seen Columba, it would still have been famous in its own right. It is a beautiful island, only three miles long by one wide, but with numerous beaches of white shell-sand on the north, west, and east coasts. The southern third is rough moorland edged by sea-cliffs. This south part is uninhabited. The people, numbering 100, live in the central farm-land, most of them in or near the village on the east side facing Fionnphort.

Iona Cathedral (the old abbey was raised to the dignity of a cathedral in 1500) is reached from the jetty by walking half a mile north on the road above the Village. This leads you past the thirteenth-century Nunnery of St. Mary, built (like the old abbey) by Somerled's son Ragnall (or Reginald), King of the Isles. His sister Beatrice became the first prioress. It is the most beautiful ruin of the whole seaboard. The stone is mostly pink granite quarried from the cliffs of the Ross, varied with black schist and creamy sandstone. The low walls, rising and falling between tall pointed gables, have become a natural rock-garden. The cut-grass floors bear in their corners tall red sidalcea and valerian.

Farther along the road, on the left-hand side, MacLean's Cross stands ten feet tall, a slim but solid-headed schist shaft of the fifteenth century, carved on both sides with delicate tracery. Just before reaching the cathedral you see, on your right-hand side, St. Oran's Chapel and the Reilig Orain—the Graveyard of Oran, who was one of St. Columba's disciples. The graveyard looks like many another of its ancient kind, long disused; recumbent on the ridged ground are numerous stone slabs, much weathered, none erect or showy, and none seemingly of distinction. All is very simple and plain. But in this ground are buried forty-eight kings of Scotland, four of Ireland, and eight of Norway. The Scottish kings include Kenneth MacAlpin, the first to unite Scots and Picts in 843, and MacBeth and Duncan. Beside them lie Reginald and other kings and lords of the Isles. It is recorded that in 1549 the Reilig Orain had three tombs like small chapels engraved *Tumulus Regum Scotiae*, *Tumulus Regum Hiberniae*, and *Tumulus Regum Norwegiae*. These have long since vanished by neglect following the Reformation—in 1561 the reformers stripped the cathedral and threw into the sea all but three or four of Iona's three hundred and sixty crosses.

St. Oran's Chapel was built in 1074 by Queen Margaret, wife of Malcolm III (who slew MacBeth) and sister of Edgar Atheling. In 1250 she was canonized. Her chapel, the oldest building on the island, has been re-roofed by the Iona Community. The windowless walls are of pink granite pierced only by a Norman doorway. When the door is opened a silver Celtic cross flashes from the east wall above the sandstone altar.

The **cathedral** stands on a meadow between the hill of Dun I, 332 feet, and Iona's east shore. You approach it along the Street of the Dead, on which kings and chiefs were borne for burial. Columba's sixth-century monastery—it is not known whether he built in stone or wood, more likely both—was destroyed in a Viking raid of 759, was rebuilt and destroyed in 801, again levelled in 806, when the Vikings massacred sixty-eight monks at Martyr's Bay, two hundred yards to the south of the jetty, yet again in 825, and finally in 986, when they murdered the abbot and fifteen monks on the sands of the north point, now called the White Strand of the Monks. As a consequence of these five raids, no relic of St. Columba survives in Iona. Some were taken to Kells in Ireland, others dispersed around Scotland. At the Reformation of 1560, it is said that the monks ferried their priceless library to the Treshnish Isles and buried it on Carn Burg. If so, it still lies there.

Already several times rebuilt, certainly in stone from the ninth century onward, the monastery was restored in 1074 by Queen Margaret. In ruins again by 1200, it was completely rebuilt by Reginald as a Benedictine abbey dedicated to the Virgin Mary. His abbey of 1203 formed the present foundations.

A bishopric of the Isles was created in 1430, and when the abbey was raised to a cathedral in 1500 the church was once more largely rebuilt; this structure is the greater part of the one you see above ground to-day. After the Reformation, Iona was seized by MacLean of Duart in 1574, and by Campbell of Argyll in 1688. Argyll still owns it. In 1899, the eighth duke gave the then roofless buildings to the Church of Scotland, who between 1902 and 1910 restored the church, and between 1938 and 1965 restored the monastic buildings—cloisters, refectory, infirmary, chapter house, and the Michael Chapel.

The cathedral as you see it restored to-day is a splendid building— not in elegance of spire or flying buttress, but in the fitness of its simple design to rough-hewn granite, the good proportion of its small size to the site (the church is none the less the largest in the West Highlands), and the relation of stout walls to windy coast. Cathedral and island perfectly harmonize. Iona gets plenty of sun, and this is needed to reveal the sparkling rosiness of the granite, which might still have seemed heavy in so great a mass had it not been relieved by creamy Carsaig sandstone and dark green schist. The church forms a Greek cross, with a short square tower rising seventy feet above the crossing. The main doorway facing west dates from 1500. In front of it stands the tenth-century Celtic cross of St. Martin, its tall whinstone shaft richly carved with Daniel and the Lion, David playing before Saul, the Virgin and Child, and numerous other figures. The 'glory' encircling the short arms is cut open, and the only other of its early kind is the Kildalton Cross in Islay. The Druidic Celts worshipped Bel the Sun God, and used the circle as their symbol of eternity, which the Celtic Christian sculptors carried forward on to their own crosses. Iona was a centre of Druid religion (and was named after them Innis nan Druinich) long before the coming of Columba. St. Martin's Cross perpetuates the link.

Alongside the west doorway is the tiny chapel of St. Columba, rebuilt on what is believed to be the site of his own cell. In front of it there was erected in 1970 a concrete replica of the ninth century

St. John's Cross, which had repeatedly blown down in gales. Exact as the replica is, it looks pseudo and cheapens the west front.

Pass through the west door into the nave and walk down to the crossing, whose north and west arches and piers date from the thirteenth century. Among the earliest stonework to survive is the Norman east wall of the north transept. On this wall there hangs a superb oil-painting by Le Maitre of Christ crucified. The transept is ill lit, but the painting, not formerly seen to good advantage, has now been given artificial lighting. Beyond the choir, on the north side of the chancel, take note of the fine sacristy doorway. Its Romanesque arches, formed as triple mouldings recessed one behind the other, were fashioned in 1500 from Carsaig freestone. The altar under the east window is a great slab of Iona marble veined with green serpentine, quarried from a little bay on the south-east coast. On the south side of the choir, an aisle leading back to the south transept has pillars of 1500 curiously carved on the capitals with an angel weighing souls, a devil tipping the scales, and crucifixion scenes.

Returning to the nave, pass through one of its two north doorways to the cloister. The sandstone arcades have a slim refinement of line, contrasting markedly with the rough granite and strong outer walls, but appropriate to the important centre of life in a medieval abbey. The garth is grassed. At the centre stands a large bronze sculpture of the Virgin Mary, bearing on its back the inscription: 'I, Jacob Lipchitz, a Jew faithful to the faith of my fathers, have made this Virgin for a good understanding among all the people of the earth. That the Spirit may reign.'

The statue is modern, was erected here in 1959, and its presence has been a subject of much controversy ever since. The world of nature is represented at the base by a blind lamb newly emerged from coils of writhing substance, which lift up and support the hooded and hollow-skulled Virgin, who stands with open arms, swollen belly, and wide-spread legs. Above her head a downward-poised dove pours forth a stream that envelopes the Virgin with a heart-shaped structure, which spins under her feet to return upward through belly, breast, and head to the dove. The meaning is plain enough—the impregnation of the Virgin by the Holy Spirit, from whom is to come the birth of Christ. Or in different words, the descent of the Spirit to inspire man and to fill the world with life and light.

There is no doubt in my own mind that this is an excellent

sculpture. Others whom I respect think it plain ugly. Some people find that although it has grace of line it seems too squat and heavy, but I think that this weightiness is needed—that nothing more elegant could express so well the power of the descent. I do not believe, however, that the cloister garth of Iona is the right site for display: a clash of modern bronze with medieval stone-work.

Doorways opening off the east side of the cloister lead to a coffee and tea room, and to an information room selling tourist trinkets and literature. The detached building, several yards to the east of the cathedral, is the old infirmary, now a museum exhibiting some of the more important of Iona's carved stones.

The cathedral's island setting is best appreciated from north or south, outlined then against the Sound of Iona, when the Paps of Jura or the nearer Ben More of Mull form the background. White fan-tailed doves, re-introduced in 1966, wheel between the great tower and the meadow. Their presence adds the final touch to the now completed work of restoration. St. Columba's name was Calum, often rendered Calman, meaning Dove, for which Columba is the Latin.

For a thousand years after Columba, Iona was everywhere called I-Chaluim-cille, the Island of St. Calum. In his own time it was variously named Hia, Io, Hi, Hii, and Ioua, these being spellings used by Adamnan, Bede, and many others as if trying to give phonetic rendering to a word that is not Gaelic. If scholars are correct in believing that this coast had been much sailed by the Vikings before the start of the first millenium (see page 257), the original name might well have been the Norse Hiöe (pronounced Eea), meaning Den Island. The brown bear, named by the Romans Ursus Caledoniensis, was then abundant. In Northern Norway it survives to this day and in autumn the she-bear habitually swims to a small off-shore island to hibernate and to cub in the spring. There is no more fiercely vicious animal than a she-bear with cubs, and the name Hiöe given to any such island serves warning. The early Ioua, changed by typographical error to Iona, came back into general use in the eighteenth century.

The summit of Dun I (pronounced Ee) is only half a mile to the cathedral's north. From a farm-house below you can climb to the top in ten minutes, and see the whole length of the Inner Hebrides from Islay to Skye—110 miles. Better still, you see Iona itself, purpled southward by heather, rimmed northward all round the coast by green machair and white sand. The island of Staffa rides the sea like a grey warship seven miles to the north. The cliffs are 135 feet high, riddled by caves of which Fingal's can be clearly seen as the biggest at the south point—66 feet high and 76 yards deep.

Staffa is the Norse for Stave Island, for the Norsemen built their houses of tree-trunks set vertically like the island's basalt columns. The cave is named from the third-century Irish hero Fionn MacCoul, called by the Scots Fingal (Fionn na Ghal, Chief of Valour), who according to the Irish annalists defended the Hebrides against early Viking pirates. He died in battle near the river Boyne in A.D. 283. His cave is in Scotland unique of its kind—lined with black hexagonal columns, which on the left wall rise 40 feet in perfect symmetry. Calm weather is required for a landing. You can sail out from Oban by steamer or from Iona and Ulva by motor-boat. If funds allow, take a private hire and avoid Wordsworth's unhappy experience here in 1833:

> We saw, but surely in the motley crowd
> Not one of us has felt, the far-famed sight;
> How could we feel it? Each the others blight,
> Hurried and hurrying volatile and loud.

Fingal's Cave is far more than a 'show-piece'. It inspired Mendelssohn, when he visited Staffa in 1829, to write the overture *The Hebrides* (Fingal's Cave).

CHAPTER 14

Ardgour and Morvern

Ardgour, Morvern, and Ardnamurchan are the last lands of the Argyll mainland, the most remote and westerly, cut off from the rest of their county by the long arm of Loch Linnhe. **Ardgour** is the most highly mountainous of the three. Lifting abruptly from the north-west shore of Loch Linnhe, its hills extend eleven miles west to Loch Shiel. Its north frontier is Loch Eil, its south the isthmus of Glen Tarbert between Loch Linnhe and Loch Sunart, from which two wings spread out to seaward—Morvern to the south, Ardnamurchan to the west. All land to the north is Invernessshire.

Ardgour is roadless except around its perimeter. Since the fifteenth century it has been held by the MacLeans of Ardgour, an offshoot of the Duart MacLeans, but their holding is now much reduced. The interior is deer forest in the hands of sporting proprietors. Much land is now owned by the Forestry Commission between Glen Tarbert and Salen. This is the most sparsely inhabited parish of Argyll. Work is given by several farms and a score of crofts, mainly on sheep and cattle rearing, and by the Forestry Commission. Approaching from the south, you have a choice of three routes. From Oban, there is the car-ferry to Loch Aline in Morvern by way of Mull, and this route is best if you choose to omit the Appin coast and to move on from Morvern through Moidart to Morar. If you include the Appin coast or Glen Coe, the quickest and best route is to cross the narrows of Loch Linnhe by the Corran ferry, thus to arrive in mid-Ardgour. If you want to see north Ardgour, you can instead go to Fort William and pass round the head of Loch Eil, which in fact is a western dog-leg of Loch Linnhe.

This last route adds forty miles to the journey if you come from the south. It brings you on to the Ardgour shore of Loch Eil, where the road immediately narrows, traffic vanishes away, and you pass

190

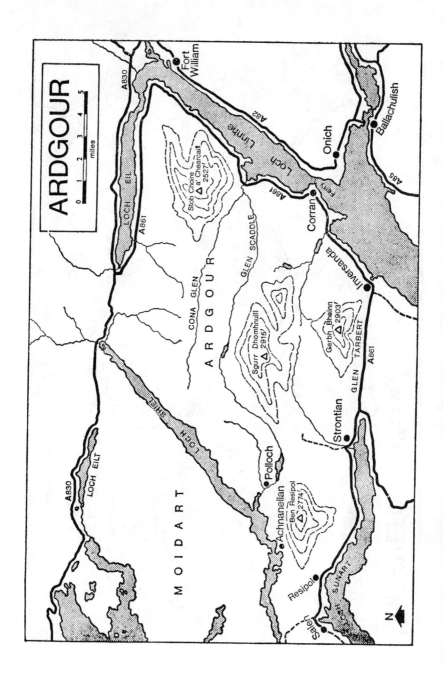

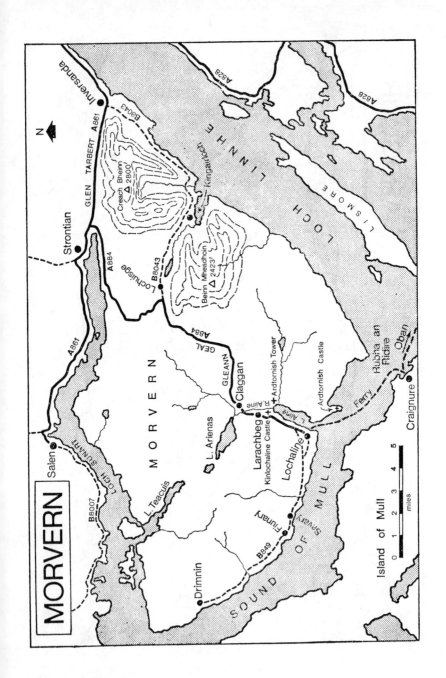

MORVERN

Inversanda
GLEN TARBERT A861
B3043
Creach Bheinn
△ 2800'
Kingairloch
A884
Strontian
Lochuisge
B8043
Beinn Mheadhoin
△ 2423'
LOCH LINNE
LISMORE
A828
A828
A861
A884
GLEANN GEAL
MORVERN
Claggan
R. Aline
Ardtornish Tower
Ardtornish Castle
L. Aline
Rubha an Ridire
Oban
L. Arienas
Larachbeg
Kinlochaline Castle
Lochaline
Savary
Ferry
Craignure
LOCH SUNART
Salen
B8007
L. Teacuis
Fiunary
B849
SOUND OF MULL
Drimnin

Island of Mull

miles
0 1 2 3 4 5

through quiet woods by the water's edge. As you turn the corner into Loch Linnhe's shore you see the massive head of Ben Nevis pushing up through the swell of Lochaber.

At **Corran** the road widens again, for the main traffic comes over the ferry. The Corran Narrows are only a quarter of a mile wide, but a fast tide-race goes through and may give a rough passage if it sets against a high wind. In the days before the last war the ferry-boat sank more than once. The only risk now is that splendid new highway on the Ardgour side. One might speed along at a hundred miles an hour suddenly to be faced by a narrow continuation, the very entrance to which will not admit two passing cars. This danger is becoming yearly more frequent on West Highland roads as long or short stretches are widened.

South of Corran there are marvellous views across Loch Linnhe to the Appin hills of Beinn Bheithir and Bidean nam Bian. At Inversanda you turn rightward on to the Morvern isthmus named Glen Tarbert, which runs six miles to the west coast at the head of Loch Sunart. The glen is open moorland on its south side, but to the north is closely flanked by **Garbh Bheinn.** If you want exercise, there is no better way than to stop half a mile beyond Inversanda and climb Garbh Bheinn, 2,903 feet, by way of Coire and Iubhair. The glen is rugged and its upper stretch walled by 1,000-foot cliffs on the mountain's north-east face. You can see these by walking three miles to the head of the glen. If you prefer to go to the summit, turn leftward before reaching the cliffs into the high eastern corrie. At the top you enter a world of bright skies and brisk winds; cloud-winged mountains soar above broad-waters. In Ardgour there is no finer watch-tower than Garbh Bheinn, but it has a rival in Ben Resipol eight miles west, to which I turn later.

From the head of Loch Sunart you strike south into **Morvern.** The peninsula is diamond-shaped. Three of its sides are twelve miles long, but the fourth measures twenty along the sound that so narrowly separates it from Mull, and which gives Morvern its Gaelic name—A' Mhorbhairn, the Sea-Gap. The whole interior is hill and moor of undistinguished shape and rarely exceeding 1,800 feet. Morvern is seen at its best from the steamer between Oban and Fort William. The road rises up from Loch Sunart to an expanse of desolate moor, then drops to Gleann Geal, the White Glen, perhaps named from its river and waterfalls (there is no other whiteness) rumbling through woods to join the valley of the river Aline. At this point you swing south through Claggan to plantations of pine and larch, the latter a feathery green in early summer. The clachan of Larachbeg, to the left-hand side of the road, is on croft-land given to the people of St. Kilda when they were evacuated in 1930.

Half a mile beyond, again to your left-hand side, **Kinlochaline Castle** stands on a little crag at the head of Loch Aline, close above the old bridge over the river. This fifteenth-century square keep was the seat of the chiefs of Clan MacInnes when they were subject to the Lords of the Isles. Their coat of arms had for its crest 'A thistle proper and thereon a bee sucking the flower', and a motto unique in the Highlands: 'Work gives pleasure'—brave words that brought no good fortune. Their lands of Morvern and Ardgour were given by the Lords of the Isles to MacLean of Duart, and later the castle, which they retained, was breached and fired by Cromwell's army. It was restored in 1890.

Entry is by a stone staircase to a door six feet up—probably reached in early days by a ladder that could be raised as required. Above the door are the usual machicolations for pouring lead and oil on besiegers. The walls are forty feet high to the parapets and nine feet thick. On the ground floor, a handsome fireplace on the north wall has a nude woman sculptured on a panel above. Stairways lead down to a cellar and dungeon. A pit in the south-west corner is said to be an oubliette. Near the guardroom to the right of the main door a stair spirals up in the thickness of the wall to the hall. A second flight of stairs continues for ten steps then forks, one branch to the battlements, the other to a low corridor giving a descent at its farther end back to the hall. The battlements have one feature not usually retained to the present day—a fireplace for heating up lead and oil within the parapet projecting over the main door.

The outlook is excellent. Looking north up the valley of the Aline, road and river snake through a green and wooded strath towards hills receding in tiers. Southward, you see down the two-mile length of Loch Aline to its bottle-neck mouth, then across the Sound of Mull to the island's mountains. At this bottleneck lies Morvern's principle village, Lochaline. Its pier is on the open sound, where the main road ends. Car ferries cross to Mull.

Lochaline used to be one of the more delightful villages of Argyll. Its setting gave it every natural advantage: forested hills behind, and in the foreground a land-locked bay, whose rocky shores are traversed by an old road through natural woods. The ground there is a confusion of mossy boulders, primroses, and burns. The loch is scoured by numerous divers and diving duck, most usually the merganser, red-breasted with dark green head and crest, and red- and black-throated diver; more rarely a great northern diver, which takes off from the water with great difficulty, but then flies very fast and straight.

Loch Aline is now much spoiled by sand-mining and timber-felling. As long ago as 1925, the Geological Survey had noted at Lochaline a bed of white cretaceous sandstone, eighteen feet thick. When war broke out in 1939, this Morvern sand became Britain's only source of optical glass, which had hitherto come from Europe. When mining began, the sand was proven pure and free of iron. Between sixty and seventy thousand tons are extracted annually from twenty-seven miles of tunnel. The rock is drilled, blasted, screened, washed, stored in bunkers, and loaded to steamers by conveyor-belt. Lochaline is made hideous in the process. Lorries come and go for the timber, for the land to the west is now owned by the Forestry Commission and the Department of Agriculture.

These industries may make us despair at the despoliation of natural beauty, but they arrest depopulation. The district had suffered heavily in the Clearances, when former large townships at the north-west point were wiped out. The population of all Morvern is less than 500, so the employment of 45 men on mining and 30-odd in forestry is of no small importance. The Department of Agriculture lets four farms, and near Drimnin, eleven miles west along the coast, there are four crofts. The Ardtornish estate, from which the sand is mined, has a herd of dairy cattle supplying milk to the village. Cattle and sheep are shipped to Oban for auction.

One fine scene that can never be taken from Lochaline is that down the Sound of Mull to the distant coast of Lorn. Two long points thrust boldly out from either shore of the sound; the more distant is Duart, crowned by MacLean's castle, and the nearer Ardtornish, reaching out from the Morvern shore to oppose Duart with a castle of the Lords of the Isles. Between the two, Lady's Rock appears like the hull of a low ship.

Ardtornish Castle is reached by ferrying across the narrows of Loch Aline, leaving you with a pleasant walk across moorland to the point. In the twelfth century Morvern (then called Kenalbin) was in the possession of Somerled as King of Argyll, and belonged thereafter to his heirs, the Lords of the Isles, who granted much land to MacLean of Duart and others. Sir Walter Scott sets the first canto of his *Lord of the Isles* at Ardtornish Castle, which was built in the fourteenth century, probably by John, the first Lord. He died there in 1380, and here, in 1461, John II, the fourth and last Lord, signed the Treaty of Ardtornish with Edward IV of England, arranging dismembership of Scotland. This conspiracy, when it became known, lost John the earldom of Ross and much else. MacLean of Duart owned the castle in the seventeenth century. There is no record of its destruction, yet to-day it is only a ruckle of stones, shorn of every architectural feature save for the basement walls of a quadrilateral keep, 10 feet thick by 15 high.

Close above Lochaline village, a church dedicated to St. Columba deserves a visit for its site overlooking the Sound of Mull. In front stands a nine-foot Celtic cross of the fifteenth century. The ruin in the churchyard (known as Kiel) is that of a pre-Reformation church.

Return to Loch Sunart and round the head of the loch to enter Ardgour at its western end, named Sunart. Two miles down the north side you arrive at the first of the shore's thirty bays, where the little village of **Strontian** snuggles in the fold of Strontian glen. A few boats lie on a beach of red sand rimmed by green turf. There is one hotel by the main road, and numerous neat cottages lying out of sight up the glen. The Minister of State for Scotland announced in 1968 that the first of a series of redevelopment experiments to bring new life to small villages would begin that year at Strontian. The first phase has now been completed with the erection of a central building containing a shop, tearoom, house, information kiosk, and other facilities, designed to form the new village nucleus. This will soon be followed by new village houses, a school, an old people's home, a football park and showfield, and a caravan park.

Strontian, pronounced Stron-teé-an, gives its name to the metallic element Strontium and to the mineral strontianite. In the upper glen there are lead mines, and here strontianite was first found in 1764 and later discovered to be a distinct mineral. In 1787, while at Strontian, Cruickshank discovered in the mineral the element Strontium. Its yellow metal, isolated in 1808 by Davy, is hard yet ductile, and is used in the manufacture of fireworks since it burns with a brilliant crimson flame.

A car may be driven up the glen to a point close below the mines, which after their closure in 1904 have now been reopened. They lie on the flank of the long hill ridge that links Sgurr Dhomhnuill, 2,915 feet, with **Ben Resipol**, 2,774 feet. Resipol is an obligatory climb for all who can make it. The mountain rises on the westernmost fringe of Ardgour, the last high hill beyond which the land drops sharply away in low peninsulas. The ridge leading up to it from the east has one superb view of Loch Moidart, narrowly twisting, long and glittering, pointing straight out towards the islands of Eigg, Rhum, and Muck. The Scuir of Eigg thrusts out of the sea like a Dolomite tower, better seen from here than from any other angle. To the right are the blue-black Cuillin of Skye, and far beyond them the Outer Hebrides from Harris to Barra. When I last saw them from Resipol on a July day, they were slightly hazed but bathed in a brilliant sunshine that laid over them the peculiar lustre seen on old Italian paintings, as though the sun were a paradisal sun, shining forever.

From Strontian ten miles west to Salen, Loch Sunart becomes increasingly lovely. The road winds along its shores through woods of scrub oak, ash, and birch, fringed by rocky outcrops and a profusion of golden whin. At every bend the view changes until you reach Salen, where there is a hotel and a tiny village at the back of a narrow bay. Salen Bay cuts deeply into the neck of land, only two miles wide, dividing Loch Sunart from Loch Shiel to its north. All ground to the west is now Ardnamurchan.

CHAPTER 15

Ardnamurchan

From its Salen neck, Ardnamurchan runs seventeen miles into the
Atlantic. The name means Point of the Great Ocean. During the
Ice Age, the highlands of Ardgour sent a big glacier westward,
sweeping the soil off the Ardnamurchan rock. The west end extends
three miles past the north butt of Mull and protects the sound. It
seems fearsomely exposed, yet high winds are the land's salvation:
they blow inland from its shell-sand beaches sufficient lime to give
a calcareous soil on its coastal strip, on which grass and livestock
thrive (on a small scale). Throughout Ardnamurchan there is only
one industry—agriculture, organized as a few farms and many
crofts. A once prosperous fishing industry collapsed under three
heavy blows: the first was lack of manpower following the Clearances, when alien landlords evicted people and cattle to make way
for sheep; the second, an unexpected change of course by the herring
shoals; and third, trawlers poaching inside the three-mile limit
ruined the banks for line-fishing. Salmon fishing round the coasts
still employs several men in summer. Many of the crofters now take
work at Sunart with the Forestry Commission, who can employ
nearly all men available and allow them time off at harvest.

Two roads lead in from **Salen**. One goes north to Loch Shiel,
the other west along Loch Sunartside. From this latter, two side-
roads branch off later to the north coast, which for the most part is
roadless but not trackless.

On leaving Salen, your road westward is dull for five miles (by
Loch Sunart standards), but thereafter, from Laga Bay five miles to
Ardslignish, it rivals the very best of Loch Lomond and Loch Awe.
Narrow, bumpy, and twisting, this much maligned road is crowded
close by trees and crags, and by a mossy stone wall along the edge of
the loch. Slow and afflicted by bends though it may be, it is in itself

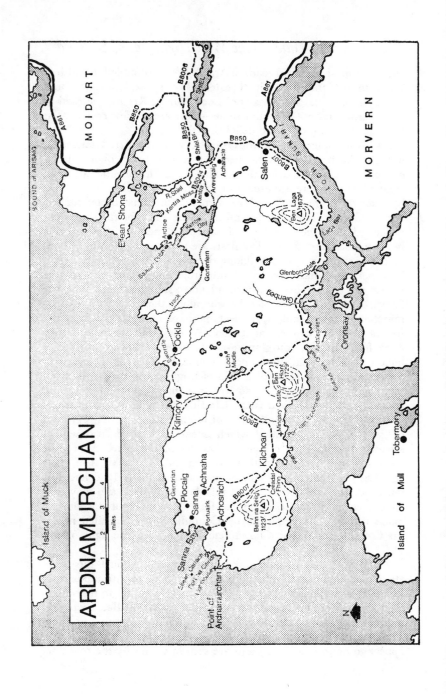

one of the most beautiful roads of Argyll. Were it doubled in width to speed tourist traffic (as is threatened) the development would destroy a principal scenic asset of Loch Sunart. Regard the road as adventurous but not as troublesome—there are too few roads left in Scotland that can offer the delights of this one.

Half-way along, at **Glenborrodale**, you pass a red sandstone hotel at the back of a bay where the road is lined for a mile by massed banks of rhododendron. They make a splendid array in June. Offshore there are numerous islands used as breeding stations by eider duck, goosander, merganser, and of course oystercatcher, tern, and gulls. The nests are all in the heather, for the shores are naked rock. Huge numbers of sandpiper nest on the lochside between road and shore. The nests are woven into clumps of bog-myrtle and heather, or set among dense grass and bracken.

At **Ardslignish**, whose south-projecting point marks the mouth of Loch Sunart, you turn inland to side-step Ben Hiant, the Holy Mountain, which bars the way along the coast. It is Ardnamurchan's highest hill, 1,729 feet, perhaps named holy from the Bay of Camus nan Geal at its foot. At the point where you turn away from the sea, you glimpse the bay deep below with a grassy hollow at its back facing the now open firth. It arrests the eye with a flash of clean silver sand, a field of bright green turf, and on all three sides steep slopes of 250 feet that give it unusual seclusion. At the centre of the field is the **Cladh Chiarain**, or graveyard of Ciaran. Here stands a tall pillar of reddish stone, perhaps granite or gabbro, on the front of which is carved a large cross with a separate boss in each of the four angles of the arms. Above the cross, a dog is sculpted with up-turned tail. The shaft is of great age. On 9th September, 548, St. Ciaran died in Ireland and was buried there. The dedication of this Ardnamurchan site may well have been made by St. Columba, for Adamnan records a journey made through the peninsula by Columba when he sailed north. To Columba on Iona, Ciaran remained always 'the light of this isle'.

When the road goes inland from Camus nan Geal the scene altogether changes. The peninsula grows bare to Ardnamurchan Point. You move now through smooth-cut, green hills to the water-shed at 400 feet and to the moors around **Loch Mudle**. There you suddenly see below the now familiar outlines of Rhum and Eigg. The loch has good fishing and the moors teem with deer, or would appear to do so when the herds are seen in winter by the roadside.

A few golden plover may be heard, their note a liquid *tlu-i,* often elaborated, and their flight fast and straight, unless when displaying, when they fly like bats.

A mile beyond Loch Mudle, a side-road goes off to Kilmory on the north coast. Leaving this meantime, you turn south-west over the moor and drop again to the coast. Half a mile before you reach Kilchoan, a side-track leads to the ruin of **Mingary Castle** at the water's edge. This thirteenth-century castle stands on the east side of a rocky bay named Port nan Spainteach, or Bay of the Spaniards. The prominent point on the west side has a pier, visited thrice daily by MacBrayne's ferry from Tobermory in Mull. The castle has a fine site, especially if seen in June against a dancing sea, when bluebells thickly carpet the field alongside. The hills behind rise away in succeeding folds to 1,400 feet.

It is recorded that in 1292 the King of Scots, John Baliol, gave Ardnamurchan to Iain, the youngest son of Angus Mor of Islay. The truth seems to be that such a grant by a king of Scots was mere formality. Angus Mor of Clan Donald was King of the Isles. Ardnamurchan was already in his hands and his castle built, probably during the reign of Alexander III. It remained the stronghold of the MacIains of Ardnamurchan for four hundred years.

The curtain-walls are hexagonal but with rounded corners, on four sides surrounded by sea, and on the two others by a ditch cut into the basaltic rock on which the castle is planted. The main gate is to seaward, where the rock forms a natural causeway from which rude stairs mount to the walls. One can enter instead by a landward port, where the ruin of a stone bridge crosses the ditch. The interior is hardly worth even casual inspection—full of weed and rubbish, and of dilapidated buildings, which are probably the work of eighteenth-century Campbells.

When the Lordship of the Isles was forfeited, James IV held two courts at Mingary, first in October 1493 and then in May 1495, to receive the allegiance of the island chiefs. Of these, only MacIain of Ardnamurchan made full and lasting submission, for which the other chiefs held his family in small respect. Their subsequent attacks on Mingary did much to ruin the walls. Sir Donald Mac-Donald of Loch Alsh laid siege to the castle in 1517. In 1588, Lachlan MacLean of Duart brought a hundred Spaniards from the galleon at Tobermory and besieged it for three days without success—hence the name Bay of the Spaniards. In 1644, Colkitto MacDonald stormed and took it for Montrose and King Charles, and then held it against a full siege by the army of Argyll. At the rising of the '45 it was held by Campbell of Achinduin, who sent messengers to London giving the first warning of Prince Charlie's landing in Arisaig.

Half a mile farther you pass through **Kilchoan,** the principal village of western Ardnamurchan. It looks out across the firth to the north point of Mull, to the immediate left of which the mile-wide semi-circle of Bloody Bay is made a dominating feature by tall cliffs rising sheer from the sea. The bay was named from a sea-battle between John, the last Lord of the Isles, and his son Angus. Incensed by his father's loss of land—Ross, Kintyre, Knapdale, and much else—Angus tried to take the Lordship at once by force. He won the battle, but while doing so his one new-born son, Donald, was abducted from Islay and imprisoned by Colin Campbell (the infamous first earl) at his Castle of Innis Chonnail on Loch Awe. The boy was held for fifteen years and Angus never discovered where.

Beyond Kilchoan, the road strikes inland again to avoid **Beinn na Seilg,** 1,123 feet. Near its top, this splendid little hill has a number of gabbro crags that give excellent if short rock-climbs. On its lowest, south-east slopes, only a quarter of a mile from the point where the road turns inland, is the Greadal Fhinn, or Fingal's Griddle. These prehistoric remains are marked on the map as *Stone Circle.* No circle now stands, but the vestiges of probable socket holes have been found on the ground surrounding two groups of stone, which are recognizable as the denuded cists of a chambered cairn. Earthenware urns were found on the site. The stones of the cairn were probably stripped off for local wall-building. The sepulchre has been dated to the late Stone Age, around 2000 B.C., but if standing stones were indeed set around the cairns at the time of their building the date would be 1600 B.C.

The road continuing north-west across the bare back of the peninsula to Sanna Bay forks twice en route. The first, right-hand branch goes to Sanna at the north end of the bay, the central line goes to Portuairk at the south end, and the left-hand branch winds through bleak moor to the lighthouse on the **Point of Ardna-murchan.** The lighthouse tower is of grey granite 118 feet high, but set on a 60-foot cliff, the light thus being raised 180 feet above sea-level and visible for eighteen miles. The point is the most westerly of the British mainland, twenty-three miles farther west than Land's End. The keeper shows visitors through the tower and generating room. From ground-level one can see Coll and the Treshnish Isles on one side and Rhum and Eigg on the other. More than a dozen islands are visible on a good day, including Barra and South Uist in the Outer Hebrides. Gannets dive offshore. North-east of the point are the series of beaches for which Ardnamurchan is famous. The first of these is **Port na Cairidh**. At the south end it has an old pier, formerly used for supplying the croft-houses and lighthouse. The bay, half a mile wide, has rock, reef, and sand, enlivened by fast-flying sandpipers, busy ringed plovers, and lazy seals. If you walk between the shore and its yellow flags to the farther end, you find, behind Eilean Carrach, the Bay MacNeil (not named on the O.S. map). A guide to it is a small burn flowing off the hill behind, its banks thick with flowers before it drops underground on approaching the shore. Eilean Carrach guards this sandy cove from the Atlantic swell, and the MacNeil who gave it name was MacNeil of Barra, whose men landed their cattle here en route to the annual Tryst of Falkirk in Stirlingshire.

It is easy to continue your walk round the coast to Portuairk, the tiny village at the south end of the mile-wide Sanna Bay. Instead you may return to Achosnich by the lighthouse road and drive to Portuairk, where the road ends on the beach. **Sanna Bay** is the most delectable of Ardnamurchan, for it is really four bays separated by rocky points, each different from the others except in the pure quality of white shell-sand. Good fishing may be had by rod from the rocky points. Sanna at the north end of the bay is the site of an ancient crofting community, once heavily inhabited when the people of Swordle, farther along the coast, were evicted and here given ground thought to be valueless. Cows still graze the machair, but the once numerous thatched cottages have gone. Sanna can also be reached by road through the farmland of Achnaha, if you take the first side-road on the right after leaving Kilchoan.

Half a mile to the east of Sanna, **Plocaig Bay** is of totally different character. At the tiny crofting clachan of Plocaig above its south shore the cottages before the last war were thatched. Now they too are gone. No doubt they were primitive, but at least they positively improved a landscape already beautiful. New cottages, like those at Portuairk, do not. They detract from a scene in which they are incongruously set. Plocaig Bay is rocky. Instead of the vast sweeps of sand found at Sanna, you have low cliffs, which rise to their highest at the farther end, where the maps mark the Glendrian Caves. The shore is a cruel one of seething reefs and black razor-edged rock, but the sea between them is brilliantly green, for white sand lies at the bottom, to emerge only when the tide is out. Only then can the caves be explored, but they are mere fissures and quite without interest—their appearance on maps being apparently due to some past surveyor's never-corrected misjudgment. Around the bay, the gorges splitting the cliffs are noticeable for their huge clusters of yellow rose-root.

The coast continues rocky for four miles east to the village of Kilmory, which stands on high ground above another excellent bay. To reach it by road you return to Kilchoan, climb to the top of the moorland pass, and descend north to the scattered village. The grassland dropping to the bay is extraordinarily rich in flowers, mostly red and white clover, buttercup, bird's-foot trefoil, dense packs of eyebright, and great pads of purple thyme near the beach. Among this mass of blossom you can find yellow rattle, and butterfly orchid shooting tall with leaves like those of lily of the valley. Most of the houses stand high beside the road. Lower down, two thatched cottages are sited in nooks facing the sea.

The north-facing bay is deeply U-shaped. Rocky arms enclose far-running sands, which are effectively screened from storm-seas by a multitude of rocks and skerries, many of which emerge at low tide. Sheld-duck rear young on the bay in May and June. As at Sanna, the view is to the Small Isles, Rhum, Eigg, Muck, and Canna, but with the Cuillin of Skye showing much clearer. The next, more open bay to the east has a cave, which by local tradition was used by Columba on his visit to Ardnamurchan. He found the cave occupied by robbers, converted them, and baptized them in a natural basin. The cave has two entrances gained from a ledge on which the waves break at high water. The basin is a shallow pool within the first entrance. The healing properties ascribed to the water, consecrated by Columba, have drawn sick people as pilgrims until recent times. They left offerings lying on the rock.

The road continues two miles east from Kilmory through Swordle to end at **Ockle** farm. Swordle or Suardaill, meaning Grassy Field, is the scene of the notorious eviction of 1853, when the sixteen tenants were cleared by the landowner immediately after they had been forced to build themselves new houses at their own expense. No compensation was allowed. Forty years later the sheepfarm had failed.

At the broad hayfields of Ockle, a sign-post points the way north-east down a track to a big bay on the coast (the track is not marked on maps). The bay is rocky and without sand. In summer, long salmon nets will be seen running out from the rocks to which they are lashed. An extensive system of underground caves has recently been found in the nearby sea-cliffs. Behind the farm, another track runs six miles east across the moors to Kentra Bay near Acharacle. Near the start it enters a green hollow cupping a large and almost perfectly circular water-lily loch. The lilies form a complete ring round the perimeter, separated from the shore by a similar circle of reeds. Thereafter the track keeps to high bare ground well away from the coast, and if transport can be arranged at the far end is worth walking for its splendid views out to sea and up the Moidart coast. Towards the end it falls to the sea at Gortenfern, formerly a farmhouse and now derelict in a new forestry plantation. It has one of the best sandy coves of the whole peninsula and looks straight across the outer Kentra Bay to Ardtoe on the Kentra peninsula. The track leads through woods for another three miles to Arevegaig at the head of the inner Kentra Bay, and there joins the main road to Acharacle.

As seen from its head before you reach Arevegaig, **Kentra Bay** is a finely-shaped sea-loch. The pointed peaks of Rhum seem to bar its mouth, distant as they are. The flanking hills are to the left-hand side low and wooded, to the right-hand bare and knobbly. Grassy islands lie out on the water. The inner bay dries on the ebb, and was formerly crossed at the head by fords. These need no longer be used. A new forestry road (not marked on maps) has recently been made to Gortenfern. It is closed to cars but remains a right of way.

From Ockle, you return to Salen on Loch Sunart. Acharacle is reached across the two-mile isthmus to Loch Shiel. The road climbs up through woods to the top of a steep hill, levels out past another fine water-lily loch, and finally drops to Loch Shiel at Acharacle. The houses stretch out thinly along the road for one mile from the hotel to Shiel Bridge. It is a village without any distinctive character. Within itself it has nothing of interest, but its hotel makes an excellent centre for fishing and for exploring western Moidart, the north-east coast of Ardnamurchan, and Loch Shiel.

Loch Shiel runs seventeen miles in bow-shape from Glenfinnan in the north to Acharacle. Its centre-line is the frontier between Ardgour and Moidart, and between Argyll and Invernessshire. From its foot, the serpentine Shiel flows three miles into Loch Moidart, a broad slow river, greened by its flanking trees and rich in fish for the angler. It is spanned by Shiel Bridge near the site of an old ford called Ath Thorcail, or Torquil's Ford, where a Norse warrior fell in battle and gave his name to Acharacle.

A few hundred yards short of the bridge, a branch road strikes three miles west across the Kentra Moss on to the low and bare Kentra peninsula, to end at Ardtoe on the open sea. The extremely craggy coast, grassed between its ribs, is here nibbled out into several sandy coves. Close to the first is a huddle of crofts in a green hollow between rocky hillocks. This is the clachan of Ardtoe. From its high ground you look out to Rhum and the Scuir of Eigg. A few hundred yards to the north, a long sandy creek called the Sailean Dubh has been used since 1965 for an experiment in fish-farming by the White Fish Authority, with help from Strathclyde University. Five acres were enclosed near the head of the creek, and 200,000 inch-long plaice released into it in an attempt to grow the fish to marketable size. The Sailean Dubh had been chosen because it had the right depth, clean sand, and good shelter from storm. Most of the plaice were killed by crabs and eels, and by too much fresh water flowing into the creek from the burn at its head. Counter-measures were taken, and the scheme is now successful.

From Acharacle there were, until 1967, sailings twice daily in summer, and once in winter, run by David MacBrayne Ltd, to Glenfinnan at the head of the loch. These have been abandoned following the opening of a new forest road on the south shore. It may be that cruises may be run in summer only. Inquire at Acharacle Hotel. The shores of Loch Shiel were roadless until 1965–66, when the Forestry Commission made a new road down the Ardgour bank from Glenfinnan to Polloch. It may be that in due course this will be taken over by the District Council and opened to public traffic. Meantime, the track provides access to the hills on the east bank, especially to Ben Resipol, which is only six miles from Acharacle. The approach from here is much easier than from the Sunart shore. The mountain is best climbed from Achnanellan.

Moidart now summons you across Shiel Bridge, but before moving there I return you to Loch Linnhe to enter Inverness-shire by its west coast town, Fort William in Lochaber.

CHAPTER 16

Lochaber

When you cross the Ballachulish bridge to the north side of Loch Leven you enter Lochaber, and now really are in the 'Land of the mountain and the flood'; every feature of the landscape is carved on the grand scale. Lochaber is spread at the foot of the Great Glen of Alban (the greatest in Scotland), at the head of one of her two biggest sea-lochs, bears Britain's highest mountain, and is furrowed by rivers and lochs whose names are famous: Garry, Arkaig, Eil, Spean, and many another. At the Ballachulish Narrows you are given no reason to suspect the presence of this magnificence. All of it lies hidden behind the foothills of Mamore. You drive along outer Loch Leven through the village of Onich, your eyes taken the while by regions you already know seen from new angles—the mountains of Appin and Ardgour across sparkling blue sea. Onich is a sun-trap with several pleasant hotels, a clean stony beach, and a lower rainfall than anywhere else in Lochaber. Onich is the threshold.

NETHER LOCHABER

On turning north from Loch Leven you emerge on Loch Linnhe-side at Corran Narrows and hold to the wooded shores for six miles to enter **Fort William** by its suburb of Achintore. There you pass under a long line of new villas and come abruptly into the old town —'the Fort' as it is now jocularly called. At first sight it appears to consist of a narrow High Street a mile long, sandwiched between the steep slopes of Cow Hill and Loch Linnhe. Neither hill nor loch can be well seen, for the houses rise tall to either side, forming at ground level an unbroken line of shops. On the hillward side, the street is indented by small squares like riverside bays. One may dodge into these and be out of the heavy main stream—for in summer the street is jammed with traffic. From these havens you get glimpses uphill to the residential part of the town, stone-built

207

houses of good size with gardens and views across the head of Loch Linnhe. Neither from here nor the High Street can you see Ben Nevis, although the foot of the mountain is barely two miles east. Cow Hill, 942 feet, hides all. The Fort thus lacks the splendid situation of Oban, although it has been opened out by a new through road along the sea-front, which uses the space formerly occupied by the railway (the station is now at the north side); nor has it Oban's handsome buildings and spacious air. It seemed cramped, without being too unsightly except on its outer north fringe.

The chief town of Lochaber, and sited in the most important industrial centre of the west seaboard, Fort William is Oban's closest rival as a tourist and shopping centre—and is fast developing. Thus far, it lags behind the towns of Argyll and Bute in hotel accommodation, and I am unable to recommend a restaurant. Good food is served in hotels, more particularly the Alexandria and the Station.

Fort William's population is around 3,000 and growing. This figure does not reflect the importance of the region, for many more live at the new housing schemes around the head of the loch at Inverlochy, Banavie, and Corpach. These serve the aluminium factory under the north-west slopes of Ben Nevis and the great new pulp mill at the Annat point of Corpach. Harris wool and knitwear and tweeds can be bought in Fort William in greater variety of pattern than anywhere else in the West Highlands. One shop at the south end of the town has a permanent Scottish crafts exhibition displaying wood, iron, stone-work and much else.

At Cameron Square, near the middle of the High Street, the West Highland Museum has the best collection of relics on the west coast. The exhibits are seen in four floors. In the ground-floor hall are relics of early man: stone axes of the Neolithic Age, and vitrified rock. In a room off the hall are more modern weapons of war and tools of husbandry. They include the trooping helmet worn by James Graham, the great Marquis of Montrose, swords from Culloden, pistols and battle-axes, the caschrom or crooked spade, and the wild animals of Lochaber (stuffed). In the basement are relics of a crannog, or wooden lake-dwelling, from Loch Treig. The second floor exhibits a reconstructed croft-house kitchen of the nineteenth century, and beyond it a Jacobite room with numerous personal relics of Prince Charles Edward Stewart and the '45. The Jacobite wine-glasses are especially notable. One well-known curio is the secret portrait of the prince. It looks like a painter's palette

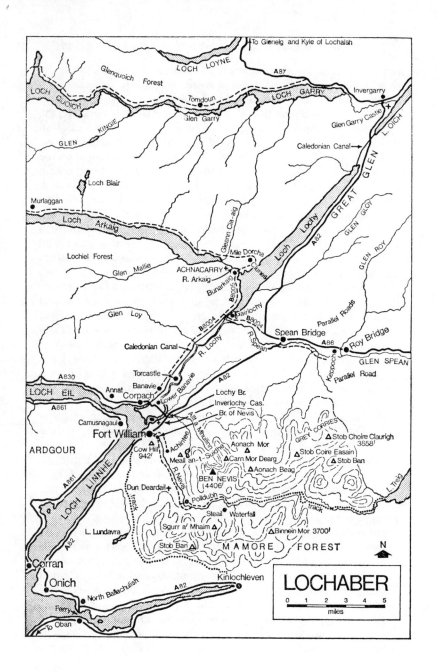

To Glenelg and Kyle of Lochalsh
LOCH LOYNE
A87
Glenquoich Forest
Tomdoun
LOCH GARRY
Invergarry
LOCH QUOICH
Glen Garry
Glen Garry Castle
Caledonian Canal
L. OICH
GLEN
KINGIE
GREAT GLEN
Loch Blair
GLEN GLOY
Murlaggan
Loch Arkaig
Loch Lochy
GLEN ROY
Lochiel Forest
Glen Mallie
Mile Dorcha
ACHNACARRY
R. Arkaig
Bunarkaig
Parallel Roads
B8005
Glen Loy
Gairlochy
B8004
Spean Bridge
A86
Roy Bridge
Caledonian Canal
R. Lochy
B8004
R. Spean
GLEN SPEAN
A830
Torcastle
Keppoch
Parallel Road
Annat
Banavie
A82
Lower Banavie
Lochy Br.
LOCH EIL
Corpach
Inverlochy Cas.
A861
Br. of Nevis
Camusnagaul
Allt a' Mhuilinn
GREY CORRIES
Fort William
Stob Choire Claurigh 3858'
ARDGOUR
Cow Hill 942'
Achintee
Aonach Mor
Stob Coire Easain
Meall an-t-Suidhe
Carn Mor Dearg
Stob Ban
LOCH LINNHE
Aonach Beag
A861
Dun Deardail
R. Nevis
BEN NEVIS (4406')
L. Treig
A82
Polldubh
Corran
track
Steall   Waterfall
Onich
L. Lundavra
Sgurr a' Mhaim
Binnein Mor 3700'
track
N
Stob Ban
MAMORE   FOREST
Kinlochleven
North Ballachulish
A82
LOCHABER
Ferry
0   1   2   3   4   5
To Oban
miles

The Companion Guide to the West Highlands of Scotland

until a metal cylinder held against it reflects the portrait. On the third floor are spinning-wheels, a clarsach or harp, brooches, and a display of the clan tartans of Invernessshire.

More towards the north end of the town, on the hillward side, the episcopalian church of St. Andrew is one of the most beautiful on the west coast, deserving more ground-space than the planners have given it. In 1966 a further and more disastrous encroachment on the site was made by the erection of a supermarket alongside, screening and darkening the only good building that Fort William possesses. In 1819 the site was given to the church by the War Office, who had held the ground adjoining the old fort. At first a small chapel was built, replaced in 1880 by the present church of pink granite with tower and tall spire. The building is simple, given a grace and dignity by excellence of proportion and high quality workmanship. The altar frontal is decorated with huge cairngorm stones.

Opposite the church, where the river Nevis flows into Loch Linnhe, is the site of the fort—no longer extant—built in 1654 by General Monck. In course of time it was to give the town its present name, but the original and much better name given by Monck himself was Inverlochy. That name had long been given to the estuary lands of the river Lochy, where a much older Inverlochy Castle was the symbol of the region's geographical importance as a hub of communication lines, the control of which, till after Culloden, gave the key to power in the West Highlands.

Whereas Oban's importance is based on its harbour and sea-links, Fort William's is from its site at a natural cross-road. It is inland, being twenty miles from the open coast at the Sound of Arisaig, yet with a seaport from which a canal goes right through Scotland to the east coast by way of the Great Glen. **The Great Glen** is a geographical freak of the first order. This huge rift, which splits Scotland from the Firth of Lorn in the south-west to the Moray Firth in the north-east, is a fault or movement line along which the north block of Scotland moved sixty-five miles to the south-west in relation to the south block. Three lochs fill forty-five miles of its bed—the Ness, Oich, and Lochy—and these are linked from sea to sea by twenty-two miles of the Caledonian Canal, cut by Thomas Telford, who had built the Crinan Canal. Work began in 1803 and took nineteen years to complete. There are twenty-eight locks. At Banavie near the south end, a series of eight locks are called Neptune's Staircase. Small ships can thus sail between the North Sea and Atlantic coasts without having to make the stormy passage round

Cape Wrath. Fort William thus has direct land and water links with Inverness, the capital of the Highlands. Close to the town's north, the Spean valley gives a pass to Strathspey; to its south, Glen Coe links it to Argyll, Perth, and the Lowlands; and to the west, Loch Eil links it to Mallaig and the Hebrides. The West Highland railway from Crianlarich across the moor of Rannoch was opened in 1894 and then extended to Mallaig. The Inverness line up the Great Glen has long been closed, but in compensation the road has been made excellent.

The rift of the Great Glen is the central axis of Lochaber. Opening off it on its west side are three long, roughly parallel glens, each bearing a long loch: Loch Eil, Loch Arkaig and, Loch Garry. Lochaber extends twenty-four miles from Loch Leven in the south to Loch Garry in the north. From west to east its lands spread from the head of Loch Arkaig to Loch Laggan in Glen Spean, at which point it borders on Badenoch. In ancient days Lochaber was still wider territory, stretching from the Atlantic coast to Strath Spey. The name derives from Latin words in Adamnan's *Life of St. Columba*, in which he writes of men who were living 'in the region bordering Loch Aporum'. His name Stagnum Aporum is thought by some scholars to refer to Loch Eil, but we should note that he usually used 'stagnum' of tideless inland lochs, which here would be Loch Lochy and its river: Apor is from the Gaelic Aber, an estuary. In brief, Stagnum Aporum equals Inverlochy.

The exploration of Lochaber is best accomplished in three stages: (1) the low ground close around Fort William; (2) Nether Lochaber, or the country to the south of Glen Spean, which includes the Mamore Forest, Ben Nevis, and the Grey Corries; and (3) Upper Lochaber, or the country to the north and west of Spean Bridge.

Any attempt to forage close around Fort William tends to be defeated by the very facilities at hand for exploring farther afield. The once popular cruise to Coruisk in the Cuillin of Skye has been withdrawn, but there is a weekly steamer cruise to Iona by way of Oban, the Firth of Lorn, and the Ross of Mull, with time allowed ashore on Iona; and to the Sound of Sleat and South Skye by daily train to Mallaig, thence by car-ferry to Armadale, bus to Kyleakin, ferry to Kyle of Loch Alsh, and steamer next day to Mallaig; or on certain days of the week you can vary that tour from Kyle of Loch Alsh onwards by taking the bus to Kintail and Glen Garry and back to Fort William. There are twice-weekly cruises down Loch

Linnhe to Oban, and circular tours that include the seventeen-mile sail down Loch Shiel from Glenfinnan. Motor-boat cruises are daily available on Loch Eil and Loch Linnhe, and thrice a week on Loch Ailort, the Arisaig coast, and from Mallaig. Motor-coach tours spread across the Highlands to Glen Coe and Inveraray, Glen Affric and Inverness, Glen Spean to the Cairngorms and Pitlochry, and even to Arndamurchan Point. These and much more besides tempt the motorist far out of Fort William. Resisting their temptations, take to your feet.

You can make no better first reconnaissance than the ascent of **Cow Hill,** which has been obscuring the view. The simple topography of Nether Lochaber can then be seen at once and fixed in the mind. The easiest way to reach the summit is to turn off the High Street near its south end at the Grand Hotel, walk uphill past the church, turn right, then follow the first road to the top where a track leads past a big new housing scheme on to the open hill. At the summit, the vast flank of Ben Nevis confronts you across Glen Nevis, the toothy Mamore range fills the head of the glen to the south, northward the strath of the river Lochy rolls from the Great Glen to Loch Linnhehead, and westward, Loch Eil divides the hills of Locheil from Ardgour. The cramped streets of Fort William give no notion of this spacious setting, nor of the scale on which Lochaber is cast.

The Ardgour side of Loch Linnhe looks attractively close, but since the road makes a twenty-mile detour round Loch Eil, many people think it too far to reach on foot, unaware of the daily ferry-service from Fort William pier. The town pier is not the long one extending far out from the Inverlochy shore (that belongs to the British Aluminium Company) but is the pier close to the big car park near the south end of High Street. A motor launch (passengers only) crosses several times daily to the Ardgour shore at Camusnagaul —which offers a good anchorage for yachts and fishing boats. In a few minutes one can be away from Fort William's bustle, on a quiet and wooded shore. Beside the town pier is a slipway, which can be used by dinghy-sailors. Loch Eil and Loch Linnhe offer good sailing with the chance of exploring islands, bays, and sandy beaches not otherwise seen or readily accessible. The Lochaber Yacht Club is centred at Corpach and welcomes visitors.

One of the most famous of Highland glens lies within a mile of the town's centre. Glen Nevis, which opens off the Inverness road, is in its lower part spoiled for the walker by a constant stream of sight-seeing cars. Another but harder way to visit the glen on foot is to go five miles over the Peat Track. A short way south of the railway station, the Lundavra road strikes leftward uphill. Follow it half a mile or more till a sign-post points to the Peat Track on the left. The path climbs four hundred feet to a broad hill-ridge, where Ben Nevis bursts upon you. It is not from this angle a shapely mountain. Bludgeon-like it makes its presence felt by sheer mass. You cross a stile over a deer-fence and go down through pine forest to the floor of the glen.

The Lundavra road on which you started out is a motor-road running five miles to **Loch Lundavra** under the west end of the Mamore range. The old military road there continues seven miles to Kinlochleven. This walk can be recommended for its excellent views across Loch Leven to the mountains of Appin and Glen Coe. It can be walked in the reverse direction by taking the service bus to Kinlochleven. Get off at the school (before rounding the head of the loch), where a right-of-way footpath leads up to the military road. At Fort William, one may hear (or read) the local tradition that MacBeth died in a castle at Loch Lundavra. In hard fact he was killed by Malcolm III at Lumphanan, Aberdeenshire, in 1057. But the body was shipped to Iona for burial, and while waiting for a galley down Loch Linnhe would be held, as was the custom in Lochaber for many centuries, at Corpach, 'the place of the dead'. His general, Banquo, was Thane of Lochaber, and by tradition lived near **Torcastle**, about three miles up the river Lochy on the right bank. The wooded bank above rocky pools is still called Banquo's Walk. As the finest reach of the river Lochy, it ought to be visited.

To get there, you drive or take bus or train three miles to Banavie Station on the left bank of the canal. The canal runs parallel to the river and to its west. At Lower Banavie, you climb past Neptune's Staircase and then walk a mile and a half up the bank of the canal to Torcastle Farm. The ruins of Tor Castle stand on a rock overlooking the Lochy. It was built by the thirteenth chief of Clan Cameron in the early sixteenth century and remained the family seat till the Restoration, when Sir Ewen Cameron of Lochiel built his better-known castle at Achnacarry near Lock Arkaig.

The Lochaber castle of greater historical fame was **Inverlochy**, near the mouth of the river, where it flows broad and deep only a mile north of Bridge of Nevis. It should not be confused with a modern mansion house, also and misleadingly styled Inverlochy

Castle, a mile still farther north up the Inverness road. The ruins of
the old castle on the left bank are reached from Fort William by
driving (or taking the Corpach bus) three-quarters of a mile north
of Bridge of Nevis to an unsignposted side-road that strikes left to
the Lochy nearly opposite the private road leading to the aluminium
works. This side-road, by which you can drive to the castle's gate,
is the first on the left several hundred yards beyond the new Milton
Hotel.

The building of Inverlochy was the work of the Comyn family,
who first arrived in Britain as companions of William the Conqueror.
One branch of the family came to high office under the King of
Scots in the twelfth century. In the thirteenth they acquired the
Lordship of Badenoch and Lochaber. The Black Comyn, Sir John,
was made regent of Scotland and later made a vain claim to the
throne. He is credited with having built the castle at Inverlochy
around 1260, although there may well have been an earlier fort on
the site. It was his son, the Red Comyn, whom Bruce stabbed to
death at Dumfries. The estates passed to Bruce through lack of
issue in 1313 and were later granted to the family of Gordon, earls
of Huntly. The existing castle can be dated to the later thirteenth
century.

Ringed by sycamore beside the dark river, the castle is square,
its curtain-walls now reduced to 20 feet (from an original 30) but
still with a tower at each angle. They enclose a courtyard of 100
feet by 90. The castle was formerly surrounded by a moat forty feet
out from the walls, and some remains of old masonry show the site
of a drawbridge. The main gateway faces the river. An unusual
feature is a second gate, by which you enter, in the wall exactly
opposite, both of which had a portcullis. The four towers communicate with the battlements and the central yard. Each has a
staircase within its wall's thickness and all have sally ports. Comyn's
Tower is the biggest one at the north-west angle.

The flat ground to the south-west of the castle was the site of one
of the most famous battles in the military history of the Highlands,
when the great Montrose overthrew the covenanting army under
Campbell of Argyll in 1645. Montrose's royalist army was gathered
from Clans Donald, Cameron, and Stewart. In January 1645 he
was returning by way of the Great Glen to Aberdeen after ravaging
Argyll, and was encamped near the present Fort Augustus (not
then built) at the head of Loch Ness, when the Bard of Keppoch,
Iain Lom MacDonald, arrived hot-foot with the news that the

covenanting army was close on his tail. He had watched them pitch camp around Inverlochy Castle—three thousand Campbells and Lowland levies under command of MacChailein Mor. This Iain Lom was later to become Poet Laureate under Charles II, the first and last poet writing in Gaelic to be so honoured.

Montrose took a hard decision. He had only eighteen hundred men, but he resolved to go back and attack. On 31st January he led his men on the toughest march in the military history of Scotland. Had he held to the Great Glen, the march of only twenty-five miles would have spared his men fatigue but have allowed Campbell full warning. He instead made a great eastward detour through the roadless mountains of the western Monadhliath, first up Glen Tarff, which opens south-east off the head of Loch Ness, then over the maze of snow-covered mountains at its head by way of the Corrieyairack pass at 2,500 feet to the headwaters of the Spey. He had now crossed Scotland's watershed to its east side, but zig-zagged back over it by way of a pass between the Spey and the river Roy, descending thus to Glen Spean, where he crossed the river and came down on Inverlochy through the northern foothills of the Grey Corries and Ben Nevis. Some writers have averred that from Glen Spean he might have crossed the Grey Corries and descended through upper Glen Nevis. The feat might not have been impracticable, for a main factor in the success of this forced march at the height of winter was the clansmen's hatred of Clan Campbell. All things had become possible. Led by James Graham, however, they did not do so: he was too good a soldier to squander so much time and energy at the last moment. His army's sudden appearance on 2nd February on the banks of the Lochy caused the utmost consternation. Argyll was no soldier. His chiefs persuaded him to retire to his galley anchored off Camusnagaul and leave his army to fight under Campbell of Auchenbreck. Despite a two to one superiority they were routed on Montrose's charge. Campbell of Argyll was rowed away to safety while half his army was slaughtered.

In two years, Montrose in a brilliant series of campaigns had won six pitched battles against the Covenanters. His victory seemed complete. The country lay at his mercy. And at this point his Highland army melted away. His men's too long neglected lands called them louder than a national cause. In September, General Leslie overtook his denuded force and cut it to pieces at Philiphaugh near Selkirk. In 1650 Montrose was betrayed by MacLeod of Assynt and hanged in the Grassmarket, Edinburgh, while his lifelong enemy, Campbell of Argyll, looked on (appropriately from behind curtains).

Cromwell now sent General George Monck to Lochaber to restore law and order. Monck decided to build and garrison strongholds at either end of the Great Glen. Not liking the site of Inverlochy Castle, he built a new fort on the left bank of the river Nevis where it flowed into Loch Linnhe. In a letter to Cromwell, he declared the fort's birthday precisely as Thursday, 22nd June, 1654, and named it Inverlochy. There were no houses there, but a village naturally began to grow around the garrison fort. On the accession of Charles II the fort fell into disrepair, and then, on the accession of William of Orange, it was repaired by MacKay of Scourie, who renamed the village Maryburgh after the Dutch usurper's wife; thus it was known till the nineteenth century, when the Duke of Gordon as landowner called it Gordonburgh. The name never caught on, nor did the name Duncanburgh given by Sir Duncan Cameron when he later bought the Gordon estate. The village was dominated by its fort, and Fort William it was called by the people. They honoured the Dutchman. The post office and county council finally acknowledged a *fait accompli* and fixed the name.

In the years between the two risings of 1715 and 1745, General Wade built the road from Fort William to Inverness, and again after the '45 General Caulfeild made the road by Loch Lundavra to Kinlochleven and Kingshouse. At the '45, Prince Charles raised his standard only thirteen miles away at Glenfinnan at the head of Loch Shiel. After his retreat from Derby, Fort William was besieged by Cameron of Lochiel in March 1746, but he had to raise it a month later to join the prince at Culloden. Thereafter Lochaber suffered deeply. The clan system was destroyed, and with it a social system. The men emigrated. In the nineteenth century the glens were further denuded of human life to make way for sheep. Huge numbers of men emigrated to America, Canada, and Australia. But gradually industries developed. Fort William for a while became a fishing port; the canal was made through the Great Glen; the railway line was opened in 1894, and to make room for it along the sea-front the old fort was demolished. A distillery had been founded in 1823, and now a second followed. At the end of the first world war, the British Aluminium Company built a large factory at the foot of Ben Nevis on the Inverness road. They dammed Loch Treig and Loch Laggan and drove a fifteen-mile pipe-line through the lower slopes of Ben Nevis to feed the power-house. This factory is an eyesore rivalled only by Kinlochleven's, but the Company make the greater part of Britain's aluminium. As the chief employer of labour in Lochaber they give work to several thousand men.

More recent developments that have greatly improved the appearance of Lochaber are the reclamation of land between Inverlochy and Loch Lochy, followed by the setting up of the Great Glen cattle ranch, and the afforestation of the glens. The enormous growth of forestry in Scotland since the Commission was established in 1919 led in 1966 to the opening of a huge pulp mill at **Corpach,** two miles north-west of Fort William. This is the biggest industrial development in the Highlands since the arrival of the aluminium factories. It cost twenty million pounds to build, and is designed to use all the timber that Scottish forests can produce, and to save the country many millions a year on imported pulp and paper. Its greater importance is the retention of skilled men and women in the Highlands. The mill occupies eighty acres at Annat Point. The only one of its kind in the United Kingdom, it produces pulp and paper in a continuous process. It is thus an enormously long factory (pulp mill 400 feet, paper mill 540 feet, and finishing house 530 feet) with a power-house tower rising to 168 feet at one end. The design is modern with much glass and looks surprisingly well, all things considered, when seen against Ben Nevis across the loch. It does not look so well from the slopes of Ben Nevis. From there it seems a hideous monster belching out smoke between vast stacks of wood chips. The entire Inverlochy plain is becoming a monumental example of the ill-effects of haphazard planning: a splotch of factories and housing schemes.

Highland Games are still held in early August or the end of July. In late August another event of the season, which draws many visitors to Fort William, is the Agricultural Show.

In Nether Lochaber, the outstanding feature apart from mountains is **Glen Nevis.** It links Fort William to Loch Treighead with a pass of twenty-two miles and gives access to more than forty mountain tops. Along its south flank, dividing it from Loch Leven, the Mamore range stretches seven miles in sixteen peaks. The tops are bold and pointed, for they carry quartzite caps that protect the mica-schist beneath. On the glen's north flank and dividing it from Glen Spean, sprawls the tallest mountain group in Britain: Ben Nevis, Carn Mor Dearg, Aonach Beag, and Aonach Mor. The first three all exceed 4,000 feet and the last falls only one foot under. They link

217

up with the Grey Corries, whose seventeen peaks stretch east to Loch Treig.

The river Nevis rises on Binnein Mor at the extreme eastern end of the Mamores. In the course of its fourteen-mile run to Loch Linnhe it flows at first through desolate moorland at 1,000 feet, then below Aonach Beag enters a grassy strath where it meanders to the cottage at Steall. Close above Steall on the left flank, a huge **waterfall** surges down the lowest cliff of Sgurr a' Mhaim. It is 350 feet high and one of the three biggest in Scotland (the other two are the Falls of Glomach in Kintail, 350 feet, and Eas a' Chùal Aluinn in Sutherland, 658 feet). Close below Steall, rock spurs project into the glen from either side, seeming to bar the way and to pinch off the upper glen from the lower. The river bursts through the barrier by a gut, then drops four hundred feet down a gorge to lower Glen Nevis.

The lower glen is of quite different character. The river is flanked by green fields. On one side, woods planted by the Forestry Commission rise to the slopes of the Mamores; on the other, a bare mountain wall swells steeply to the vast back of Ben Nevis. The glen between makes a pleasant contrasting scene, more pastoral than mountainous, although the mountains lend the only claim to distinction in the lower part. Near Bridge of Nevis the scene close to the road has been rendered unsightly by a new housing scheme of poor design, for which Fort William Town Council must take the blame, but greatly improves as one moves upward. Sgurr a' Mhaim apparently closes the head of the glen five miles away, attended by the graceful peak of Stob Ban to its right. Their quartzite caps are often mistaken for snow.

The road, a good one, runs south up the glen to the foot of Stob Ban, where it turns sharply east at Polldubh, to end two miles farther at a car park 450 feet above sea-level. At this point the open slope on your left runs four thousand feet to the summit of Ben Nevis at an angle of thirty-five degrees—the longest and steepest hill-slope in Britain. Down it rushes the Allt Coire Eoghainn, after rain one of the more spectacular water-slides in the Highlands. It issues from the invisible floor of a corrie fifteen hundred feet above, giving a visible slide of 1,250 feet in half a mile, showing intensely white against dark rock.

Beyond the road-end, a footpath continues one mile through the **gorge of Glen Nevis** to Steall. The Nevis gorge is the finest example of its kind in Great Britain. It is only four hundred feet high, but the immense walls to its right and left are wooded in pine, oak, birch, and rowan. These sprout in profusion from the crags, giving the rock gorge a Himalayan character not seen elsewhere in this country. The apparent height is greatly increased by the wide flash of Steall waterfall, which shows through the V-shaped cleft on top. The rocky path goes up the right bank, sometimes by the water's edge, so that you can see into its deep and tortuous channel. The gorge resounds to its thunder. Great gouts, twisting and churning round gigantic boulders, have gouged pots and cauldrons out of the rock bed. At other times, high among the trees, you are allowed clear views across the ravine to the wooded cliffs of Sgurr a' Mhaim, and upwards through the throat of the gorge to Steall waterfall. At the top, the path comes close to huge boulders in the gut, where crenellated crags tower. Suddenly the scene alters. A flat and grassy meadow spreads far ahead to the next big bend of the glen. Following so unexpectedly on the gorge, the bright green flats with a brown river snaking through in slow bends makes a most happy change. The Nevis gorge taken alone is without counterpart in this country. Its Himalayan character arises from a peculiar combination of cliff and woodland and water. When one adds to the spectacle the Eoghainn waterslide below and the Steall waterfall above, and the transition to meadow on top, the whole becomes one of the great sights of the Highlands. The path itself is most lovely in its own right.

The origin of the name **Ben Nevis** has aroused much conjecture, mostly wide of the mark. It derives from a Gaelic compound word Beinn-neamh-bhathais. Neamh means the heavens or clouds; bathais, the top of a man's head (between crown and brow). A free translation is 'The mountain with its head in the clouds'. As seen from anywhere in Glen Nevis it is seen at its worst due to foreshortening—a shapeless lump. From Corpach you can better grasp something of its hulk-like shape and size, especially when whitened by winter snows. One might still not suspect, viewing it thus from the west, that its north side was walled by the tallest and most splendid cliff in Britain. This precipice can be seen in part from the Inverness road between Fort William and Spean Bridge.

The Ben is very nearly an isolated mountain. At the south-east shoulder alone does a thin ridge sweep eastward and then north to Carn Mor Dearg, 4,012 feet, the two thus forming a gigantic horseshoe, whose open end is to the north-west. The innermost recess is Coire Leis, whence the Allt a' Mhuilinn (pronounced Voolin)

flows down to the river Lochy. You can see into Coire Leis from the
road and glimpse the cliffs towering out of it, but a full appreciation
of their size and magnificent architecture cannot be had unless
you walk between three and four miles right up the Allt a' Mhuilinn
to the corrie.

The walk up starts behind the Ben Nevis distillery at the foot of
the burn. Alternatively (and this is much the easier route to find on
a first visit), you may start from lower Glen Nevis, cross the bridge
to the right bank, and follow the road to Achintee Farm. The footpath to the summit starts there. At 1,800 feet you reach Lochan
Meall an-t-Suidhe (pronounced Mellantee), whence you descend
north-east into the Allt a' Mhuilinn glen. Either course leads you
beneath cliffs unmatched even by the Cuillin of Skye. Two thousand
feet high, they stretch two miles in a series of deeply riven buttresses
and ridges, towers and pinnacles, each with its distinctive name—
Observatory Ridge, Tower Ridge, the Comb, Trident Buttress,
Castle Buttress, and a score of others. One, Gardyloo Gully, takes its
name from the ancient Edinburgh street cry of *Gardez l'eau*, used
when householders heaved their slops out of the window, for the
gully's top wall was the refuse tip for the old Observatory. The snow-
fields seen at the base of the cliffs normally remain all the year
round, and may still be thirty feet deep in August. Summer and
winter, the cliffs offer a huge variety of rock, snow, and ice climbs,
which attract mountaineers from all parts of the United Kingdom.

Many thousands of people climb Ben Nevis annually, for the
ascent is easy by the path up its back. A normal time to the summit
is three and a half hours, plus two for the descent. At the summit-
plateau it is necessary to keep a sharp look-out in mist: gullies in
the north cliffs cut deeply into the plateau and in winter and spring
their mouths are masked by snow-cornices projecting ten to fifteen
feet over the lip (cornices are liable to collapse when stood upon).
The summit is a flat desert of boulders. On a fine day the view
ranges from Ben Lomond to Torridon, and from the Cairngorms to
the Outer Hebrides. On exceptional days, Ireland can be dimly
discerned a hundred and twenty miles away. You can now most
clearly see that the Scottish Highlands are simply a level plateau,
from which mountains have been carved by water-erosion. The
winter effect is much like that of a storm-sea frozen. The most
dramatic view is across Glen Nevis to the quartzite teeth of the
Mamores.

The old Observatory near the cliff's edge was built in 1883 to gather meteorological data over a sunspot period, and closed down in 1904. Later it was used as a hotel but is now a total ruin. Since the mountain lies in the storm-track of North Atlantic hurricanes, the records are of extraordinary interest to mountaineers, and important to everyone who proposes to climb Ben Nevis by whatever route. Atmospheric condensation tends to cover the summit with a cloud-cap when the rest of the sky is clear, hence it gets an average of only two hours bright sunshine per day and an annual rainfall of 157 inches. The mean monthly temperature is half a degree below freezing point. Snow may thus fall on the mountain at any day or month of the year. The permanent winter falls begin in October. By July the melting snows have usually left the summit clear, but in hollows under the cliffs the snow accumulates in beds over a hundred feet deep. If the mountain were a few hundred feet higher it would run a glacier.

The most important records of all as they affect human life are of wind. Cold in itself is no very great menace, nor for that matter is wind, but the two combined are of deadly effect. They have taken a heavy toll of life on Nevis. The summit area has an average of two hundred and sixty-one gales per annum. Many of these reach hurricane force. At sea-level such winds are infrequent. Above 3,000 feet there is a great step-up in velocities; on Ben Nevis in winter, hurricanes blow annually and often at 100 m.p.h., gusting to 150 and more.

No one should climb Ben Nevis even by the path unless he carries plenty of warm clothing, wears good boots, and carries a one-inch map and compass. He should not be tricked into taking the mountain lightly by noting that harriers wear singlet and shorts on the annual race up to the summit from Fort William, for that event is run under special auspices on the first Saturday of September. (The record for the race was made in 1973, by Harry Walker of Blackburn, in 1 hour, 29 minutes, 38 seconds there and back). It should be kept at the back of the mind that nearly fifty men and women have been killed on Ben Nevis in the last fifteen years, and in the forefront that a mountain is better enjoyed if one is equipped.

UPPER LOCHABER

Ten miles to the east of Nevis, Loch Treig marks the boundary of Nether Lochaber. Between lies the range of the Grey Corries, which are most easily seen and reached from Glen Spean. On the other side of the valley, the hills of Upper Lochaber, the old country of MacDonald of Keppoch, spread to the Corrieyairack pass. From these hills two long glens, the Gloy and the Roy, fall to the west end of Glen Spean. All three glens are famous for the geological phenomena known as Parallel Roads high up on their hillsides. These terraces are seen more clearly in Glen Roy, which opens off the Great Glen at Roy Bridge.

Glen Roy in its lower half is of almost lowland character—not a rough, steep-sided highland glen but green and wide with low hills sparsely wooded. It offers good picnic spots. The **Parallel Roads** appear early, but are seen best from the highest point of the road where there is a big car-park. This overlooks the upper half of the glen, which takes a long sinuous curve bordered by grassland along the river, before rising at the valley's head to steep, scree-covered mountains. On your left-hand side, three successive mountain flanks are heather-covered. Traversing their brown flanks, three Parallel Roads stand out vividly green. The Middle Road is a third of the way down from the top Road. On the right-hand side of the glen, on the farthest hill, three identical Roads exactly 'meet' the Roads on the left-hand side where the two opposing walls converge as the glen bends eastward.

The origin of these parallel terraces puzzled our forebears for several thousand years. In Glen Roy they appear at 857 feet, 1,068 feet, and 1,149 feet. They were formed towards the end of the last ice age when a great glacier, flowing northward off the Ben Nevis massif, dammed the outlets from the glens. The mountain waters flowing in behind formed deep lakes, and the Parallel Roads are the beaches. As the ice retreated, or was breached, the water-level sank and new beaches were formed at successively lower levels. You can climb on to one of the old beaches a hundred feet above the car park. The surface slopes gently and is covered in grass or bracken, but never by heather.

West of the Great Glen lie the true West Highlands, which might be said to stretch from Ardnamurchan to Loch Carron. Their straight eastern boundary of eighty miles contrasts with the extreme length of their west coast, which from Morvern to Loch Carron is nearly three hundred and fifty miles. This highly splintered coast fringes a multitude of close-packed mountains, sixty of which rise above 3000 feet. From the low Morvern hills they increase in height northward to reach little less than 4,000 feet at the west end of Glen Affric. The whole of this mountain fastness is deeply moated by zig-zag lochs, both sea-water and fresh. The scenery of the long, twisting glens is of a high order, so many rivalling one another in claim to the greatest beauty that hardly two men can be found to agree which wins. Prior to the activities of the North of Scotland Hydro-Electric Board, almost all granted the highest award to Glen Affric. But the building of the dam there and the flooding of the former shores of Loch Beneveian have deprived that glen of pre-eminence.

A great part of this delectable region was the scene of Prince Charles Edward's wanderings after Culloden. You enter it, bound for Loch Arkaig, by crossing the Great Glen at either the foot or the head of the river Lochy. If from Fort William, you take the Mallaig road across Bridge of Lochy to Banavie, then up the right bank of the canal; if from Spean Bridge, you cross by the Bridge of Mucomir close to Loch Lochy. On leaving the village of Spean Bridge, the road climbs steeply up to the Gairlochy road-fork. On top of this hill stands the Commando Memorial raised in 1952 and designed by Scott Sutherland. A group of three bronze soldiers stands on top of a short stone pedestal looking west to the Cameron country of Lochiel, where they were trained during the Second World War. This sculpture is excellent—an original work of art that has been given the site it needs.

On approaching Gairlochy, you should halt at the bridge over the river to view the **falls of Mucomir.** The river Lochy bursts out from the loch above in tumultuous flood and plunges through dense woods into the river Spean (which now also becomes the Lochy). A splendid view can be had from the parapet of the bridge. Passing over the canal beyond, you drive three miles north up the forested shore of Loch Lochy to a beautifully wooded bay called **Bunarkaig,** where Loch Arkaig flows into the Great Glen. The view across the farther arm of the bay to the Grey Corries of Nether Lochaber has a foreground of birch trees trailing like willows over the face of the broad river. The river, only a mile and a half long, flows through a wide-spreading, undulating forest. At the centre of it, amid broad lawns on the right bank, stands **Achnacarry House,** the home of Cameron of Lochiel since 1660. The original Achnacarry Castle was laid to ruin in 1746 by the Duke of Cumberland, and the present house built on its site by the twenty-second chief in 1802. During the last war it became the Commando training base—and was severely damaged by fire. The house was restored and partly rebuilt in 1952.

The original architect employed by Lochiel was James Gillespie.

He has used a tawny whinstone and built a square two-storeyed house in classical style with Gothic decoration. A crenellated parapet runs round the top of the walls below the attic with turrets at all corners. Round towers at the north and west sides rise from the ground to roof level. The tall windows, square-cut, are varied with oval tops above the front door, and with narrow Gothic windows to its sides. The setting among woods now at their prime on a riverside park amid mountains is no less than magnificent. This is the only fine building of Lochaber and one of the most pleasing in the Highlands. The interior has space and light and is furnished with treasures collected over four centuries of family history. It is now the home of the twenty-sixth chief and is not open to the public.

The road to Loch Arkaig goes by the river's left bank through the old and famous **Dark Mile**, a tree-lined avenue connecting the two lochs. The exclusion of light by the interweaving beech branches overhead gave the place its name, but would not do so to-day. Its fame depended on an old and narrow road, whose unique quality vanished with the building of the new road, the felling of trees by storm, and the recent planting of conifers. The Dark Mile still shows a fine combination of deciduous with coniferous forest.

In August 1746, Prince Charlie spent two weeks beside the Dark Mile 'hiding in sundry fast places'. One of these was a big tree on the left-hand side of the road and still marked on one-inch maps. His tree was blown down with the others many years ago. His second hiding place was a cave at 800 feet on the hillside above the Dark Mile, close to the re-entrant of Gleann Cia-aig (pronounced Caig). The glen has a strong burn tumbling down to the foot of Loch Arkaig. Close above the road it issues from a ravine to thunder over a short fall among birch and hazel.

The road continues twelve miles along the north shore of **Loch Arkaig**, at first among deciduous trees and later under bare hill-slopes, where the eye is held by the high mountains to the west, for they rise sharply from gleaming water. They stand along the watershed narrowly dividing Loch Arkaig from the sea at Loch Nevis, which is only seven miles away. The southern slopes of Loch Arkaig were formerly pine forest, devastated by fire during the last war. Now they are bare, and the scars have not yet healed.

At Murlaggan, a mile and a half from the head of the loch, Jacobite treasure is said to have been buried either in the loch or on ground nearby. Immediately after Culloden, two French ships

Above Ardnamurchan Point, the most westerly of the British mainland,
23 miles west of Land's End. The name means the Point of the Great Ocean. The
lighthouse tower is of grey granite 118 feet high and set on a 60-foot cliff:
its light is visible for 18 miles. *Below* Mingary Castle, near Kilchoan,
Ardnamurchan, built in the 13th century by Angus Mor of Clan Donald, King of
the Isles. In 1292 the King of Scots gave Ardnamurchan to Angus Mor's youngest
son Iain. The castle remained the stronghold of the MacIains of Ardnamurchan
for 400 years. The curtain walls are hexagonal with rounded corners, on four
sides surrounded by sea, and on the other two by a ditch cut into the basaltic
rock on which the castle is planted. The main gate is to seaward, where the
rock forms a natural causeway.

Above Sgurr Choinnich Mor, 3,603 feet on the Grey Corries of Lochaber,
a range of seventeen peaks that flank the north side of Glen Nevis.
These peaks all give excellent ridge-walking in winter. *Below*, Ben Nevis and
Glen Nevis seen across the head of Loch Linnhe. The small town is the Inverlochy
extension of Fort William.

arrived off the Arisaig coast laden with arms and 35,000 louis d'or. They were much too late to aid the rising and were caught by three English frigates (which were beaten off). But before action took place the treasure was landed and carried, probably by boat up Loch Morar, to Glen Pean and through to the Cameron country, where the main bulk was buried. Needless to say there is no record of its subsequent disposal. A few optimists have thought some might still be there.

From the head of Loch Arkaig there are two passes to the coast, each with a footpath: Glen Pean to the west, Glen Dessary to the north-west. From the road-end there is a good track for four miles up Glen Dessary, degenerating to a rough and rocky path over the wild pass of Mam na Cloich Airde at 1,000 feet. The path is well-marked: it has been used for many centuries. As it drops to Loch Nevis, it passes below the highest peak of Knoydart, Sgor na Ciche, 3,410 feet. The Glen Pean track to Loch Morar is boggy and much inferior in its mountain scene, but is much lower at only 400 feet. This was the fast route taken by Prince Charlie. Culloden was fought at one o'clock on 16th April and lost thirty minutes later. With half a dozen horsemen the prince rode all day and most of the night for the Rock of the Raven, MacDonell of Glengarry's castle on Loch Oich. Resting there from early morning till the afternoon, he rode on with three men by the Dark Mile and Loch Arkaig to the house of Donald Cameron of Glen Pean, stopped there for the night, then went on by foot to Loch Morar and the Outer Hebrides.

It is the principal attraction of Loch Arkaig that no work of man has yet defaced its natural beauty. The big glens to north and south, Glen Garry and Loch Eil, are main highways loaded with traffic. Glen Garry would have been preferred to Loch Arkaig for its varied beauty until a few years ago, but not now unless in its lower part. Arkaig remains an old Highland glen, remote from the pressures of industrial development. Although, alas, not free of tourist development in the shape of caravan sites. Its quiet bays and woods and hills breathe a peace not to be sensed so markedly in any of the other glens that radiate west from the Great Glen.

North to Invergarry the road follows the east side of Loch Lochy to its head, then crosses the glen to the west side of Loch Oich by a swing bridge over the canal. Half a mile north of this bridge keep a lookout on your right for the **Tobar nan Ceann**, or Well of the Heads. The monument raised above the well by the twenty-seventh chief of Glengarry in 1812 is a tall pyramid on a square column, carrying a cluster of seven men's heads on its peak. It is hardly beautiful, but a curio in commemorated vengeance.

In 1663, the young MacDonald of Keppoch and his two brothers were murdered in the castle in Glen Spean by guests and kinsmen. The stone monument records the punitive action taken by Sir James MacDonald of Sleat, high chief of the clan of which Keppoch was a branch. The four sides of the column bear inscriptions in Gaelic, French, Latin, and English, correctly stating (after a windy pre-amble, in which the punitive action is ascribed to the wrong chief and hence to the wrong century): 'The heads of the seven murderers were presented at the feet of the noble chief in Glengarry Castle after having been washed in this spring, and ever since that event, which took place in the early sixteenth century it has been known by the name of Tobar-nan-Ceann, or Well of the Heads.' The well has vanished, overlaid by the widening of the Inverness road.

A mile farther you reach the north boundary of Lochaber, where Glen Garry cleaves the western mountains twenty-six miles to Knoydart. Two great sheets of water fill its bed from end to end—Loch Garry and Loch Quoich (pronounced Kooich), which discharge by the river Garry into Loch Oich. Loch Oich at 105 feet is the summit of the Great Glen and canal. At Invergarry, on the flat ground between the road and the loch is the former mansion and now country house hotel of Glengarry Castle (recommended). Close to its left are the remains of the old Glen Garry Castle of MacDonell. Built on Creagan Fhithich, the Rock of the Raven, it sheltered Prince Charlie before and after Culloden, hence was burned down by the Duke of Cumberland. On the north bank of the river, where 'The Road to the Isles' strikes left to Loch Garry and Glen Shiel, the Invergarry Hotel is the region's centre for deer-stalking, grouse-shooting, and fishing. On all the great lochs and rivers of Lochaber, there is excellent fishing for salmon, sea-trout, and brown trout. Boats are for hire on at least eight of the big fresh-water lochs, including the Oich, Garry, and Quoich.

Loch Garry has woodland and splendid river scenery that fully equals if it does not excel the beauty of Loch Arkaig. The road up the north shore has recently been widened. The extraordinary beauty of the old one, twisting along the rocky shore as a lane between broad-leaved trees, which being well-spaced obstructed no view over the water, owed much to its narrowness—a slow road, on which travel-lers saw far more than they do now. The chance offered them by the new road to double their old speed is too strong to resist, and men forget what it was that they came to see and enjoy. Travel slowly on this road. There is no other glen opening off the Great Glen that can give one so much delight.

Five miles from Invergarry, a new road to Kintail and the Isles rises north over the hills. The Loch Garry road continues to **Tomdoun**, where the old Road to the Isles formerly struck north; from there westward the scene deteriorates. It looks well from a distance —indeed, from the heights of the new Kintail road, upper Glen Garry and Loch Quoich, ringed by the Knoydart mountains, is one of the more enthralling sights of the West Highlands—but does not bear up to close inspection. Loch Quoich and its tributaries are incorporated in a big hydro-electric scheme comprising several dams; and the dams, pylons. wires, and the loss of woodland by flooding, have shorn upper Glen Garry of its old worth. The scheme should thrive in what is notoriously one of the wettest districts in Scotland. A rain gauge gives a fall of 200 inches. At the bare western end of Loch Quoich there are two passes over the watershed, one south-west and trackless to Loch Nevis, the other north-west by motor-road to Loch Hourn, where it ends. I shall deal later with Loch Hourn under Glenelg and Knoydart.

Glen Garry and Loch Arkaig have thus no through roads at their western extremities. But Loch Eil to their south gives a pass right through to the sea at Loch Ailort and carries both road and rail, which turn up the Morar coast to Mallaig. This too is one of the roads to the Isles, and the journey by observation car (scrapped and not replaced in 1968) was scenically the most rewarding offered by Scottish railway lines. The excellencies lie in the Moidart and Morar half. You meet this Moidart frontier at Glenfinnan, at the head of Loch Shiel.

CHAPTER 17

Moidart

From Loch Shiel to the sea all land is Moidart. Low but hilly in its
south part, it rises mountainously in the north in two ranges:
Rois-bheinn, 2,887 feet, whose six tops overlook Loch Ailort, and
Beinn Odhar Bheag, 2,895 feet, whose twin peaks flank upper Loch
Shiel. Moidart owes its peculiar beauty and fame to the water-
filled glens framed by these ranges.

Until recently, Moidart's only roads were along its north and
south frontiers. These are now linked by a new road near the west
coast. Another road made by the Forestry Commission 11 miles
down the south side of Loch Shiel has not been completed to
Acharacle.

You arrive on the north frontier at **Glenfinnan**. Around the
head of the loch, green fields spread broadly, bearing near the
centre the monument to the '45—a grey round tower in baroque
style, on top of which stands a bearded stone Highlander, repre-
senting not Prince Charles Edward but his clansmen. The shape of
the column is not unlike that of Ardnamurchan lighthouse. One
can even climb up inside by a spiral staircase. The famous view down
Loch Shiel, whether seen from the monument's parapet, or better
still from the hill-slopes behind, is given its startling beauty by its
mountain frame. The wide nearer waters are broken by an island
curved like a boomerang; trees on its broad back throw strong
reflections on to green water. The mountains receding behind thrust
spurs into the loch with sufficient irregularity to give the distant
waters an apparent double twist. The eye thus seems to be led
farther and the loch to penetrate deeper than could be possible
were its shores straight.

The grassy fields near at hand, especially when viewed from
above, can be seen to be heavily furrowed. They are the site of old
lazybeds. Such beds used to be common all over the West Highlands
when the glens were well populated. They are a method of tillage

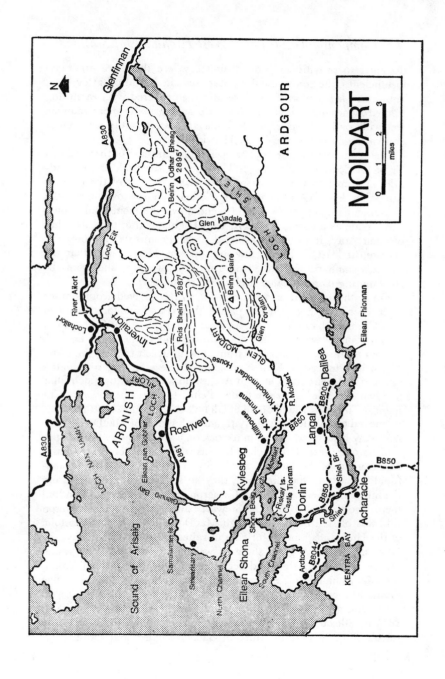

N

MOIDART

0 1 2 3
miles

Glenfinnan

A830

ARDGOUR

LOCH SHIEL

Beinn Odhar Bheeg
2895'

Glen Aladale

Beinn Gaire

Glen Forslan

Rois Bheinn 2887'

GLEN MOIDART

Loch Eilt

River Ailort

Lochailort

Inverailort

Kinlochmoidart House

Eilean Fhionnan

R. Moidart

B806 Dalilea

LOCH AILORT

ARDNISH

LOCH NAN UAMH

Eilean nan Gobhar

A830

Roshven

A861

St. Finnans
Millhouse

B850

Langal

B850 Shiel Br.

B850

Samalaman Is.

Kylesbeg

Loch Moidart

Dorlin
Riskay Is.
Castle Tioram

R. Shiel

Acharacle

Smeararry

Shona Beag

Eilean Shona

South Channel

Ardtoe
B8044

KENTRA BAY

North Channel

Sound of Arisaig

designed to provide soil and drainage where these are otherwise insufficient. The seed—usually potato or oat, but also barley, hay, and corn—is sown on the surface and then covered with earth dug from trenches alongside. The beds are not normally more than six feet wide or less than three. Nowadays they are rarely seen under cultivation except in the Outer Hebrides.

The monument to the '45 has been under the care of the National Trust for Scotland since 1938. They have a car park at the roadside, and an information room with a wall-display of the prince's campaign from Glenfinnan to Culloden. To my own eyes, the monument impairs the splendid scene down the loch. Had it only been made as a cairn, in accord with Highland tradition, like that of Glen Aray, it would have fitted perfectly into its environment. Its site, at least, is historically appropriate. Here it was that the prince's standard was raised on 19th August 1745, and from the surrounding country came his immediate support.

On 25th July, the armed brig *Du Teillay* arrived from France with the twenty-five-year-old prince aboard and anchored in Loch nan Uamh, a bay on the Arisaig coast. MacDonald of Clanranald, whose country was Moidart and Morar, and Cameron of Lochiel, arrived to dissuade the prince from action but left to raise the clans. The prince moved to Kinlochmoidart House while the summonses to the rising went out. On 18th August he was rowed up Loch Shiel to Glen Aladale, a strath under Beinn Odhar Bheag, where he spent the night at MacDonald of Glenaladale's house. Next morning he moved on to Glenfinnan. With only a handful of MacDonalds for company he arrived at eleven o'clock on a wet Monday morning to find no one there. For a while he was in despair. Some time later, MacDonald of Morar appeared with a hundred and fifty Clanranalds. Early in the afternoon, they heard the sound of pipes from the hills of Locheil, and at last Cameron arrived with seven hundred men. The Bratach Bhan, the Stewart banner of white and crimson silk, was blessed by Bishop Hugh MacDonald, the Vicar Apostolic of the Highlands, and unfurled and raised by William Murray, the Duke of Atholl. A great shout of welcome went up to the young prince. By evening they had been joined by the Stewarts of Appin, the MacDonalds of Keppoch, and many others to a total of five thousand men.

On the ground where they stood, the monument was built in 1815 by Alexander MacDonald of Glenaladale. Plaques set in the surrounding wall are inscribed in Gaelic, English, and Latin.

West of Glenfinnan, the Mallaig road has been widened and gives fast driving through a nine-mile glen to Loch Ailort. The bleakness of the hill-scene is likely to be relieved in time by afforestation, and is much lightened now by the long waters of Loch Eilt, from which the river Ailort flows west to the sea. On passing the foot of the loch you enter at once into Arisaig. Above the head of Loch Ailort, a branch road forks left to Inverailort, and so by the new road round the Moidart coast. Most people prefer instead to explore Moidart through its south approaches. For the present, then, I return you to the point where I broke off in Chapter 15, at the south end of **Loch Shiel.**

Entering Moidart from Loch Sunart and Ardnamurchan, your best centre for exploration is just outside its frontier at Lochshiel Hotel (Acharacle Hotel was destroyed by fire in 1967). Moidart has crofts, farms, and lobster-fishing, but the district is very largely given over to game-fishing and shooting. There are few houses other than the big lodges, the gamekeepers', and the crofts'—and the only hotels are at Loch Ailort and Glenuig.

From the jetty behind Lochshiel Hotel a motor launch used to leave every morning and afternoon for Glenfinnan until the service was abandoned in the winter of 1967. We must hope that summer cruises will take its place. In good weather, this is the only satisfactory way of seeing Loch Shiel, which is too narrow—never so much as a mile wide—to be appreciated from its own banks; mountains hem its upper two-thirds. At the narrows of the twisting lower third lies the tiny island of **St. Finan,** properly called Eilean Fhionnan. He is said to have come here from Kilchoan, and from him Glen Finnan is named. He died in 575. His cell became famous and drew great numbers of pilgrims. The present church, 70 feet long, was built in the sixteenth century by Allan, Chief of Clanranald. From earliest times the island has served as a burial ground for Moidart, Sunart, and Ardnamurchan, and is still occasionally so used today. The church and two little chapels are in themselves of no architectural merit, but on the stone altar of the church there stands a remarkable Celtic bronze bell, seven inches high and quadrangular. Only seven of these survive in Scotland. Pick it up, and hear its beautiful ringing note.

Rank grass and nettles grow around the church, but in spring the island becomes a blaze of golden broom. Blackcock nest here, and greenshank are numerous along the shores. Unlikely though it must seem, this minute island had a school in the eighteenth century, financed by the Society for the Propagation of Christian Knowledge. Its schoolmaster was the most famous of all Gaelic poets, Alexander MacDonald (Alasdair MacMhaighstir Alasdair). He held the school from 1729 for nine years, but like many another young poet (he was also a son of the manse) he found himself writing verse of which a society for propagating Christian knowledge could hardly approve. He therefore resigned his office. Later in life he became a fervent Jacobite. He was born in 1700 less than two miles down the loch at Dalilea on the north shore. His father, Alexander MacDonald, the first of Dalilea, had graduated in Arts and Divinity at Glasgow. Although he lived in Dalilea House his church was at Kilchoan. It is an interesting comment on the toughness of Highland priests that the Reverend Alexander thought nothing of rising in the early hours of a Sunday morning, fording the bridgeless river Shiel, and walking by the north coast of Ardnamurchan twenty-five miles to Kilchoan Church. He is buried on St. Finan's Isle and his gravestone is distinguished by the carved figure of a skeleton.

When you cross the Shiel Bridge from Acharacle the road forks. The main road goes over the hills to the head of Loch Moidart; instead, hold to the broad and wooded river, following it to Dorlin at the outer loch. On Sundays and Wednesdays a motor-boat (based on Loch Ailort) calls at the jetty to take visitors cruising on Loch Moidart and round the coast to Glenuig. The outer loch is divided into north and south channels by the island of Shona. The passage across the loch from the Dorlin Woods, first past Riskay Island to Shona Beag, and thence down the north channel, is one of exceeding beauty when the sun shines, especially in the early morning before the wind gets up: the water lies almost still, gently rippled so that colours from the hills' and islands' trees are broken into a myriad fused spots, reminding one of a Monet painting.

Close to Dorlin, but offshore in the south channel, stands the fourteenth-century **Castle Tioram** of the MacDonalds of Clanranald. Its island is tidal, linked to the mainland except at high water. With high curtain-walls and turreted keep, it remains at least outwardly in a good state of preservation. You cross the sands to find that the old masons, who were expert in tailoring a castle to fit its underlying crag, have here made it pentangular. The entrance lies on the north side facing Riskay. You pass through to a small courtyard. Above and beyond, a rocky terrace rises 5 feet, to which roughly-hewn steps give access. The castle has a hall, kitchen, and a satisfyingly dank dungeon. But all seems rather cramped.

Moidart

Tioram Castle was built in 1353 by Lady Anne MacRuari, the divorced wife of John MacDonald, first Lord of the Isles. From their son Ranald sprang the great Highland family of Clanranald. The chiefs ruled both sea and land, and in early days all enemy attacks came by sea. Perhaps for this reason the seaward walls have no windows. The castle was never taken by siege, but once was temporarily seized by the earl of Argyll. He had won a commission from the government to harry Clanranald, and for five weeks his galleys hung around, latterly anchored hard under the west walls. Argyll broke off and pretended to sail for Ardnamurchan Point. Clanranald flew out of his cage. The too wily Campbell hastened back and took the empty castle. But Clanranald had not flown far—only far enough to send out the fiery cross and rally the clan. He returned with speed to the slaughter and not one Campbell survived.

The castle's end came at Clanranald's own hands. At the rising of 1715, when Allan Dearg led out his clan to fight for the Old Pretender, he rightly feared that if he died in battle his ancestral seat would be seized by Campbell of Argyll. He gave orders that it should be fired, but could not bear to stay to see this done. Only the shell remains, yet like nearly every old castle it lends a grace to our age.

The road to Kinlochmoidart from Shiel Bridge falls close to Loch Shiel at **South Langal**, where there is an excellent sandy beach with a hayfield for tents and caravans. A short way beyond, it breaks north over a low hill-pass to Loch Moidart. Before crossing the pass you can, if you so wish, fork right to **Dalilea**, and to the pier at the lochside. From this point Prince Charlie embarked in a galley on 18th August to be rowed up the loch to Glenfinnan. The house standing high above the pier was built around the end of the eighteenth century by the grandson of the Rev. Alexander Mac-Donald. The house is an excellent example of Scottish baronial style, showing how effective that can be when all is kept simple. It has a plain dignity quite absent from the enlarged and heavily embellished imitations built by eighteenth and nineteenth-century English industrialists, who wanted not a home but a 'laird's' status-symbol.

Alasdair MacMhaighstir Alasdair did not live at Dalilea (to which his elder brother succeeded), but the poet planted the oak-tree that still stands near the kitchen. When Prince Charlie arrived here from Kinlochmoidart, he came not by the line of the present motor-road but by the foot-track directly behind the house. It leads two miles over the hill to Glen Moidart, which it joins two miles from the foot. On its moorland pass, the numerous big cairns one sees by the trackside are the points where men rested when carrying coffins over to Loch Shiel for burial on Eilean Fhionnan. Many an empty whisky bottle will be found inside them. And no whisky was harder earned, for many of these coffins had been carried six or ten miles, or even more, before they reached this pass.

The main road to Loch Moidart crosses the hill a little farther west. From its top you have a clear view into **Glen Moidart** and to the peaks of the Rois-bheinn range standing round its head. From their slopes the river Moidart flows six miles south-west into the head of Loch Moidart. The wide lower glen is sheltered ground, most beautifully wooded in lime, beech, and chestnut, all well-grown, and especially so in the grounds of Kinlochmoidart House. You can drive or walk from the loch's head two miles up this fertile glen till a step in the valley-floor separates it from the barer but surprisingly still more lovely upper glen. There you must take to your feet on a good track. A freshwater loch fringed by reeds and water-lilies and flanked by a deciduous wood around Moidart House, is backed by the bare hillside of Rois-bheinn and on the east side of the glen by the white gout of a waterfall coming off Beinn Gaire.

Around the head of Loch Moidart are wide sandy flats that dry out for nearly a mile on the ebb. Behind them, wide grasslands, where cattle graze, merge into the woods of the glen. Here stands **Kinlochmoidart House**, once the seat of the MacDonalds. No family in Scotland gave such devoted service to Prince Charlie on his landing at Arisaig. The prince stayed in old Kinlochmoidart House from 11th to 17th August attended by a body-guard of fifty men of Clanranald while he laid his plan of campaign. The modern house is not open to the public. The approach to it from St. Finnan's Kirk goes through a series of tree-shaded avenues, finally under a short avenue of plane-trees called Prince Charlie's Walk. Near the garden are four splendid yews, under the shelter of which Cumberland's soldiers camped when they came to burn down the old house. Kinlochmoidart's mother was then lying seriously ill in bed. The soldiers dragged her out and set her beneath these trees to watch her home go up in flames. Her family then carried her up to Glen Forslan, where you saw the waterfall in upper Glen Moidart.

Between Loch Moidart and the Sound of Arisaig, Moidart

234

projects into the sea as a broad and hilly peninsula. To reach its north coast you drive nine miles down the loch to the shore at **Millhouse,** which is marked by a post office and a tea-room (whose home-baked food I can recommend). A quarter of a mile south-east of the post office, seven beech trees stand on a meadow by the lochside. They were planted to commemorate 'The Seven Men of Moidart' who accompanied Prince Charlie from France. Only one of the seven men, Aeneas MacDonald, was in fact born in Moidart. The trees planted in line astern look stout and gnarled, but one in the middle has been dwarfed by the others.

The motor-road formerly ended at Millhouse, only a foot-track continuing along the shore to Kylesbeg at the inner end of the north channel, where it broke over the hill-pass to Glenuig Bay on the Sound of Arisaig, and thence to Kinlochailort. This walk made an excursion excelling all others on the Scottish west coast. Its extra-ordinary merit lay not in the seaward vistas but in the track itself. It was a period-piece, an old Highland road through natural woods, narrow, flagged, closely overhung by the branches of the trees and by crags, and most worthy of preservation for its own sake. This old and famous road has been destroyed by the building of a wide new motor-road, which opened in 1966. It has a wonderful surface for fast driving, and the scene has been rendered suitably dull. One or two fragments of the old road survive to one side or the other, but they are not worth following, since they are very short, neither readily gained on foot nor seen from the main road. This wanton destruction was made solely in the interests of tourism— and for no other reason: the natural and faster outlet for the people of Glenuig was by Kinlochailort. Again and yet again in the High-lands, the planners' blindness is leading them to destroy, for the sake of the money-disgorging visitor, those rare things that should most have rejoiced his heart.

At **Glenuig Bay** there are now only eight or nine houses. Had the new road to Kinlochailort been made fifty years ago, emigration might have been halted and the village been more populous to-day; but new roads in the West Highlands are not made for the con-venience of men living there. Glenuig, being no longer an end in itself, has lost much of its old character as a remote and peaceful clachan. The passing tourist is hardly likely to look at it twice. But something of the old-time Glenuig is still to be found if you leave the new road at the head of the bay and follow the old coast-track west, past St. Agnes's Roman Catholic Church to Samalaman Bay.

It is the best bay of the Moidart coast. From its sandy, well-shaped beach you look north-west over the back of a low island to the Cuillin, Rhum, Eigg, and Muck, and north across the sound to a trackless Arisaig peninsula. The seascape is so delightful that one wants to lie back on the sand and watch it for hours. Samalaman Island, a hundred yards or so offshore, is grazed by horses and foals. The strait has a sandy bottom all the way across and the water is shallow. At low tide I have waded half-way over and swum the rest. The track along this coast from Glenuig continues two miles, at first to Glenuig House and its woodland, then across wind-swept open moor to the old crofting community of Smearisary. Its half-dozen cottages lie in a green hollow fringed by rocky bays. Long deserted by the original crofters, the houses are now all in the hands of enterprising holiday-makers from England, who have restored and re-roofed them. It is a most exposed shore, on which Atlantic rollers forever crash white, but the view out to the isles and to Ardnamurchan give high reward.

Moving in the opposite direction from Glenuig, you follow the seven miles of new motor-road along the north shore of Moidart to join the Fort William to Mallaig road at Kinlochailort. **Loch Ailort** is five miles long, a double-twisting sea-loch between the Ardnish peninsula of Arisaig and the mountain slope of Rois-bheinn. Its name is from the Norse All-fjord, meaning Eel Fiord or Deep Fiord. Eilean nan Gobhar at its mouth has a vitrified fort—one of several in the Sound of Arisaig. The summit of Rois-bheinn is easily gained in two miles from the roadside by way of its west ridge. The climb is worth making for its wide view of the West Highland coast, the sea-lochs, and the Inner Hebrides.

At **Kinlochailort,** a few hundred yards before you join the Mallaig road, a jetty in a cove is the passengers' embarking point for cruises along the Moidart coast. The M.V. *Jacobite* sails to Glenuig on Tuesday, Thursday, and Saturday, leaving at 12.45 p.m. and returning at 6 p.m. In 1966 a fish-farm was started at Kinlochailort to breed sea-trout and salmon. If the pilot scheme, which at first employs only five men, proves successful, it will be followed by a big development financed by Unilever Ltd., and will give much needed employment to the men of the surrounding country.

CHAPTER 18

Arisaig and Morar

Morar is the peninsula between the Sound of Arisaig and Loch Nevis. It is a wide one, nearly a double peninsula, split up the middle by the freshwater Loch Morar. The names North Morar and South Morar are thus given to the hill-ground on either side. Arisaig may be loosely defined (for there is no hard frontier) as the broad and low coastal strip between South Morar and the Sound of Arisaig. Mallaig at the north-west tip is the west coast's most important fishing port after Oban.

The **Sound of Arisaig** is a huge bay biting ten miles into the land. The inner sound is divided by a small peninsula called Ardnish, forming Loch Ailort to its south and Loch nan Uamh (pronounced Ooa) to its north. From the head of Loch Ailort you enter Arisaig through a glen at the back of Ardnish. If you drive this road, as most people do, you lose nearly all that is best of Arisaig. You ought instead to walk its fourteen miles at least as far as the river Morar. Only this way can you begin to know Arisaig: the scent of honey-suckle lingering among the drooping birches, the herons fishing on a lochan of water-lilies, the roe-deer and sometimes red standing in the ferns and moss under the rowan-trees and oak, the seals swarming among the rocks near the Back of Keppoch, the curlews crying along the foreshore where the yellow irises grow thick, and finally, the silver sands of Morar, stretching bay upon bay in front of five miles of dunes and machair. Of all the west coast, Arisaig is the land most deeply related to the stirring decisions of July 1745 and the fate of Prince Charles Edward. When he arrived off the coast aboard the *Du Teillay* on that summer's day and first set foot on the glittering shingle of Loch nan Uamh, where the oystercatchers swoop screaming over the rocks, he must surely have thought this a country worth fighting to win. The **Prince's Beach**, as it has since been called, is not where the road meets the head of the loch, but a

mile and a half farther on where the Borrodale Burn flows into the
bay beside the point of Rudh Ard Ghamhsgail.

Two burns debouch on the north shore of Loch nan Uamh: the
Beasdale and Borrodale. The road turns inland, first to cross Glen
Beasdale, whose woods gave shelter to the prince after Culloden,
and then runs a mile to Borrodale at a point half a mile from the
shore. Here, at **Glen Borrodale House**, then the farmhouse of
Angus MacDonald, Charles stayed for a week guarded by a hundred
men of Clanranald. He met the doubtful clan chiefs and inspired
them with his own enthusiasm. The decisive moment was his conversion of Donald Cameron of Lochiel, who more than any other
man at that time swayed the West Highlanders. On 11th August,
Charles sailed to Glenuig Bay, thence to the narrows of Loch
Moidart's north channel, where he landed and walked to Kinlochmoidart House. When he next returned to Glenborrodale farmhouse
in April he came as a fugitive by way of Loch Morar, four days
after Culloden. In hope of gaining a French ship he was rowed out to
Benbecula in the Outer Hebrides. The Hanoverian navy and army
closed in, and only by the resource of Lady Margaret MacDonald of
Skye, who organized his escape, and of Flora MacDonald who
brilliantly carried her plans into effect, was Charles brought back to
Skye in June, and thence to Mallaigvaig on the Morar coast.

He arrived at Glenborrodale House to find it burnt down by the
navy, and Angus MacDonald living in a hovel alongside. Troops
swarmed everywhere. Charles skulked in various caves both by the
Glenborrodale shore and inland. The name Loch nan Uamh means
the Loch of the Caves, and although one of these is marked on the
maps as Prince Charlie's Cave, the fact is that none can be identified
as certainly his. He at last managed to break through the cordon into
the mountains, and with £30,000 upon his head played a grim
game of hide-and-seek with the Redcoats until September, when
word reached him at Cluny's Cage on Ben Alder that two French
ships had arrived in Loch nan Uamh. On 19th September, the
prince and a large company boarded *L'Heureux*, which sailed for
France shortly after midnight on Saturday, 20th September, 1746.
A cairn by the lochside marks the spot where he embarked.

The house at Glenborrodale was rebuilt with the old stones to the
old plan, and is thus substantially the building in which Charles held
his first court. His bedroom was one with a small window at the
extreme right of the upstairs' front, shaded by two elms. The old
house should not be confused with the modern mansion house built

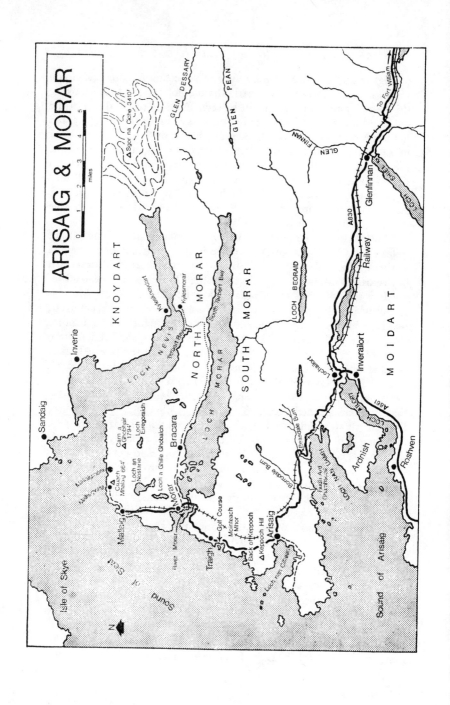

ARISAIG & MORAR

on higher ground. A very good view of its setting may be had if you walk to the summit of Rudh Ard Ghamhsgail, 100 feet, overlooking the shore where eider duck will be seen. At the hollowed top of the hill there is a vitrified fort of the Iron Age, more than forty yards in diameter. Like its better-known neighbour on Eilean nan Gobhar in Loch Ailort, it has a fortified spur below the main fort. Four miles west towards the Point of Arisaig, two other vitrified forts on Eilean na Ghoil and Eilean Port nam Murrach, make four all told in the Sound of Arisaig. Linked by beacon, they would command the sea from Ardnamurchan to the Sound of Sleat and be able to give warning of approach by hostile ships.

West of Glen Borrodale the road keeps inland for two and a half miles across the back of Arisaig peninsula. You come to the sea again at the little village of Arisaig on the shore of **Loch nan Cilltean**. The name means Loch of the Churches: at the back of the bay the tower of the Roman Catholic Church of St. Mary is certainly a landmark from sea, but this is a relatively modern church; beside it lie the ruins of the sixteenth-century church of Kilmory, which was dedicated to St. Maelrubha (who gave his name to Loch Maree in Ross). In the graveyard is buried the poet Alasdair MacMhaighstir Alasdair of Moidart, whose intended burial on St. Finan's Isle of Loch Shiel was prevented by a great storm. It was on Loch nan Cilltean—and not on Loch nan Uamh as is often said— that the engagement took place after Culloden between three English frigates and two French ships laden with belated arms for the rising and 35,000 louis d'or. After landing the money at Borrodale they managed to fight off the English warships and get clean away.

Thus far the coast of Arisaig has been beautifully wooded, but from here northward the land grows bare to Mallaig, except for one wooded glen at the river Morar, which marks a change in the character of the coast-line. To the north all is rocky and to the south sandy—a pure white silica sand, not shell-sand like Ardnamurchan, which is creamy. You arrive at the silver sands from Arisaig by crossing a pass on the hill of **Keppoch**, descending thence to a crofting community called the Back of Keppoch. A series of at least twelve coves and bays now stretch four miles to the Morar estuary. Their sands flash white across the sea to Skye, Rhum, and Eigg, from which points the Morar coast can be identified at a glance. Long lines of inshore skerries make a ragged foreground to the Cuillin. Behind some of the bays rise sand-dunes bound by marram, behind others slope level green machair, or the hayfields

Above the Great Glen, which splits Scotland from the Atlantic to the North Sea. It is the line of a geological fault, caused by the north block of Scotland moving 65 miles to the south-west in relation to the south block. Three lochs fill 45 miles of its bed: Loch Lochy (foreground), Loch Oich (middle distance), and Loch Ness may just be discerned in the farthest background. These are all linked by 22 miles of canal. *Below*, Prince Charlie's Monument at Glenfinnan, where he raised his standard in 1745. The figure on top is not Prince Charlie, but a bearded Highlander. You can climb up inside and stand beside him.

Castle Tioram on Loch Moidart, the seat of MacDonald of Clanranald. Built in 1353, the high curtain walls and turreted keep remain in a good state of preservation. The castle was never taken by siege, but once was temporarily seized by the Earl of Argyll. His galleys hung around for five weeks under the seaward wall, then he broke off and pretended to sail for Ardnamurchan. Clanranald flew out of the cage. Campbell hastened back and took the empty castle, but Clanranald had sent the fiery cross round his clan. They returned with speed to the slaughter and not one Campbell survived.

of croft-land where corncrakes will be heard each evening. At some bays the road traverses close to the foreshore, from which only a narrow strip of grass separates it. These are the most crowded beaches. People, it would seem, do not like to walk; yet by walking only half a mile I have found deserted coves even at the height of summer. The most readily accessible bays are circled by tents and caravans. At sunset in fine weather the campers are drawn to the beaches to watch the volcano-blaze of sky above the spikes of Rhum and the Cuillin and the sea spread from them to the Morar coast like a lava-flow, lapping molten red on black skerries.

Inland from the shore, a low, boggy plain called the **Great Moss** (Mointeach Mhor on the map) stretches two miles to the first craggy hills. Half-way between Back of Keppoch and the river Morar you come to a nine-hole golf course on the machair bordering the moor, and at this point the road holds farther inland to avoid a deeply in-cutting bay where Loch Morar discharges into the sea. Loch Morar is nearly but not quite a sea-loch. A narrow land-barrier separates it from the Sound of Sleat, and through this barrier the river Morar bursts in once-famous falls, now harnessed by the ubiquitous hydro-electric scheme. The river is only three hundred yards long, a wide and heavy stream, little of whose water now comes over the fall. In an effort to spoil a former beauty-spot as little as possible, the engineers have built the powerhouse into the cliff of the left bank, where little of it is visible, and the water used for generation is returned to the river below. Despite these commendable efforts at preservation, the scene is no longer of outstanding quality. It really did need its waterfall, and that gone it is nothing. The dam is of blue metal. Alongside the powerhouse, a fish-ladder of nine steps mounts to the loch. There is no public road on that side, but the rocks of the fall are normally so dry that one may cross to examine the ladder at close quarters.

Morar Bay has a long strand, very shallow and sheltered and filled with pale green water when the tide floods. It is exceedingly popular with tourists, for its south shore is continuous silica-sand backed by dunes easily accessible from the road. People use it more for sun-bathing than sea-bathing: the sands dry out a long way on the ebb. At the narrows, nearly a mile out from the bay's head, it is possible to wade across and be no more than chest-deep.

Loch Morar, barely a quarter of a mile inland, is yet another of Scotland's geological freaks. Its depth is 1,017 feet—although it lies close to shallow seas that reach no equivalent depth until the dip of the continental shelf a hundred and seventy miles north-west between St. Kilda and Rockall. It is thus the deepest water in Britain. But how was this chasm gouged? It is a problem still to be solved.

The loch is twelve miles long. The road up its north side goes only three, ending at the tiny village of Bracora. A track continues to the mountainous head of the loch, where two passes lead over to Loch Arkaig. The track gives an excellent walk for the first four and a half miles to South Tarbert Bay, where a side-track strikes north across a half-mile isthmus to Tarbert Bay on Loch Nevis. From the high ground on that bay's eastern arm, you obtain a fine view of the loftiest mountain in this part of Scotland: Sgor na Ciche (pronounced Keeh, with glottal aspirate), 3,410 feet. It has been rather fancifully likened to the Matterhorn, and seen from seaward is indeed one of the sharpest peaks in Scotland.

The west end of Loch Morar is thickly wooded, especially the half-dozen islands humped high off Bracora. There is excellent fishing on the loch, for both sea-trout and salmon. Boats may be hired from the Bracora crofters, who will act as ghillies. The biggest fish in the loch is Morag, a legendary monster. No vulgar creature like her mate on Loch Ness, who exhibits himself to all and sundry, Morag appears only to foretell the death of a MacDonald of Clanranald. Less ambitious but free fishing for brown trout may be had on the hill-lochs to the north of Bracora—Loch an Nostarie, Loch Eiregoraidh, and others.

The village of **Morar** sits on the breast of a hill close above the river's estuary. Like Arisaig, it has its own hotel within easy reach of the silver sands. The road and rail northward now keep well away from the shore till they end at **Mallaig** three miles farther. The road makes a sharp descent to the harbour, set on the west side of a rock-bound bay, protected by hilly headlands and facing north into the Sound of Sleat. The stone-built houses, mostly white-washed, cluster mainly on the west side above the harbour, but extend more thinly right round the bay. The population is 1,000—a number doubled in summer by visitors. There are two hotels, the West Highland on top of the hill, and the Marine close to the harbour and railway station; in addition to which are numerous guesthouses. The Jacobite Restaurant, opposite the West Highland Hotel, is the best within a radius of forty-five miles.

The harbour is the centre of all activity, much more so than at Fort William or Oban. Mallaig is a specialized fishing port, and to fishing all else is subservient. The value of the catch in 1971 was over £2 m.—nearly double Oban's, although Oban is several times the size of Mallaig with thrice its population. People tend to gather on the piers and quays, not to watch the passenger steamers and ferries bound for the Hebrides but to enjoy the intense activity of the fishing fleets, and the bustle of landing the catch and dispatching it south. Fifty herring boats use the harbour and the lobster fleet fishes two thousand miles of coast-line, making Mallaig the most important herring and shellfish port of the west coast and of Great Britain: in these catches (which are worth several million pounds annually) she far excels Oban, whose more valuable landings are whitefish. On Saturday mornings around eight o'clock, you can see 10,000 lbs of lobster auctioned on the quay.

On Friday mornings, around nine or ten o'clock, the harbour is congested with boats unloading herring and prawn. The prawns, packed in wooden boxes, are lifted by derrick out of the holds. Two men waiting at the quay's edge beside each boat have boxes of crushed ice and a spade. One man slowly spills the prawns from the ship's box into empty tea-chests while the other shovels in ice, a spadeful to each layer. Then the chests are nailed and loaded on to waiting lorries. The prawn catch goes to Whitby and other centres, and not to Billingsgate.

The herring boats come in with brimming holds. The scene here is of much greater activity, the air clouded with screaming gulls. Lorries wait piled with crushed ice. The boats' derricks swing the herring ashore in round baskets, straight on to the lorries. At each lift, the fish in mid-air spill back on to the deck, drop into the sea and on to the quay (leaving the baskets still full) while the gulls go mad. They swoop, gobble, gulp, fight, and pursue each other in a state of frenzy. On the lorries, one man tips each basketful into wooden herring boxes while another shovels in ice. The filled boxes pile high on the lorries' backs. Thus far the gulls pick the spilled fish out of the sea, and are most wary of coming close to pick them off quay or deck. They know the drill: as the lorries fill up, and the lorrymen's attention slackens, or is diverted elsewhere, suddenly the gulls settle on the stacked boxes. They hastily peck through the ice, each to extract one, two or even three whole herring, gulping them down at incredible speed. The men take notice and wave them off: but now they are reluctant to fly and hover only to return. At last the men make a determined move; they advance on the gulls and throw ice-chips, at which the gulls get nervous and

243

The Companion Guide to the West Highlands of Scotland

may even drop a herring from the beak. And so the contest goes on.

Tucked away around the village are lobster ponds, kippering kilns (one may buy fresh and excellent fat kippers at the quayside), deep-freeze plant, and an ice-factory. Those of us who wish to catch our own fish can hire boats at the harbour. The rest of the port's activity is given over to passenger services. MacBrayne's steamers sail two days a week to Eigg, Rhum, and Canna, but now no more to Raasay and Portree in Skye. Their car-ferry plies daily to Armadale in Skye, but now no longer to South Uist and Barra. The former sailing to Stornoway now goes from Ullapool. Motor-boat cruises abound: to Loch nan Uamh and Loch Moidart, with time ashore to visit Castle Tioram; to Loch Scavaig in Skye, with time ashore to visit Loch Coruisk; to the islands of Eigg, Rhum, and Canna; to Loch Duich in Kintail, with time to visit Eilean Donan Castle; to Loch Hourn in Knoydart; and more importantly for the exploration of Morar and its neighbourhood, to Loch Nevis twice daily on four days of the week. This latter excursion allows one to land at Inverie in Knoydart, or on Mondays and Fridays at Tarbert, whence one could enjoy a ten-mile walk back to Mallaig down Loch Morarside. Motor-boats can be chartered privately to go anywhere along the coast.

On the east side of Mallaig Bay, a narrow road runs a mile round the coast to the tiny crofting community of **Mallaigvaig** on the outermost lip of Loch Nevis. It was here that Prince Charlie landed on his escape from Skye on 5th July 1746. A track high up on the steep hillside continues three-quarters of a mile round the corner to the croft-house of Mallaigmore. Known as the Burma Road, this track was made with enormous labour by the Mallaigmore crofter aided by army engineers. His white croft-house nestles in a little bay of Loch Nevis, from which a green glen runs up into the hills. A cow and some sheep graze on close-cropped fields. Half-way along the Burma Road you can climb directly up to the top of a hill called **Cruach Mhalaig,** 664 feet. This simple feat is strongly recommended for its wide view across the inner isles and the Knoydart mountains on the far side of Loch Nevis. Lower Loch Morar can be seen with its heavily wooded islands. Above them, the hill-lochs of Nostarie and Ghille Ghobaich form a beautifully twisting pattern adorned by several small islands. All along the outer Loch Nevis coast of North Morar, you can see salmon nets running out from the shore; lobster-pot buoys dot the sea in a long

244

sparse line till they vanish east. Southward, the coast of Arisaig spreads seaward peppered with skerries and fringed by its dozen sandy bays.

The horn of Sgor nan Ciche is not there to complete the scene. For that you must climb higher still. Close to your east rises Carn a' Ghobhair, 1,794 feet, a bare rocky hill whose foot is best reached by following the Burma Road all the way to Mallaigmore croft. The vast seaward panorama from the summit ranges south to north from the distant point of Ardnamurchan westward over the Small Isles to the great horse-shoe of the Cuillin, then far up the Sound of Sleat to Kintail. It commands the entire lengths of Loch Morar and Loch Nevis, and the cirque of mountains round their heads. Especially near and clear are the hills of Knoydart, that remote land, well-nigh roadless and without hotel or any other accommodation for the visitor, to which you are now bound.

CHAPTER 19

Knoydart

The Rough Bounds of Knoydart is the only big peninsula of the West Highlands to retain to the present day its ancient isolation. Not even General Wade and his successors, responsible for the pacification of the Highlands between the two risings and after, made any attempt to break in by road. Nor has any local authority tried since. No touring motorist may sully its thirty-six miles of shore or its five mountain glens and passes. Knoydart is still the wild west; herein is a great part of its fascination for walkers, and no small part of its beauty, whose peculiar quality is given less by the interior glens than by its two great sea-lochs and their mountain setting.

Knoydart is a knuckled fist of land rooted in the long arm of Glen Garry and bounded north and south by Loch Hourn and Loch Nevis, each thirteen miles long—the lochs of Hell and Heaven. The names are apt. Both share the typical sea-loch form, a wide outer loch separated by narrows from a narrow inner loch, but there all likeness ends. **Loch Hourn** is sombre even on days of sun; steep mountains flank it; they rise to 3,000 feet and more on both sides, scree-covered on the sharp slope of Ben Sgriol of Glenelg, and faced with thousand-foot cliffs on Ladhar Bheinn (pronounced Larven), which towers to 3,343 feet above the Knoydart shore. The inner loch is much narrower than Nevis's, twistier, and sharply sided with forested crag. No sun shines on the Knoydart shore for five months of winter. These close-crowding mountains give Loch Hourn the forbidding majesty of a Norwegian fiord seen nowhere else in this country so markedly. While they shadow Loch Hourn from the southward sun, they offer shelter from the north to **Loch Nevis**, which has for its southward wind-break the low but sufficient hills of Morar. Hence Nevis wears a totally different aspect, fair, open, sunny, and bayed, yet sheltered. No big mountains lend drama to the outer reaches, but the head is ringed by mountains of unusual beauty

246

as seen from the west. Sgor na Ciche, 3,410 feet, lifts to the clouds a spire sharper than any other of the mainland coast and is gracefully supported by lesser peaks.

These mountains border the head of Glen Garry and Loch Quoich. They are, as I noted earlier, the region of heaviest rainfall in the Highlands. The west half of the peninsula is less wet, but still gets eighty to a hundred inches, for the near neighbourhood of Skye, only three miles across the Sound of Sleat, does not help matters—the Cuillin are notorious cloud-gatherers. Despite rain, the Loch Nevis shores are among the kindliest of the west coast, and this is particularly true of **Inverie Bay** on the outer loch: a wide and spacious bay, but well-guarded by hill and headland. Growth is luxuriant. The hill-slopes above the village were splendidly wooded till a year or two ago, when they were clear-felled. One hopes they will be replanted. The land is potentially good for crops and live-stock, which used to be vegetables, corn, and cattle, sufficient, together with fishing, to support a thousand people. But these days ended at the Clearances. The principal land-use is now sheep-farming, deer-stalking, and some crofting and forestry work.

Around Inverie Bay and up the nearer glens there are short roads used by vans, tractors, lorries, and Landrovers on estate business. Otherwise all travel in Knoydart goes on foot. No accommodation is available. If you wish to explore the region fully you must camp, for while you can travel daily from Mallaig to Inverie by motor-boat, you would have only three and a half hours ashore.

From Inverie, three glens radiate into the mountains. The principal track cuts through the central mountain group by way of **Gleann an Dubh Lochain** to Barrisdale Bay on Loch Hourn. This glen is the central axis of Knoydart. Big mountain ranges lie to its either side: to its seaward, Ladhar Bheinn; to its Glengarry side, a chain of four, lifting in the middle to Luinne Bheinn and Meall Bhuidhe, both around 3,100 feet. These latter give a most enjoyable walk and are easily gained from the Dubh Lochan (Small Dark Loch) in the middle of the glen. They are linked by a continuous ridge enclosing a north-west corrie, which displays a spectacular example of glaciated rocks.

The second main track leads off Gleann an Dubh Lochain two miles from the Inverie pier. It strikes east up **Glen Meadail** then over a pass of 1,709 feet, whence it falls to the head of Loch Nevis. Walkers bound for Kinlochnevis may feel tempted to go instead by the shore of Loch Nevis, feeling that although it is nine miles (two more than by Glen Meadail) it saves a climb of 1,700 feet. Let them be warned: the shore track ends at Kylesknoydart (the narrows of the loch). The remaining four miles are tough going. The district's title of 'The Rough Bounds' has not been earned for nothing. They will be quicker and fresher at the end if they go by the hill-pass. The ideal way to reach Kinlochnevis is to use the Mallaig motor-boat. It sails from Inverie to the head of the loch on Mondays and Fridays around 2 p.m.

The third track from Inverie leads north over Mam Uidhe, 445 feet, to **Gleann na Guiserein**, a broad strath that runs from the base of Ladhar Bheinn to the west coast. Ladhar Bheinn is the most westerly Munro of the mainland. Its views over Loch Hourn to Kintail, and over the Sound of Sleat to Skye and the Isles, are worth much effort to win in fine weather. The name means the Forked Mountain, for the two-mile long-summit ridge sends a big secondary ridge two miles north-east. The ascent is made easily from upper Gleann na Guiserein by way of the mountain's south slope. Mountaineers will find that the more interesting route is from **Barrisdale Bay** on the north side. But Barrisdale is hard to reach. The best way is to approach it through Glenelg to Arnisdale on the north shore of Loch Hourn. The postman sails from there to Barrisdale thrice weekly and will take passengers. This north-east face of the mountain has in Coire Dhorrcail one of the deepest and most craggily splendid of Highland corries. From Barrisdale, move into the corrie by a path leading to the right bank of its burn, then make for the Bealach Coire Dhorrcail, 2,300 feet, on the left of the main ridge.

Other good tracks from Inverie lead westward round the coast to the numerous bays and old crofting communities overlooking the Sound of Sleat at Sandaig, Doune, Airor, Inverguseran, and so right round to Loch Hourn. From Barrisdale, two tracks lead inland up Glen Barrisdale and over the hills to Loch Quoich. A third and much more important track goes along the shore of inner Loch Hourn to Kinlochhourn, where it meets the **Glengarry** road-head. This point is the only one at which a motor-road touches the Knoydart border, and is the only one (in my own experience) where the few people inhabiting made it plain, without being hostile, that visitors were not welcome. The attitude so violates the known character of the Highlander that I must suppose it due to very strict instruction from the English estate-owner. It may therefore be worth noting that the tracks in and around Knoydart are rights of

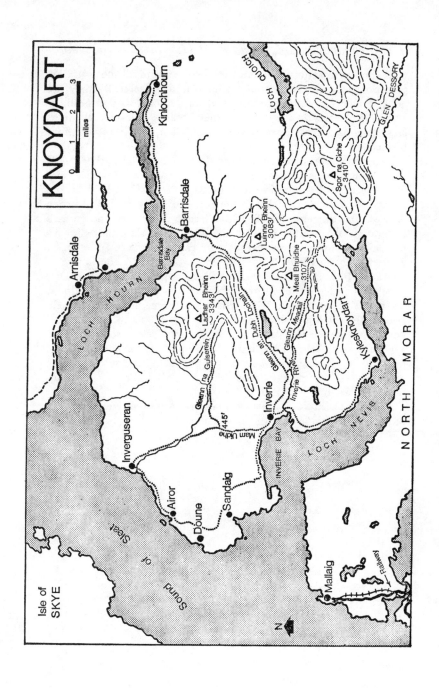

KNOYDART

miles
0 1 2 3

Isle of
SKYE

LOCH HOURN

Arnisdale

Kinlochhourn

LOCH QUOICH

Barrisdale
Barrisdale
Bay

GLEN DESSORY

Sgor na Ciche
3410'

Ladhar Bheinn
3343'

Luinne Bheinn
3083'

Meall Bhuidhe
3107'

Gleann na Guiserein

Dubh Lochan

Gleann an Dubh Lochain

Gleann Meadail

Inverguseran

Inverie
Inverie RN
INVERIE BAY

Mam Uidhe
1445'

(Kyles)Knoydart

Airor

Dóune

Sandaig

LOCH NEVIS

NORTH MORAR

Sound of Sleat

Mallaig

Railway

N

way. These numerous glens and tracks, free from all motor-traffic, give excellent walking through wild country. Scenically they are not a match for Kintail to the north or Moidart to the south, or lower Glen Garry to the east, but they breathe a peace that others lack; they have remoteness without desolation, and beauty without blemish.

In the days when population neared a thousand, the land belonged to the MacDonells of Glengarry. After the '45 there followed a long-drawn period of emigration to Canada, but the chief held his old ground from the Great Glen to the Sound of Sleat until 1840, when Aeneas, the sixteenth chief, sold all save Knoydart and himself emigrated to Australia. In 1846 there were still six hundred of his people in Knoydart, but in that year came the first of a series of disasters. Potato blight caused famine, worsened by the failure of migrating herring to arrive in Loch Nevis in their old number. Dire poverty then forced further emigration. Aeneas returned to die at his home at Inverie in 1852. His widow, Josephine MacDonell, cleared the remaining humans to make way for sheep, her purpose being to enhance the value of her property before selling it to a Lowland ironmaster. Four hundred people were evicted by force from Airor, Doune, Sandaig, and Inverie. Their holdings were destroyed and the people driven like cattle aboard a waiting transport supplied by the British government.

When we visit Knoydart we find that the brisk air of sea and mountain has made the land new again.

CHAPTER 20

Glenelg

From the Great Glen at Invergarry, the road to the Isles is your road to Glenelg, and also for that matter to Kintail, Applecross, and all the way up the seaboard to Cape Wrath. Glenelg is the huge headland between Loch Hourn and Loch Duich. Its outer coast is on the Sound of Sleat. The principal feature of its hinterland is the long chain of eighteen mountains that line the south flank of Glen Shiel on the frontier of Ross. The main mass of Glenelg is thus in Invernessshire, but the north shore is in Kintail of Ross. For practical purpose I include that ultra-montane strip of Glenelg as Glenelg itself: all is one headland.

You leave the Great Glen by Loch Garry. On climbing north up the new double-carriageway to the heights overlooking Loch Quoich, you cross a hill-pass above **Loch Loyne**—a long pass from which the mountain chain fringing the Ross frontier is seen to westward as a wild tangle of crowded peaks rather than the orderly range it is. When shadowed by cloud the peaks loom dark and desolate across the silver sheet of Loch Loyne. You are now crossing their eastern end to come round to their north side. The road falls to the river Moriston, which drains from Loch Cluanie to Loch Ness. **Loch Cluanie** means the Loch of the Meadows, but the former meadows have mostly vanished following the damming of the loch. Below the dam you turn sharp left to enter the county of Ross. Loch Cluanie is seven miles long. At its head stands the old Cluanie Inn, beyond which you cross the broad backbone of Scotland to the head of **Glen Shiel** at 889 feet.

The main geographical feature of the region is this enormous trough cutting forty miles over the Highland watershed from Loch Alsh on the west coast to the Great Glen by way of Loch Duich, Glen Shiel, Glen Cluanie, and Glen Moriston, thus to Loch Ness and the Moray Firth. Both sides of Glen Cluanie are flanked by

251

mountain ranges. On the south, seven tops exceed 3,000 feet, on the north ten tops, which thrust spurs equally high into upper Glen Affric. They are grassy hills with little visible rock. Their height and distance from the coast give them a heavy cover of snow into late spring, when the traverse of the seven linked summits on the south side becomes one of the better ridge-walks of the West Highlands. All Cluanie is under deer, hence hill-walking may be restricted in the stalking season (mid-August to mid-October). The best centre for exploring these hills and fishing on the loch is Cluanie Hotel. A quarter of a mile beyond the hotel on the right-hand side, vestiges can be seen of the military road built between 1750 and 1784 by Wade's successor, General Caulfeild, to link Fort Augustus with the Bernera barracks at Glenelg.

The old narrow road that used to writhe its way down Glen Shiel has now been replaced by one of double width. It gives an exhilarating plunge as though down a titanic Cresta Run in a trough whose walls are over 3,000 feet high, and draw so close at one stretch that there is barely room between them for road and river. The most inspiring sight of all from upper Glen Shiel is to a lance-like peak in the lower glen. This is Faochaig, whose grace of form shames its name, which means the Whelk. Its relative nearness obscures the greater and craggier virtues of the Saddle. Together they appear to block all exit from the glen. Half-way between Cluanie and Loch Duich, and close below Glenshiel Wood, you cross the river Shiel for the first time at **Bridge of Shiel**, and here enter Kintail. A battle was fought at the bridge in 1719 between the Redcoats and the Jacobites, whose force included two hundred Spaniards. I deal with this incident in the chapter on Kintail, noting it here to explain that from these Spanish troops came the name of the mountain directly above Bridge of Shiel on the north side—Sgurr nan Spainteach, the Peak of the Spaniards. It is the first top of the Five Sisters of Kintail. They extend six miles down the glen, rising to their highest point on Sgurr Fhuaran, 3,505 feet. Despite their distinctive name, they are in fact only the western (and not even the highest) tops of a continuous ridge running twenty miles from Glen Moriston. As seen from the shores of Glenelg they are one of the more memorable sights of the seaboard.

At the foot of the glen, the river Shiel spreads out in a little loch, whose shores are in June gay with yellow-flags, and just half a mile farther flows under Shiel Bridge at the head of Loch Duich. Here you fork left for Glenelg. Almost at once the road again forks, the

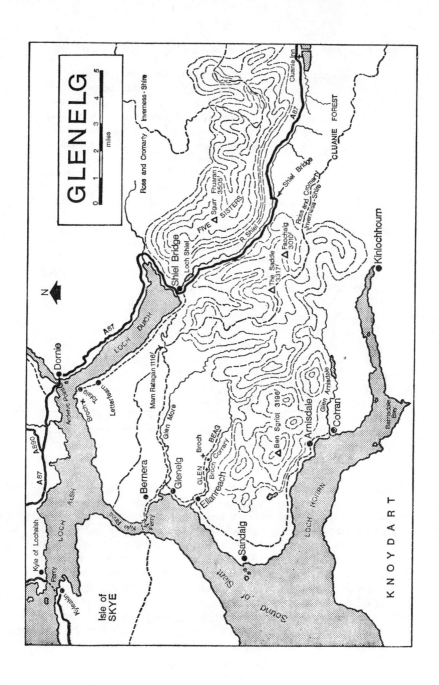

GLENELG

miles
0 1 2 3 4 5

N

Kyle of Lochalsh
Ferry
Kyleakin
Isle of SKYE

A890
A87
A87
LOCH ALSH
LOCH DUICH
Dornie

Kirk's Point
Totaig
Broch +
Letterfearn
A87
Mam Ratagan 1116'
Glen More
Bernera
Ferry
Bernera Barracks
Glenelg
GLEN BEG
Broch +
Broch Corary
Ellanreach
Sandaig
Sound of Sleat

Shiel Bridge
Loch Shiel
FIVE SISTERS
Sgurr Fhuaran 3505'
R. Shiel
The Saddle 3317'
Faochaig 3010'
Shiel Bridge
A87
CLUANIE FOREST
Cluanie Inn

Ross and Cromarty Inverness-Shire
Ross and Cromarty Inverness-Shire

Ben Sgriol 3196'
Glen Arnisdale
Arnisdale
Corran
Barrisdale Bay

LOCH HOURN
KNOYDART
Kinlochhourn

left-hand branch over the frontier mountain-range by way of the
Mam Ratagan pass, and so to Glenelg proper, and the right-hand
branch along the Kintail shore to end five miles away on the point
of **Totaig**. Totaig marks the junction of Loch Duich with Loch
Alsh and is matched by Ardelve Point on the farther shore. The
ferry that used to cross the narrows to Dornie, passing close to
the walls of Eilean Donan Castle, no longer exists.

Totaig has a fort of its own, the remains of an Iron Age broch,
three-quarters of a mile west (one must walk) near a little bay of
Loch Alsh called Ob-Inag. All brochs are built as circular tapering
towers, and this one is named Caisteal Grugaig. The traditional
story is that the owner was a lady whose sons, Telve and Trodden,
built or possessed the two more famous and better-preserved brochs
in Gleann Beag, in central Glenelg. I postpone discussion of brochs
till we visit the latter, noting meantime that the Grugaig broch
differs from the others by its thicker walls (nine feet), bigger stones,
and by its having a huge triangular block, which cannot weigh
less than a ton, above the four-foot doorway.

The road back towards the head of the loch takes you through the
clachan of Letterfearn. You look out between birch and alder
groves to the Five Sisters, lightly veiled, it may often be, in blue
haze. Dead bracken and the fresh green of birch along the shore
reflect fierily in the nearer water, mostly in tiny bays, but towards
the centre of the loch the colours dim in the brightness of the rippled
surface: there the mountains lie inverted, their flanks, corries, and
every shadowed crag spreading subtly different tints—all this giving
depth and distance in what otherwise might seem short space—
until suddenly the land leaps up. The scene is no less excellent from
the top of **Mam Ratagan at 1,116 feet**. The climb up is one-in-six
with hairpin bends but a good surface. The once superb views to
be enjoyed on the way up and down this hill have been lost by the
ill-service of the Forestry Commission, who have planted their
conifers hard alongside the road. Little can be seen till you near the
top, where you clear the treetops. The pass is the county boundary.
From this point the Five Sisters are seen at their best, standing in
file over the long pool of Loch Duich, and holding their heads stiffly
upright. Sgurr Fhuaran dominates the group, her face lifted back,
averted from the dark defile of Glen Shiel.

When you cross to the west side of the pass, you drop through the
Ratagan Forest to the slopes of Glen More and win a glimpse from
the high ground of Glenelg's interior. Like Knoydart it is rough and

mountainous country. The principal mountain of Glenelg is **Beinn Sgriol**, 3,196 feet, on the shore of Loch Hourn, to which it presents an extremely bare face of crag and scree. From all other angles it is a bold peak of good shape, hollowed by immense north corries.

Three important glens penetrate these hills and radiate paths into the farthermost corries. Two strike in from the coast, and the first and greatest of these is **Glen More**, where we now are. It is heavily forested in its upper part, and becomes a farmed strath in its lower. The second is **Gleann Beag**, two miles south from and parallel to Glen More. It gives access by path to the north face of Ben Sgriol, to Arnisdale on Loch Hourn, and to Kinlochhourn. The third is Glen Arnisdale, running east from Loch Hourn to give a backstairs route to Kinlochhourn. Numerous other tracks allow much opportunity to walkers who wish to penetrate wild and lonely country.

You descend to the flat floor of Glen More. Half a mile short of Glenelg village a road forks two miles right to Glenelg ferry, first through the fields bordering the Sound of Sleat, where you pass the ruins of the old Bernera barracks, in which Hanoverian troops were quartered for seventy years from 1722, and then along the rocky shore of **Kyle Rhea**. The road ends at the ferry, and Skye lies only five hundred yards across the strait. In former days cattle were ferried from Skye across the kyle, then over the Mam Ratagan to the great cattle trysts of Falkirk. This was the route to Skye taken by Dr. Johnson and Boswell on their Highland tour of 1773. It can still be the quickest ferry for the motorist. The more usual route to Skye is across Kyle Akin, at the farther, north-west shore of Loch Alsh, where the ferry-boats are bigger and numerous. But the very popularity of that route means that on busy days long queues forming at Kyle of Loch Alsh cause much delay. In such conditions it may be better to cross at Glenelg. But this ferry does not run in winter.

The strait is named from Riadh, a Fingalian hero of the third century, whose brother Acunn may have given his name to Kyle Akin between Skye and Lochalsh.

The village of **Glenelg** lies on a bay at the foot of Glen More. You approach through a wooded avenue to find a dozen harled houses set under a low heathery hill among deciduous trees. It has a post office, store, and a church that last century gave the village the name of Kirkton. The houses have no frontage to the sea. Access to the stony beach is cut off by fenced hayfields, but just behind the village the road breaks to the shore where a small harbour for rowing boats and dinghies is formed by shingle spits.

One mile south you reach the foot of **Gleann Beag** at Ellanreach House. A narrow side-road runs two miles east up the glen to the brochs of Dun Telve and Dun Trodden. These call for careful attention, for they are the best of their kind on the mainland. The floor of the glen is flat, and for this part of Scotland, luxuriant. A river flows down from its distant source high in the north corrie of Ben Sgriol. All down its lower reaches the fields are deep in grass and hay, their green and gold contrasting with the dark pines and larches of Ellanreach Forest on the south hill-slope. The road winds through woods of hazel and alder, which become bright in springtime with primrose and massed bluebell. It is then a road to be walked, not driven.

The first broch, **Dun Telve**, is beautifully sited beside the river, where four ancient sycamores stand on flat grassland. The tower rises to 33 feet, but only a third of the circumference reaches that height. The rest has been plundered for local building long before the brochs were taken under the care of the Ministry of Works. The great skill and patience shown by these Iron Age masons is a matter for marvel. The walls are made double, coursed by galleries spiralling up within their thickness, narrowing as the walls taper to the top, where they become a single wall. The tower, like others of its kind, would originally be 40 or 50 feet high and unroofed. On the outer wall there are no windows or other opening except the doorway, about 4 feet high. These hollow walls are well exposed to view since the broch is now a half-section. The outer wall has been built concave: it slopes gently inward to half its own height, then slopes gently out to become vertical or slightly overhanging. The surface is unbroken, the stones being laid without gaps despite lack of mortar.

You enter the broch on its west or down-river side between large stones that once gave an approach-passage 13 feet long, 4 feet wide, and 5 feet high. The door has socket holes to each side with a guard chamber on the right. The courtyard within is approximately 33 feet in diameter, overlooked by two windows on the inner wall. One can no longer climb up the inner galleries, but it seems clear that these were too small ever to have been used as living quarters. They were for shelter during defence, more especially at night. At the base and again at the top are two stone ledges, the purpose of which is one of the many puzzles that all brochs present.

The date given for Dun Telve is 'Iron Age', which in Scotland means 450 B.C.–A.D. 400, qualified by the words 'during the Roman occupation', which in Scotland began in A.D. 80 and lasted till the end of the second century. Archaeologists and historians do not agree on the purpose of brochs, of which there are five hundred in Scotland. Most of them lie in the north—Shetland and Orkney Islands, Caithness, Sutherland, Ross, the Outer Hebrides, and Skye, diminishing in number as far south as Tiree, and nearly all are by the shore, not inland as in Gleann Beag. A few authorities argue that the brochs were both offensive and defensive posts used by sea-robbers, but the evidence routs that notion: for there is good evidence from the relics found in them that the occupants farmed the land and were not only seafarers. That being so, the brochs would most likely be built by the Picts who would use them as temporary keeps, or places of safe-keeping for themselves, their women and children, and (less likely) livestock. Where set on advantageous points on the coast they would also serve as look-out towers to give warning of enemy approach. The interior yards are by no means big enough to enfold a community's livestock—these would more probably be driven off into the hills when a raid threatened.

The intriguing question is, who was the enemy? Viking settlements did not occur on the north and west coasts until A.D. 800. But there is now ample evidence that their raids began very much earlier, probably as early as 100 A.D., and this is substantiated by the pattern of the brochs' distribution. They are concentrated in the north, which would be the first land subject to raids from Norway—and from nowhere else. There was no organized kingdom in Norway in these days. The early Vikings were illiterate sea-rovers who kept no records. But rock-carvings of 1000 B.C. and earlier in both Norway and Sweden depict multi-oared longships capable of long ocean voyages. That such men and ships failed to arrive off Scotland in considerable numbers until nearly two thousand years later is not to be believed.

It would appear, then, that the brochs were built for protection against Viking pirates on hit-and-run raids. They were clearly never intended to withstand a long siege—they are too cramped for space, nor are wells often found in them. The protection they gave was excellent, their design cunning. The outer walls were unscaleable, and any unfortunate raiders who were unlucky enough to gain the interior yard would find themselves trapped there, as if at the bottom of a deep well, completely at the mercy of the defenders above.

The second broch, **Dun Trodden**, lies only a few hundred yards up the glen on the hillside above the farm of Corrary. Like its brother, it is incomplete. Following inhabitation by the Picts, Glenelg became one of the earliest lands of the MacLeods of Skye, who derive their crest, a bull, and their motto *Hold Fast*, from Malcolm, the third chief, who armed with a dagger fought and slew a wild bull in the woods of Glenelg. Later, Glenelg was occupied by the Clan MacRae, and came under the sway of their allies the MacKenzies of Kintail, earls of Seaforth.

From Ellanreach at the foot of the glen, the main south-going road keeps to high ground all the way down the west coast till it finally descends to **Loch Hourn**. It thus commands wide views of the Inner Hebrides down the Sound of Sleat, but the seaward views have repeatedly been screened off and their enjoyment lost to us by forestry fences and the planting of conifers against the road. This unfortunate encroachment threatens further loss as the trees grow taller.

At Loch Hourn, you traverse a bayed shore between several islands and the vast, scree-strewn slope of Ben Sgriol. The road passes through the village of **Arnisdale** to end at the crofts of Corran. A rough and stony footpath continues four miles farther up the lochside to the narrows, giving at last a clear view into the splendid north-east corrie of Ladhar Bheinn. That north coast of Knoydart is accessible by the postman's motor-boat from Corran to Barrisdale Bay.

Set on the south shore of its little bay, Corran is one of the most beautiful of West Highland clachans. The peaks of the Black Cuillin, although distant, are seen to better advantage from here than from anywhere else on the mainland coast. From a foreground of short turf and wild roses, or of fields of buttercup and clover, or of simple cottage gardens crowded with flowers, almost every peak of the range can be seen through the wide mouth of Loch Hourn.

CHAPTER 21

Skye

The Island of Skye is so nearly a part of the mainland that recently there has been much talk by local authorities of bridging the half-mile strait of Kyle Akin between the villages of Kyleakin and Kyle of Lochalsh. The more southerly strait of Kyle Rhea, off Glenelg, is only half as wide, but not considered for bridging because the main traffic goes by the north route, served by better roads, a railway from Inverness (which carries cars and is linked with the car-sleeper train from England), and a steamer pier beside the Kyle ferry. Convenient as the bridge would be, let us hope it may never be built. Skye owes much of its fame and attractive power—nearly half a million people cross the straits annually—to an island magic that any bridge would diminish. It would become another peninsula.

Sixty miles long, yet so riven that no land is more than five miles from the sea, Skye has little body and more arms than the Goddess Kali. Six big peninsulas spread out into the Minch: Trotternish and Vaternish northward, Duirinish and Minginish westward, and to the south, Strathaird and Sleat (pronounced Slate). The Gaels, who had a quick eye to the shape of land as seen from the hills, called it the Winged Isle (Eilean a Sgiathanach). The Vikings approaching by sea saw no wing-like shapes. Like all seamen before and after they saw land heavily capped with cloud over the Cuillin. They named it Skuyö (pronounced Sky-a), the Cloud Island.

Skye is for the greater part bare and treeless, the interior high and hilly and almost all of it grazed, for Skye is the most heavily crofted ground of the inner seaboard. Its 7,500 people live on the coastal strips. At the private estates of the MacLeod and Mac-Donald chiefs, at Dunvegan and Armadale, there are large woodlands, and elsewhere the Forestry Commission has 9,000 acres of conifer plantations, but most of Skye is in the hands of farmers and crofters. If you cross to Skye by the car-ferry from Mallaig to

Armadale in Sleat, your first impression is of likeness to Mull at Craignure, for this is sheltered ground, several weeks ahead of north Skye at harvest-time.

Half a mile north of the pier, Armadale Castle standing deep in deciduous woods was built in 1815 as the seat of Lord MacDonald, who still owns. It is not open to the public. A short way beyond, a side-road crosses Sleat to the west coast. Leaving this meantime, continue north up the coast to **Knock Bay**, four miles from Armadale. On a rocky mound by the shore you see the ivy-clad stump of Camus Castle, which belonged originally to the MacLeods. When Norway formally ceded the Isles to Scotland in 1266, Skye went to Angus I, King of the Isles, who made grant to Leod, son of the Norwegian prince, Olav the Black. But in the late fourteenth century Clan Donald took Sleat back from the MacLeods by force and reoccupied Camus Castle. When William of Orange sent two warships to the Sound of Sleat in 1690 to try to bring in Sir Donald MacDonald, his clan fared better than their brothers of Glen Coe. They captured the naval landing party—who had burned down the chief's old house at Armadale—and strung them on gibbets made of their own oars on the beach by the castle.

Less than a mile on from Knock, another side-road strikes across Sleat. Take this one if the sky is clear, for the west coast offers better views of the Cuillin than you can have from sea-level at any other place in Skye. You reach the coast at **Ord**, where there is a small hotel above a bayful of islets. A mile and half south at the Tokavaig crofts there is a bay with a red sandstone shore. The north point has an islet-stack crowned by the ancient ruin of Dun Sgathaich (pronounced Skaich), once the most important stronghold in Skye. First it belonged to the Norse kings of Man (from where they ruled the Hebrides), then to the MacLeods and finally the MacDonalds. You cross to it by scrambling over a rock moat, for the arched bridge is unsafe, then up to grassy battlements. They give, like Ord, Sleat's finest view of the Cuillin. You look out over Loch Slapin and the back of Strathaird peninsula to the twenty-odd peaks of the main ridge, and to the Red Hills to their right—one of the great sights of Scotland when the sun sets behind them. A mile and a half farther you pass Tarskavaig, the largest crofting community of the Sleat coast; there the road turns inland back to Armadale.

Three miles north of Knock, **Isleornsay** is Sleat's finest village. It lies five hundred yards off the main road in a backwater, where a small headland with pier and inn faces the tidal island of Ornsay.

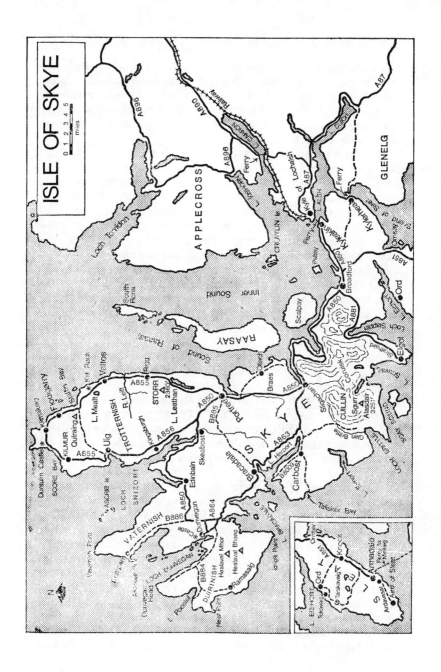

ISLE OF SKYE

0 1 2 3 4 5 miles

APPLECROSS

GLENELG

Loch Torridon

Railway

A896

A890

A896

Ferry

Inner Sound

Ferry

Kyle of Lochalsh

A87

Ferry

Kyle Akin

A87

Kyleakin

A890

Balmacara

Broadford

Kyleakin

Plockton

A851

Ord

Loch Slapin

Elgol

Strathaird

Loch na Cille

South Rona

RAASAY

Sound of Raasay

Scalpay

A850

A881

SLIGACHAN

A863

CUILLIN

Sgurr
Alasdair
3251'

Glen Brittle

LOCH BRITTLE

Soay Sound

Braes

Ollach

A855

Storr
2360'

L. Leathan

R. Lealt

Kingsburgh

A856

L. Mealt

Quiraing

KILMUIR

DUNTULM

SCORE BAY

Staffin Bay

Kilt Rock

Valtos

Uig

TROTTERNISH

Portree

B885

Sligachan

Skeabost

Bracadale

L. Harport

Carbost

B8009

Talisker Bay

SKYE

Edinbain

A850

B886

Dunvegan

Castle

A864

VATERNISH

SNIZORT

LOCH DUNVEGAN

Waternish Point

DUIRINISH

Healaval Mhor

Healaval Bheag

B884

Ramasaig

Dunvegan Head

MacLeod's Tables

L. Poolitiel

Neist Point

Idrigil Point

N

(inset)

SLEAT

Ord

Isleornsay

Knock

Armadale
Ferry to
Mallaig

Tarskavaig

Ardvasar

Point of Sleat

L. EISHORT

A851

The croft-houses line a road running south, from which their tiny crofts stripe the slope falling to another bay named Camas Croise. The whole forms one of the few bits of old-time Skye now remaining on this developing island. Your view across the sound is to Knoydart, where the mountains of Ladhar Bheinn and Ben Sgriol stand high to either side of Loch Hourn.

The north-going road now crosses the Sleat isthmus to the east coast and runs out on flat green fields at **Broadford.** An airstrip three miles to its south between road and sea is served by thrice weekly *Loganair* flights from Glasgow and Inverness. Broadford is Skye's biggest crofting township, a long straggling village formed by the coalescing of several smaller townships—it is hard to know where it begins or ends or is called something different. It 'has several good hotels and shops, and is a convenient centre from which to explore south Skye. Close-to it appears a drab place—Skye has no modern buildings worth notice—redeemed by the Red Hills to the west, Beinn na Caillich to the east, and Applecross in front. The main east coast road from Kyleakin to Portree runs through the centre, but the road you should explore first is the one westward to Strathaird and Elgol.

Strathaird peninsula divides Loch Slapin from Loch Scavaig. The narrow and hilly road out of Broadford turns the Red Hills to their south then falls to their west shore at the village of Torrin on Loch Slapin. Here the Red Hills and the first of the Black Cuillin confront each other across the head of the loch. Both are igneous rock, but the Red Hills are rounded, made of a pink and crumbly granite, whereas the Black Cuillin are spiky, appearing plum-black only in shadow—the true colour of the rock varies from pale grey to chocolate brown. The two Cuillin peaks you see across Loch Slapin are Blaven, 3,042 feet, and its north top Clach Glas, 2,590 feet, outliers of the main range that lies behind them, and from which they are cut off by the seven-mile length of Glen Sligachan. The traverse of Blaven's pinnacled ridge is one of the best in the Cuillin, but that is work for rock-climbers. An easy way to climb Blaven is by its long south ridge from Camasunary at the Loch Scavaig end of Glen Sligachan. You can reach **Camasunary** by walking two miles along the hill-track to Coruisk, and find the start of this track four miles down the Loch Slapin road on the hill beyond Kilmarie burn. It crosses the peninsula's back close under Ben Meabost. When you breast the pass you see the Black Cuillin at five miles' range—the most dramatic introduction you can have—

unless you climb Ben Meabost, 1,128 feet, whose top is only a mile south.

Beyond Camasunary, the track contours round the base of Sgurr na Stri to the shore of Loch Scavaig, and so to Loch Coruisk at the heart of the range. Half a mile short of Coruisk is the famous 'bad step' across the face of a crag. The usual mistake made is to try to cross too high. The step is free of any difficulty at 15 feet above high water mark.

The easiest approach to Coruisk is from the road-end at Elgol. Elgol is the point to which Prince Charlie was guided in July 1746 by the aged chief MacKinnon, whose clan had held Strathaird since 1354, and so escaped back to the Morar coast. A minor road from Elgol goes a mile and a half across the tip of the peninsula to the east coast facing Sleat, and there you can visit the famous Spar Cave, described by Scott in his *Lord of the Isles*, Note 22. The cave (marked on both one-inch and half-inch maps) can also be visited from Elgol by motor-boat. It lies under much fissured cliffs below the crofts of Glasnakille. The lofty roof and walls used to be hung with semi-transparent stalactites, which have been destroyed by tourists. The inmost chamber has a circular pond like white marble.

In summer, motor-boats sail from Elgol daily to **Loch Scavaig**, and land passengers on the rocks near the Scavaig river, which flows out of Loch Coruisk. Loch Scavaig is one of the three main gateways to the Cuillin. The other two, Sligachan and Glen Brittle, are little less spectacular, but not like Scavaig leading directly into the middle. When inner Loch Scavaig is entered, the nearer peaks hide the others behind. The bay is studded with skerries, which make entry difficult for a big ship. The innermost islet, Eilean Glas, guards the mouth of Scavaig river and gives excellent protection to small boats, which can lie safely in the channel even in high southerly winds.

Loch Scavaig, seen from the rocks of its shore, is green, deep, and clear—a perfect swimming pool, if a chilly one, complete with a sandy beach on its east side under Sgurr na Stri. **Loch Coruisk**, on the other hand, ringed by the Cuillin horse-shoe, is of royal blue rippled with silver. The loch is a mile and a half long by a quarter of a mile wide, and its surface 26 feet above sea-level. From the landing stage at Scavaig a boggy track leads up to its mouth, where stepping-stones allow one to cross the river, if not in spate. Rough stony tracks lead up both sides of the loch to Coire Uisg, the Water Corrie, usually abbreviated to Coruisg, which extends two miles to the main ridge, flat and grassy for the first mile, then steepening to the great upsurge of naked rock.

Nearly two-thirds of Skye place-names come from the old Norse. The name **Cuillin** is a plural noun from Kjöllen, meaning Keel-shaped Ridges, and is accurately descriptive. Ranges of the same name are found in Iceland and Sweden. The pseudo-derivation from Cu chuill fhionn (or Cuchullin), Hero of the Fair Hair, is from the Gaelic story-tellers.

The Cuillin are made of two rocks, a coarsely crystalline gabbro, dear to the heart of mountaineers because tough and reliable, and a smooth basalt, which they detest because slippery when wet. The two rocks are present in the Cuillin in equal surface quantity: both originate in lava flows. The basalt has cooled rapidly from the lava poured at the earth's surface; the gabbro has cooled slowly under its cover, taking thus a crystalline texture. The gabbro has since been exposed by water erosion, sculpted by glaciers, and proving more resistant to weather than basalt now projects on twenty-four sharp peaks, which form this seven-mile horse-shoe. The traverse of the main ridge gives 10,000 feet of ascent and the best day's mountaineering in Britain.

A hundred years ago, artists were more numerous around Loch Coruisk than climbers, drawn here by the publication of Sir Walter Scott's *Lord of the Isles*. There was a time when almost every British landscape painter of eminence felt bound to do Coruisk—Turner, Horatio MacCulloch, MacWhirter, Alfred Williams, George Fennel Robson, and many another. They and the writers of the time so falsified the face of Scotland that there was later difficulty in convincing visitors of the evidence of their own eyes. It is still necessary to explode the myth of 'Gloomy Coruisk' (except in foul weather). Far from being shadowed and overhung by beetling crags, the loch has a fairly open situation, for the Cuillin lie a couple of miles back. In spring and summer it is sunlit for the better part of the day, for it faces south ('Here the sun never shone since creation', wrote Dr. John MacCulloch in his *Western Islands*). In summer the banks of the loch are alight with wild flowers, green shrubs, and long grasses, and the great bowl of Coruisg becomes a green oasis ('No tree, nor shrub, nor plant, nor flower', wrote Scott, 'Nor aught of vegetative power'.)

The principal peaks of the Coruisk horse-shoe, as you see them from the Scavaig river, are:

1. At the two outer ends, Gars-bheinn, 2,934 feet, on your left-

hand side, and Sgurr na Stri, 1,623 feet, on your right-hand side.
2. Behind Gars-bheinn on the left arm of the horse-shoe, Sgurr
Dubh na da Bheinn, 3,069 feet, and Sgurr Dubh Mor, 3,089 feet,
from which a long rock ridge falls toward Loch Coruisk.
3. Circling the head of the great corrie, from left to right, Sgurr
na Banachdich, 3,167 feet, Sgurr Thormaid, 3,040 feet, Sgurr a'
Ghreadaidh, 3,190 feet, with huge buttresses falling to Coruisg,
then Sgurr a' Mhadaidh, 3,010 feet, with four tops, and well to its
right the sharp and double-pointed Bidein Druim nan Ramh,
2,850 feet. From Bidein a long south-east ridge runs down the side
of Coruisk to end at Sgurr na Stri on Loch Scavaig.

More than half the Cuillin, including their highest point, Sgurr
Alasdair, 3,251 feet, is thus invisible. But nearly all the peaks can
be seen if you climb Sgurr na Stri from its north-west side, and then
follow its long ridge towards Bidein Druim nan Ramh. Return the
same way—attempt no short cuts.

The road from Broadford to **Sligachan** at the north end of
the Cuillin passes Sconser, which has a passenger ferry to the isle
of Raasay. Sligachan Inn is one of the best hotels in the Highlands,
strategically placed on the ring road that circles Skye's central
'body' and links Dunvegan on the west with Portree on the east.
Sligachan used to be the main centre for Cuillin climbing, but that
has shifted west to Glen Brittle. The inn is famous too for its trout
and salmon fishing. Three miles to its south rises Sgurr nan Gillean,
3,167 feet, the northmost peak of the Cuillin, more heavily pinnacled
on its subsidiary ridges than any other Scottish mountain and rising
to a fine spire at the summit. To its left-hand side, Glen Sligachan
runs south to Loch Scavaig, giving access by footpaths to Blaven
on one side and to the main Cuillin ridge on the other, or to Loch
Coruisk (seven miles in three hours) over the Druim Hain ridge.

Few of the Cuillin tops can be reached without rock-climbing.
But one that can is Bruach na Frithe, 3,143 feet, in a four-mile
walk of three hours from Sligachan. Follow the track south-west up
the Allt Dearg Mor to the Bealach a' Mhaim, 1,132 feet, then climb
the mountain's north-west ridge to the summit. The view is among
the best of the Cuillin. Return by walking down east towards the
Bhasteir Tooth, then descend the grassy Fhionn Choire back to
Sligachan.

The path up to the Bealach a' Mhaim, if followed onward, leads
to **Glen Brittle** on the west side of the range. The motor-road goes
west to the head of Loch Harport, then south over 600-foot hills

through new conifer plantations at the head of Glen Brittle. The north Cuillin peaks are now close and every fissure of their stark rock is seen clearly. Lower Glen Brittle is farmed, the finest and most fertile glen of the Minginish peninsula. It ends on the great bay of Loch Brittle. In all Skye there are no more than four or five sandy beaches, mostly grey-black, and Glen Brittle has the best of them. The foreshore in summer may carry 150 tents or more, and nearly all the campers are climbers. The very best of the Cuillin rock-climbing lies at this end of the range, especially on the 1,000-foot face of Sron na Ciche—a south-west spur of Sgurr Alasdair. If you want to climb Alasdair—the highest peak in Skye and the finest viewpoint in the Highlands and Islands—you can do so without rock-climbing. Follow the path from the camp-site into Coire Lagain, which is like the courtyard of a giant's castle, and from there climb the Great Stone Shoot to the left of the summit-buttress. This gully has more than a thousand feet of loose scree, the ascent is drudgery beyond compare, and if you haven't dropped dead you will regret none of it at the top.

At the head of Loch Harport, the ring road turns north up the Bracadale coast to **Dunvegan**. Here two peninsulas, Vaternish and Duirinish, thrust seven or eight miles into the Minch, and Dunvegan lies between them, at the head of Loch Dunvegan. Duirinish to the west is distinguished by the two truncated cones of 1,600 feet named MacLeod's Tables. From the top of the farthest, one can see the full length of the Outer Hebrides from the Butt of Lewis to Barra Head (130 miles) and every Cuillin peak across the wild shores of Loch Bracadale.

Dunvegan has more variety of scene than any other region of Skye in its mountains, woodland, crofts, and moors, and rugged shores and islands; above all these it is famous for a building of no unusual architectural value, but of an historical interest that attracts many thousands of visitors annually—**Dunvegan Castle**, the seat of Clan Leod. It is the oldest inhabited castle of Scotland. The MacLeods have lived here continuously for seven hundred years, and still do.

The castle stands on a crag facing the sea, split off from the land by a natural moat scarped by hand. This rock was the site of a ninth-century Norse fortress. On the annexation of the Hebrides by the King of Scots in 1266, Olav the Black's son Leod married the daughter of the Norse jarl whose seat was Dunvegan, and thus founded the Skye dynasty through his son Tormod MacLeod. The castle you now see was begun in the fifteenth century, consisting then of a great wall of enceinte (like Mingary) of which only a detached ruin survives at the west point of the rock. The keep was built in the first half of the sixteenth century by the seventh chief, Alasdair Crotach, or Hunchback—he had been wounded in battle by an axe-blow between the shoulders. The dungeon wing of this keep was carried up as a lofty square tower, which gave the building most of the good effect it possesses. Alterations and additions continued into the nineteenth century, despite which many early features have been preserved. The ancient gateway and portcullis are on the south side of the rock facing the sea. The modern doorway, by which you enter, is on the landward side, where the moat is now bridged. The castle is open daily in the afternoons only, except on Saturdays and Sundays.

The old keep with its 9-foot thick walls is now modernized, and the hall on the first floor has become a drawing room. A guardroom off the drawing room has a dungeon under its floor—a vertical shaft 6 feet wide cut 16 feet deep into the castle's rock. A flagstone trap covers the mouth, but this is removed on visiting days. These rooms were the scene of a frightsome incident in 1558. The MacLeods produced a peculiarly rich crop of chiefs powerful in noble or evil character. The worst specimen (perhaps) was the bastard tenth chief, Iain Dubh. When John the ninth chief died in 1557 he left a daughter Mary as only child. While John's brothers and kinsmen were away at the funeral, Iain Dubh seized Dunvegan. When the mourners returned he killed his two brothers and three nephews and threw the others into the dungeon. They were still lying there when Campbell of Argyll intervened to safeguard the interest of Mary, of whom he was guardian. Iain Dubh invited eleven of the Campbell chiefs up to Dunvegan to discuss this delicate matter, and pretended to accept their terms. At a farewell banquet in the hall the Campbells were served at the end with goblets of blood, then dirked where they sat.

Among the treasures displayed are Rory Mor's drinking horn and the Fairy Flag. Sir Rory Mor was the famous thirteenth chief, who ruled around 1620. His horn appears to be that of a long-horned Kyloe ox, rimmed with chased silver and holding five pints. At the inauguration of a chief it is filled to the brim with claret, which the new chief must down in one draught. To make this feat possible nowadays a false bottom is inserted.

The Fairy Flag, properly called the Bratach Sith, is the most famous relic in Skye. By traditional story it was given to William, the fourth chief, by his fairy lover. Originally of strong yellow silk with red elf spots, it is now extremely fragile but retains a delicate beauty of colour. Over the centuries portions have been torn off by thieving visitors and the tattered banner is now protected behind glass. It has three principal properties: unfurled on the battlefield it brings MacLeod victory; spread on his marriage-bed it grants children; and hoisted at Dunvegan it brings herring into the loch. The gift of the Bratach Sith was made on condition of its display on only three kinds of emergency: when the clan faced defeat in battle; when the sole heir was in danger of death; or when the clan was near extinction. Thus far it has been displayed twice in battle and victory followed. It is thought to be a consecrated banner of an order of Knights Templars, and during the Crusades to have been taken as a prize from the Saracens.

The woods east of the castle are open to the public. They were planted in 1780. If you have been long in the treeless Hebrides you will be glad of this chance to walk once again among old beech, oak, cherry, and chestnut, and to scent pine and cypress. If your preference is for sea-cliffs, go out to Moonen Bay on the west coast of **Duirinish**, where the cliffs of Waterstein Head rise 967 feet— the highest in Skye. Neist lighthouse on the bay's north side is on Skye's most westerly point. The nearer, Dunvegan shore of Duirinish was for nearly two hundred and fifty years the site of MacCrimmon's world-famous school of piping. The MacCrimmons were first patronized by Alasdair Crotach, who in 1540 granted them rent-free land at Boreraig.

Four miles north of Dunvegan, at the outer point of the inner loch, are two coral beaches, small in size but the best of their kind in Scotland. Vaternish, shooting eight miles north-west from the outer loch, is scoured by wind. The road ends at **Trumpan** above Ardmore Bay. On the bare plateau above, the ruined walls of Trumpan Church still point a gable to the sky. It was burned down by the MacDonalds of Uist in May 1578 in revenge for the previous year's massacre at the cave of Eigg. The people of Trumpan were in church on a misty Sunday morning when the MacDonalds landed, barred the door, and fired the thatch. All inside perished. But the alarm reached Dunvegan. MacLeod's war-galleys sped north. The Uist fleet was seized on the beach and the Bratach Sith unfurled. The MacDonalds set their backs to a dry-stone dike at the north shore and were cut to pieces. The wall was tumbled on top of them and can still be seen as a low grassy ridge above black sands. In north-westerly storms the old wall has sometimes been breached and bones exposed.

In the churchyard near the north wall of the chapel, a grey rectangular slab marks the grave of that pitiful creature Lady Grange. She is the only Scotswoman known to have had three funerals, and her strange story demonstrates once again how little the king's law ran in the Highlands, even so late as the eighteenth century. Wife of James Erskine of Grange, the Lord Justice Clerk, whose brother, the earl of Mar, had led the 1715 rising, she was a bad-tempered woman, bitterly opposed to her husband in politics. One night in 1731, when Jacobite conspirators met at Lord Grange's house in Edinburgh, she eavesdropped from under a sofa and foolishly burst out with a threat to denounce him and his friends. He judged her capable of that betrayal. The lives of men of great family and high position were at stake. MacLeod of Dunvegan and MacDonald of Sleat agreed to hold her fast in the remote parts of their islands. She was promptly abducted to Skye, where MacLeod lodged her in a poor man's hut (earth floored and chimneyless) at Idrigill on the Duirinish peninsula. News of her death was spread abroad in Edinburgh, where a mock funeral was arranged at Greyfriars Church. MacDonald later shared the burden of holding her for two years on the lonely island of Heisker off North Uist, then MacLeod sent her for a seven years' term to his oceanic island of St. Kilda. As danger was thought to lessen she was brought back to Uist, then to Assynt, and to Skye, where she learned to spin wool. The local spinners sold their yarn at Inverness, and she managed to hide a letter in a clew of her own yarn sent to market. The buyer forwarded the letter. Her relatives, appalled, assailed the government, who at last despatched a warship to search the coast of Skye. MacLeod immured her in a cave at Idrigill—a fine sandy cave, used by fishermen till last century for sleeping, net-drying, and fish-curing. Feeling the site to be unsafe, MacDonald shipped her to Uist, attended on passage by a man with a running noose lashed to a heavy boulder, ready to sink his prisoner if the warship came in sight. After a long spell on Uist, Lady Grange was returned to the Vaternish peninsula and held there till she died in 1745. Fearful that an exhumation might still bear witness against them, the conspirators filled a coffin with turf and staged a second funeral in the churchyard of Duirinish, while her body was secretly buried at Trumpan.

The ring road out of Dunvegan undulates across green moors to Edinbain, one of Skye's fairest crofting villages on Loch Greshornish, then past the wooded head of Loch Snizort to cross the five-mile isthmus to **Portree**. Portree is the capital of Skye with a population of 2,000. Its fine harbour running two miles and more into the land is protected by the twelve-mile length of the Island of Raasay. A steamer no longer calls from Kyle of Lochalsh.

Portree was given its name of Port Righ, or King's Harbour, after the visit of King James V in 1540, when he tried to end the feuds between the MacLeods and MacDonalds. Before that time Portree Bay was called Loch Chaluim-cille. The room in the old inn where Flora MacDonald took leave of Prince Charlie is now part of the Royal Hotel.

Portree lies at the base of Skye's biggest and best-populated peninsula. Trotternish runs twenty miles north and is eight miles wide between Loch Snizort and the Sound of Raasay. From a spine of brown hills the land falls away to a green coast, which carries continuous crofts and a ring road. The spine has two projecting vertebrae exhibiting two more of the Highlands' geological curios —the Quiraing and the **Old Man of Storr**. The Storr is a hill of 2,358 feet at the south end, and the Old Man the biggest of a dozen monolithic pinnacles low down on its east flank. It is clearly seen against the sky from the south side of Portree Loch, and is a landmark for ships in the Sound of Raasay. It is easily reached from the roadside by walking 900 feet up the hill. The pinnacle is 160 feet high, balanced precariously on a rock plinth on the rim of a green corrie. The rock is a light grey basalt, black round the overhanging base. Impossible though it seems, it was climbed in 1955 by Don Whillans and James Barber. On the corrie's lower rim stand the other pinnacles, one of them a slender corkscrew of 100 feet pierced by three natural arches. At the back of the corrie, unclimbed cliffs rise 600 feet to the summit of the Storr.

The **Quiraing** (pronounced Kooraing) at the north end of the range is quickly reached from the back of Staffin Bay by a side-road crossing the hills to the west coast. At a height of 500 feet, leave the car and walk north up a terrace till the spires appear. Castellated crags on the right are called the Prison. Above on the left is the Needle, 100 feet high and unclimbed, behind which you enter a grassy gulf between rock walls. These are slit to seaward by huge 'windows' facing on to the mountains of Ross and Sutherland. On top of a short central crag is a meadow like a football pitch called the Table. The name Quiraing is from the old Gaelith Cuith Raing, meaning Pillared Stronghold. Its strange rock-formation is the result of a side-slipping of the hill's summit-cliff.

The east coast of Trotternish is coastal landscape on the grand scale. On the vast shelf between the parallel cliffs of sea and hill, the road often winds close to the edge of bluffs, where brown basaltic columns, topped by smooth green turf, tower out of the sound. You can see the best example of this cliff-scenery at the **Kilt Rock**, two miles south of Staffin Bay. Leave the car at Loch Mealt and walk north along the cliff-top. The Kilt Rock is named from the tartan pattern of the stratification—vertical basalt columns based on grey Jurassic sediment laid horizontally. The cliffs continue north to Staffin at a height of 350 feet or less.

Two miles north of Staffin Bay you can see below you on the right the house of Flodigarry, now a hotel. When Flora MacDonald was released from imprisonment on the passing of the Indemnity Act of 1747, she married Allan MacDonald of Kingsburgh, by whom she had seven children, and lived at Flodigarry for eight years. Your road now crosses the north tip of Trotternish to the west coast at **Duntulm**. On the edge of the sea-cliff at Duntulm Bay, the ruins of Duntulm Castle look over the Minch to Lewis and Harris. Built on the site of an early Norse fortress, it was held first by the MacLeods, then taken by MacDonald of Sleat, who moved his seat here from Dun Sgathaich in 1539. On the failure of the 1715 rising, MacDonald was forfeited for the second time in rapid succession. The Crown never managed to take Sleat, but did take Trotternish, and Duntulm fell into disrepair. The stone was quarried to build the family a house five miles south at Monkstadt, from where (still incorrigible) they rendered great service to Prince Charles Edward. The old castle is no longer worth the trouble of close inspection, but looks well from the road.

A mile and a half south of Duntulm are the wide crofts of **Kilmuir**. The tomb of Flora MacDonald stands on high ground east of the road. Her original tombstone has long since been broken up by tourists and removed piece by piece till not a chip remains. In its place there has now been raised for monument a big Celtic cross, a most deplorable example of its kind. The cross is ugly but the site excellent—it looks far out over the Minch to her birthplace on Uist. On the shaft is engraved Dr Johnson's spoken praise: *A name that will be mentioned in history, and if courage and fidelity be virtues, mentioned with honour.*

It has been customary to give Flora all the credit for Prince Charlie's escape from South Uist and Sky when the Hanoverian net was closing in. But there were men in Uist and Skye who died, or were ruined or tortured for his sake, and of whom nothing is now said. The £30;000 reward on his head was held in contempt by the poorest Highlanders. His escape was organized from Monkstadt by the chief's wife, Lady Margaret MacDonald. Flora, then aged twenty-three, was her principal agent in fetching him back from Benbecula to Trotternish, and who showed such quick wit and courage in extracting from the Hanoverian commander, whose men had arrested her in South Uist, a pass back to Skye for herself and her maid 'Betty Burke'. Five men of Uist rowed Flora and the prince to Trotternish on a night of storm—thirty-three miles in an open boat through a screen of patrolling warships—landing at noon on the shore below Monkstadt, where Lady Margaret was lunching with the officer commanding the Hanoverian forces. The boat's crew were seized on their return to South Uist, confession forced, and Flora arrested. In London she was treated well and released two years later. She died in 1790 at the age of sixty-eight, two years before Allan, who lies at her side.

Kilmuir has Skye's first museum, opened in 1965. An old croft-house has been renovated and re-thatched, and although the exhibition is necessarily small it is worth seeing. Two of the more interesting exhibits are a Paisley shawl covering a cradle and still flawless although nearly three hundred years old, and the communion cup used at Trumpan Church in 1578.

This west coast of Trotternish is the richest land of Skye, for the soil is basaltic loam and the ground tight with crofts. It has one good bay at Uig, which has recently become an important fishing port. A car-ferry sails daily to Tarbert in Harris and Lochmaddy in North Uist. The road from Uig back to Portree gives long views twenty miles south across hill and shimmering moor to the Cuillin, which from all the wide-spread wings of Skye are so constantly seen that one comes to accept them as the Skye backdrop, no longer consciously noticed—ignored unless at Sligachan or Glen Brittle. Elsewhere in the world, when a man thinks of Skye, the first mental image he forms is the Cuillin outline. Or perhaps, if he is a seaman, it is the great cloud-cap on top, visible from far below the horizon, the white banner of Skuyö.

Above Dunvegan Castle in Skye, the seat of Clan MacLeod, the oldest inhabited castle of Scotland. The MacLeods have lived here continuously for 700 years. The rock on which it stands was the site of a 9th century Norse fort. The present castle was begun in the 15th century, consisting then of a wall of enceinte like Mingary, of which only a detached ruin survives at the west point of the rock. The keep was built in the 16th century, and the dungeon wing was carried up as a lofty square tower, which gives the building the only good effect it possesses. The more ancient gateway and portcullis face the sea on the south side. *Below:* the heights of Trotternish above Staffin Bay. Trotternish is Skye's biggest and best populated peninsula. It carries an 18-mile spine of brown hills, from which the land falls to a green coast bearing continuous crofts. The rock is basalt, which breaks down to good soil.

The Five Sisters of Kintail from the south shore of Loch Duich. They run six miles along the flank of Glen Shiel, which can be seen behind the trees. Despite their distinctive name, they are only the western tops of a continuous ridge running 20 miles to Glen Moriston.

CHAPTER 22

Kintail and Lochalsh

Wester Ross, the seaboard of the county of Ross and Cromarty, is in my own opinion the most splendid region of the Highlands. You enter it at Kintail if you come by road, or at Kyle of Lochalsh if you come by sea, and stay with it to the Sutherland frontier sixty miles north.

From the Inner Sound of Skye, two arms of the Atlantic, Loch Alsh and Loch Carron, break fourteen miles into the mainland coast. They isolate Lochalsh peninsula from Glenelg to the south and from Applecross to the north. Loch Alsh where it narrows splits at Dornie, sending one branch south-east as Loch Duich, and another north-east as Loch Long. The land enclosed by these two sea-lochs (and by their continuing glens) is Kintail, named thus from the Gaelic Cean Da Shaill, or Head of Two Seas.

Three long mountain ranges terminate around the head of Loch Duich. Between the ranges, three glens send parallel rivers into the loch's opposite corners. We have already seen Glen Shiel, giving the only road-link with central Scotland. The second is **Glen Lichd** between the Five Sisters and Beinn Fhada (Long Mountain). Its floor is flat and exceedingly bare, but is coursed seven miles by the river Croe, which becomes open and lightly wooded in its lower part around and below the farm of Morvich. Here Glen Lichd is renamed Strath Croe. At Morvich, the river is joined by a big tributary flowing down **Gleann Choinneachain**, our third converging glen and the finest in Kintail. Its rushing, tumbling burn carves the north side of Beinn Fhada in a series of short waterfalls and clear pools. The woods of Inverinate Forest on its north flank, the pastures of the lower strath, the clean, sweeping skylines of Beinn Fhada's north corries, and that broad outlook across Loch Duich, all combine with its lively river to give distinction.

Gleann Choinneachain divides near its middle at the keeper's cottage at Dorusdain. The main glen runs east to the Bealach an Sgairne giving access east to Glen Affric, or north by way of three lochans to the Falls of Glomach. The line of descent to the falls is clear and gives a dramatic view of the burn's abrupt plunge. The falls may also be reached from Dorusdain by the path up a side-glen, first northward through a forest of spruce and larch, then north-east over the Bealach na Sroine at 1,700 feet. The final drop to the falls is sharp. These routes are for long-distance walkers. The falls are more quickly reached from the head of Loch Long than Loch Duich, hence I delay an account till later.

The entire tegion of 15,000 acres comprising the Five Sisters, Beinn Fhada, and the Falls of Glomach, is held for the nation by the National Trust for Scotland. The Trust has also the western half of the Lochalsh peninsula, known as Balmacara. Their beneficent rule has preserved the amenities of a region that has no superior in Scotland, although it has its peers. In our long journey up the sea-board from Kintyre to Kintail, the variety and majesty of scene has steadily mounted even as the low hills to the south have grown in height. In Kintail everything culminates. Nothing lacks. It is the epitome of the West Highland scene. You have already seen much of the best of Kintail—the descent of Glen Shiel, the view of the Five Sisters from Ratagan, the glens of Beinn Fhada—but there is more to come, both in inner Kintail (the Trust's property) and in outer Kintail (from Strath Croe to Loch Long). The main mass of outer Kintail is private land owned by sporting proprietors, who naturally require to exclude intruders at the fishing and shooting seasons. The Trust has the salmon and sea-trout rights on the south bank of the river Croe and makes these available to visitors on certain days of the week. Permission may be had from Morvich farm. Salmon fishing on the river Shiel may be adversely affected by netting at the mouth. The higher value of Trust ownership is that you have access at all times of the year to an interior whose beauty is outstanding. The best centres for exploring the region are Kintail Lodge Hotel at Invershiel, or from Dornie Hotel if one has a car, or from the camping and caravan site at Morvich. This latter has been provided by the National Trust for Scotland behind a screen of trees on the banks of the Croe. Freedom to camp farther up the river-bank has been found to spoil the fishing, and has therefore been withdrawn.

The mountaineer and hill-walker have many rewards in Kintail.

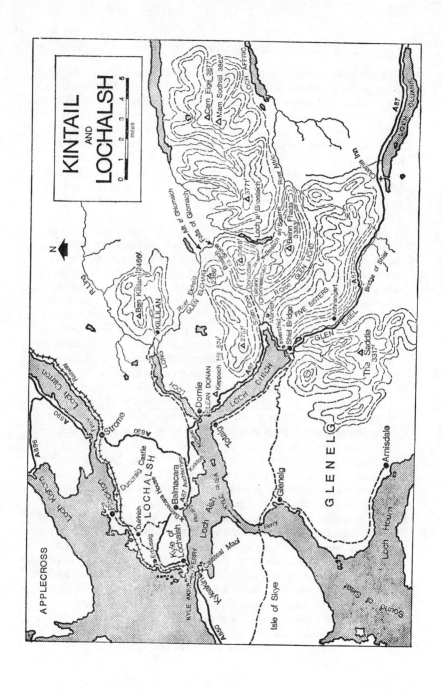

KINTAIL
AND
LOCHALSH

miles
0 1 2 3 4 5

N

APPLECROSS

Loch Kishorn

Loch Carron

River Ramsay

A896

A890

Strome

A890

Loch Long

LOCH LONG

Duncraig Castle

Balmacara House

LOCHALSH

Balmacara

A87

Erbusaig

Plockton

Duirinish

Kyle of Lochalsh

KYLE AKIN

Kirkton

Auchtertyre

Loch Alsh

Glas-ailt

Dornie

EILEAN DONAN

Kyleakin

Casteal Maol

FERRY

Isle of Skye

FERRY

Glenelg

GLENELG

Arnisdale

Loch Hourn

Sound of Sleat

Ben Killilan 2466′

KILLILAN

RUINS

River Ling

River Elchaig

GLEN ELCHAIG

Falls of Glomach

Alt a′ Ghlomaich

Carn Eige 3877′

Mam Sodhail 3862′

LOCH AFFRIC

△ 3771′

Loch a′ Bhealaich

River Affric

△ 3066′

Ben Sgriol

Sgurr na Ceathreamhnan 3771′

Loch a′ Bhealaich

Beinn an Socaich

Beinn Fhada 3383′

GLEN LICHD

Sgurr Choire Dhomhnuill

R. Croe

△ 2757′

Keppoch Hill 574′

Invershiel

Morvich

Shiel Bridge

FIVE SISTERS

GLEN SHIEL

A87

Achnangart

Bridge of Shiel

The Saddle 3317′

TORR A′ CHOIN

LOCH DUICH

Ratagan

Totaig

Glenshiel

Cluanie Inn

A87

LOCH CLUANIE

The traverses along the crests of the three principal ranges are unsurpassed as ridge-walks west of the Great Glen. They should be made from east to west, facing the Hebrides, to win the fullest enjoyment. The Saddle is the best mountain of the region both in distant shape and on close acquaintance. Its summit ridges dwindle to knife-edges and burst in pinnacles; its corries show ice-worn rock; its flanks are precipitous. The summit is truly a saddle slung between two peaks of equal height. The most sporting route of ascent goes up the Sgurr na Forcan ridge, which is reached by way of the stalker's path above Achnangart farm between Shiel Bridge and Bridge of Shiel.

Bound for Lochalsh, you round the head of Loch Duich and cross Strath Croe to the north shore. A new road made in 1969 goes six miles by the shore to Dornie. If you take the old road you rise high above the water to 574 feet on the **hill of Keppoch,** and at this point you should halt. The view back to the head of the loch is hardly superior to that from Mam Ratagan, but it does give an even better notion of Kintail's character. The scope is greater. The loch runs far and deep into a wild tangle of spiky mountains, whose immense spread succeeds in conveying a sense of the interior's real seclusion and loneliness, while the nearer intermingling of wood with water and scarred hill reveals the extreme beauty of its detail, which in the storms of winter, when sea-devils spin across the whitened surface of the loch and clouds race between snow-capped peaks, can be no less astonishing than now, in summer's serenity.

Descending north from Keppoch, you soon catch sight of **Eilean Donan,** crowned by its castle. It projects out of the water at the meeting place of all three lochs, Alsh, Duich, and Long. No other castle in Scotland enjoys a site quite so idyllic. Becoming too familiar with the scene in picture-postcards, I always feel in some danger of 'not seeing'. Yet each time I see Eilean Donan set in its living scene I find that after all it has lost none of its old power to move me. Most bewitching of all is the evening scene down Loch Alsh, when a low sun is flushing the clouds over the Cuillin of Skye. Against that unearthly light the water burns like a river of fire, writhing outward between sharp capes and bays, at last thinning to a distant trickle and vanishing into the jaws of the Cuillin, for these gape like caves against the sky. There is nothing in all Kintail to match the scene. The opposite view up Loch Duich to the Five Sisters, with the castle in the foreground, is splendid enough in all conscience, but it can be matched in several of the great sea-lochs. The view west

276

from Eilean Donan, in such lighting, is an experience altogether different.

Loch Duich was named from St. Dubhthach, an eleventh century bishop of Ross, and Eilean Donan from the much earlier Saint Donan, who in 616 founded a monastery in the island of Eigg and with his fifty brothers was there massacred by pirates. No castle had then been built on Eilean Donan, but it was already the site of a prehistoric vitrified fort, a few remains of which are to-day shown to visitors. The existing castle is a restoration of 1932 built to the plan of the original thirteenth-century building. That first Norman castle was completely surrounded by water, but the new is linked to land by a triple-arched bridge and causeway. The castle was built around 1230 by Alexander II for defence and aggression against the Norsemen who were in full occupation of Skye. His son, Alexander III, gave it in 1266 to Colin Fitzgerald, a son of the earl of Desmond, for his services at the battle of Largs three years earlier. Colin is thought to be the progenitor of Clan MacKenzie, whose chiefs became lords of Kintail and earls of Seaforth, although there is no record of a MacKenzie at Eilean Donan till the fifteenth century. The earl of Moray had it in 1331, when he draped the walls with the heads of fifty victims. The earl of Huntly took it for the king in a rising of 1504, but thereafter it reverted to MacKenzie of Kintail.

Meantime, the old Ross clan known as the Wild MacRaes had migrated to Glenelg and Kintail in the mid-fourteenth century and now became such devoted allies of Clan MacKenzie that they were commonly called 'MacKenzie's shirt of mail', and from 1520 were hereditary constables of Eilean Donan (the MacKenzie's chief seat became Brahan Castle at Conor Bridge, near Dingwall).

The MacKenzie's power grew greatly after the forfeiture of the Lords of the Isles. Donald Gorm of Sleat mounted a big attack on Eilean Donan in 1553 with a fleet of war galleys and four hundred men, but the constable, Duncan MacRae, saved the castle by killing Donald Gorm with an arrow-shot. After a long and bloody history the castle's downfall came in a little-known Jacobite rising of 1719. William Murray, the young Marquis of Tullibardine (who twenty-seven years later was to land with Prince Charlie at Arisaig) and William MacKenzie, the fifth Earl of Seaforth, were in April holding the castle for James III, the rightful King of Great Britain, against George of Hanover. Murray was commander-in-chief of the Jacobite forces in Scotland. The pair had sailed in March from

France with 300 Spanish troops to lead a Scottish rising as part of a much greater landing on the English west coast, which was the stronghold of Jacobitism. The English expedition was being led by the Duke of Ormonde, whom Cardinal Alberoni of Spain was backing with an armada, 5,000 Spanish troops, and arms to equip 30,000 English Jacobites.

Murray and MacKenzie garrisoned Eilean Donan and formed magazines there and at Strath Croe. The main body camped nearby, where they were joined by Lord George Murray, Lochiel, Clanranald, MacDougall of Lorn, and later by Rob Roy MacGregor and others to a total of 1,100 fighting men. Early in May ill-tidings reached Murray from Edinburgh. The armada from Cadiz had fared no better than its greater predecessor. Storms had shattered it off Finisterre. He was warned to re-embark the Spaniards and to disperse his men as fast as he could. While he read these dispatches, three English frigates sailed into Loch Alsh and bombarded the castle. They reduced it to ruin and captured the Spanish garrison and stores. News of these disasters quickly spread through the Highlands and the clansmen refused to rise. Murray was trapped.

A Hanoverian army under General Wightman advanced from Inverness on Kintail. On 9th June the Jacobites took up a strong position at Bridge of Shiel, where they occupied the hill-slopes to either side of the river-gorge. The right wing under Lord George Murray held the south bank. The left wing under Tullibardine held the north, and this was the main force of 1,000 men, consisting largely of Seaforth's MacKenzies, who were placed high on the hill, and 200 Spaniards placed low near the gorge. The battle began at 5 p.m. Wightman opened by mortar-shelling Lord George's position, then made three fierce onslaughts, which were repulsed. Lord George held out for two hours, but receiving no support from the Spaniards across the river, and the heather having been set ablaze by artillery fire, his men had to give way and retreat.

Wightman now strongly attacked the left wing at MacKenzie's position. Before Murray could reinforce him, MacKenzie fell dangerously wounded. At this the Kintail men lost heart and retired uphill, carrying their chief with them. Everyone then joined the retreat, pursued by the government troops till nightfall, by which time the Jacobites were nearly at the top of the mountain, which has since been named Sgurr nan Spainteach. The Spaniards surrendered to Wightman next day.

The greatest family of the north-west Highlands was here brought to ruin. MacKenzie's lands and titles were forfeited and never restored. For his grandson a new earldom of Seaforth was created in 1771, but the old was allowed to lapse. He raised the famous Seaforth Highlanders, but in 1781 the title died with him—all heirs were to the old title, not the new. Eilean Donan remained a ruin until 1912, when it was rebuilt by the family of MacRae as hereditary constables. The restoration, which cost a quarter of a million pounds, took twenty years to complete.

The causeway and bridge are reached in a quarter of a mile from Dornie by the shore road. At the main gate you pass under a portcullis to a high-walled and embattled courtyard. The two principal rooms open to the public are the billeting room of the great keep, into which you enter direct from the courtyard, and the banqueting hall above it. The billeting room housed the fighting men. Its remarkable feature is the huge arched roof built of rough stones. The banqueting hall has an old Highland magnificence. Bare stone walls show off the elegance of Chippendale and Sheraton furniture and the family portraits of bygone MacRaes. The stone canopy above a massive fireplace is emblazoned with the MacRae coat of arms, and is flanked by the banners of the Black Watch, with whom the restoring MacRae (a colonel) no doubt served. Historically, the banners displayed seem odd in MacKenzie country, for the Black Watch were enemies to the Jacobites, being recruited from the Whig clans and first used in the Highlands to enforce the disarming act. From the timbered roof hangs a wrought-iron chandelier, designed in tiered circles bearing candles. At various points in the wall to either side of the fireplace are concealed slits, to allow guards outside to observe suspected guests—a real need as shown by the castle's history. Around the room are numerous relics of interest. Before leaving you should go upstairs to the battlements; every new view of Loch Alsh gives a fresh delight.

Dornie was once a thriving fishing village, densely populated along the east shore of Loch Long. When the fishing died crofting replaced it, but never on a large scale. The larger farms remained in the hands of the big landowners. A hotel and good shops make the village a most convenient base for exploring Kintail and Lochalsh. A bridge spans Loch Long to the neighbouring village of Ardelve from which no ferry now plies to Totaig. Ardelve has a camping and caravan site by the shore. This tends to fill up rapidly in the evening, when one may fare better by moving on four miles to a similar site, more pleasantly situated, at Reraig. No visit to Kintail is complete without a visit to the most spectacular waterfall in Britain, the **Falls of Glomach**. Yet be warned: it draws many tourists but few ever reach or see the waterfall, for it is also well-named the Hidden Falls, hard of access at the last stage of approach. It is best reached from Ardelve by way of Loch Long.

Two great glens converge on the head of Loch Long from either side of Ben Killilan. The right-hand or south-east glen is Glen Elchaig, whose river is joined five miles up by the Allt a'Ghlomaich, The Burn of the Chasm. The Glomach's source at 1,200 feet is a loch above the head of Glen Affric, from which it flows level for three miles north, then plunges nearly five hundred feet down a chasm. The fall at the top is 350 feet. That is not, as has too often been said, the highest waterfall in Britain, but it takes one of the biggest single leaps, and no other is anything like so impressive.

The public road goes five miles up Loch Long through farmland to end at the foot of Glen Elchaig, half a mile short of Killilan House. The second stage is rough going through thick alder woods. The road is gravelly, full of potholes, and marked *Private* at the start. But the owner of Killilan House grants motorists permission to drive five miles on to the Allt a'Ghlomaich. For the rest, boots are essential. You cross the river Elchaig by a footbridge built by the Rights of Way Society, and with 800 feet to climb follow a path up the left bank of the Glomach Burn. The hillside above looks grassy, with some birch-scrub in the deep-cut ravine, but the path is boggy in the lower part, then rocky where it traverses the flank of the ravine. The burn below has several brown pools under small waterfalls—each a tempting bathing spot on hot days. A point is at last reached where the top of the Falls of Glomach at 1,100 feet may be glimpsed, and now the track divides.

One branch keeps high on the easier, outer slopes to the top of the great chasm. This track does not give any good view of the fall. For that you must climb down a very steep zig-zag track on the west flank of the chasm to a platform, from which the upper and middle part of the fall can be well seen. The second branch is a lower track suitable only for mountaineers. It traverses into the upper chasm on precipitous, rocky, and grassy flanks. The route is often exposed and dangerous unless one is wearing climbing boots and the weather is dry. Do not use the route in wet weather. The narrow track ends on a horizontal rock-rib, from which one suddenly looks down into the cauldron under the great waterfall. The river comes over the brink in one gigantic spout of 80 feet, hits the top of a buttress, and there splits with deafening roar into two falls, which in heavy spate may coalesce. These plunge 220 feet in weighty curtains down the smooth-faced buttress to a misted rock-pool, then on again to a 50-foot fall that cannot be seen. The cauldron formation is unique in Scotland in the combination of its hidden character with extreme narrowness and great depth.

Lochalsh, west of Loch Long, is a land of low green hills typical of an outlying peninsula. It is beautifully wooded along the shores, where promontories give delightful views of Skye across Loch Alsh and Kyle Akin. After leaving Ardelve your road keeps inland for four miles till you reach Balmacara Bay. Half-way there you pass the road-fork to Strome Ferry, giving access around Loch Carron to the North-West Highlands. At the back of Balmacara Bay are the twin villages of Reraig and Balmacara, where the National Trust for Scotland maintains an invaluable information centre. Balmacara means the Village of the Rock, but the name is now given to the whole western half of the Lochalsh peninsula. The Trust has possession here of an 8,000-acre estate, comprising most of the land and including Kyle of Lochalsh, but excluding the north-eastern hills and Strome Ferry. Take note that Strome no longer has a ferry. The service was withdrawn when a new road was made round the head of Loch Carron.

The road west to Kyle (five miles) again strikes inland, rising to 500 feet and twice sending side-roads three miles north to **Plockton**, one of the most beautiful of Highland villages. Set on a bay of outer Loch Carron, its cottages, sheltering under low green hills, look eastward across island-studded sea to the wild crags and woods on the farther shore flanking Duncraig Castle. This modern house has become a residential school of domestic science, giving a one-year's course. The haven of Plockton has long attracted yachtsmen and landscape painters. Up and down the coast are many other little bays and islands. Last century, before the railway was built through Strath Carron from Inverness, Plockton was a port for schooners trading from the Baltic and used by tough Hebridean fishermen, who made light of rowing seventy miles across the Minch to Stornoway. It is a fishing port no longer, but its waters are still lively in summer with yachts and sailing dinghies. Many of its houses are now holiday homes for townsmen. In 1966, on the rough grazing adjoining the village, the Army's Royal Engineers made an air-strip, which is now being used to give the district an air ambulance service.

The Companion Guide to the West Highlands of Scotland

The west coast of Balmacara is fringed by a maze of skerries and islands. The main road and the railway to Kyle come on to this rock-strewn coast at the bay of Erbusaig. Few people are aware that between the rocks of the shore lies a bank of coral sand. At low water small branches of the coral, usually cream-coloured but sometimes pale pink or purple, may be freely picked up among the coarse sand.

Less than two miles south down the shattered coast, road and rail end at the western extremity of the peninsula. There you enter the village of **Kyle of Lochalsh,** only half a mile from Skye across the strait of Kyle Akin. Kyle has many shops, two garages, and a good hotel, but above all it is the busy ferry-point for Skye. Motorboats may be hired for cruises around the neighbouring sea-lochs, and MacBrayne's steamer calls on its way to and from Mallaig. The business of Kyle and its railway has been greatly increased by work at the huge yard for building oil-production platforms at Loch Kishorn.

According to tradition, Kyle Akin was named from King Hakon, who (as we know from the thirteenth-century Hakon Saga) anchored in the strait during his voyage to the Firth of Clyde in 1263. There is however another tradition, which might be older, that the strait is named from Acunn, brother of Riadh, who was active on this coast a thousand years before Hakon. Acunn was a follower of the Irish leader Fionn MacCoul, called Fingal in Scotland, whose task was driving the piratical men of Lochlann (Norsemen) off the west coast.

On the Skye shore of Kyle Akin you can see the worn stump of Caisteal Maol, Castle of the Mull (or Point). Formerly called Dunakin, it was built in the thirteenth century, allegedly by the daughter of a Norse king to exact toll on ships using the strait. She married a MacKinnon, whose fortress it thereafter became. Originally it was probably three storeys high, and the walls, still 9 feet thick, enclose a space of 30 feet by 17.

In these days the whole of Lochalsh belonged to the Clan Donald Lords of the Isles as earls of Ross, and was ruled for them by MacDonald of Lochalsh until 1518, when MacDonnell of Glengarry inherited the Loch Carron half. You see evidence of this when you head for Loch Carron across the broad back of the peninsula and descend on Kyle Strome, where Loch Carron narrows before opening out to the sea. Until 1970, a car-ferry plied to the farther shore, where the ruins of Strome Castle lie behind the jetty. Like Caisteal Maol, it is too small a fragment to be of architectural interest.

It belonged to MacDonnell of Glengarry, but his Lochalsh property was surrounded by that of MacKenzie of Kintail, who, after the MacDonalds' forfeiture of the earldom of Ross in 1475, came to hold a vast territory stretching from Applecross to the Moray Firth, and from Sutherland to Glenelg. In 1603, after a century of the most cruel and bloody feuds, Kenneth MacKenzie of Kintail captured and blew up Strome Castle and seized the land. The MacKenzie earldom of Seaforth (created twenty years later) became the most powerful north of the Great Glen. The remains of the castle hardly repay inspection, but serve as a reminder of things past that affect the present. The MacKenzie shield displayed a stag's head and their crest was a burning mountain. These are still appropriate symbols of the North-west Highlands, whose frontier is Loch Carron. But the stag stands now for the sporting proprietor, to whom the land belongs, and the burning mountain for the spring heather-firing, needed to renew the crop for the sheep and deer that have driven out and almost wholly replaced MacKenzie's clansmen.

CHAPTER 23

Loch Carron and Applecross

Loch Carron and Glen Carron, striking north-east into the middle of Scotland, mark one of the decisive frontiers of the Highland seaboard. South of it, the West Highland zone is softer country with softer weather and more open to the North Atlantic Drift, both because it is more riven and because the North Highland zone is partially screened from the Drift by the Island of Skye, which fans out forty miles from Lochalsh like a vast dam. North of Carron the land hardens. The rock becomes Torridon sandstone, Archaean gneiss, and Cambrian quartzite, none of which breaks down into good soil. Over great tracts of country, this rock increasingly crops out until it forms a landscape peculiarly wild, windswept, and empty of human life. The seaboard becomes much more compact, less indented by sea-lochs in the sense that although numerous they are short, usually around six miles long and exceeding twelve only at Loch Broom. Hence the North-west is poor farmland and lacks timber, yet its very ruggedness has a beauty of its own.

You might hardly anticipate this change when you first come to the shores of **Loch Carron.** You cross the hillocky back of Lochalsh to high ground above Strome, and see Loch Carron lying as still as a freshwater loch, enfolded by hills that rise to mountainous stature round the head but are green along the farther shore with natural ash and alder, and with darker conifer plantations relieved by grass fields. The Strome Narrows protect it from storm-sea; Raasay and Skye shield the outer loch from much wind; and Kyle Akin like a sluice lets through a modicum of the Gulf Stream.

There is a railway and a road up the south side of the loch to Strathcarron. The traffic demands on the ferry in summer had become too great for it to bear—delays had sometimes extended to several hours. A new road round the loch was therefore planned and built in 1970.

284

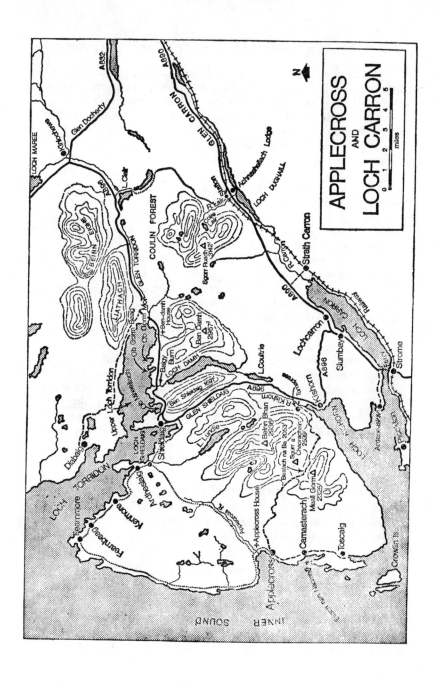

APPLECROSS
AND
LOCH CARRON

N

0 1 2 3 4 5
miles

LOCH MAREE

Kinlochewe

Glen Docherty

A832

A890

GLEN CARRON

Achnashellach Lodge

A896

Glen Torridon

L. Clair

Coire Lair

R. Lair

Upper Strath

LOCH DUGHUILL

Strath Carron

BEINN EIGHE

LIATHACH

COULIN FOREST

Sgorr Ruadh
3142'

R. Carron

A890

GLEN TORRIDON

Ob Gorm Mor
Ob Gorm Beag

+Ben-damh
House

Ben Damh
2957'

LOCH DAMH

Balgy
Burn

Railway

Lochcarron

LOCH CARRON

Slumbay

A896

Strome

Balnacra

L.Coultrie

Ben Shieldag 1691'

GLEN SHIELDAIG

A896

R. Kishorn

Kishorn

LOCH KISHORN

Ardan-aise

Loch Kishorn

Plockton

LOCH SHIELDAIG

Upper Loch Torridon

Diabaig

LOCH TORRIDON

Kenmore

Fearnmore

Fearnbeg

Ardheslaig

Shieldaig

Lundie

Beinn Bhan
2936'

Bealach na Ba 2053'

Sgurr a
Chaorachain
2539'

Meall Gorm
2325'

Applecross R.

+Applecross House

APPLECROSS

Camasterrach

Toscaig

Eilean nan naomh

INNER SOUND

Crowlin Is.

Loch Carron presents the same benign aspect if you approach instead from Inverness. Your route from there goes north-west to Garve, then follows the same route as the railway to Kyle, first through Strath Bran to Achnasheen, then breaking south-west over the watershed moors to Glen Carron. Along its fifteen-mile course to the sea, the river Carron in the bed of the glen is swollen by innumerable torrents pouring off the mountain flanks; half-way down at the woods of Achnashellach it is joined by the river Lair, which drains a great mountain cirque of the Coulin Forest to the north. At Achnashellach the Carron spreads out as Loch Dughaill, discharging thence into a mile-wide strath, down whose flat bed the continuing river meanders back and forth, thus giving its name 'to glen, strath, and sea-loch, for Carron means Winding Stream. Thus whether you come by the glen or by Strome you appear to be in mild and fertile country.

Near the head of the loch, a side-road strikes south across the strath to Strathcarron Hotel and railway station. These used to lie in a quiet backwater, and will change in character now that the new road has been made to Strome. The northerly main road continues two miles down the shore of the loch to **Lochcarron** village (sometimes called Jeantown). It has two small hotels and several boarding houses amid a long string of white cottages facing the shore. The gardens are all neat and bright with carnations, hydrangeas, and roses. At the south-west end, where the road branches off to Applecross, Loch Carron runs into the twin village of Slumbay, which has a good harbour. Fishing was once the mainstay of life in the parish of Lochcarron. It was recorded last century by the parish ministers that Lochcarron had a population of 2,100, and Applecross 2,892:

'In a calm summer evening, when hundreds of boats are seen shooting their nets, and scores of vessels lying at anchor, Loch Carron exhibits a scene of rural felicity and of rural beauty that is seldom to be witnessed.'

The men of the North-west Highlands heavily inhabited the coastal strips and lived by teeming seas. The rivers too yielded a rich harvest:

'In the river Carron . . . a common fisher could easily take with the rod twenty salmon in a day.'

This abundance vanished in the mid-nineteenth century. The great herring shoals no longer came into the sea-lochs; the runs of salmon and sea-trout dwindled. And the population was decimated. The people had lived in poverty. Their food was potatoes and herring twice daily, and oatmeal gruel for supper. Only the better-off could afford mutton, butter, and cheese. Their stone cottages were roofed with turf and chimneyless. Smoke reeked out of the door. The windows had wooden shutters but not glass. The floors were mud, and the cattle shared the interior. Such were the housing conditions in Wester Ross in 1845. It could be misleading to judge former poverty by modern standards: it seems clear that the people enjoyed life in communities much more lively than any to be found in Wester Ross now. Quiet and delightful as you will find Loch-carron, it is in terms of human population a shadow of its former self. When you move out of it, the land is empty.

Before moving west to Applecross you should walk in the **Coulin Forest**—a deer- not a tree-forest—between Glen Carron and Glen Torridon. Six miles up the glen at Achnashellach there is a railway station, and behind it an excellent right-of-way track up the river Lair, which foams in waterfalls through a narrow gorge overhung by twisted pines, leading thus to the foot of Coire Lair, where the river takes its source. The main track swings north-east over the Coulin pass to Glen Torridon (eight miles) by way of Lochs Coulin and Clair. On no account should this walk be omitted from any exploration of the region. The views from the Coulin woods and across the lochs to the far side of Glen Torridon, where the white quartzite summits of Beinn Eighe and Liathach are reflected in the water, fringed by pine, birch, heather, and bracken, have no superior in Wester Ross.

The road west out of Loch Carron rises to 450 feet on a hill-pass purpled in August by ling heather, and giving a fine view north-east to the craggy mountains of Ben Damph Forest. You are now in red Torridon sandstone country, but many of the peaks are given a grey look by quartzite caps. You descend to **Kishorn** village on the shores of Loch Kishorn, a branch of outer Loch Carron. Kishorn is almost lush country, or seems so among the flowered grass and big hayfields at the shores of its loch; the hinterland is brown heath. The scene is marred by an oil industry yard on the west shore. Beyond the head of the loch, which dries out a mile on the ebb, you see the massive eastern bluffs of Bein Bhann. Below its nearest top, at Tornapress, the road forks: the main road continues north to Shieldaig on Loch Torridon, the principal village of Applecross; the left fork leads to the west coast over the Bealach na Bà, the Pass of the Cattle—the highest road in West Scotland—climbing from sea-level to 2,053 feet in six miles.

Applecross is a fish-tail peninsula between Loch Kishorn and Loch Torridon. Its west coast facing Raasay across the Inner Sound is sixteen miles long and surprisingly little indented save for Applecross Bay near the middle. The inland boundary ten miles east is a fold in the mountains filled by Loch Damh and the river Kishorn. The ground between is deer forest except on the coastal fringe where the people live. The eastern part is a high plateau of Torridon sandstone presenting bold cliffs to the Shieldaig road but falling away gently north and west to the sea. That eastern half has three mountains, Beinn Bhan, 2,936 feet, Sgurr à Chaorachain, 2,539 feet, and Meall Gorm, 2,325 feet, and all three at their south-east ends slope straight into Loch Kishorn.

The road up the **Bealach na Bà** climbs between the last two mountains, at first high above the sea with views across Loch Alsh to Glenelg and Skye, and then burrowing deeply into the corrie between the cliffs of Meall Gorm (the Blue Mountain) on the left and the vast screes of Sgurr à Chaorachain, on which the road becomes a slender ledge above a drop of several hundred feet. At the back of the corrie it zig-zags in hairpins with a maximum gradient of one in four, and at last breaks out on to the plateau. You can then look over the lower tops of Meall Gorm to Skye. Thus far the cliff-scenery of Meall Gorm, the sudden dropping away of ground as you look back from the edge of the plateau, the wide vistas across Loch Alsh, have given the Bealach na Bà close resemblance to an Alpine pass. The plateau is a desert of stone, moon-like in its desolation. The hilltops are from here readily accessible and give extraordinarily rough walking. There is found here a kind of beauty utterly different from that of lake and woodland, and worth experiencing—a beauty of desert, wide skies, strong rock. It is harsh and stern, yet enchanting. In the glens and coastal fringe, all the needed relief and contrast are found.

The road descends much more gently to Applecross village, latterly through woods near the approaches to Applecross House, which lies at the back of the bay beside the Applecross river. A motor-road continues north, made by the crofters with government support, and goes all the way round the west coast to Shieldaig. From the right bank of the river, another track to Shieldaig, this one for walkers only, crosses the hills by a pass at 1,213 feet.

From Applecross the motor-road turns four miles south down the

Above The Saddle of Glen Shiel, 3,317 feet, rising over the glen's foot. The most sporting route of ascent goes up the Forcan ridge, seen falling rockily from the summit (see p276). *Below* Eilean Donan Castle, on Loch Duich. The long and bloody history of this islet goes back to prehistoric times when it carried a vitrified fort. The original castle was built around 1230 for defence and aggression against the Vikings, then in Skye. From 1266 it was held by the MacKenzie Lords of Kintail, until 1719, when they fought a government army at Bridge of Shiel. English frigates reduced the castle to ruin by bombardment. It was rebuilt in 1912.

Above Highland cattle, Ross-shire. *Below* the Bealach na Bà, the Pass of the Cattle, between the cliffs of Meall Gorm, the Blue Mountain (background) and the vast screes of Sgurr à Chaorachain, on which the road, gradient one in four, becomes a slender ledge above a drop of several hundred feet. From the plateau on top one looks out to Skye.

coast to **Toscaig,** passing clachans on small bays, where it is finally
revealed that from Kishorn onward you have left the West Highlands behind and are now in the North. Their atmosphere is quite
different from that of any present-day West Highland village save
Corran on Loch Hourn. Time no longer matters. There seem to be
no fences or prohibitions. Wild irises and foxgloves and roses grow
by the roadside as elsewhere, but the fields are tiny, arrayed in
strips of changing colour—corn, the heavy green of potato, the hay
a riot of brightness rarely seen in the south, full of huge oxeye
daisies and buttercups, red and white clover, and bright yellow
charlock, all crowded together and their scents mingling with the
scent of the sea. The very air seems freer as you draw away from
the more heavily indented coastline south of Skye. You have come
to a different country. The work of crofting and fishing gets done,
but in leisurely fashion. The people seem more friendly. The clachans
have the charm of remoteness and isolation.

The most valuable bay of the coast is not Applecross but Camusterach two miles to its south. It has a natural harbour in which
fishing boats can lie protected by the green back of Eilean nan
Naomh, the Holy Isle, on which St. Maelrubha is said to have first
landed while he reconnoitred the district. Toscaig at the road-end
has a long south-facing bay from which the hills of Skye appear
beyond the Crowlin Islands.

The sense of isolation in Applecross is in large part an effect of
the Bealach na Bà. But much more than that is implied in the old
name of the peninsula, which was Comeraich, a Sanctuary—the
only name known in the language of the people themselves. It was
first made a sanctuary by the arrival here in 673 of St. Maelrubha,
and continued under the church as a recognized sanctuary for all
manner of fugitives in succeeding centuries till the Reformation.
The bounds of the sanctuary lands, centred on the river's estuary,
were marked by a six-mile arc of stones. All these have gone. The
most southerly stone was a cross eight feet high, which used to
stand on a promontory at Camusterach. This was deliberately
smashed by a mason repairing the Free Church.

The name Applecross is from Apor-crossan, first mentioned in
Tighernac's Latin Annals. His Crossan is the Applecross river,
which is still locally known as the Crossan. Apor is from the Gaelic
Aber meaning Estuary. Tales have gained currency, principally
through an error repeated in the Third Statistical Account of 1845,
that the name Applecross arose on the break-up of clan territory,

when the new proprietor of the estate re-named Applecross after planting five apple-trees crosswise in his garden. When examined in 1854, all but one of these trees were found to be chestnuts. The modern name Applecross first appears in Papal documents of 1275—clearly a written corruption of an ill-heard 'Abercrossan'.

St. Maelrubha built his monastic huts and church at the mouth of the Crossan, perhaps where the present kirk and manse stand to-day on the north bank, but no trace remains. Like those on Iona, they were destroyed in Viking raids of the ninth and tenth centuries. The ruins of an ancient chapel, to which no date has yet been assigned, still stand within the churchyard.

Maelrubha's name is from Mael, meaning Tonsured, and Rubha, a variant of Ruadh meaning Red, from which it may be inferred that he was red-headed. In the general esteem in which he was held in the West Highlands he ranks second only to St. Columba. He was directly descended from the Irish King Niall of the Nine Hostages. Born in County Derry in January 642, he sailed to Scotland in 671 at the age of thirty. In the following two years he founded six churches along the west coast before settling with his company of monks at the foot of the green and wooded glen of Abercrossan. He ruled as abbot for nearly fifty years. In that time he and his brothers carried their civilizing work across Ross and Cromarty into Sutherland. On one of these northern journeys he died in 722 at Skail in Sutherland, aged eighty. His body was carried back to Applecross for burial. Two round-shaped stones close below the chapel are traditionally said to mark his grave, which before the Reformation had been marked by a carved Celtic cross of red sandstone. This cross too was broken up by a protestant mason, and incorporated in the walls of the new manse. Two fragments of an ancient sandstone cross, probably Maelrubha's, were found some years ago in the churchyard and are now preserved in the kirk.

From Tornapress at the head of Loch Kishorn, the road north to Loch Torridon climbs up Glen Kishorn to open moor before descending through Glen Shieldaig to the Torridon coast. The Kishorn glen is flanked to the west by Bheinn Bhan, whose several deep corries are walled by cliffs stratified like Cyclopean masonry— a form typical of Torridon rock. In the lower bowl of the middle one, Coire na Poite, lies a lochan to which high spurs run out from the main face; between them a burn cascades over a rock-terrace from an inner corrie, whose ice-worn floor holds two smaller lochans, green and crystal clear. Behind them, cliffs of purple sandstone rear up to 1,200 feet.

On crossing the pass into **Glen Shieldaig**, you approach Loch Damh, only to turn away from it on a road much widened in parts, but happily reverting to its ancient narrowness alongside Loch Dughaill. This loch is a broad sheet half a mile long, flanked like the road by gnarled Scots pines and ling heather—a wood typical of its Torridon kind. Immediately beyond and just before you reach Loch Shieldaig, a new road to Kenmore breaks west, and half a mile farther another new road to Torridon breaks east. You continue past both forks into Shieldaig village. Whitewashed and harled, and mostly of two stories, the houses spread in line along a curving road between the blunt cone of Ben Shieldaig, which rises close above to 1,691 feet, and a shore of red sandstone. Offshore is Shieldaig Island, pine-covered. The bay and village are no less beautiful than those of Plockton, much quieter, and with better surrounding country. Here also, too many houses are becoming holiday homes. At one time the bay was famous for its herring fishing; in the days of Norse rule it was given the name of Sild-vik, or Herring Bay, from which the Gaelic Shieldaig derives. There is no hotel, but the boarding house next to the post office keeps a high standard of service, food, and courtesy.

The walk west along the coast goes on a switchback track, first through pines then across rough hillsides above a dozen lovely bays, from which one looks across Loch Torridon to the long rocky points of Diabaig and the towering peaks of Torridon Forest. The old crofting communities at the back of these bays—Ardheslaig, Kenmore, Fearnbeag, and Fearnmore—are still inhabited, but so sparsely that one wonders how long they can survive. The people's innate love of the land has so far made them resist proposals of evacuation. Their new road progresses slowly, only a little being made each year as the men find time.

From Shieldaig, one of the most beautiful **paths** in Rossshire goes six miles east along the deeply-bayed coast to Glen Torridon. As far as the first bay, Ob Mheallaidh, this old track has recently been replaced by a new double width road; thereafter the new road keeps higher than the old. After crossing the Balgy Burn, the foot-track twists through woods of mixed conifer and broad-leaved trees at the back of two craggy inlets named Ob Gorm Beag and Ob Gorm Mor, and so through increasingly magnificent woods to Ben-Damph House (now Loch Torridon Hotel), where it joins the new road through Annat to the head of the loch. Much of the old track has been saved, but five miles have been lost at start and finish. The loss has been a despoliation.

On the new higher road, motorists who drive in blinkers are able to cruise at sixty miles an hour and to cross from Shieldaig to Torridon in six minutes. 'Walking is for horses', I once read in an American advertisement: 'Quit horsing around—buy yourself a Cadillac'. If you choose not to walk you must at least stop at the highest point of the road and look. The hillsides above you are bare and craggy, not even heathery, but below is that wonderfully wooded shore and the old footpath that makes motoring seem a vanity. You can see that like Applecross Torridon is country in which to walk, fish, sail, climb, or wander, or to shoot stags in September; all these are permitted, but fast driving, no. On the far side of the loch, Torridon House crouches in a pinewood under the west ridge of Liathach; to its left, the white croft-houses of Inver Alligin lie under Beinn Alligin like quartzite boulders fallen from its pinnacles. All these may be Torridon, not Applecross, but for once the two are wedded by the loch between, and are not divided.

CHAPTER 24

Torridon and Gairloch

Gairloch is the parish name of all country between Loch Torridon and Gruinard Bay of Loch Broom. Within its bounds are Loch Maree, Loch Ewe, the sandy bays of Gair Loch, and the mountain ranges to either side of Glen Torridon and Loch Maree. Water and mountain lend to each other beauties of shape and setting that make this district the most popular touring country of the North-west Highlands. All the greater features can be seen from points of vantage by the roadside, and to help you see the greatest of all, stalkers' paths and old drove roads penetrate the mountain fastnesses.

You have already made an approach through Applecross. The more usual route for travellers moving up from south or east Scotland is from Inverness, then west by road or railway through Strath Bran to Achnasheen. Passengers by rail are there met by bus. By this route you enter Gairloch above the west end of Loch a' Chroisg, where you cross the Highland watershed at 815 feet. You descend through the defile of **Glen Docherty**. Its walls rise a thousand feet to bare escarpments, but open below on to Loch Maree in the floor of the valley. Your first intimation of an usual splendour is the sight of Slioch, 3,217 feet, towering over the loch, and later a glimpse of a shoulder of Beinn Eighe round the corner to the left, where Glen Torridon slices west. Loch Maree is world-famous for its beauty. It seems all the greater crime that its approach in lower Glen Docherty should be marred by hydro-electric pylons and telephone wires, of which the latter are the worst offenders. They carry a heavy cable slung as thick as a hawser from pole to pole, giving the effect of a giant fence from which the eye cannot escape.

Two miles from the head of the loch, the glen widens to a farm-land strath broken by groves of oak and alder along the banks of Kinlochewe river. The river is formed by three tributaries flowing

293

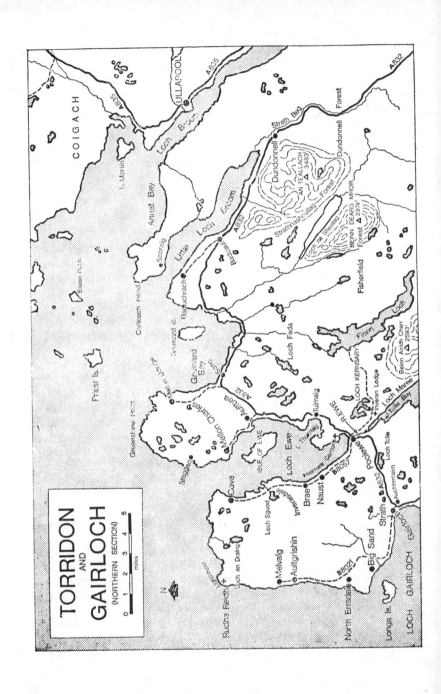

TORRIDON
AND
GAIRLOCH
(NORTHERN SECTION)

miles
0 1 2 3 4 5

N

COIGACH

ULLAPOOL
A835
A835
Loch Broom
Strath Beg
Dundonnell
AN TEALLACH △ 3483'
Dundonnell Forest
A832

Is. Martin
Annat Bay
Scoraig
Little Loch Broom
Badcaul
A832
Strathnasheallag Forest
Loch na Sheallag
BEINN DEARG MHOR △ 2974'
Forest

Cailleach Head
Badluchrach
Fisherfield

Eilean Dubh

Priest Is.

Greenstone Point
Melvin Charles
Gruinard Is.
Gruinard Bay
Sand
Aultbea
A832
Loch Fada
Loch Ewe
Loch Kernsary
LOCH KERNSARY
Inveran Lodge
Loch Maree
Tollie Bay
Loch Tollie
BEINN AIRIDH CHARR △ 2593'
Loch Fionn

Slaggan
Cove
Mellon Charles
ISLE OF EWE
Inverasdale
Thurnaig
Tournaig
Poolewe
A832
Auchtercairn
Strath

Loch Sguod
Inveriscaple
Naust
Brae
Midtown
Camas
B8057

Rudha Reidh
Loch an Draing
Melvaig
Aultgrishin

B8021
Big Sand
North Erradale
Strath
Longa Is.
LOCH GAIRLOCH

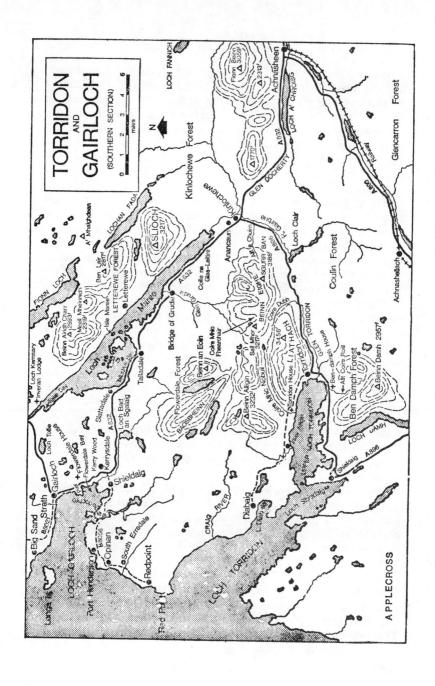

TORRIDON
AND
GAIRLOCH

(SOUTHERN SECTION)

N

miles
0 1 2 3 4 5

LOCH FANNICH

Fionn Bheinn 3059'

2131'

1770'

LOCH A' CHROISG

Achnasheen

A832

GLEN DOCHERTY

A890

Glencarron Forest

Achnashellach

R. Fiunnlid

Kinlochewe Forest

LOCHAN FADA

SLIOCH 3217'

Kinlochewe

Kinlochewe

LETTEREWE FOREST

A' Mhaighdean

Ben Lair 2817'

Letterewe

Isle Maree

Coille na Glas-Leitire

A832

Anancaun

R. Garbhe

Loch Clair

Coulin Forest

FIONN LOCH

Loch Kernsary
Inveran Lodge

Beinn Airidh Charr 2593'

Meall Mheinnich 2319'

LOCH MAREE

Glen Grudie

Bridge of Grudie

Benn an Eoin

Coire Mhic Fhearchair

Beinn EIGHE

Sgurr Ban 3188'

A' Choinn

3456'

Coire Dubh

Coire Mhic Nobuil

BEINN LIATHACH

GLEN TORRIDON

Ben-damph House

Coire Poll

Beinn Damh 2957'

LOCH DAMH

Loch Tollie

Talladale

Slattadale

Kerry Wood

Kerrysdale

Loch Bad an Sgalaig

Flowerdale Forest

BROSBHEINN

Sail Mhor 3217'

Beinn Alligin 3232'

Torridon House

UPPER LOCH TORRIDON

Shieldaig

A896

Big Sand

A832 Strath

Gairloch

LOCH GAIRLOCH

Port Henderson

Opinan

South Erradale

Redpoint

B8056

Flowerdale House
Flowerdale Bay

Shieldaig

CRAIG RIVER

Diabaig

LOCH TORRIDON

Red Pt

APPLECROSS

Luinga Is.

OLD ROAD

west down Glen Docherty, south from the Heights of Kinlochewe, and north from the Coulin Forest. Where they meet lies the village of **Kinlochewe**, at the foot of Beinn Eighe. Kinlochewe is named from the loch, which many hundreds of years ago was called Loch Ewe. The name would probably be changed to Maree to distinguish it from the sea-loch into which it flows. The village, with its hotel at the road-fork to Glen Torridon, is well-placed strategically for exploring the Torridon or southern part of the region. Nearby are a boarding house, a caravan park, and a few bed-and-breakfast cottages. Fishing for brown trout may be had on numerous hill lochs, for salmon and sea-trout on Loch Maree, and for salmon on the river Gairbhe, which flows in from the Coulin Forest. Climbers are drawn to the region in even greater numbers than fishermen. The big ridges and rock buttresses of the Torridon mountains, and of Letterewe Forest to the north side of Loch Maree, give much of the best mountaineering in the North-west Highlands.

These mountain ranges have often been described as the world's oldest mountains, which is not strictly accurate. As we have noted earlier, they were raised as a plateau and carved to present shape only thirty million years ago. In outer form they are no older than the Alps. It is the rock of the original chain, now exposed on these hills, that is so extraordinarily old. That original chain was heaved out of the sea four hundred million years ago. It may have been of Himalayan scale and was certainly of Alpine, but was reduced to a sea-level plain by erosion. When 'Scotland' finally rose, the root-rocks of the old chain rose with it. Its sandstone sediment was deposited earlier than the Cambrian rock (the first in which fossils occur), which now caps many of the Torridon peaks with quartzite. These quartzite caps are at least six hundred million years old, the sandstone below them is older still, and the platform of gneiss on which the mountains stand, and which forms so many of the wild moors of Wester Ross and Sutherland, is aged two thousand six hundred million years. This is Britain's oldest rock. It several times forms summits and cliffs of itself, notable on the Letterewe range on the north side of Loch Maree.

In 1967, Torridon Forest was given to the National Trust for Scotland. Its 14,000 acres extend westward from Sail Mhor (the peak at the west end of Beinn Eighe) to Inver Alligin on Loch Torridon, and northward from the river Torridon to Beinn Dearg. The eastern boundary thus marches with that of the Nature Conservancy's reserve on Beinn Eighe.

You could not have a better introduction to Torridon mountains than that given by the approach from Kinlochewe. Three miles up the river Gairbhe, halt by the roadside at Loch Clair. To the right of the road are two of the finest mountain ranges of Scotland: **Beinne Eighe** (pronounced A as in Aim) and **Liathach** (pronounced Leeagach). Beinn Eighe means the File, and truly its seven tops on their seven-mile ridge seem from a distance not unlike one. Both mountains are largely red sandstone, but Beinn Eighe's four eastern tops are entirely of Cambrian quartzite, giving an aspect of white sterility, yet enhancing the grace of the sharp summit ridge swinging from peak to peak. Liathach, 3,456 feet, means the Grey One. It too has seven tops, four of them quartzite. A ridge of five miles links them, but from Loch Clair one has eyes for only one. It is the most soaring peak of the North; a mountain of sombre sandstone, it springs to an arrowhead of white quartzite more than 3,000 feet above the road. It appears close above, but in fact is four miles away. If you have not already followed the foot-path over the Coulin pass from Glen Carron, you should follow it now in the reverse direction, at the very least for two and a half miles to the head of Loch Coulin. The path leaves the main road beside Loch Clair and follows the shores of the two lochs through woodland past Coulin Lodge. The view back to Beinn Eighe, described in the Lochcarron chapter, is not one to be lightly missed.

Several centuries ago, **Glen Torridon** was thickly wooded from Kinlochewe to the sea. The Coulin trees are no more than a remnant, the rest having been clear-felled. As a result, the Torridon pass is bleak ground of scraggy heather and bent. In recent years the Forestry Commission have leased and planted some three hundred acres on the lower slopes of Beinn Eighe. Small as the forest is, it is big enough to give (in time) diversity to a hillside peculiarly bare; it includes local pine, and the Nature Conservancy, who own the ground, have helped matters by adding small enclosures of other trees native to the country.

The great single feature of Beinn Eighe cannot be seen from the roadside. This is the **Coire Mhic Fhearchair**, pronounced Veek Errecher, at the north-west end of the range. Any approach involves a long uphill walk, but anyone who penetrates to this mountain recess wins a high reward. It is one of the half-dozen most magnificent corries of the Highlands. In the North-west its only possible rival is the Coire Toll an Lochain of An Teallach. Around its stony floor circles a cliff on which three huge buttresses, split from each other by gullies, tower thirteen hundred feet above a lochan. Their lower halves are red sandstone, their upper white quartzite. They give good rock-climbing. The encircling arm on your left-hand side rises to the summit, Ruadh Stac Mor, 3,309 feet. On your right is Sail Mhor, 3,217 feet, shaped like the fin of a shark, but meaning Big Heel. Access to the corrie may be had either from Bridge of Grudie on Loch Maree, by way of a track up Glen Grudie to 900 feet, then a thousand feet up an open hillside to the floor of the corrie, or else from Glen Torridon by way of Coire Dubh. You reach Coire Dubh, which is the narrow glen dividing Beinn Eighe from Liathach, two and a half miles west of Loch Clair at the head of Glen Torridon. A track goes up the right bank of the burn to 1,100 feet, after which you must contour round Sail Mhor to the corrie. Either route involves a walk of five miles in two and a half hours.

Passing down Glen Torridon, you have on your right-hand side the sharp peaks of Liathach, precipitously flanking the glen and appearing inaccessible till they fall away at the shores of Loch Torridon. On your left are the Coulin and Ben Damph Forests—a dozen red sandstone mountains, some with quartzite caps; none rival their great neighbours across the glen, but several show splendid cliffs on their east faces. Between them are beautifully shaped corries scooped like quaighs (Scottish drinking cups) holding a score of glistening lochans. The whole being deer forest, it is served by numerous stalking paths extending to fifty miles; these are a great boon to the walker at the start and finish of each day, for the lower slopes of the hills are as rough as the Rough Bounds of Knoydart. Access can be had from all sides and the tracks are marked on the one-inch maps. In exchange for these excellent tracks you should respect the rights of the proprietors who maintain them. The Coulin Forest is closed for deer-stalking from 20th August to 10th October. The path over the Coulin pass from Loch Clair is of course open at all times.

At the foot of Glen Torridon, where the National Trust for Scotland has an information centre, you can walk up Beinn Damph, 2,957 feet, by turning left through Annat to Loch Torridon Hotel. At the back of the house a good track climbs through a forest of Scots pines on the left bank of a deep-cut gorge, down which the Allt Coire Roill cascades in high waterfalls. The pines on the left bank become dwarfs high up, allowing views across the loch to **Beinn Alligin**, 3,232 feet. The name means the Jewel Mountain, and does seem peculiarly apt in springtime, when its cluster of four snow-capped peaks shine like diamonds on blue sky or in the still deeper blue of upper Loch Torridon. The Loch Torridon Hotel below offers all facilities for stalking, fishing, and riding.

At the head of the loch, the main road narrows and goes nine miles down the north side of the loch to end at Diabaig on the outer loch. You pass first through the tiny village of Torridon, at whose west end a shore road (not to be used by passing motor-cars) goes two miles to Torridon House, which is hidden in a pinewood at the foot of Coire Mhic Nobuil, the glen dividing Liathach from Beinn Alligin. The shore track continues another two miles to the crofting township of Inver Alligin, where the Alligin burn enters the sea. The track deteriorates, but may still be used past the Shieldaig Narrows, climbing high above the bays of the rocky coast to reach Diabaig. As far as Inver Alligin, this quiet track is one that you ought to walk on a good day—or a moonlit night, for my own most lingering memory is that of a yellow harvest moon flooding over the Applecross mountain-tops.

As seen from the sea, **Loch Torridon** is the hub from which the hills of Applecross, Beinn Damph, and Torridon run out like spokes and by their presence make it the most superb sea-loch of the North-west. A score of lovely bays along the shores maintain this excellence. An attempt should therefore be made to hire a motor-boat from Shieldaig or Diabaig—possible only if the fishermen are free of work.

The new road to Diabaig climbs above the old to pass behind Torridon House, where the Coire Mhic Nobuil burn is the best point of access to both Liathach and Beinn Alligin. The traverse of Liathach's five-mile summit-ridge over the pinnacles of Am Fasarinen (the fourth top) is rivalled on the mainland only by the Aonach Eagach of Glen Coe and An Teallach of Little Loch Broom. The route goes up the stalker's path on the left bank of the burn through a gorge wooded with old Scots pines. Waterfalls, guts, and cauldrons punctuate the river's bed. When clear of the wood you take to the open hillside; or instead, you may follow the path to the mountain's north side, where the cliffs rise near to the perpendicular for five hundred feet. They give good rock-climbing, especially from the depths of Coire na Caime, the mountain's grandest feature.

Beinn Alligin is a relatively easy mountain, best approached from the right bank of the same burn. The east face is carved in elegant corries, and the views from the summit excel those of its greater neighbours. They extend from Cape Wrath to Ardnamurchan. The west slopes fall away in bluffs to Loch Diabaig, a mile-long bay of outer Loch Torridon enfolded by arms of naked rock. Your descent by road to Loch Diabaig is abrupt. You wind your way down a steep grass slope on which is set a crofting village looking out to Skye and the Outer Hebrides. On a coast where loveliness is met at every turn, **Diabaig** is remarkable. The road ends at a small pier used by the crofter-fishermen, but a foot-track continues seven miles north up the coast to Red Point, where there is another crofting village, a sandy beach, and a motor-road to Gairloch. This track gives a most enjoyable coastal walk. It faces the Trotternish peninsula of Skye, fourteen miles across the Minch. There is no hotel at Diabaig, but a cottage may be able to give you a room.

At Kinlochewe, there is at Anancaun farmhouse (half a mile from the hotel towards Loch Maree) a residential field station of the Nature Conservancy. In 1951, when the Nature Conservancy bought the eastern half of **Beinn Eighe** comprising nearly 11,000 acres, it was their first Nature Reserve in Britain. Their primary purpose was to preserve and study a 700-acre remnant of Caledonian pinewood at Coille na Glas Leitire on the lower north slopes above Loch Maree.

Less than a thousand years ago, the glens of Wester Ross were heavily forested. As in Argyll and Invernessshire, the land was devastated by fire and felling. The Beinn Eighe forest suffered further felling during the last war and after. Although it was one of the finest stands of aboriginal pines remaining in Scotland it would have been lost to the nation had the Conservancy not intervened. Although Scots pine predominates, there is also much birch, rowan and alder. The Conservancy's aim is to recreate a natural woodland of mixed species, so far as possible self-regenerating and harbouring a varied plant and animal life.

One of the more interesting animals finding refuge in Coille na Glas Leitire is the pine-marten. Centuries of persecution and destruction of forest brought the marten in peril of extinction in Britain. In the Highlands, it found refuge last century by adaptation to treeless hill country in Sutherland around Foinaven, but now it is again increasing in numbers on Beinn Eighe. The marten is long and lithe with dark brown fur and a yellow throat. The tail is a foot long and the body around eighteen inches. Dr. J. Morton Boyd writes of the Beinn Eighe Reserve:

'Individuals can occasionally be seen at dusk, and they present a wonderful sight bounding along the paths or ascending and descending the old pines with incredible speed.'

On the hillside opposite Anancaun, an old pony track runs from the roadside into the heart of the Reserve at 1,400 feet. Far above are the north-eastern corries of Beinn Eighe, deserts of pale quartzite screes, from which crags rise to the summit of Sgurr Ban. Lesser tops of the massif rise closer to the west; between them spreads rough pasture grazed by red deer, which in winter come down to the pinewood for shelter. Here too are ptarmigan, wild cat, fox and the golden eagle. When you climb up to higher ground, you can see across Loch Maree to range upon range of rockily savage mountains spreading north to Loch Broom: in the forefront, Slioch, in the background, An Teallach. You can, if you wish, go on to the summit of Sgurr Ban from this side and traverse the long ridge westward. An easier route to the main ridge is from the mountain's east side: go three-quarters of a mile from Kinlochewe down the Glen Torridon road, then follow the right bank of the Allt a' Chuirn into Coire Domhain.

The Nature Conservancy welcomes visitors to the Reserve and has a new information centre at Aultroy. Anancaun has sleeping accommodation for nine people, much used by visiting naturalists. Parties buy food and cook for themselves. Kitchen equipment, cutlery, and beds are provided for a small charge. By the roadside the Conservancy maintins a car-park and camp-site.

Loch Maree is twelve miles long and one of the three most excellent of Scotland's big inland waters. Its only possible rivals are Loch Lomond and Loch Awe, neither of which has a mountain with so powerful a presence as Slioch, nor the Scots pines and heather that distinguish the shores of Loch Maree. The others have gentler country. Loch Maree exhibits the wilder and rougher forms of mountain country, although deciduous trees happily alternate with coniferous.

You pass three miles through the woods of Coille na Glas Leitire to open heathery hillside split by **Glen Grudie**, where the river Grudie falls from Coire Mhic Fhearchair. You can use the path high above the left bank either to reach that great north-western corrie or to climb to the summit of Beinn Eighe, or to cross the pass to the head of Coire Mhic Nobuil and walk down under the long northern cliffs of Liathach to Loch Torridon. This latter route of fourteen miles gives one of the most rewarding mountain walks in Wester Ross. Beyond Bridge of Grudie the woods of the Reserve are followed by several more miles of open hillside to the bay of **Talladale**, from which the forest of Slattadale spreads four miles west. At Talladale Bay is Loch Maree Hotel, one of the more famous fishing hotels of Wester Ross. Its jetties and boat-house lie close to the door. The boats are equipped with big landing nets, for the sea-trout in Loch Maree run up to 20 lb. Ten beats are fished in rotation. The salmon-run is in April and May, the sea-trout season from 1st July to Mid-October. A catch of seventeen sea-trout weighing 79 lb. has been recorded.

Offshore from Talladale lie a spatter of islands big and small— at least a score—of which a dozen are wooded. Close to the Letterewe shore is the tiny **Isle Maree**, from which the loch is named. It has gravelly shores and is wooded in oak, holly, ash, willow, pine, birch, and hazel. Pagan rites involving the sacrifice of a bull occurred here as late as the seventeenth century. These are recorded in the church records at Dingwall, when a Hector MacKenzie and his two sons and grandson were summoned to appear before the Presbytery. Long before the days of St. Maelrubha the island had been a sacred place of the Druids, who are said to have introduced the oak as one of their religious symbols. When St. Maelrubha arrived in the seventh century he is likewise said to have planted the holly. At the centre of the island are the remains of his chapel or monastery in the form of a circular dike, an ancient graveyard, a deep well (now dry and filled in), and beside it the wreck of an old tree. Each has a story of its own.

At the height of Norse power in the eleventh and twelfth centuries, the whole of North Scotland down to Inverness lay in Norwegian hands, until wrested from them in 1196 by William the Lion, King of Scots. It was perhaps during this occupation that a Norse prince married the daughter of a Celtic chief in Wester Ross. Left too much alone during his necessary absence on expeditions, she began to doubt his love and resolved to test it. On his next return home she pretended to be dead. On hearing this news and seeing her apparently lifeless he stabbed himself to the heart. In a frenzy of remorse the princess plucked the dagger from his breast and plunged it into her own. They were given burial in Isle Maree and their graves marked by two slabs standing face to face, each incised by a cross.

The well was for centuries a place of pilgrimage. Its water was believed to have a powerful curative effect on people suffering mental disorders. Until the end of the eighteenth century, all such people in Wester Ross were brought to the well to drink. During his tour of Scotland in 1772, Thomas Pennant visited the island and recorded that a patient first knelt before the altar while attendants made an offering of money; he then went to the well and sipped the holy water, when a second offering was made. After that he was dipped thrice in the loch. The performance might be repeated daily for some weeks. Pennant adds, 'It often happens that the patient receives relief.'

The well was also a wishing well, and beside it grew an ancient wishing tree. After wishing at the edge of the well, one went to the tree to make an offering, which could be either money or a scrap of one's own clothing. If money, the coin was hammered edgeways into the bark, if cloth, the fragment was nailed to the trunk. The tree was still alive in 1877 when Queen Victoria called—she wished her wish and drove in her coin—but has since died a death hastened by the mass of embedded metal.

The **Letterewe** shore, to which you are now so close, is even more beautiful than the south side of the loch, or so it seems because here there is only a footpath. The walker feels closer to every growing thing and to the elements, and being free of cars, tarmac, and petrol fumes, has leisure to observe closely. The hill-flanks are wooded along a narrow strip by the water. In the old days they were heavily forested. Around 1700 veins of iron ore were discovered and worked near Letterewe House, which lies a mile to the east of Isle Maree. The forest was then felled for iron-smelting. There is no ferry service across the loch; Letterewe is a private estate. But the path is a right of way to which you have access from either end. Before the opening of the Inverness to Lochalsh railway, the whole mail for the Outer Isles used to be carried on foot down the Letterewe track from Kinlochewe to Poolewe. The eastern end of the track gives the best means of access to Slioch and to Loch Fada under the mountain's north side.

Slioch, 3,217 feet, is named from Sleagh, a Spear. By its south-east ridge it is easy to climb. The views from the top embrace a vast tract of rocky mountains: south to Torridon and Flowerdale Forests, east to the still higher peaks of Fannich Forest, and north into the wildest region of the Scottish mainland—the Forests of Strath na Sheallag and Fisherfield (the older and better name for which is Achaniasgair). Letterewe Forest, on the crest of which you now stand, is the continuous mountain ridge bounding Loch Maree's north shore. The four principal summits are Slioch, Beinn

Lair, 2,817 feet, Meall Mheinnidh, 2,391 feet, and Beinn Airidh
Charr, 2,593 feet. Like most mountains to north and south, Slioch
is a sandstone pile set on a plinth of gneiss; this gneiss rises to the
summits of Beinn Lair and Airidh Charr, buttressing their north
sides with great cliffs, which on Beinn Lair extend two miles. These
give excellent rock-climbing.

The **Letterewe ridge** is moated by long lochs on each side. On
the north are Loch Fada and Fionn Loch, and beyond them that
mountainous maze, which in appearance rather than in fact is not
paralleled throughout Scotland in its savage complexity. An
Teallach bounds it to the North. Between lie more than a dozen
other mountains, some of sandstone, others of gneiss, all exposing
much rock. They are stark, rugged hills, unexpectedly adorned very
high up in folds under the peaks by lochans that flash in the sun or
shine dully through shifting mist.

Unlike the old Letterewe track, the main road on the south side
does not continue down Loch Maree to Poolewe. From the middle
of Slattadale Forest it bears west over the hills to Gairloch, topping
the pass at 427 feet, and then skirting the shore of Loch Bad an
Sgalaig. This loch is fed by a river draining the mountains of Flowerdale Forest, Baosbheinn and Beinn an Eoin, which rise three miles to
your south and are close neighbours of the Torridon hills. The loch
offers good angling for brown trout and pike. Gairloch Angling
Club have the fishing rights. Out of this loch flows the river Kerry,
plunging three miles to Gair Loch through a glen formerly of quite
exceptional beauty, called **Kerrysdale**. The falls near the top were
a sight superior to the bigger falls at Steall, Glomach, and Eas a'
Chùal Aluinn in the beauty of hillside woods and the surge of water
through them. The river has been dammed at its exit from the loch
by the North of Scotland Hydro-Electric Board. The old river-
course under the dam is dry and ugly. Big pipe-lines, painted an
unnatural green, run horizontally through the woods beside the
road; the old waterfalls are silent, mocked by the merest trickle. A
half-hearted attempt has been made to screen the pipes by the
planting of saplings. They give pathetically inadequate cover. The
former beauty of the glen has not simply been lost; it has been
replaced—and this was not necessary—by the very kind of ugliness
that causes men to flee industrial towns. The power-house a mile
below the dam is of excellent design in red stone.

Soon you see the gleam of the **Gair Loch** through the tree-tops.
The loch is named from the Gaelic Gearr, meaning Short, for it

bites only four miles into the land. Half a dozen bays and coves at its back, and several islands, give to its shores a pleasing irregularity, and to visitors an exploratory interest. Towards the foot of the glen, a road forks leftward past two of these bays on the south shore, Loch Shieldaig and Badachro, and thence to Red Point. Leaving this road meantime, you pass on north through Kerry Wood to the Flowerdale bridge. On your left is an inlet harbouring the pier of the Gair Loch fishing fleet, and on your right through the trees, **Flowerdale House**, the ancient seat of the MacKenzies of Gairloch. It was known as An Tigh Dige, the Moat House, until last century. House and Harbour are intimately connected. There were no clearances in Gairloch in the nineteenth century. To the contrary, the MacKenzie family subsidized the fishing industry by buying wood for local boats and guaranteeing sale-money for catches. Gairloch now ranks sixth among the fishing ports of the Highland coast.

The greater part of **Gairloch**, between outer Loch Torridon and Loch Ewe, had been held by the MacLeods till the seventeenth century. They were chiefly an island clan of Skye, Raasay, Lewis, and Harris, but their mainland territories of Glenelg, Gairloch, Coigach, and Assynt brought them into feud with the MacKenzies, who came to hold most of Ross. The MacKenzies first won footing in Gairloch in 1494 after long feuds conducted by Hector Roy, the progenitor of their house of Gairloch, against the MacLeods of Raasay and Gairloch. Hector's sister had married Allan, chief of the Gairloch MacLeods, in 1480. She had two sons by him, but her husband's brothers so hated the MacKenzies that one summer's day, when Allan was fishing on the river Ewe and his wife and children were on an island on Loch Tollie a mile to the west, they murdered their brother by the river bank, and then went to Loch Tollie and murdered the two boys; they stripped the boys and threw their blood-stained shirts at the mother. She went straight to her father at Brahan Castle. MacKenzie sent his brother Hector Roy to the king; the king gave Hector a commission of fire and sword. And that was the end of the MacLeods of Gairloch. The descendants of Hector Roy occupy Flowerdale House at the present day.

When the boats are in, the bustle at the pier is as fascinating as at Mallaig, although on a smaller scale; whitefish boats from Stornoway jostle with the lobster-boats and salmon-netters and ringnet herring-boats calling in from the farthest Hebridean seas. The auctioneers ring their bells to draw attention and be heard above the noise of gulls and lorries and the shout of seamen. The times to visit are in the forenoon when the salmon catch is landed, and the evening when the fleet enters to unload whitefish, prawns, lobsters and crabs. The value of the fish landed at this little inlet amounts to several hundred thousand pounds a year, comprising mainly white-fish and shellfish.

Beyond Flowerdale Bridge you pass on the left a nine-hole golf course—an unusual feature on the north-west coast—and rise to a hill-top. The Gair Loch opens out to your west. Across the back of its islands you can see the north point of Skye, and forty miles across the wrinkled Minch, the long isle of Lewis and Harris lifting its ridge of gneiss along the earth's rim. Close below you comes the sight of a new bay—a quarter-mile curve of perfect sand leading the eye on to the village of Gairloch. The nearer point of this bay breaks west in a promontory on which stood the old fort of the MacLeods of Gairloch. Before their time it had been the site of a vitrified fort, of which the barest trace remains.

Gairloch is a village of some 300 people. This small figure mis-represents the real importance of Gair Loch, for it does not include the crofting townships that extend nine miles north along the coast at Strath, Big Sand, North Erradale, Aultgrishin, and Melvaig, nor those extending nine miles south-west at Shieldaig, Badachro, Port Henderson, Opinan, South Erradale, and Red Point. Gairloch is simply the central village of twelve, developed to give services in its shops, bank, garage, church, school, and so on, and developed too as a tourist centre. The real population is nearly 1,800. Gairloch is dominated by its huge hotel—or one that looks huge (53 bedrooms) in a village so small. It has fishing rights on Loch Maree, and free trout-fishing on five other lochs, and (again most unusual in the north-west) a private tennis court. Other smaller hotels will be found at the head of Flowerdale Bay (The Old Inn), and at Shiel-daig Bay (Shieldaig Lodge Hotel). There is no lack of house-accommodation. Permits to fish on Loch Bad an Sgalaig and two other lochs may be had from the Gairloch Angling Club at the Wild Cat Store.

The district of Gairloch, although it measures approximately thirty miles by twenty-two, has a coastline of nearly one hundred. You begin to explore it by moving south to Red Point. From the shores of the Gairloch there is a magnificent panorama across the great bay to the Torridon mountains. It is in this direction you now go, through birch and oak woods of the south shore through Shieldaig

Torridon and Gairloch

(not to be confused with the Applecross Shieldaig) and on to open country at Badachro. Bare gneiss everywhere protrudes as in Sutherland, and with little soil between the stone, yet gaily tufted by late August heather. Badachro has a perfect haven in its north-facing bay, guarded from storm by a breakwater of over-lapping islands. It is much used as an anchorage by cruising yachts and fishing boats. An old inn at the sea's edge is so close to the water at high tide that one feels afloat if one looks out.

Two miles west, the road turns south at Port Henderson and passes through succeeding crofts at Opinan and South Erradale to end at Red Point. All four have beaches of clean sand, safe for bathing. Red Point is the outermost point of Loch Torridon. Two sights most worth seeing from here on a clear morning or evening are the views down the Inner Sound (between Applecross and Raasay) to the Cuillin of Skye, and south-east across Loch Torridon to the mountains of Kintail.

Between Gair Loch and Loch Ewe, the peninsula of **Rudhe Reidh** (the Level Point), projects ten miles north into the Minch. The main road from Gairloch strikes east over its broad neck to Poolewe, but a side-road winds nine miles along the peninsula's west shore to Melvaig. By this road you at once enter Strath, which is virtually a part of Gairloch with shops, hotel, and boarding houses. Two miles west the road turns inland, by-passing the crofts of Big Sand and North Erradale. If you walk down to the shore south of Big Sand you will find a good sandy beach at Little Sand, and a cave in the rocks of North Erradale. A memorable feature of this coast, if you are in luck, is the sunset over the Hebrides. At Melvaig the public road ends, but a private road owned by the Northern Lighthouse Commission continues three miles to the lighthouse of Ru' Re' (as it is usually abbreviated). Permission to use the road should be obtained from the lighthouse keeper, telephone Gairloch 81.

Leaving Gairloch by the Auchtercairn hill, you cross to Poolewe over a barren moor peppered with gneiss outcrops, relieved only by a pinewood at the west end and **Loch Tollie** at the east end. Loch Tollie, the Loch of the Hollow, has a crannog, or artificial island made of stone and rubble raised on a timber platform, which was used by the Clan MacBeth as a refuge and stronghold. The road now falls away to the river Ewe, passing a track that forks sharp right to Tollie Bay of Loch Maree. Here you should halt and climb a hillock by the roadside. The whole of Loch Maree is revealed. The scene is a moving one, partly by its unexpectedness after the bleak

307

moor, but more by the natural splendour of the islanded loch and the mountain range lifting from its shore. All the peaks can be seen from Beinn Airidh Charr (the Mountain of the Rough Shieling) to Slioch.

Poolewe is a land of crofts and small farms at the estuary of the river Ewe, to which are added two hotels, the Stage House caravan park, and the Inverewe Gardens. At the very brink of the river, where it surges into Loch Ewe, stands the Pool House Hotel, with salmon and sea-trout rights on the river and trout fishing on several lochs. Poolewe hotel stands above it on the side-road down the west shore of the sea-loch. **Loch Ewe** is nearly twice the size of Gair Loch, fully eight miles long and three wide, enclosed by two big peninsulas, the Ru' Re' and Greenstone Point. Like Gair Loch it is embellished by a multitude of small bays, but all on bigger scale. The road down the west shore gives an excellent view of the loch from its highest point (point 176 on the Ordnance Survey map), on which stands an old concrete gun-site two miles north of the road-fork. The gun-site is a relic of the last war, when Loch Ewe was a naval base of importance. The road continues through the scattered crofting townships of Naust and Inverasdale to a fine sandy beach, deep-sunk under a rocky bluff opposite Isle of Ewe. The road thereafter loses interest and ends at Cove, where there is another sandy beach, eight miles from Poolewe. Much peat-cutting is done on the hills along this road in late spring and early summer. The aromatic scent of peat-reek from the croft-house chimneys can be one of our pleasures all around Loch Ewe when we forsake the main road.

Across the head of the loch and facing Poolewe are the world-famous Inverewe Gardens. Between the two shores and facing down the loch, the Stage House has been built by the National Trust for Scotland and the Shell Oil Company to serve as a caravan park luxuriously equipped with hot showers, drying room, electric washing machines, and power-points for electric shavers and irons. The five concrete sheds that line the road-front, when added to the length of the filling station, make a rather long blank wall. It looks well from the far distance. Near-to, the bare walls topped by corrugated asbestos cement are in need of masking; this would be achieved in time if trees were planted in front in sufficient number.

The **Inverewe Gardens** were created last century by Osgood MacKenzie, a son of the twelfth chief of the Gairloch clan. In 1862, the point on the eastern shore, Am Ploc Ard (the High Round Promontory), was barren ground on which grew only one bush, a

308

willow three feet high. MacKenzie, a man of energy and imagination, accepted that ground as a challenge and the bush as encouragement. Sour peaty ground was drained. Rock excavated. Trees were planted as shelter-belts. His estate workers were employed to carry soil in their peat-creels to fill the troughs in the rock and to build up beds. He planned it as a wild garden: any other kind would have been out of place in this mountainous landscape. In the course of sixty years he made that rocky desert one of the best sub-tropical gardens in North-west Europe. The work was continued after his death by his daughter, Mrs Mairi Sawyer, until in 1952 she handed over the garden to the National Trust for Scotland. Under their highly skilled direction, further improvements and additions have been made. An information centre and a licensed restaurant have been built to serve the flood of visitors. Before the Trust took over the garden was visited by several hundred people annually. It now draws 100,000.

Inverewe is a woodland garden. The windbreak trees are mostly conifers, pine predominating, but among them are magnificent Monterey pines, Australian tree ferns, a larch tree on which a hydrangea climbs fifty feet, rhododendrons and many other exotic shrubs from China, Tasmania, Chile, the Himalaya, Ceylon, South Africa, the Chatham Islands in the Pacific—and all this seeming miraculous when one remembers that Inverewe lies near the 58th parallel, which cuts through Hudson Bay and Siberia. The wealth of rare plants and trees under their shelter offer beauty, colour, and constant surprise to the visitor at every season of the year. A feature of the garden is magnolia trees. In March, the *Magnolia campbellii* blossoms in delicate pink flowers on leafless branches. The *Magnolia stellata* is thought to be the world's largest—28 feet high and 75 feet in circumference. Eucalyptus rise to 98 feet. August at Inverewe is the month for hydrangea, first brought from Japan to Scotland in 1790. Its near relative, *Hydrangea paniculata grandiflora*, blooms in spikes of white flower in early September, when its branches arch along the waterside. In September, South African *Agapanthus* show tall umbels of blue or white, while its compatriot *Watsonia beatricis* displays from high spikes fiery flowers that last into December. In September, too, look for the Chinese rowan, *Sorbus vilmorinii*, nearly smothered in pink berries, and for *Eucryphia* x *nymansensis*, which becomes a pillar of white blossoms with flowers like camellia.

Spring and early summer, when the flowers common to Scotland

—primula, daffodil, heather, azalea, rhododendron, and a host of rock-plants—outdazzle all exotic bloom, is of course the most rewarding season in terms of colour-blaze, but every other season offers so much of interest that the garden must be regarded as a unique national asset. The paths winding through 2,000 acres of low hills and woods cover much more ground than you are likely to estimate. A morning or afternoon visit will not allow you to see all at leisure. Allot a full day to a first exploration. The gardens are open throughout the year from 10 a.m. till dusk, on Sundays from 1 p.m. till dusk.

The garden has for its background the mountains of Flowerdale and Letterewe, not crowding in close but lying far back in spacious spread. Beinn Airidh Charr, the nearest, stretches a long shoulder down to the foot of Loch Maree. Under its north flank lies **Fionn Loch**, one of the more delightful hill-lochs of the Highlands, not known as widely as it should be because one must walk to see it, but famous among anglers as one of the best trout lochs in Scotland. Osgood MacKenzie records a catch last century of twelve trout weighing 88 lb., and the fishing has not fallen off seriously. In 1963 one rod took twenty-one trout weighing 63 lb., of which one weighed 11 lb. There are nò salmon. The walk in to Fionn Loch is six miles. The route follows at first the track to Loch Maree, and this track is worth walking for its own sake.

Start at the bridge over the Ewe, near Pool House Hotel. The road strikes in along the right bank for a few hundred yards to a gate marked PRIVATE. NO ADMITTANCE TO VEHICLES WITHOUT PERMIT. You pass through. The river is only two miles long, but flows deep and wide. In August the banks are ablaze and scented with ling and bell heather. Craggy sandstone hills rise a thousand feet on the far side, and from three neat crofts below them the reek of peat fires drifts over the river. Opposite the last croft-house there is a hidden drop in the river-bed where the flood quickens. This the salmon love and they may be seen jumping in August, big ones three or four feet long coming clear out of the water.

The road now leads through woods of scrub-oak, birch, and alder to Inveran Lodge at the upper end of the river. Here the track turns above the house and strikes north-east across rough open moor to Loch Kernsary. For permission to fish, apply to the croft-house above the loch. At the river below the cottage you have a choice of route. If you wish to go to Loch Maree, turn sharp right up the left bank; if to Fionn Loch, keep straight on uphill to the cottage.

The **Loch Maree** track is at first invisible on open grass, but you soon see it by the river's south fork. It is the roughest track I have ever walked in Scotland, surpassing the worst I have known in the Himalaya. In compensation it crosses open moorland under Beinn Airidh Charr, now close and rugged, with fine views across Loch Maree to the Torridon Hills. The summit of Beinn Eighe is clearly seen as a huge quartzite cap sitting on top of red sandstone. There is no need to descend to Loch Maree (where the views are inferior) unless you are intent on the long walk to Kinlochewe. The best return is to Inveran along the flat hill-tops north-west—dry walking not one half so rough as that path back to Kernsary.

The track to Fionn Loch curves uphill from Kernsary, swinging leftward far across wide moorland heavy with the scent of heather. The track is fair, the going dull, and the end worth all effort. You finish at a boat-house and jetty. The view is good, the water laps on the rocky shore, trout jump and ring the surface, but much the better view is from the top of a rocky hillock 150 yards to the north of the boat-house. The whole five-mile length of Fionn Loch is now seen. It lies deep between the mountains of Fisherfield and Letterewe Forests; the broad waters dotted by islets, some rocky, others grassy or heathery, are alive with light and dappled by passing clouds. Capes, bays, and points sculpted out of the shores make a wildly ragged foreground to an arc of rock peaks enclosing the loch's head. On the right, the cliffs of Letterewe plunge a thousand feet to the glen. At the centre, a rock cone marks the end-point of the loch; and close to its left, **A' Mhaighdean**, the Maiden (pronounced Ah Vyéjen), is Scotland's finest mountain of gneiss. It soars in a pillar of naked rock from the water's edge to 3,000 feet.

From the peaceful seclusion of Fionn Loch one returns with reluctance to the busy thoroughfare of Poolewe. The main road north goes six miles down Loch Ewe, then rises over the back of Greenstone peninsula to Gruinard Bay. On passing Inverewe Gardens you climb at once on to a rocky moor, on which dense outcrops of Torridon sandstone are the same deep pink as the ling heather growing thickly from their crevices. A lochan on your left encircles, with the heather of its banks and the waterlilies of its fringe, an islet of rhododendrons at the centre. You drop to the shore of Loch Thuirnaig, a bay of Loch Ewe, and immediately beyond rise to a hill-top. Here you should stop to enjoy a vast eastward and southward panorama. The mountain ranges of Fisherfield, Letterewe, Flowerdale, and Torridon are spread before you, their peaks crowding the sky.

Three miles farther the road forks: the main road north-east to Gruinard, a side-road north-west through Aultbea to Mellon Charles. You should not omit the latter, for you will see here something you have not seen before on the mainland coast, and will not see again on your way to Cape Wrath—a large crofting community on a traditional pattern that is dying out elsewhere on the mainland, but is here thriving through the good offices of the Royal Navy.

Along this three-mile strip of coast are five crofting townships, with Aultbea (pronounced Aultbay), the Burn of the Birches, at one end and Mellon Charles at the other. The name **Aultbea** is commonly used to include them all. From dark heathery moors behind, the crofts undulate in green and gold strips down to the sea, where the shore forms a big double bay, divided by a central spit with a pier, and sheltered by the Isle of Ewe. The Outer Hebrides can be seen through the mouth of the inner channel.

The navy is further developing its former war-time base. More piers and quays are being built, pipe-lines laid, and numerous big buoys moored offshore. This work, and the naval establishment at Mellon Charles, are giving the crofters the security of employment and income that crofting alone cannot provide. The community thus has an air of prosperity; the white-washed cottages are neat and clean and scent the well-tended fields with peat-smoke. The Aultbea Hotel and the smaller Drumchork Lodge Hotel both have a good reputation.

From Aultbea, a broad new road crosses the moorland back of the peninsula to Gruinard Bay. The western half of the bay is politically in Gairloch district, but is geographically part of Loch Broom, and more properly described under that heading.

CHAPTER 25

Loch Broom

Between the seaward peninsulas of Greenstone Point and Rhu
More Coigach, which lie fourteen miles apart, **Loch Broom** drives
twenty-one miles into the mainland—the longest sea-loch of the
North-west Highlands. And between its **Gruinard Bay** and the
Coigach shore, more than thirty islands spread across the ten-mile
width of the outer loch. Most of these islands lie in two groups, the
Summer Isles under the wing of Rhu More, and the **Priest Island**
group at centre. At the back of the outer loch, two narrow inner
lochs pierce nine miles south-east into the mountains. The more
southerly is Little Loch Broom under the flank of An Teallach, and
the more northerly, Loch Broom, whose head lies under Beinn
Dearg, in the Inverlael Forest. The ground dividing the two is a long
hilly peninsula projecting into the middle of Outer Loch Broom
at Cailleach Head.

The surrounding district of Lochbroom, 400 square miles, is one
of the largest parishes in Scotland. Its capital is **Ullapool**, a fishing
port on inner Loch Broom, and the best centre for exploring most
of the district. The southern shores—Gruinard Bay and Little
Loch Broom—are more conveniently explored from Dundonnell
Hotel at the head of Little Loch Broom: this to obviate the twenty-
five mile detour from Ullapool, not only round the heads of the two
lochs, but also to turn their far-running valleys, Strath More and
Strath Beg, and to cross the hills between.

The most direct approach to Lochbroom from south and east
Scotland is from Inverness through Garve, then over the Highland
watershed to the Diridh Mór, or Great Ascent, as the west side of
the pass is called. The pass at 1,000 feet is dull and dreary moorland,
greatly improved since 1950 by the five-mile length of Glascarnoch
Loch, created by the North of Scotland Hydro-Electric Board as a
reservoir. The Diridh Mór slopes from there down to Braemore at

the head of Strath More, where the road divides, one branch to
Loch Broom and the other to Little Loch Broom. This route is
served daily by a bus from Garve to Ullapool (33 miles), and by
another less frequently from Inverness. Your approach through
Gairloch, although served by bus only once a week, would be the
line chosen by anyone on tour up the west coast. If you approach
from the north through Assynt, you can now use an excellent new
road from Kylesku to Ullapool, but on this road no public transport
is provided. These west coast districts are largely isolated from each
other in business and social life; their life-lines, like those of the
Hebridean islands, run east to market and not north and south
between themselves. The development of good north to south roads
is recent, and almost entirely in the interest of summer tourist
traffic.

When whatever your line of approach, you soon discover in Lochbroom
three completely different kinds of scenery. The low-lying ground
towards the sea, at Gruinard and the north-west coast of Coigach,
is a wilderness of pale grey hillocky gneiss. But these gneiss-deserts
are small compared to those of Sutherland. Immediately behind rise
the cones and pyramids of red Torridon sandstone, only half the
age of the gneiss but nearly eight hundred million years old. At their
highest they rise to 3,483 feet on An Teallach, but even when a
thousand feet less on the coast of Coigach, they are carved to conspicuous shape, monuments to a vast denudation. They strike to
the eye. Most *Munros* of the south and central Highlands seem tame
by comparison. Behind them again, towards the eastern parts of
Lochbroom, more rounded peat-moor hills spread through the
Forests of Dundonnell, Inverlael, and Rhidorroch to the Cromalt
Hills. These are mountains of schist, named Moine Schist from the
Gaelic word Moine meaning Peat-moor. They have been pushed
westward over the top of the sandstone and gneiss on an incline
called the Moine Thrust Plane, and thus cover most of North-west
Scotland except the seaboard.

When you cross from Loch Ewe of Gairloch over the back of
Greenstone peninsula you come down on Gruinard Bay at Laide.
The coast is lined with old crofting townships of strange-sounding
names—Mellon Udrigle, Laide, Sand, First Coast, Second Coast,
and others. The name **Gruinard** is from the Norse Grunna Fjord,
meaning Shallow Fiord. Four miles wide by four long, its shores are
indented by a dozen coves, most of them rocky, but several having
sweeps of pink sand that contrast markedly with the ash-grey gneiss

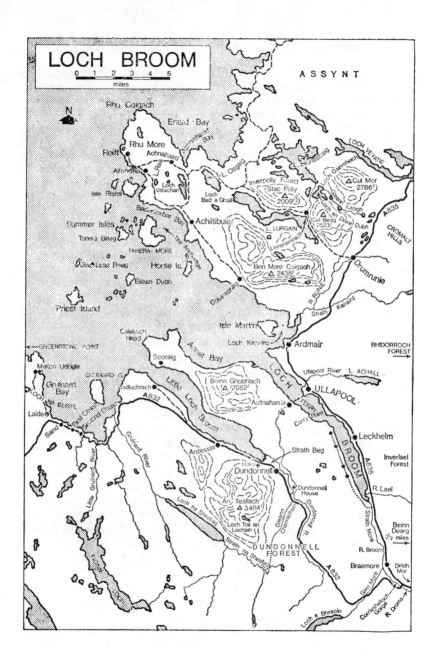

LOCH BROOM

0 1 2 3 4 5
miles

N

ASSYNT

Rhu Coigach

Enard Bay

Rhu More

Achnahaird

Reiff

Achnahaird Bay

Altandhu

L. Rae

Isle Ristol

Loch Vatachan

Loch Bad a Ghaill

Inverpolly Forest

Stac Polly
△ 2009'

LOCH VEYATIE

Loch Gainmheich

Cul Mor
△ 2786'

Gleann Laoigh

A835

Summer Isles

Badentarbat Bay

Achiltibuie

L. Osgaig

Sionascaig

Loch an Doire Dubh

Cul Beag
△ 2523'

CROMALT HILLS

Tanera Beag

TANERA MORE

The Anchorage

L. LURGAIN

Linneraineach

Glac Dhorc Beag

Horse Is.

Eilean Dubh

Priest Island

Culnacraig

Ben More Coigach
△ 2438'

Drumrunie

R. RUNIE

Strath Kanaird

Cailleach Head

Isle Martin

Loch Kanaird

GREENSTONE POINT

Annat Bay

Ardmair

RHIDORROCH FOREST

Scoraig

Little Loch Broom

Beinn Ghobhlach
△ 2082'

Ullapool River L. ACHALL

Melton Udrigle

GRUINARD IS.

Badluchrach

A832

Badcaul Croft

Laide

Sand

Great Cuan

Little Gruinard River

Gruinard River

Aultnaharrie

LOCH   BROOM

FERRY

Corry Point

ULLAPOOL

Leckhelm

A835

Gruinard Bay

NA BEISTE

Ardessie

Hotel
Dundonnell

Strath Beg

Dundonnell House

Inverlael Forest

R. Lael

An Teallach
△ 3484'

Loch na Sealga

Loch Toll an Lochain

Strath na Sheallag

Gleann Chaorachain

Dundonnell R.

DUNDONNELL FOREST

Strath More

R. Broom

Beinn Dearg
2½ miles

Braemore

Diridh Mor

A832

Glen More

Corrieshalloch Gorge

R. Droma

Loch a Bhraoin

inland and have made the bay celebrated throughout the west coast. None of these sandy bays of Ross and Assynt have the creamy shell-sand that you found at Ardnamurchan, but are formed mostly of red sandstone, which replaces gneiss around the shores. The sandy bottom offshore is rich in flounders, which draw to Gruinard several great northern divers, who love flounder so well that they have learned how to swallow them whole. In winter, the most common sea-duck is merganser, which go up the Dundonnell river to breed. Long-tailed duck hunt among the shoals for shellfish, and dunlin comb the sand at the sea's edge.

On reaching Laide, you turn north up the coast past croftland to arrive in three miles at **Mellon Udrigle**. Here the road ends. This delightful cove is ringed by short green turf and by low sandstone hills. Broad sands stretch into green seas. Six cottages at its back have small gardens packed with flowers, notably roses.

To get the best view, you should walk on to the bay's left arm. From there you can look south-east across the breadth of Gruinard Bay into Strath na Sheallag, which runs deep into the mountains between An Teallach on the left and Beinn Dearg Mhor on the right. Between the two mountains but hidden from sight lies Loch na Sheallag, the Loch of the Hunts, named thus from its ancient fame as a hunting ground. The strath at its head is still strongly populated with red deer. Even more impressive is the outward view across Loch Broom. Eastward on the back of the Cailleach Head peninsula, Beinn Ghoblach, the Forked Mountain, rears twin peaks of 2,000 feet, appearing in their abrupt rise and shapeliness far higher and steeper than they really are. This same virtue shows with still more cause on the ranges of Coigach and Assynt to the north, where Ben More Coigach lifts from the very shore of Loch Broom, backed by Stac Polly, Cul Beag, and Cul Mor, all close to its left, by Suilven and Canisp beyond, and in the farthest background, the five tops of Quinag. The horizon bristles like a harrow. One cannot think of these peaks as the relatively low hills that figures indicate, but at once grant them the status of mountains.

On your return to Laide you pass on your right **Loch na Beiste**, the Loch of the Monster, one mile from Mellon Udrigle and only a hundred yards from the road. The loch received its name from an incident that local people rejoice to tell, and which Seton Gordon records in his *Highways and Byways*. One Sunday morning the monster emerged to astound township elders on their way to church. Fearful of its possible depredations, they asked and received from their laird permission to drain the loch. Prolonged effort at drainage having left them defeated, they carried a boat to the loch, and after taking soundings resolved to try to kill the monster in his den, which they had determined must be a hole in the middle. To this hole they ferried out fourteen sacks of lime and tipped them in. And the monster was never seen again.

Beyond Laide you pass through the crofts of Sand and First and Second Coasts to top Gruinard Hill at 328 feet. You are now at the back of the great bay and should stop to climb a hillock on your left; it gives a clear view across the three principal beaches, whose red sands are creamed by sparkling surf and fringed by the emerald of foreshore grass. Wild crags of gneiss rise behind, receding inland to the sandstone pile of An Teallach. No camping or caravanning is now allowed at these wonderful beaches. The result has been nothing but good. The litter that spoiled their appearance ten years ago has vanished away. The sands are spotless, giving more delight to more people.

The road plunges to the Little Gruinard river, which bursts white along the edge of a pinewood, given a furious life by the boulders congesting its bed. An unsolved mystery of the river is why the salmon and sea-trout that run annually up its five-mile length will not enter Fionn Loch, from which it flows free of obstacle. One suggestion is that if salmon were to breed in Fionn Loch the brown trout there, which are exceptionally big and numerous, would devour the smolt. But if so, how do the salmon know this?

A mile or so beyond Little Gruinard, the road twists between gneiss crags to cross the river Gruinard. Here there is a track up the left bank to Loch na Sheallag, with right of way up the strath at its head. The road returns through woods to the coast, where it links the second and third sandy beaches. On this stretch of road you are warned by notice-boards that Gruinard Island, which lies three-quarters of a mile offshore, is contaminated, and must not be approached by boat. The island is no more than a mile long by half a mile wide. The prohibition on the use of its good pasture and fine beaches has long aroused the wrath of local people and the curiosity of visitors. The notice-boards offer no explanation.

During the last war, the Microbiological Research Establishment of the Ministry of Defence used the island for an experiment in germ warfare. This was a defence measure taken on intelligence reports that Germany was investigating the subject as an offensive weapon. At Gruinard Island, anthrax was disseminated in aerosol

317

form to determine whether that could cause the infection of sheep and cattle. The answer was affirmative for sheep, and one result was the development of an effective vaccination against anthrax for both man and beast. The experiments ended with the war. New experiments have since shown that Gruinard Island could be cleaned, but at so high a cost that the government is unwilling to spend the money. The director of the Microbiological Research Establishment is reported as saying that a hundred years might pass before the island is free of infection, but that any earlier clearance will be publicly announced. Meantime, his staff make annual inspection.

The road now swings east over the back of a headland to **Little Loch Broom**. From the top at 585 feet, you can survey all the high mountains encircling Lochbroom. They afforest the sky; southward, the ranges of Fisherfield; eastward, An Teallach; at the head of Loch Broom, the dozen tops of Inverlael; and then the lesser host of Coigach. As you move in towards them, rainfall-averages swiftly rise—72 inches at Dundonnell at the head of Little Loch Broom, 100 inches at Strath na Sheallag, whereas Ullapool, only four miles north of Dundonnell but free of cloud-gathering mountains, registers 48 inches.

This mountain rain has given loch and parish their name. High in the hills of Dundonnell Forest, above Strath Beg and Strath More, lies Loch à Bhraoin, meaning Loch of the Showers. From Braon (Bhraoin is the genitive) the word Broom derives. The Dundonnell river, which flows down Strath Beg, was in early days called the Little Broom, distinguished thus from the river Broom flowing directly out of Loch à Bhraoin down Strath More to the main loch. The name Dundonnell is a relic of early history, when the parish was Clan Donald country. Lochbroom was held by the Donald Lords of the Isles as earls of Ross, and ruled for them by the MacDonalds of Lochalsh even after the forfeiture of 1493. In 1518, MacDonell of Glengarry inherited one half and MacKenzie of Kintail purchased the other half. The deadly feud between the two lasted through the sixteenth century. In 1603, Glengarry surrendered to Kintail all his lands in Ross.

The western shore of Little Loch Broom is the barest of croft-land, sustaining several small townships. In striking contrast, Strath Beg (like Strath More) is finely wooded with much natural growth of birch, rowan, hazel, oak, and alder. It is one of the virtues of private ownership, as distinguished from state ownership, that rich men plant for beauty. Thus, in the neighbourhood of **Dundonnell**

House, as also around the several mansion-houses of Strath More, the ground has been planted with elm, lime, beech, chestnut, sycamore, and oak, none of which is thought profitable by the Forestry Commission, whose official eyes seem unable to rise above the limits set by material profit and loss. For the woodland beauty of Highland glens we owe a great debt to men of a past age.

Half a mile to the east of both Dundonnell House and Hotel, hill-tracks give quick access to the slopes of **An Teallach**. The name means the Forge, from the smoke-like mists that curl round its eleven tops. The main ridge of the chain is three miles long and rockily pinnacled. The traverse of these pinnacles in winter is the best of its kind on the mainland. In summer the rock-scrambling is easy, but a rope should be carried and used if required. The rock is rough and sound. The geologists call it red, but in fact the colour is chocolate brown, appearing as pink only in rare patches. Laid down in successive layers, it weathers to a piled pancake formation, pinnacles emerging as stepped pyramids, which are a distinguishing feature of An Teallach's crest.

The summit may be reached without any rock-work if one starts up the track near the hotel and aims for the north-east ridge. If the thought of climbing to the top is too daunting, an effort should at least be made to walk up to its eastern corrie, for that is one of the half-dozen most elegant examples of mountain architecture in the Highlands. The track starts near Dundonnell House up Gleann Chaorachain. It goes all the way to Strath na Sheallag, but two miles up at 1,200 feet you leave the track and strike west-north-west over moorland into the corrie. Its floor is filled by the black water of Loch Toll an Lochain. From an apron of tumbled screes, the cliffs circling it spring 1,300 feet in divided towers; they break against the sky like a wave-crest. The summit-ridge is much favoured by golden eagles, whose talon-prints often mark the winter snow at the brink, from which they launch themselves over the great precipice. On the south side of the mountain, Strath na Sheallag gives the extraordinary contrast of a flat green valley, meandering and gently flowing rivers, and the long mirror of Loch na Sheallag in the trough between An Teallach and Beinn Dearg Mhor, 2,974 feet, whose eastern corrie is like that of Toll an Lochain in miniature, and often mistaken for it in photographs.

Where the lowest slopes of An Teallach meet the sea, by the roadside two and a half miles west of Dundonnell, the waterfall of Ardessie makes a sight worth seeing after rain. The principal falls of the district, the most spectacular in Ross after the Falls of Glomach, are the Falls of Measach at the head of Strath More. You pass them on the way to Ullapool. The journey to Ullapool is twenty-five miles by motor-road but for the walker this can be shortened to little more than five if he takes the cart-track from Dundonnell northward; it climbs to 800 feet on the back of the Cailleach Head peninsula and drops thence to **Aultnaharrie** on the south shore of Loch Broom. From there a ferry for passengers only plies to Ullapool, sailing six days a week in summer at intervals of two hours from 10 a.m. to 8 p.m.

The long route for the motorist climbs from wooded Strath Beg on to the bleak moors of Dundonnell Forest at 1,110 feet. This road is known throughout the North-west Highlands as Destitution Road, for it was made during the potato famine of 1851 to give work to starving men. Near Loch à Bhraoin it descends to Glen More, but where that opens out to Strath More the road takes a big eastward swing to turn the Corrieshalloch Gorge of the river Droma, which cuts in from the right to join the Broom. The Droma flows down the pass of the Diridh More between two high mountain ranges. To its north is the Braemore Forest, whose summit is Beinn Dearg, 3,547 feet, and to its south is the Fannich Forest, whose main summit is Sgurr Mor, 3,637 feet. These two massifs and their outliers were in the Ice Age covered by an ice-cap several thousand feet thick, from which glaciers flowed to the Atlantic. The ice smoothed and striated the rocks of Strath More and Strath Beg, and as the ice-cap melted, the water roaring down to Loch Broom cut the mile-long gorge of **Corrieshalloch** through solid rock. The gorge is now in the care of the National Trust for Scotland.

The road skirts the south edge, executes a hairpin bend at the head, and returns down the north edge. The two sides are connected near the middle of the hairpin by a bridge and footpath. You can walk out on to the bridge between sheer rock-walls and see the river Droma burst from the chasm close above and plunge down the Falls of Measach into the gorge two hundred feet beneath your feet. A short way below the bridge, a wooden platform built out from the north wall allows you to view the gorge to best advantage. The vertical sides are thickly grown with dwarf rowan, hazel, birch, and alder. To appreciate the gorge to the full you should walk a few hundred yards up the narrow woodland path on the right bank. Rough grass slopes rising from the gorge to the roadside are heavily planted with larch, which are mixed along the path with all the

320

trees above noted and with pine, holly, a few oak, and sycamore. This variety gives much beauty to the scene. The path winds through the woods, for the most part holding closely to the sheer wall and granting exciting vistas down to pools in the river or to side-streams hurtling down the left wall. The path dwindles away where the river-bed is split by a 100-foot vertical stack crowned with heather and two dwarf larches. The gorge is small compared to that of Glen Nevis, but north of Lochaber is the finest (though not the biggest) of its kind on the Highland seaboard and the most readily accessible.

From Braemore, where the river Droma becomes the Broom, you descend Strath More to broad park-land bearing stands of nobly-proportioned trees around the bigger houses. Rhododendron now lines the road, showing at its best at Leckmelm, two and a half miles down the loch. Near the head of the loch a branch road goes left to the crofting villages on the west shore. The main road keeps to the east side, below the Lael forest of the Forestry Commission, where a track up the river Lael gives access to the north side of the Beinn Dearg range. Five miles on you top the hill of Corry Point and suddenly find **Ullapool Bay** below, dotted all over with red and white buoys. The town shines white along the south shore of the farther point, massed behind and to either side of its long pier. No building emerges prominently from the seeming huddle; only a few tree-tops appear over the roof-tops, and the hills behind are feature-less. The beach is shingle. Out through the mouth of inner Loch Broom you glimpse the long low Summer Isles.

Town and setting have a clean bareness, the air a sub-arctic clearness, that I associate with the old Norse lands of the outer and northernmost Hebrides: a quality that distinguishes Sutherland and this Coigach border of Ross from lands farther south, perhaps by reason of smaller rainfall and higher wind, for the north-west coast is the windiest of the British Isles. Appropriately, Ullapool's name comes from the Norse for Ulli's Steading. The present village, sited on a late Ice Age beach fifty feet above sea-level, was founded by the British Fisheries Society in 1788. Its life then and prosperity since it owes to herring.

The appearance of huddle vanishes when you enter the village, which is neatly laid out in streets of criss-cross pattern. The population is nearly 600—half of the population of Loch Broom's 400 square miles. In summer one might think the village was first and foremost a tourist resort, for it has several well-furnished hotels, nearly forty boarding houses, a caravan site, and much to offer the visitor in well-organized sea-fishing, pony trekking, and of course the most excellent loch and river fishing for brown trout and salmon, both close at hand on Loch Achall and on the river Ullapool flowing from it, and in Coigach to the north. A car-ferry runs daily to Stornoway in Lewis. Motor-boats cruise to the Summer Isles or to Gruinard Bay. Ullapool may seem crowded in July and August, but the serious business of the port is not the visitor but the herring.

At the height of the season, which lasts from October to March, a fleet of seventy boats uses Ullapool, and the value of the landings is nearly £1 million a year—almost all in herring. The whitefish on this coast are landed in the Sutherland ports of Kinlochbervie and Lochinver, to which Ullapool ranks equal. It appears that Ullapool is just a little too far from the best whitefish grounds, but ideally placed for hunting the Minch herring. When the fleet makes port it is met by a lorry-fleet, which carries the catch to Aberdeen for canning and kippering.

Many of the crofters around Loch Broom fish cod and lobster, but the size of their catch is relatively unimportant. It was different in former days. For nearly four hnudred years, from the sixteenth century to the latter part of the nineteenth, the herring fishing within Loch Broom itself was famous. The local boats went far into the outer loch to lay their nets. Unfortunately this manna from heaven was exploited by companies from England, who on receiving expert reports established fishing stations on the Summer Isles and at Isle Martin at the mouth of Inner Loch Broom. The annual herring migration does not, as has hitherto been thought, go clockwise round Scotland. The shoals are now believed to come and go, concentrating here and there round the coast, so far inexplicably. In the eighteenth century and earlier they passed Loch Broom from May till September, when they came into the loch in prodigious shoals. The *Statistical Account* reads:

'People are instantly afloat with every species of seaworthy craft ... they press forward with utmost eagerness to the field of slaughter —sloops, schooners, wherries, boats of all sizes, are seen constantly flying on the wings of the wind from creek to creek, and from loch to loch, according as the varying reports of men, or the noisy flights of birds, or tumbling and spouting of whales and porpoises attract them.'

This happy-go-lucky fishing was bridled around 1780 by the exploiting companies' planning officers. The herring, they had noted, entered Loch Broom along the Coigach shore and left by the Gruinard. By siting their fishery stations on Isle Martin and Isle Tanera on the Coigach shore they ensured that their boats need sail only one mile and be back in an hour to clear the catch. The catch was exported to Ireland and the West Indies, and the rewards were immense. The boom lasted fifty years. But even a herring will turn in the end. This localized depredation was too great. By 1830 the shoals were growing markedly less, and by 1880 they had vanished.

Meantime, the success of the island stations had caused the formation of the British Fisheries Society, which in 1788 had begun to build Ullapool three miles down the inner loch as a new station with pier, inn, sheds, and houses for the fishermen, The houses, renovated, survive to the present day. On the collapse of the industry Ullapool fell on evil times, but the Minch fishing took a new lease of life during the last war, partly through the sowing of mines on the east coast, and is now established and thriving.

Sea-angling for sport has in Ullapool its unrivalled west coast centre. When the European Sea Angling Championship was held here in September 1965, 10,716 lb. of fish were caught in one week. The many bays, creeks, sounds, and islets of Loch Broom give small boats sheltered water—and stirring seascapes, which in the outer loch are dominated by the huge cone of Ben More Coigach. Four kinds of fishing may be had: by rod from the shore rocks for cod, saithe, and mackerel; by boat from inner Loch Broom for bigger fish of the same variety, and for whiting, haddock, and skate— skate of nearly 200 lb. were caught off Ullapool in 1961; by motor-launch in outer Loch Broom with fishing parties under experienced boatmen, who sail both from Ullapool and from Achiltibuie in Coigach, and whose target is the still more plentiful and bigger fish off the Summer Isles, Gruinard, and Little Loch Broom. Lastly, there is 'big-time' sport—fishing for shark, conger, tope, and huss. All tackle for the two latter categories is provided by the launch-hirers.

A ship of unusual interest at Ullapool, one that arrived in 1966 and is likely to be a frequent visitor, is the new and experimental Royal National Lifeboat *002*. Seventy feet long, she is larger and faster than former lifeboats and of different silhouette, although painted in traditional colours. Unlike the old lifeboats she has living accommodation aboard for her crew and can work independently of a fixed shore base. This will allow her to range widely along the mainland's windiest coast. Another unusual ship, for many years past a frequent visitor to the lochs and harbours of Wester Ross, and likely to be seen at any time, is the three-masted schooner *Prince Louis* (160 tons). She has been used by the Outward Bound Sea School and by the Dulverton Trust to give training under sail to boys of sixteen to twenty years of age. The boys land and make long expeditions ashore through the mountains, and into the sea-lochs by canoe.

From Ullapool northward a wide new road has been made thirty miles through Coigach and Assynt to Kylesku. Coigach and Assynt appear to be topographically one, a landmass of gneiss hillocks (as seen from the west) and several hundred lochs and lochans, in the midst of which are set a dozen sandstone mountains, not spreading in ranges like An Teallach but each standing in a monolithic isolation and all several miles back from the twenty-mile arc of Enard Bay. Fourteen miles inland the region is bounded eastward by the mountain chain of Ben More Assynt and the hills of Cromalt. Although essentially one in character, the region is split from east to west by the **Cam Loch,** which changing its name four times as it goes, meanders ten miles between the mountains before discharging into the sea by the river Kirkaig. Its thin line gives the county boundary between Ross and Sutherland, and marks off Coigach from Assynt. The Coigach moorland is nearly all sandstone, yielding us at least one great and gentle sanctuary at the head of Loch Sionascaig: the moor of Assynt is unrelenting gneiss.

Three miles north of Ullapool you pass through the village of **Ardmair** above the shore of Loch Kanaird, which is a bay of outer Loch Broom. Isle Martin fills the bay's mouth, and Strath Kanaird breaks into the hills behind. Isle Martin, a round hill of 397 feet, is named from a Saint Martin, who built his chapel at the west side. The ruin survives, as also the ruins of the curing station on the east bay. In the early years of this century the island had a population of 30; like the people of the Summer Isles they all left at the end of the last war. On the farther side of Strath Kanaird, **Ben More Coigach** rises to 2,438 feet, no longer the shapely cone as seen from seaward but confronting you with a wall of cliffs riven by gullies. Nine miles away on its far side lies the crofting village of Achiltibuie, whither you are bound by the road detouring the mountain's northern tops. Just beyond Ardmair an old and somewhat sketchy track goes direct to Achiltibuie along the shore, winding round the spurs and creeks of the sea-cliffs, sometimes with deep green water below. It used to be walked daily by the Achiltibuie postman and still gives a fine walk for lovers of rocky ground.

Cross Strath Kanaird into **Coigach**. The name means Place of the Fifths, from an early Celtic custom of dividing land into five parts. Six miles north of Ardmair you reach a road-fork at Drumrunie. The main road continues north to the Sutherland frontier, here only three miles distant; you instead turn sharp left along the road to Achiltibuie, following a chain of freshwater lochs through the heart of Coigach to the coast, where the Rhu More peninsula juts into the Minch. If you feel impelled to climb Ben More Coigach en route, the simplest approach is to ford the river Runie one mile south of the Drumrunie road-fork. The climb by the east ridge is then free of difficulty.

Two miles west of the fork you reach Loch Lurgain, the first of the chain of lochs, which lie in a great fold between Ben More Coigach and the mountains of **Inverpolly Forest** to the north. The Forest has three peaks, Cul Beag, 2,525 feet, and Stac Polly, 2,009 feet, both alongside the road, and Cul Mor, 2,786 feet, hiding behind them. The lochs running east to west get both the sunrise and the sunset lights, whose red or silver on Loch Lurgain is four times repeated on Loch Bad à Ghaill, Loch Osgaig, Loch Raa, and Loch Vatachan, before the road drops to the sea at Badentarbat Bay. The loch-scene is matched by the flanking mountains, whose tops, sun-browned or perhaps whitened by Easter snow, appear above dark shoulders. Stac Polly at the far end is too low to hold snow except in the depths of winter, but its splintered edge on blue sky is spired like the palace of the Wizard of Oz. For Stac Polly's sandstone crest has lost its quartzite cap and been shattered by weather into thin pinnacles. Not high enough to be called a mountain, it is yet a mountain in miniature and the traverse of its half-mile summit-ridge gives an exciting walk (the pinnacles can be dodged round their sides). In little more than an hour, the top can be reached by way of a tiny corrie near its west end, a route involving some rock-scrambling near the summit, or more easily but in longer time by the eastern ridge. Stac Polly means the Stack of the Bog (although the hill is no boggier than others), perhaps because the land stretching five miles to its north is for five miles from east to west more than one half water. Inverpolly Forest is now a Reserve of the Nature Conservancy. Its three mountains form a semi-circle around a multitude of lochs and lochans, the biggest of which, and the most famous for its fishing, is **Loch Sionascaig**.

Loch Sionascaig is most easily reached at its west end from the coast road to Lochinver. A much more interesting way in is from Loch Lurgain over the pass between Stac Polly and Cul Beag. Likewise, the most rewarding mountain to climb in Coigach is **Cul Mor**, most easily reached by its eastern flank from Knockan on the main road to Lochinver—a thoroughly dull route; again, the best way by far is over the pass from Loch Lurgain, which gives the most enjoyable hill-walk in Lochbroom.

The track in from the roadside is easy to miss. Marked by a small cairn, it starts from the east side of a scattering of dwarf pines, a few hundred yards east of the cottage of Linneraineach. A short ascent brings you over the bealach, followed by a long descent over moorland to birchwoods above a great, water-filled strath. Across the valley, Cul Mor presents a craggy face, looking steeper than it really is. There are two routes of approach. Above the first birchwood the track splits, one fork going leftward to Loch Gainmheich (Sandy Loch), which flows into Loch Sionascaig through a wide channel. The better approach is by the right-hand path, leading at first through a birchwood and then by a meadow to red sands at the head of Loch an Doire Dhuibh (Loch of the Dark Wood), where it ends. Cross to the farther bank under Cul Mor.

If you choose not to climb the mountain, you can turn left down the banks of the Gleann Laoigh burn, a slow-running river fringed by trees and short turf. The meadow continues all the way to Loch Gainmheich, where the burn flows into a wide sandy bay, one of several smaller beaches all of red sand. At the loch's far end is a keeper's hut. Pass this and cross a one-plank bridge near Loch Sionascaig to join the track back to Loch Lurgain. This round is one of the best short walks in Ross. The tracks are very narrow footpaths, sometimes boggy and sometimes crossing sandstone slabs, but give a delightful introduction to the heart of a mountain cirque. The lochs, on which divers breed, are of wild shape and extreme beauty, set around by the tall towers of Inverpolly; the mountains lie well back and all is sunlit from wide skies. Grass predominates over heather. The interior is a sanctuary for greenshank and red deer, and for man when he comes. There are many deer on the hills. In August they move about in small herds of a dozen along the terraces of Cul Mor, and their hoof-marks are everywhere. The lochs offer good fishing for brown trout. On Loch Sionascaig this is made available only during April, May, and June.

Your appreciation of this sanctuary cannot be complete without an ascent of Cul Mor. The whole upper part of the mountain stands on a broad plinth, which forms a terrace a few hundred feet above Gleann Laoigh (the Glen of the Calf). As seen from Gleann Laoigh, Cul Mor has several tops. The best route is up the second from the right, which is lower than the others and set farther forward. From its top, a ridge drops leftward, marked by a gully on its left, which lower becomes a deep-cut burn. The ridge looks formidably steep and rocky, but this is an optical illusion. The way is easy. Up to the terrace the ground is grassy, beyond, heathery and rocky. The ling and bell heather gives off a rich honey-scent.

The whole length of Sionascaig is revealed as you climb. Its shoreline measures seventeen miles. A dozen islets spatter the surface and a score of bays indent the edge. Far west are low rocky hills of gneiss, then the sea. From the upper mountain you can see the ten-mile breadth of Enard Bay between the flat peninsulas of Rhu More Coigach and Rhu Stoer Assynt, where the Stoer lighthouse pricks out against the Minch.

Cul Mor has three main tops. The quartzite summit, not seen from below, stands to the north and commands a view of the Outer Hebrides, and nearby of Glencanisp Forest—Suilven, Canisp, and the hills of Assynt—best of all and close below your feet of the fantastic serpentine length of the Cam Loch, the most sinuous waterway of the Highlands. This is a better view of the Inverpolly–Glencanisp Forests than Suilven's more famous one; from Suilven you can see more lochs with a sweep of the eye, but from Cul Mor you see the main ones in fuller detail and much more impressively. This climb from Loch Lurgain is most of all superb if you choose a day at the tail-end of a gale, when sun and showers come with squally winds but the sun predominates.

Loch Lurgain flows into Loch Bad à Ghaill, at whose west end a side-road breaks north up the coast to Lochinver. You continue west past Loch Osgaig, now on open ground away from the higher hills, and head for the sandstone peninsula of Rhu More. You descend on the north end of its two-mile isthmus where Achnahaird Bay cuts in from Enard Bay. Achnahaird is a flat and windy place. Half a mile of salt-marsh, on which flocks of dunlin and ringed plovers feed, stretches to sands running fully half a mile out to sea. The seacliffs to its north-west have a big colony of shags.

Moving south over the heathery back of the isthmus, from which you look seventeen miles south across Loch Broom to An Teallach, you soon arrive at the shore of Badentarbat Bay. This is an exposed coast facing south-west but protected from the sea by the cluster of the Summer Isles. **Achiltibuie** spreads three miles along the bay in two distinct parts. At the north half are the pier, church, hotel, shops, and larger houses; at the south are the crofts in long line, their strips of hay and corn running seaward over flat ground. Beyond the croft-houses the road continues south for two and a half miles to Coulnacraig, close under Ben More Coigach. Only the shore path already mentioned goes on from there to Strath Kanaird. The pier at the extreme north end of Achiltibuie has a grassy, secluded site, where salmon nets dry on poles. Motor-launch cruises go out to the **Summer Isles** daily. Inquire at the post office.

The name Summer Isles is applied strictly to the inner group of a dozen islands off Badentarbat Bay. A few miles to their south-west, a second spatter of six islands (not counting a dozen skerries) lie around Priest Island (Eilean a Chleirich). Geologically, inner and outer are one. The rock is Torridon sandstone. None is inhabited. The nearest and biggest island is **Tanera Mor**, one and a half miles off Achiltibuie. Its 800 acres used to have a thriving community in the days of the inshore herring fishing, and held a population of more than 70 as late as 1900. The last inhabitant left in 1946. The bay on its east side, under a hill of 406 feet, has been used as a harbour since Viking times and is called the Anchorage. On a coast infamously windy, Tanera Mor being the innermost isle is richer in bird life and plants than the outer isles. Dr. Fraser Darling has listed forty-three species of bird breeding on Tanera, including buzzard, heron, sheld-duck, red grouse, and many others, none of which appear on Priest Island. Nearly all the islands are grazed by sheep, for despite wind the climate is mild.

Half a mile to the west, **Tanera Beag**, 210 acres, has a well-sheltered anchorage in the lee of a dozen islets. Seals have some-times bred there, although present among the Summer Isles in only small number. The third biggest island is **Horse Island**, 174 acres, a mile and a half south-east of Tanera Mor. There is no good anchorage. One must land on the rocks. A better name than Horse might be Goat Island, for a herd of wild goat have bred on its heather for more than a century. It might even be called Treasure Island. Gold from a ship of the Spanish Armada is said to have been hidden there in 1588, and there is a local record that last century a shepherd found a gold piece in his boot-top after a stumble on rough ground. When he returned with others to try to find the site, he failed to recognize it.

328

Priest Island lies more than six miles off Coigach and four off Greenstone Point. It thus commands a panorama of the Ross mountains from An Teallach to Ben More Coigach and beyond. With 300 acres it is less than half the size of Tanera Mor. But small and exposed though it is, rising to only 200 feet at the south end, and although landings are made difficult in its two small bays by a heavy swell, it used to have a small crofting community, and is still much visited in spring and summer by naturalists and youth organizations on camping expeditions. It has a plentiful water-supply, having no less than eight freshwater lochs. One big attraction here is the bird-life. Twenty-nine breeding species use the island. These include grey lag goose, eider, storm petrel, fulmar, snipe, razorbill, shag, and a hundred pairs of cormorant, which each year ring the changes on their nesting stations by moving as a flock to a new site on a different island. Black guillemots will be seen on Priest Island but are not breeders. The notable feature of the wild life is the presence of grey lag geese as a breeding species— and the need to protect them from being shot by 'sportsmen'.

The nearest island one mile north is **Glas Leac Beag**, or the Small Green Slab, which has a colony of several hundred black-backed gulls. These so enrich the ground with their excreta that the grass is bright green (the other islands are heather-covered). The grass draws to the island several hundred barnacle geese in winter, and in summer big numbers of grey lag. In August, the grass is speckled bright blue with scabious (*Jasione montana*).

From Achiltibuie, a short ring-road goes out north into the Rhu More and back by Achnahaird. You follow it for three miles to **Altandhu**, the most delightful crofting community in Coigach. It lies in a west-facing bay sheltered by Isle Ristol. Unlike Achiltibuie and most other coastal townships, the cottages are not strung out in line, but form a widely-deployed cluster. Between road and sea, the fields of corn and turnip are in August thickly covered with yellow corncockles, which in a southerly wind give off a sweet, heavy, but slightly pungent scent. Isle Ristol is a tidal island. At low water it can be reached by a causeway on its east side. The north point is cliffed and crowned by a hill of 234 feet. Between cliff and causeway spreads a most tempting, sandy beach—remember the tide, or go prepared for a twelve-hour day.

Beyond Altandhu the ring-road sweeps east across moorland to Achnahaird, but a side-road continues a mile and a half up the west coast to **Reiff**. Reiff Bay has sand, spattered with big boulders.

All along this shore, and on the offshore islands, the shingle and stone are pink. Reiff Bay has suffered much in appearance from a large new house, presumably a holiday-house, built alongside its beach. Close behind, a freshwater loch, the Loch of Reiff, stretches half a mile to the next bay. The small crofting township by its shore is now largely deserted and fallen into ruin, although the cottages are strongly built in red sandstone. One thatched cottage is still occupied—thatch is a rarity now on the west seaboard, although common in the Outer Isles. The coast north of Reiff has spectacular if low sandstone cliffs; huge flat platforms run round their seaward side; along their tops you have excellent walking on bare slabs and short turf. Deep creeks thrust far into the rock, some of them forming long caves impossible of access without a rope.

The Rhu More inland is a most bleak and exposed moor.

We return to Inverpolly Forest and take the road to Assynt.

CHAPTER 26

Assynt

More visitors are drawn to Sutherland by the rocky desert of **Assynt** than by any other landscape feature of a county that stretches from the North Sea to the Atlantic. If one has the good fortune first to see Assynt by sailing into Enard Bay, its magic will at a glance be made apparent, especially if one comes late in the day, when **Lochinver's** white houses at the back of the sea-loch glow in a light mellowing the great sandstone stacks behind—the Quinag, Canisp, Suilven, and the peaks of Coigach, all set widely apart and each lifting its head like some petrified monster from the gneiss billows rolling in from the coast. The scene has a fantastic quality, hard to equal in the length of the seaboard.

Between Enard Bay and Ben More Assynt, and between the Cam Loch and Loch Cairnbawn, Assynt measures fourteen miles by twelve. Small though it might appear, travel around it is long and walking within it is arduous. Your introduction to the best of it is, by road, more delayed than by sea and granted in brief but lengthening glimpses, yet more informative. From western Coigach you move in by the hill-road above Loch Bad à Ghaill, climbing steeply over the westernmost slope of Stac Polly, which seen end-on is a fine spire, and descend four hundred feet to cross the Polly river. The Polly drains Loch Sionascaig to Enard Bay and marks a geological frontier. Once across it, you leave the sandstone moors behind and are launched on the choppy gneiss. Golden whin brightens the roadside in June, heather in August, although gneiss country is not commonly heathery except in patches. The more usual plant-covering is sedge, coarse grasses, and dwarf willow. The road takes an erratic course a mile and a half inland, swooping to the sea through the woods of Glen Srathain, rising again over hillocky moor and then zig-zagging down to the coast by the river Kirkaig—for another feature of gneiss country is the tangle of little glens running here and there between the hollows, most of which hold tarns, lochans, or burns. Away from the road one can never follow a straight course over the moor to reach an objective, but must plan a tortuous route from the one-inch map on pain of entanglement in watery barriers and cul-de-sacs—or of getting lost, for the moor is featureless in the multiplicity of its rocky outcrops and humpy hills. Many of the lochans, especially near the coast, bear round the edge rings of lobelia and water-lilies, always just out of reach, for the red deer eat them from the shore, craning their necks but never wading in—the bottoms are soft peat.

At Bridge of Kirkaig you enter **Sutherland**, the South Land of the Vikings. They occupied the Orkney and Shetland Islands for six hundred years from 875 to 1469. In 1034 they overran Sutherland too, naming it Sudrland in relation to the Orkney jarldom, and holding most of it for nearly two hundred years until it was wrested from them in 1196 by the King of Scots, William the Lion. Norse place-names are thus even more numerous in Sutherland than farther south on the mainland seaboard. At the Kirkaig you also enter **Assynt**, a name most probably derived from the Norse Ass, meaning Rocky. In the course of their earlier raids the Vikings burned down all the great forests along the coast. Roots of these ancient trees are still found preserved in the bogs of what are now bare headlands. Three miles north of Inverkirkaig you enter the chief village and port of Assynt, Lochinver.

The main road from Ullapool to Lochinver is the one you left at Drumrunie, over on the eastern side of Assynt, in order to penetrate Coigach. By this route you cross the Sutherland frontier-pass at 800 feet under Cul Mor. Just south of the frontier, you should halt to enjoy the westward view through Gleann Laoigh to Stac Polly. Its spire is better seen from here than from any other angle. The road then falls from the brown pass to a green oasis at the crofts of **Knockan** and **Elphin**. This unexpected greenery is a first intimation of the limestone that occurs in far greater bulk along your route on the flanks of Ben More Assynt and its outliers to the strath of Inchnadamph at the head of Loch Assynt. From Knockan to Kylesku (at the narrows of Loch Cairnbawn), the road follows a geological boundary-line—the valley under the Moine Thrust Plane. In broad, general terms, this means that to your west the land is Archaean gneiss, and that to your right-hand side it is Moine Schist, which has been pushed from the east-north-east to come riding over the gneiss, even to carry the gneiss ahead of it in places, or turn the

ASSYNT

N

0 1 2 3
miles

The Companion Guide to the West Highlands of Scotland

old strata completely upside down. The result is a chaos of tormented rocks, the presence of which along this somewhat dreary glen the lay traveller might not appreciate, but a thing of joy to geologists for whom eastern Assynt is Scotland's Mecca. They have come in pilgrimage for the last fifty years.

The glen is not dreary at Cam Loch. A mile beyond Elphin, the road bridges the Ledmore river above its Cam Loch estuary. To the left of the road and to the right of the river, a hillock offers a view worth seeking of Suilven's twin horns across the winding waters of the loch, which flowing east from near Suilven here takes a violent bend like a shepherd's crook—Cam means Crooked—henceforth flowing west to the sea. At **Ledmore**, one mile farther, your road is joined by the Strath Oykell road coming in from the south-east. This gives an alternative approach from east Scotland by way of Bonar Bridge on the Dornoch Firth (into which the river Oykell flows). It brings you from the upper Oykell, whose source is Ben More Assynt, over the Highland watershed on Craggie Hill—and suddenly there before you are the sandstone towers of Coigach and Assynt, pricking out against the distant gleam of the Minch. On the lonely shore of Loch Barralan above the Ledmore road-fork is the fishing hotel of Altnacealgach, the Burn of the Deceiver. Beyond Cam Loch the scene becomes duller. You follow the river Leanan flowing out of Loch Awe, where in the bed of the glen there are Bronze Age burial cairns. To your left and right are Canisp and **Ben More Assynt**, the latter the highest mountain of Sutherland. But Canisp's eastern profile is not distinguished, and the top of Ben More Assynt, 3,273 feet, is hidden behind its outliers. Most people drive down the glen without giving it any attention, for it is no spiky sandstone mountain, but of well-rounded gneiss topped with quartzite. The gneiss goes close to the summit, indeed to the highest level it attains in Britain, but the lower slopes on this side are Cambrian limestone, burrowed by underground rivers and carved into caves by acid moorland water. This limestone area has been made a Reserve of the Nature Conservancy.

The caves have not grown to the great size of those found on Yorkshire moors, for the Cambrian limestone is much harder than the Carboniferous, but they draw pot-holers bent on speleological exploration, a few archaeologists, and many geologists. The caves most worth exploring are near the two principal burns: the **Traligill** flowing into Loch Assynt, and the **Allt nan Uamh** two and a half miles to its south. If you stop at the bridge over the latter, and walk

334

one mile up its left bank to the 900-foot contour, you will find three caves a hundred yards to the south of the river-bed. These were excavated by the famous geologists Peach and Horne in 1917, and by others in 1926. They found bones of northern lynx, bear, arctic fox, reindeer, and of two human skeletons that have been attributed to the Azilian period around 6000 B.C. The principal feature of the Traligill burn is the disappearing river behind Inchnadamph Hotel. A mile and a half uphill, near the 600-foot contour, the Traligill drops underground below its more ancient bed and reappears 350 yards lower. Half a mile higher, on the 750-foot contour to the south of the watercourse, there are three caves, in one of which, rather small in size (it is not always possible to stand upright) there are numerous straw stalactites. Great care must be taken not to brush against them—they take thousands of years to grow. Avoid pot-holing in Assynt during unsettled weather, for the caves can then flood suddenly.

Inchnadamph, meaning Stag's meadow, is a crofting community at the head of Loch Assynt where the good influence of the limestone is again seen in green pasture. Some of the cottages are built of white marble—for marble is simply limestone in its crystalline form. The hotel, besides being the best centre for scientific explorers from botanists to geologists, offers the angler free and excellent fishing for salmon, grilse, brown trout, and the exceedingly rare (in Scotland) gillaroo trout. The name gillaroo is from the Gaelic gille ruadh, meaning the red lad. This queer fish (*Salmo stomachicus*) comes from Ireland. One part of its stomach is a gizzard serving to crush the shells of molluscs.

Your road to Lochinver now semi-circles the six-mile length of **Loch Assynt.** The west and east halves of this loch are of quite different character: the west half takes a big southward twist, its shore broken by wooded bays and capes and the surface by tiny islands bearing old pines; the east bare and featureless land, marked only by the ruined towers of **Ardvreck Castle,** which sticks out from a grassy point on the shore a mile from Inchnadamph. Its name, from Ard Bhreac, the Speckled Point, was here made famous by the owner's capture of the great Marquis of Montrose.

There are few records of Sutherland's early history, and still fewer remains of archaeological or architectural interest. Ardvreck Castle was built in 1597 as the seat of MacLeod of Assynt. Before the Viking invasions, Assynt was ruled by the thane of Sutherland, who in the twelfth century granted the land to MacNicol of Ullapool as a reward for help against the invaders. Two hundred years later the last daughter of the line married a son of MacLeod of Lewis, and to this MacLeod the king granted Assynt by a charter of 1346. The family held the land for 326 years and lost it by the loyalty to the Covenanters of a seventeenth-century chief.

James Graham, the Marquis of Montrose, was the greatest Scotsman of his time, not only a brilliant general but a man of ideals in advance of his century. He was in the Low Countries in January 1649 when news came of the execution of his king, Charles I. The Covenanters' excesses, and their barbarities in name of an Old Testament god, had long disgusted him. Now most deeply moved, he swore to take the field once again. With the blessing of the exiled Charles II, he raised an invasion force and in March 1650 sailed for the Orkneys. Transport ships preceding him had been wrecked by winter storms, so that when he made his landing on the Caithness coast his only troops were 400 Danes, 1,000 raw levies from the Orkneys, and 40 horse. Yet his landing was not the mad act it might sound. Scotland was ripe for the restoration. Had MacKenzie been able to raise his powerful clan, as Montrose had been led to expect, his march south would have been secured, central Scotland safely gained, and once there the other great chiefs and nobles might have followed and the cause been won. But MacKenzie while in France had discovered that the king was trying to bargain with the government over Montrose's head. This double-dealing by Charles was to cost him dear. MacKenzie wondered if war were really needed. He remained abroad—and Montrose was lost. His march south was in April intercepted at Invershin by Colonel Strachan, whose still smaller force included 220 mounted dragoons. They cut the unseasoned infantry to pieces.

Montrose had his horse shot under him, but escaped up Strath Oykell and over the pass to Assynt. Three days later, starving, and with a £20,000 reward on his head, he was found by MacLeod's men and taken to Ardvreck castle. Neil MacLeod, eleventh chief, was then twenty-two and like most Sutherland men staunchly Presbyterian. Montrose offered ransom. Whatever Neil may have felt for the man James Graham, freeing an attainted rebel must have meant to him betrayal of Covenant and Parliament, not to mention the probable loss both of his own head and a large reward. He betrayed no one. He consigned Montrose to the dungeon and then had messengers sent to General Leslie at Tain. Many days later, suffering high fever caused by exposure, Montrose was led bound on

Above Loch Broom is the longest sea-loch of the North-west Highlands, driving 21 miles into the land. Here you look up the inner loch from a jetty at the fishing village of Ullapool (*below*) which was founded in 1788 by the British Fisheries Society: its life then and prosperity now it owes to herring.

Above Loch Assynt and Quinag, 2,653 feet. The road to Lochinver holds to the right-hand shore of the loch for its full six-mile length, passing gradually from bare land to woodland. *Below* Stac Polly from the shore of Loch Lurgain, Coigach, close to the Sutherland border. The hill is a mountain in miniature, for although only 2,009 feet, its sandstone crest has lost its quartzite cap and been shattered by weather into thin pinnacles. The traverse of its half-mile summit-ridge gives an exciting walk (the pinnacles can be dodged round their sides). Loch Lurgain is one of a chain of five lochs leading through the heart of Coigach to the coast.

horseback through the length of Scotland to Edinburgh, and there, on May 21st, hanged in the Grassmarket.

The MacLeod's 300 years of good fortune now ended. It is recorded fact that the government awarded Neil £20,000 in Scots coin, which they never paid. They gave him 400 bolls of oatmeal. Unfortunately for him and his family, he had made a life-long enemy of his mighty neighbour, the MacKenzie Earl of Seaforth, who not only ruled all Ross but was a royalist conscience-stricken at Montrose's death, which he might have averted. He devastated Assynt from end to end and made off with 9,000 head of cattle, sheep, and horse. It is interesting to note that in dealing with minor plunder he destroyed (and did not hold for his own cellar) a whole ship-load of MacLeod's wine and brandy worth 50,000 merks (£1,250). Like most Highlanders to-day he clearly despised all but whisky. After the restoration of the monarchy in 1660, Neil MacLeod was imprisoned without trial for three years on a charge of betraying Montrose. Charles II released him. At MacKenzie's instigation he was indicted again in 1674, tried on the old charge before a royalist judge and jury, and acquitted. MacKenzie was ruthless. He seized Assynt and held it for a hundred years.

In 1760, the MacKenzies offered Assynt for sale. It was bought for the earl of Sutherland, reverting thus to the family who six hundred years earlier had given the land to a good neighbour. (The ancient Sutherland family are not to be confused with the new English family of Leveson-Gower, whose first duke of Sutherland was responsible for the Sutherland clearances). In the present century, Assynt has been sold again and re-sold.

Half a mile west of Ardvreck the road forks at Skiag Bridge. The Kylesku road rises northward over a hill-pass. The Lochinver road holds to the west by the loch's shore under Quinag, passing gradually from bare lands to wooded. A few sycamore appear among dwarf birch and rowan, the trees thickening after Lochassynt Lodge to the foot of the loch. The ling heather along the banks will surprise you in its mid-August brightness. The river Inver flows broad and deep, wriggling python-like alongside the road for five miles to Loch Inver. Its waters are full of salmon in late June when the main run begins. The woods all the while increase, becoming in the lower reaches plantations of pine and larch. You cross the river at its estuary and are suddenly in **Lochinver** village.

Loch Inver, the Loch of the Estuary, is two miles long. The island of Soyea at the mouth gives slight protection from the sea, but a harbour is luckily formed to the south side of the village by the bluff and wooded point of Culag. The entire bay is enclosed by low rocky hills, and Suilven four miles inland is not seen. The houses face west. They line the twice-curving sea-front on the inland side of the road and are made to withstand wind, some of Torridon sandstone, others harled and whitewashed. At the busy centre of the street—for Lochinver is packed with cars in summer—all gardens are set at the backs of the houses, elsewhere at the front and kept tiny. As the chief village of Assynt, Lochinver has a daily bus service to Lairg (46 miles), several good shops, a bank, police station, garage, and beside the pier the well-appointed Culag Hotel. The hotel has salmon and sea-trout fishing on the river Kirkaig, brown trout fishing on Loch Assynt among numerous other lochs, and hires out motor-boats for sea-angling. If you want fishing, join the Assynt Angling Club, thus ensuring access to nearly thirty lochs, where baskets of twenty to thirty trout are commonly caught between May and October. The first salmon and sea-trout runs start in April, and the big runs at the end of June.

The pier beside the hotel is often thronged with fishing boats from Lossiemouth, Ullapool, Buckie, the east coast, and of course Lochinver itself. As a fishing port, Lochinver ranks with Ullapool in the value of its landings—over £1 million a year. This catch is largely whitefish.

The principal playground for summer visitors is out to the north-west on the **Rhu Stoer** peninsula. It has sandy coves at Achmelvich, Clachtoll, and Clashnessie. Many walkers are drawn instead to **Glencanisp Forest,** that wild hinterland of gneiss; tracks lead in to either side of Suilven by way of Glencanisp and the river Kirkaig. For Glencanisp, start from the south end of Lochinver by a private motor-road to Glencanisp Lodge. It ends after one and a half miles by the shore of a loch, whence a pony track continues six miles east to Lochan Fada beyond Canisp. At first it keeps to the north flank of the shallow glen, then after three miles crosses the river below to its south bank. At this point you leave it, if your objective is **Suilven,** and make straight for the saddle to the left of its summit. The mountain is cliffed all round, but the central saddle has broad and easy gullies falling down either side. This north flank of Suilven comes as a surprise to anyone who has seen the mountain only from east or west; from there it appears a lone peak, for the end-top screens the serrated summit-ridge of one and a half miles. Thus it appeared to the Vikings from their Long Ships; they named it

Sul-fjall, the Pillar Mountain. The present name, like so many others on the west coast, is a combination of the Norse and Gaelic, Sul and Bheinn. From the north and south, however, it looks not at all like a pillar, but like some high-decked galleon riding the seas of gneiss.

Suilven is the name now given to the mountain as a whole. The Vikings' original pillar, the west peak or summit, 2,399 feet, is named by the Gaels Caisteal Liath, the Grey Castle. The flanks are dull red, but the summit has a cap of grey quartzite scree. The eastern top is 2,300 feet, much sharper and spire-like. The summit view is not unlike that described from Cul Mor, but the tarns starring the moor seem from here numberless, like a Milky Way (pedants will tell you there are 200). When the sky is bright they scintillate, brilliantly blue; when the sky is heavy, and grey mists twist among the mountains, they glint whitely or lie black and fathomless. The scene is never without beauty, weird or brilliant as the skies dictate.

Far away to the south-east across the highlands of Easter Ross, a sharp eye may be able to pick out the plateau of Ben Wyvis, 3,429 feet, on the other side of Scotland. Streaks of snow may be seen on the top till mid-summer. The MacKenzie Earls of Cromartie have held it from the Crown since the seventeenth century, at first for the rent of a bucket of snow whenever demanded. Just three miles to your east, Canisp rises like Suilven out of the dark water of Loch na Gainimh. Its shape is an oval cone of 2,779 feet and the ascent easy.

A still better though longer walk to Suilven goes by the river **Kirkaig,** three miles south of Lochinver. Leave the car by the Kirkaig bridge. The path goes up the right bank three miles to Fionn Loch. On the hill slopes above the bridge is the small Achins Hotel with a craft shop selling goods for the tourist. The path up-river goes at first through woods frequented by pine-marten. Two miles up you pass the falls of Kirkaig—they take a vertical plunge of 60 feet— and shortly afterwards turn north to Fionn Loch, which is the west end of the lengthy Cam Loch that splits Coigach from Assynt. Suilven now stands clear across the water, reflected there in detail if the air is still. You have to walk another two miles down the north bank but the way is plain. The wide gully falling from Suilven's saddle is steeper on this side but free of obstacle.

The northern half of Assynt, beyond the river Inver, is still more heavily congested with lochs than Glencanisp Forest. You will see little of these, however, unless as fisherman you deliberately penetrate the maze by the numerous tracks running in from the motor-road round the periphery. This steeply hilly and twisting road, which links all the crofts of the coast and sends an offshoot into the Rhu Stoer peninsula, is adventure enough for most people: along Eddrachillis Bay it makes the Loch Sunart road of Ardnamurchan seem like a motor-way. On the way out to Stoer its several sandy bays trap all but the dedicated long-distance tourer; and from its high ground, as you leave Lochinver and its river-valley behind, you can again see inland to the pillared mountains—a sight you will never forget.

The first, best, and most famous sandy bay of the Assynt coast used to be **Achmelvich,** less than four miles north of Lochinver. A side-track leads out a mile and a half to what used to be short sweet turf and a clean beach, flanked by coves to the north. It has been eroded and ruined by caravanners and by the crofter-tenants. The Bay of Clachtoll, a mile or two farther, is close by the road. Three sandy coves, all with bold rocks at the outer edges, are backed by flat machair on which salmon-nets are often laid out to dry. Low rocky hills fill the background. Round the north point of Clachtoll lies the Bay of Stoer. Its sands are much broader, with wider machair behind, but without rocky arms to give shelter: being thus too open to wind for comfort, it is empty of tents. All these bays have small crofting communities close at hand.

A short way beyond Stoer the road forks, one branch to follow the north coast to Kylesku, the other leftward into the **Rhu Stoer.** The name is from the Norse Staurr, meaning Stake, for the north point is marked by a huge sea-stack called (like its brother in Skye) the Old Man of Storr. Except for the Point of Stoer, the peninsula, four miles long by two wide, is not barren ground like the Rhu More of Coigach. Crofts spread farther inland and the road links them. The coast too is more fertile and mild, hence better populated. On moving inland, you may if you wish take a side-road back to the west shore at Balchladich Bay. Although sandy it is a bigger, more open bay than the others and unfrequented by tourists, for there is no signpost back at the main road, although there is a sizeable crofting township around a loch on the low hills above.

On the west side of Rhu Stoer the road ends at Stoer lighthouse. You may enter at the keeper's discretion. It is set on the top of a sandstone cliff. From its base, short keel-shaped ridges run out to a vertical face, 100 feet above the sea. On the ridges fat cushions of sea-pink scent the June air, narrow-winged fulmars swoop over their nests on the face, and deep beneath breakers seethe across the reefs. The tower looks across the Minch to Lewis, where the Tiumpan Head light can be seen winking on a clear night, twenty-eight miles west.

Stoer Point, projecting two miles farther north, is most bleak ground, mainly brown grass and rushes without much rock cropping out. Cliffs rise to 300 feet on the east side of the point, on the west to 200, and there the Old Man stands close in its ring of foam. The stack is 200 feet high and was declared to be unclimbable until its first ascent in 1966 by Dr. Tom Patey and Brian Robertson.

Crossing to the east side of Rhu Stoer, you find at Culkein a big open bay facing Oldany Island. It has bag-net salmon-fishing and a natural arch at the north point. From the crofting township behind, a peat-track runs into the hills to within a mile of the Old Man—the closest approach one can make by track. Peat is much used in Assynt, and peat-smoke perfumes every clachan of the Rhu Stoer, indeed of the whole Sutherland coast. Sutherland peat is of peculiarly high quality, and when dry is almost as hard as coal and as waterproof.

You may now be ready for that tough journey of fourteen miles along the north coast to Kylesku. It is a heavily-riven coast. The road keeps inland most of the way, and that means riding switch-back over the gneiss and wriggling eel-like between lochans and crags. You start at **Clashnessie Bay,** facing into Eddrachillis Bay, which is bigger than Enard Bay and teeming with islands frequented by lobster-fishermen. The name Eddrachillis is a corruption of the Gaelic Eadar Da Chaolas, Between Two Straits. Clashnessie, the Valley of the Waterfall, has indeed a fine waterfall of 50 feet, half a mile up-river from the road. The bay into which it flows is a double one, with red sands in the west bay and rock in the east. On top of the west arm sits a ruined dun. There are numerous duns along the Assynt coast, but they are not interesting specimens.

The road east from the bay is cut out of gneiss cliffs and then rises on to moorland knolls, mostly heathery and sometimes under birch-scrub. Increasingly from now on water-lilies improve the lochans. You come close to the coast again above Oldany Island, where there is excellent lobster-fishing among a score of skerries and islets trailing out east. Immediately afterwards you enter the biggest of the gneiss hollows; an islanded loch fills it, overlooked by the principal village of the coast, Drumbeg. It has a good fishing hotel and at least a dozen houses.

Half a mile beyond Drumbeg you start on the last and most violent lap. First comes a very steep descent of 300 feet to sea-level at Loch Nedd—a twisting loch heavily wooded in scrub alder and birch—then an equally steep rise to heathery moor, promptly followed by a zig-zag descent of alpine character. You are now on the hills above Loch Cairnbawn, the main sea-loch running into the hills from Eddrachillis Bay. At **Kylesku** the loch forks, the farther branch becoming Loch Glendhu, the nearer Loch Glencoul. You rejoin the main north road (Ullapool to Kylesku) just two miles short of the kyle, and descending past the clachan of Unapool (named from the Norse Steading of Uni) run out on a broad promontory to the hotel and ferry at Kylesku. The name is a pruned version of Caolas Cumhang, the Narrow Strait.

This roundabout route of twenty-seven miles from Lochinver to Kylesku can be cut by ten miles (and more than an hour) if you instead take the main road by Loch Assynt to Skiag Bridge. There you turn north, once again on the line dividing gneiss mountains from sandstone. On your left is the **Quinag**, on your right Glas Bheinn. The road between lifts to 850 feet. The Quinag has seven tops rising to 2,653 feet at the summit. The sandstone rests on a thick bed of gneiss, which attains 2000 feet at the north end but never forms an upper deck; the tops are all sandstone, a few with quartzite caps. Their linking ridges give an excellent walk and the ascent is easy. Leave the road about a mile and a half up from Skiag Bridge, then climb the east ridge. The seascapes to the Outer Hebrides are superb and change from peak to peak as the foreground changes from Enard Bay to Eddrachillis. Southward, beyond Loch Assynt, rise the splintered profiles of Suilven and the Coigach hills. The north prongs of Quinag facing Loch Cairnbawn are Sail Ghorm and Sail Garbh, meaning Blue Heel and Rough Heel, each terminated by rock buttresses. These are bold features of the mountain as seen from Wester Sutherland, and they give good rock-climbing. The cliff of Sail Garbh is appropriately called Barrel Buttress, and gives name to the mountain, for Cuinneag (there is no Q in Gaelic) means Churn or Pail.

Glas Bheinn across the road from Quinag is nearly as high, 2,541 feet, but a shapeless lump of gneiss. It may claim merit as the source of Britain's highest waterfall, the **Eas a' Chùal Aluinn** (pronounced Ess-Kool-Aulin), which is four times the height of Niagara. The name means the Splendid Waterfall of Coul. The fall lies three-quarters of a mile inland from the head of Loch Glencoul. Two parallel glens come down to the head of the loch, divided from each other by the Stack of Glencoul, 1,600 feet—a geological showpiece where Moine Schist has been thrust forward to clap a cap on top of Cambrian quartzite. The glen on the Stack's south side is a flat-bottomed and narrow gulf (the Amhain an Loch Bhig) between escarpments of 1,000 feet. On the Glas Bheinn side the waterfall shoots over the open cliff at a height of 825 feet. The vertical drop is given by the Ordnance Survey as 658 feet.

The fall is little visited because access is thought (I think mistakenly) to be too hard. There is no road along either shore of Loch Glencoul. Going in from Unapool one would have to traverse on exceedingly steep grass above cliffs plunging 200 feet to the loch. But there is a very much better and shorter way, of which few people seem to know. The route in (three miles) starts from the main road on the pass between Quinag and Glas Bheinn, and just before the long descent to Kylesku. One hundred yards beyond the point marked 849 on the one-inch map (the true pass), a track goes hard right and falls to Loch na Gainmhich, then up the right bank of a burn rising to a lochan at the Bealach à Bhuirich, 1,600 feet. The track continues east, descending through a maze of gneiss humps and hollows. Glas Bheinn above is a waste of pale grey scree. The second burn after the bealach is the Eas a'Chùal Aluinn. Descend the left or right bank to the top of the waterfall; if by the left bank, cross the river now by stones to the right bank. About a hundred yards to the east a broad easy buttress falls to the main glen. From only a short way down it, a clear view of the waterfall can be enjoyed. It comes over the cliff in much the same volume as the Glomach, dropping 500 feet in three clear leaps of white water followed by a mare's tail of 150, all gleaming in the sun. White heather may be found on the escarpment, and eagles seen soaring above the Stack of Glencoul.

The walk to the fall is three miles each way. The path is easy to follow on the outward journey from the main road, but a map and compass should be carried for the return, for the path becomes indistinct above the fall, and if then lost through some carelessness, the Bealach à Bhuirich would be almost impossible to find in mist on such rough ground.

CHAPTER 27

Reay Forest

North of Loch Cairnbawn and Glen Coul, the **Reay Forest** (pronounced Ray) extends on a broad front towards Loch Eriboll on Sutherland's north coast. The mountains of its western fringe stand eight or nine miles in from the open sea, and between sea and hill lies low ground—the roughest, most intractable of low country in the Highlands, more heavily pocked with lochs than Assynt. For all its huge extent, the Reay country is uninhabited except sparsely along the shore. Inland are a few shooting lodges. The shore is the least indented of the Highland seaboard, punctured by only two sea-lochs each of four-mile length, Lochs Laxford and Inchard. In its multitude of little bays, life used to be remarkably similar to that of the northern Scandinavian fiords: tiny shore settlements whose only lines of communication were by sea. The first road was not made till last century.

The mountains of Reay Forest were from ancient times the hunting ground of the chief of Clan MacKay, Lord Reay, whose seats were at Tongue and at Dounreay on the coast of Caithness. In 1829, Lord Reay sold the land for £300,000 to George Leveson-Gower. This 'Leviathan of Wealth' as he has been euphemistically titled, was the most hated man in the Highlands. He had been responsible for untold human misery in the Sutherland clearances of 1810 to 1820, when to make way for sheep, which he thought could be the more profitable stock on his vast estates, he evicted 15,000 men, women, and children, burning their homes and driving them to the sea. In 1833, King William IV created his subjects' oppressor duke of Sutherland. Among works to his credit is the first road through Reay from Loch Assynt to Durness. It is on this same road that you drive to-day.

Your introduction to Reay Forest is at Kylesku a happy one. The ferry across Loch Cairnbawn to Kylestrome is free and runs seven

344

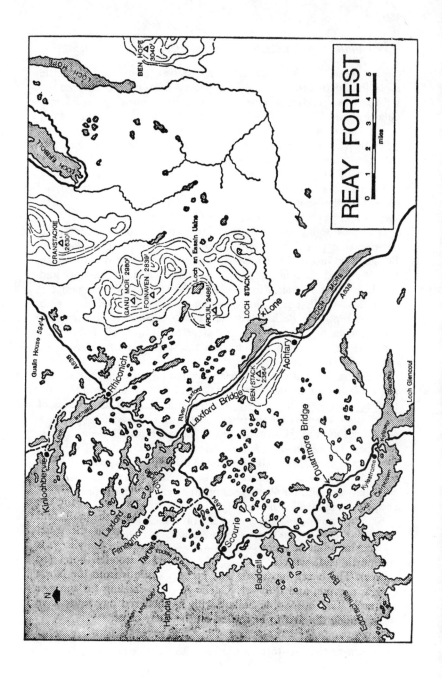

REAY FOREST

0 1 2 3 4 5
miles

BEN HOPE
3040'

LOCH HOPE

LOCH ERIBOLL

CRANSTACKIE
2630'

Loch an Easain Uaine

GANU MOR 2980'
FOINAVEN 2839'
ARCUIL 2486'

LOCH STACK

Lone

LOCH MORE

A838

Achfary

BEN STACK
2364'

Quailin House 594'+

Rhiconich

River Laxford

Laxford Bridge

Duartmore Bridge

Kirkochbervie

L. Laxford

A894

Scourie

Kylestrome

Loch Glencoul

A838

Fanagmore

Tarbet

Badcall

Handa

Loch a Chairn Bhain

Eddrachillis Bay

A894

N

days a week. The passage between the two promontories is little more than 300 yards. Several islets protect it from the sea. From the hill-road behind Kylestrome you can enjoy a clear view of Lochs Glencoul and Glendhu flowing out from either side of Beinn Leoid, 2,597 feet, which with Quinag and Glas Bheinn preside over the meeting place of the three sea-lochs. North of Loch Glencoul, you leave sandstone mountains behind. In the Reay Forest their place is taken by ranges of Cambrian quartzite, hitherto forming only summit caps as on Quinag, but now resting directly on the gneiss. Except on the island of Handa, the Torridon rock does not appear again on cliffs or hills till one nears Cape Wrath.

Distances sound so short on this coast—from Kylestrome to Scourie (the principal village) nine miles, another six to Laxford Bridge, then just five to Rhiconich before the last run of fourteen to Durness—that the motorist must be warned. He needs patience and should prepare his mind in advance. The road-surface is good but bends and knolls come close-linked and with little relief. Speeds must be kept low. Perhaps the best frame of mind to encourage is thankfulness, if not toward the duke of Sutherland (who paid £40,000 for his road), then toward the workmen who must have sweated blood on this gneiss.

A mile and a half out of Kylestrome you pass through the Duartmore plantation of the Forestry Commission, whose conifers are thriving in otherwise treeless country, and descend to a series of rocky bays screened by thirty or forty inshore islets; these make a fine foreground to the distant view of Lewis. **Badcall** is the biggest and best of the bays, enclosed by rocky hills. A small crofting community is engaged also in lobster-fishing. Close above the bay you pass a good water-lily loch; these so abound along the coast that they are commonplace, yet appear so exotic amid wind-scoured rock that one rarely fails to feel wonder.

Scourie (pronounced Scowry) lies in a wide but shallow seaside bowl. The undulating floor is covered by crofts, mostly growing the traditional crops of potatoes, hay, and corn. Between the crofts and the hills circling them, the croft-houses are not set in the usual regular lines but in staggered pattern. The 'centre' of the village is the north end, with stores, post office, and a wooden hotel (19 rooms). The beach has sand. The name Scourie is from the Norse Skóga, a copse, and the early Gaelic Airge, a shieling (or summer pasture). This hospitable hollow with its sheltered bay must have been among the first to be settled on the Reay coast.

The island of **Handa** lies two miles north-west. In 1962 it was made a bird sanctuary under the Royal Society for the Protection of Birds by agreement with the owner. It measures only one and a half miles by one mile and is uninhabited, but the Statistical Account of 1845 records that it was then occupied by twelve families ruled (like St. Kilda) by their own queen and parliament. The queen was the oldest widow on the island, and the menfolk met in parliament every morning to agree on the day's affairs. The queen's status was recognized on the mainland. The people lived on potatoes, fish, and sea-birds and their eggs. The birds made the island habitable. At the north end, cliffs of Torridon sandstone rise sheer out of the sea to 350 feet, and this cliff is the sea-bird metropolis of the north-west seaboard. The men used to cull the young birds and the eggs for food, a practice continued to this day in the Hebrides only by the men of Lewis, who by special legislation under the Bird Protection Act of 1954 are still allowed to make annual expeditions to Sula Sgeir, forty miles north-west of the Butt of Lewis, where they spend a few days in September harvesting gugas—the name given to young gannets. There is no gannetry on Handa, but a count in 1962 showed nearly 60,000 guillemot, 14,000 kittiwake, 12,000 razorbill, 4,000 fulmar, and 800 puffin. Birds alone could not support life on Handa, although they had made it possible, and the great potato famine forced the islanders to leave for America around 1848.

There is no restriction on your landing, except that if you want to camp you should ask permission from the Royal Society for the Protection of Birds, 21 Regent Terrace, Edinburgh 7. Access is had from Tarbet, a tiny clachan in a bay five miles by road north of Scourie. One of the lobster-fishermen there is the society's warden, and he (or one of the others) will ferry you out. The passage of one and a half miles down the Sound of Handa takes fifteen or twenty minutes according to tide, sea, and wind, and the landing is made on the sandy beach at Port an Eilein at the south-east corner. Long skerries give it protection.

An old graveyard close behind the beach was used not only by the islanders but also the mainlanders of the Middle Ages, for Sutherland was plagued by wolves. The site is now entirely grass-grown. A quarter of a mile inland stands an old bothy or cottage, renovated by the society for use by its ornithologists. A few hundred yards to the south-west are the tumbled ruins of the former croft-houses. These three are the only works of man now visible on

347

Handa. The whole interior is peat-bog and rough pasture. You have come for the cliffs. But if the weather is fine, resist the urge to make straight for the highest cliff at the north-west end. Instead, walk clockwise round the island starting from Port an Eilein—a round of four and three-quarter miles. This gradual approach gives a better introduction to Handa before you reach its principal feature, the Great Stack.

At the south-east and south shores you walk on green machair above several sandy beaches. Towards the south-west the ground begins to rise, the cropped turf changes to rough and tussocky grass, and the shore to rock, which gradually steepens into cliffs. Below them, flat slabs spread out in broad aprons, on which the sea crashes green to bloom in a sudden flower of spray, and seethes white endlessly back and forth. On this ground the first sea-birds appear—shags in squads of two dozen, standing on platforms just out of reach of the breakers. As the cliffs rise in height fulmars swoop up and down by the brink. Everywhere are deep chasms and inlets called geo (from the Norse gjá, a creek) and several natural arches. Handa rises to its summit at the north-west on Sithean Mor (pronounced Sheean More), the Big Hill of the Fairies, 406 feet. The top is near the cliff's edge and gives a bird's eye view over the island.

There are five lochans on the moor, each under clear skies a luminous navy-blue. The scent of peat-smoke wafts out from the mainland. You may wonder where the hidden clachans are, for the land seems empty of human life and is seen for what it is—a wildly contorted and rocky waste, which if the rock is wet shines bright as steel. The Old Man of Stoer is most distinct on the far point of Eddrachillis Bay, seeming at this distance as thin and tall as a pikestaff; you can see the coast from there northward to a point eight miles short of Cape Wrath. Eastward, two mountain peaks stand out from the ruck of the Reay Forest: Foinaven and the pointed cap of Arcuil coupled by a long ridge.

The sea-cliffs of Handa reach their highest point close under Sithean Mor. They stretch as a long smooth wall ending at a curious amphitheatre called Am Bonair at the farthest west-north-west bluff, where there is a natural arch. On the east side of the bluff is a geo with vertical walls of 350 feet. The Great Stack stands close between them to almost equal height, a massive pillar with under-cut sides and a flat turf roof. The gap measures 80 feet on the narrowest west side. It was first crossed in 1876 by Donald MacDonald of Lewis. The first crossing this century was made in 1967 by Dr. Tom Patey of Ullapool. He carried the ends of a 600-foot rope outwards on either side of the geo till the rope's middle lay across the top of the stack. He anchored one end to a boulder, the other to iron spikes driven into rock. The shortest rope-length over the gap was then 150 feet, which he crossed using sliding clamps attached to waist and foot. Companions secured him with a safety line. (MacDonald had crossed hand-over-fist without aids).

If you visit the stack in August you will find it deserted, for few of the nesting birds stay on the island. If you come in May or June the wild clamour while you are still far off will prepare you for the amazing sight when you look over the brink. The ledges below are so packed with auks—brown guillemot and black razorbill—that seen from above their rows of glossy backs almost hide the rock from sight. These spartan birds lay a single egg on bare rock, the razorbill's pear-shaped to prevent its rolling off. Puffin like auk and fulmar lay a single egg but never on open ledges; they use a hole or deep cranny or they burrow in turf. Puffin seen close look comically weird. Big grey rings circle the sad eyes around an enormous red and yellow bill flattened on the vertical plane, which shows brightly against the black back or white front. When it whirrs off it splays out vermilion legs behind. The kittiwake colonies build seaweed nests for their two or three eggs lower down on the cliffs, but fulmars like auks prefer a bare ledge nearer the top.

A great number of other birds breed on Handa in relatively small number, principally shag and herring gull, but also a few black guillemot, some with the eye bridled in white as though wearing a monocle and cord, and eider and oystercatcher. Among the birds breeding in only one or two pairs are sheld-duck, raven, golden plover, peewit, and arctic tern. The only birds of prey are peregrine falcon and kestrel (one pair of each). Golden eagle and buzzard may be often seen but do not nest on Handa. Last century the cliffs had numerous white-tailed sea-eagle, but these became extinct in Scotland during the period 1879–90.

When you move away east of the Great Stack, the cliffs decrease in height and finally vanish away at the south-east where the sandy bays begin near your landing place. In addition to landing on Handa, or at least as an alternative to it, you should cruise round the island by motor-boat, for the cliffs seen from below are not less enthralling. The fishermen charge about £2 for landing a party and returning for them on the same day, and only a little extra for circling the island.

Tarbet is only a mile south-west of **Loch Laxford,** the most heavily bayed and islanded loch of the Reay coast. A footpath from Tarbet goes over the hill to its shore, where two crofting and fishing communities, much like Tarbet itself, are less pleasantly sited at Fanagmore and Foindle. You can reach them by car up a side-road on your way back to the main road, but the excursion is not recommended. In three more miles you arrive at Laxford Bridge. The name figures prominently on maps, but not because there is any village or hotel—the land around is the bonniest of the coast, a majestic desolation, made colourful by its pink and quartzy rock and heather-clumps. Laxford Bridge is an important road-junction. It is linked to Lairg near the Dornoch Firth by a continuous water-way save for one brief gap at the watershed.

The road from Lairg follows this north-westward running line by way of Loch Shin, then through the Reay Forest by Loch à Ghriama and Loch Merkland, descending at last to the sea by Loch More, Loch Stack, and the Laxford river. The name Laxford is from the Norse Lax-fjord, or Salmon Fiord. It has remained famous for its salmon fishing to the present day. When you stop by the bridge and look east, three shapely mountains loom close and huge amid the low hills around. From south to north these are Ben Stack and Arcuil (to either side of Loch Stack) and Foinne Bheinn, the White Mountain, commonly called Foinaven, thus named from its white quartzite screes. Laxford Bridge has the most impressive landscape between Assynt and Cape Wrath, and this is best appreciated from one of the summits, preferably Arcuil or Foinaven.

Arcuil is a hollow mountain, in the sense that although it looks so massive from a distance its thin summit-ridge forms a three-quarter circle round an immense corrie containing Loch an Easain Uaine, the Loch of the Green Falls. The mountain is thought to have been named Ark-fjall by the Norsemen, allegedly for its resemblance to an ark. Arcuil is the later Gaelic version. A seven-teenth-century account of the Reay Forest states that all stags on Arcuil have forked tails, but this mutation of the species, if it ever existed, has died out.

To approach Arcuil, drive six miles up the Lairg road to a point near Achfary, and then take a side-track round the head of Loch Stack to a bothy at Lone. An island on Loch Stack used to be the summer house of the chief of Clan MacKay. A footpath from Lone leads north-east on to the main ridge, from which you can look down its north side to the great corrie and its loch surrounded by screes of glaring quartzite. The sight is worth seeing as an extreme of its kind. Exasperated climbers often damn further ascent as that of a shale-bing, but this confusion of boulders is the haunt of snow-bunting and pine-marten, the latter having adapted itself as described in chapter 22.

You may choose to keep on the ridge four miles north to Foinaven, but if you prefer to climb Foinaven direct from the road (thus avoiding the three intervening tops), you should travel north from Laxford Bridge through Rhiconich to the top of the wide pass between Foinaven and the hills of Parph. From Gualin House on this pass, make your way south across the moor to the bealach on the north side of Ceann Garbh, which is Foinaven's north peak, then up and along the ridge to Ganu Mor, the summit at 2,980 feet. By this route you spare yourself the pain of climbing on quartzite scree, and reach your goal in five hours. The emptiness and loneliness of Wester Sutherland is now fully revealed. To your south-west spreads 120 square miles of gneiss moor more heavily congested with lochans than Assynt. Try to count them: the hundreds mount up and you are still not across the Laxford river. Like the minute scales on a butterfly's wing they cover the moor in iridescent blue. Reay Forest is eagle country *par excellence*. Their well-nigh boundless view you now share, from An Teallach in the south to north-coast surf breaking on sandy beaches around Durness. The narrow Kyles of Durness and Loch Eriboll run deep into the land, even to within six miles of Foinaven. Nearer still than these, you look down on Loch Inchard, the last of the sea-lochs on Scotland's west coast. Only four miles long, it clearly defines the north-west corner of Sutherland. It belongs not to Reay, but Cape Wrath.

CHAPTER 28

Cape Wrath

Rhiconich at the head of **Loch Inchard** has only a small hotel and a few houses, but like Laxford Bridge it is a name well known in Sutherland. Here the main Durness road sends a branch four miles out along the shore of the loch to **Kinlochbervie**—the most important fishing port of the North-west Highlands—and to several crofts and sandy bays beyond. When you turn off the Reay moors to Kinlochbervie you enter brighter, more fertile country. The northern slopes of Loch Inchard are crofted throughout their length. The hillsides remain gneiss and their low tops bare-crowned, but they face south and centuries of husbandry have made every hollow and trough green, unless where darkened by potato strips or yellowed by hay.

Kinlochbervie is a tiny, quiet village despite all the activity down at the piers. Its few houses bestride a hill separating a mile-long freshwater loch from a peninsula of Loch. Inchard. This little peninsula is triangular, giving the port the advantage of two bays with harbours and piers to either side of the isthmus, which is only 300 yards wide. Men are daily at work there on the nets, which hang drying on great stakes. Both bays are protected by their own twist and by long arms of the hills. The principal bay is Loch Clash on the peninsula's north side, where big sheds flank the pier-head; alongside them the fishermen's cars and mini-vans are lined up awaiting the fleet's return. Around two or three o'clock on a Thursday afternoon in normal weather, the boats begin to appear, heralded by the screaming of gulls, which flock as a cloud-canopy over each boat. As soon as the catch is landed the young men emerge dressed for town, nip into their cars, and are off to Inverness, Banff, and Buckie, for most of the crews come from the Moray Firth coast. The value of the year's catch is about £1 million, nearly all of it whitefish.

Left
Razorbills nesting on the face of the Great Stack of Handa Island, a bird sanctuary off the Sutherland coast. At the north end, cliffs of Torridon sandstone rise sheer out of the sea to 350 feet. This is the seabird metropolis of the north-west seaboard. A recent count showed 60,000 guillemot, 14,000 kittiwake, 12,000 razorbill, 4,000 fulmar, and 800 puffins.

Below
An Atlantic grey seal pup at Loch Eriboll, Sutherland, the only place on the Scottish mainland where Atlantic seals breed.
All other breeding colonies are on islands. The world's rarest seals, they arrive in the last four months of the year and haul out to calve, mate, and change coat. A pup weighs 30 lb at birth and grows to 80 lb in two weeks.

Balnakeil Bay on the Sutherland coast, looking due north. No more land lies between Cape Wrath and the North Pole.

The Garbet Hotel on the hill above the harbour is the best centre for exploring the Inchard coast, a wild, unspoiled country with superb beaches and good fishing. The hotel was burned down a year or two ago but has now been rebuilt. The proprietor owns seventeen lochs and has fishing privileges on another thirty, including Loch Stack and Loch More, both famous for their salmon and sea-trout. Except on the last two lochs, hotel residents fish free. Brown trout angling starts at the end of April, and for salmon and sea-trout after the first spate in July. Boats can be hired for sea-fishing on Loch Inchard and the open sea—trolling for sea-trout is often very successful on Loch Inchard. A quarter of a mile behind the hotel on the far side of the hill lies the freshwater loch of Innis na Ba Buidhe, the Meadow of the Yellow Cattle, named from a yellow herd once bred by its shores.

Beyond Kinlochbervie a narrow road continues four miles north-west to the crofts of Sheigra on the outermost headland. Less than two miles along this road is one of the most excellent sandy bays of Sutherland. It lies directly under the crofts of **Oldshore More**. In the thirteenth-century MS of the Hakon Saga, it is recorded that King Hakon anchored here in August 1263 at the start of his invasion of Scotland. His fleet of a hundred ships had newly rounded Cape Wrath from the Orkneys, and this, his first port of call, was named Asleifarvic, of which Oldshore Bay is a bad corruption.

The sands are half a mile wide, broken at centre by a long black rib. The west side of the bay is sheltered by a tidal island, Eilean na h-Aiteig (pronounced Hattick), whose green back ends on a vertical rock nose to seaward, somewhat like a lizard. Beyond this island lies the smaller bay and beach of Oldshore Beg. The low hills ringing Oldshore More are rockily green. They slope to a small machair flowery with harebell, red clover and knapweed, and buttercup and dandelion. Broad marram dunes then lead down to a sea dark blue out on the Minch, rapidly greening on the inshore sand, and finally torn white where the rollers drive far up the curved beach.

Along the two miles of road beyond Oldshore More, you pass four more crofting clachans at Oldshore Beg, Blairmore, Balchreic, and Sheigra, where the road ends. The men of all these crofts work also at lobster-fishing. Cape Wrath now lies ten miles to the north, and Sheigra is the last inhabited ground of the coast.

Between Sheigra and Blairmore, a peat-track runs four miles north over the moor to the most justly famous bay of the whole seaboard, **Sandwood Bay**. The name is again a corruption of the Norse Sand-vatn, meaning Sand-water. Behind its broad belt of marram dunes lies the large freshwater loch of Sandwood, which sends a short river through the dunes into the centre of the beach, which is almost two miles wide. The bay is rarely visited: few car-owners are willing to walk eight miles there and back, least of all on a rough track through dark bog. From this unbroken solitude comes much of Sandwood's charm, and its value to mermaids as a hauling-out point. A fully circumstantial and verbatim report of one of the sightings of a mermaid by a local shepherd will be found in *Wade the River, Drift the Loch*, by R. Macdonald Robertson. Briefly it is this: Sandy Gunn was rounding up his sheep for clipping when he happened to walk over the sands with his dog. About half a mile from the south end, a spur of rock runs out into the sea. The dog showed unease on approaching this rock, and hung back. Sandy Gunn went on to within twenty yards and discovered the mermaid on a ledge at the seaward end. His collie was now terrified. When the mermaid looked up and saw him, Sandy Gunn took no further chance and withdrew, but he used his eyes and was later able to paint a detailed verbal portrait.

At the south point of Sandwood stands a tall stack of red Torridon sandstone, called Am Buachaille, the Herdsman. The shore-rocks are here rich in semi-precious stones, embedded like currants in a bun: a natural treasury, it would seem, for lapidaries.

Between Sandwood and Sheigra are numerous peat-banks. In summer the peat-stacks will be seen awaiting collection along the track to Sheigra, and by the roadside down the whole length of Loch Inchard, and on the main road too from Laxford Bridge all the way to **Durness** (accent on the last syllable).

When you head north to Durness from Rhiconich, and after you have climbed out of the Achriesgill glen, you will suddenly notice that the gneiss bumpiness had ended. A total change has come over the character of the country. To either side the hillsides take vast even sweeps. There is less heather, more grass, and hardly a rock visible. The road climbs more easily to the watershed at 594 feet, where Gualin House stands alone, built as a hotel last century by the duke of Sutherland and now a shooting lodge. From there onward you follow the wide flat glen of Strath Dionard—a straight road with few bends to Durness.

The change in landscape is caused by another change in rock. Your road is cutting across the thick neck of Cape Wrath's huge

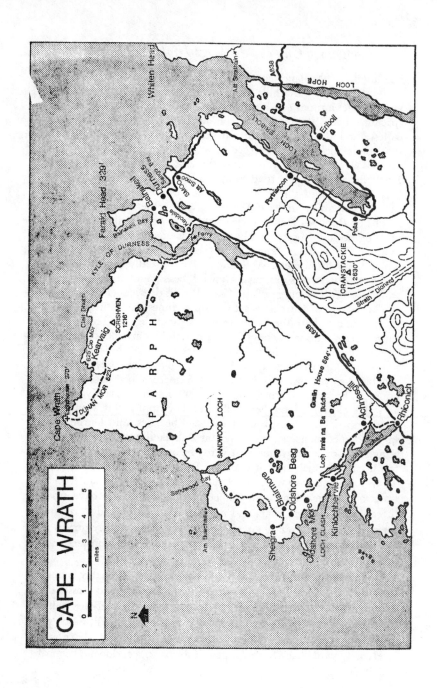

CAPE WRATH

miles
0 1 2 3 4 5

N

Cape Wrath
Lighthouse 370'

Clas Dbuibh
Clo Mor 625'
DUNAN MOR 523'

Keanvaig
SCRISHVEN 1216'

Bealach
Duiness

Farald Head 323'

Whiten Head

KYLE OF DURNESS

Balnakeil Bay

Ferry

Keoldale

SMOO
Allt Smoo

P A R P H

SANDWOOD LOCH

Sandwood Bay

Am Buachaille

Sheigra

Blairmore

Oldshore Beag

Oldshore Mor

LOCH CLASH

Kinlochbervie

Loch Innis na Ba Buidhe

Gualin House 594' X

A838

Portnancon

Loch Eriboll

Eriboll

LOCH HOPE

A838

Allt Strathain

Polla

CRANSTACKIE 2630'

Strath Dionard

A838

Achriesgill

Rhiconich

headland, a headland cut out by the sea-lochs of Inchard and Kyle of Durness. The hills are Torridon sandstone—the rock that you last met around Am Buachaille of Sandwood Bay, from which it spreads far into the moor of Parph, as the final cape's hinterland is called: and the coastland of Durness is the Cambrian limestone that made Inchnadamph so green.

At Kyle of Durness you follow the east shore for three miles to Keoldale, where a side-road branches half a mile leftward to Cape Wrath Hotel and the ferry across the Kyle. You continue north rather less than two miles to Durness. This northern butt of Scotland is split by three sea-lochs—Kyle of Durness, Loch Eriboll, and Kyle of Tongue—into three great headlands: Cape Wrath, Durness, and Whiten Head. The name Durness is from the Norse Dyra-ness, which here would mean Wolf Cape. Dyr is usually to be translated as Deer, but means primarily a wild beast, and in Viking days wolves were the scourge of the Cape Wrath district.

The village of Durness is set on top of limestone bluffs, which a quarter of a mile to the north drop in sea-cliffs, grassed on top and carved below into sandy bays. The hinterland is dark moor gradually rising for eight miles inland in a series of linked hill-tops to the summit of Cranstackie, 2,630 feet. The village has only some 400 inhabitants, yet has four hotels and numerous bed-and-breakfast houses. The pride of Durness ought to be her many sandy beaches and the clean turf on her cliff-tops. Unhappily this would not appear to be so. The sea looks after the beaches, and Durness has splendid specimens close at hand, at Balnakeil a mile to the west, Sango Bay only a few hundred yards below the village, and others towards Loch Eriboll; but man has fouled the cliff-tops eastward. They are bestrewn with the concrete foundations and wrecked walls of wartime huts and gun emplacements. These have stood there for twenty-odd years and no man has raised hand to remove them. That task could not be within the economic resources of Durness village, but certainly is within those of the county council and the government.

One curio of these cliffs is the Cave of Smoo, probably named from the Old Norse Smuga, a cleft, where the coast road crosses the Allt Smoo a mile east of Durness. A geo gashes the cliff-face half a mile deep, like a thin slice taken out of a cake. The Allt Smoo on approaching the road from the moor flows at 112 feet above sea-level; sixty yards back from the geo, it drops 80 feet down a vertical shaft and reappears through a cavern (not visible from the road) to flow out through the gorge of the creek.

Inspect the cave first from above. The river plunges down its waterfall hole immediately south of the bridge, to either side of which two more shafts allow glimpses into the cavern. Then go down into the creek by a steep path on the seaward side of the bridge. Fulmars will be seen roosting on the open cliff-face to the right of the cave. Cross the Allt Smoo by stepping-stones, then enter the outer cave under an arch 50 feet high by 120 wide. A rocky barrier now screens an inner cave on the other side of the Allt Smoo. To reach it, recross the river on stones and climb 10 feet up easy rock to a ledge, from which you can look over the barrier. A deep pool in a rock passage runs 25 yards to the 80-foot waterfall. You cannot get near enough to see the fall, but the shaft sheds light on the peat-brown water. Any further progress is for specialists. Pot-holers report that to the right of the waterfall an innermost cave goes another hundred feet and has many stalagmites. This innermost cave was first explored in 1833 but is now rarely visited.

Returning to the open air, you find on the steep east side of the geo a footpath leading up to grassy cliff-tops (free of concrete). Good walking may be enjoyed along the edge and fine views eastward across bluffs and islands to outer Loch Eriboll, and to the pale cliffs of Whiten Head on its far side. A conspicuous waterfall will be seen there, where the Allt Srathain falls over the mouth of a cave into the sea. There are several other big caves on that west side of Whiten Head, but a boat would be needed to visit them for the sea runs deep into most. The Loch Eriboll caves are the only place on the mainland where the Atlantic grey seal breeds (it is the world's rarest seal).

On the other side of Durness, the outstanding feature is a narrow peninsula of high marram dunes running out two miles north-west to Fair Aird, often called Far Out Head. It stretches a long arm around **Balnakeil Bay**—a big westward-facing bay of the outer Kyle of Durness. The shell-sand at the back of Balnakeil curves one and a half miles, and with the dunes behind gives Durness the finest beach of the north coast, excellent alike for sunbathing and swimming.

Balnakeil has another, man-made point of distinction in Balnakeil village, which at first sight might not seem prepossessing. It is the site of an old radar station. The houses are concrete blocks taken over by enterprising persons and made into a craft village

357

with pottery studio, an art gallery, coffee house, and a hotel of 19 rooms. The pottery studio under Paul Brown is producing work of high quality and design. The coffee house and hotel, named the Far North Hotel, should not be omitted from any visit to Durness. Their interior design and decoration are models of what may be done by art and imagination: for these rectangular box interiors have been transformed into rooms that delight the eye not by rich furnishing but by use of good material, tooled by good craftsmen, and by bold, unerring taste in decoration; everything is simple, yet in every feature firmly elegant—in harmony too with the Sutherland environment. The coffee house is the best of its kind on the Highland coast.

Close to the west side of Balnakeil, a ruined church of 1619 was at one time attached to Dornoch Abbey and probably gave name to the bay—Balnakeil means Place of the Kirk. The graveyard has a monument to the Gaelic poet Rob Donn, sometimes called the Burns of the North, who died in 1777. The ground farther west at the Kyle is the scene of an archaeological dig, which began in 1966 and is proving to be the most important made in Scotland for many years. The relics disclosed are of Viking, Pictish, and earlier races, but at the time of writing no detail has been made available.

Far Out Head is a good but anglicized name for **Fear Ard** (spelt Faraid on the one-inch map), which means High Fellow. There is a track all the way from Balnakeil, but this tends to get lost among the marram dunes, which are the highest and most extensive on Scotland's west mainland. You can walk instead along the beach and climb on to the track at the far end. Two miles out, the headland rises in a hill of 329 feet, on which the relics of a radar station still survive. Inland you look to Foinaven and the Reay Forest; eastward, along the Durness coast—six miles of bays and thrusting rock-fangs—to the white cliffs of Eriboll; and westward to Cape Wrath.

Cape Wrath is no easy place to reach, and we should hope it never will be. When everyone can drive his car to the cape, as he can to John O' Groats, its allure will have gone. Its present remoteness gives it the lonely character that should rightly belong to a seaboard's most northerly point. There is no public highway in from the head of Kyle of Durness. But there is a roadway of the Northern Lighthouse Commission starting mid-way down the Kyle and winding ten miles over the moor of Parph to the light-house. The road-end can be reached by a passenger ferry from Keoldale. One has to walk to the cape and back or hire a bike:

an adventurous day's work in wild or windy weather and tough at the best of times. This adventure had recently been happily modified by the owner of the Far North Hotel, who several times a day in summer ran a minibus service to the lighthouse. This service has now been taken off. Cape Wrath keeps its character.

The ferryman, who lives on the west side of the Kyle, can be telephoned from Durness post office for any private arrangement. The crossing of the Kyle in sunny weather is a most pleasant part of the Cape Wrath excursion. The water lies shallow over sand. When you look down on it from the hill on the west side, it shines luminously green, darkening to mauves and blues according to seaweed and depth.

You draw away from the sea and cross the dark rolling moor of **Parph.** The hill of Scrishven, which you pass on your right-hand side, is of Torridon sandstone gently swelling to 1,216 feet, but thrusting northward at Cleit Dubh, the biggest sea-cliff on the British mainland. The Black Cliff is 850 feet of vertical red rock, which can look black in dull weather. The cliff continues two miles westward at a height of 600 feet under the hill of Clò Mòr, falling thereafter to a beautifully sandy bay at Kearvaig, where there is one croft.

The moor of Parph behind is uninhabited. The undulating rock is a tangle of sandstone and gneiss thinly covered in peat. The word Parph is a Gaelic rendering of the original Norse name for Cape Wrath—Hvarf, a Turning Point. The English corruption is a good name in itself, but without the more practical significance of that used by the Viking navigators, whose every voyage between the Orkney jarldom and the Hebrides turned this great corner of Scotland.

The cape is hidden from you till the last moment by the hill of Dùnan Mòr, 523 feet. As you round its shoulder, you can see far south down the coast to Sandwood Bay and the slim stack of Am Buachaille. You turn north, and there at last is the lighthouse on the brink of the cape. The row of derelict stone houses that appear on your right as you descend was at one time a coastguard station. The lighthouse has no tall tower like Ardnamurchan's. Built in 1828, its short, snow-white column sits on a grass-topped cliff. The light can be seen for twenty-seven miles, for the cliff rises 370 feet out of the sea. The rock here is red gneiss veined with pink pegmatite.

From the sea-pinks at the brink you look down on three low stacks. The middle one has a natural arch, through which you glimpse the Atlantic swell bursting on submerged skerries. Four headlands recede eastward, each with numerous smaller stacks and skerries, where lobster-fishermen set their creels. Out of sight in a geo one mile east is a pier used for fuelling the lighthouse. The geologist John MacCulloch wrote in the early nineteenth century that the Cape Wrath cliffs swarmed with sea-eagles, but their only tenants now are a large colony of nesting fulmar in spring. Gannet (the biggest British seabird) will frequently be seen diving offshore, and cannot be then mistaken for any other bird—wings folded to shape an arrowhead, it plummets from a height of 100 feet or more. More often, gannets can be watched flying up the coast to use Cape Wrath, like the Viking Long Ships, as their turning point for the Orkneys, for some swing away north-east to Sule Stack, which on a clear day can be seen as a gleam of white, thirty miles north of Whiten Head; others turn north-west to Sula Sgeir (Norse for Pillar Skerry), which at forty-three miles is invisible; still more turn south-west for St. Kilda, a hundred and thirty-six miles away behind Lewis. These islands are the gannets' breeding stations, and St. Kilda with 45,000 pairs is the world's largest.

Granted clear weather, one can see very long distances from Cape Wrath, but hardly to much advantage. Lewis appears fifty miles to the south-west only as a long, low line; sixty miles east one can identify the dim cliffs of Hoy in the Orkneys, for these rise 1,140 feet at St. John's Head; more remarkable yet, North Rona, which rises only 355 feet can be seen forty-five miles north-west, although calculations demonstrate that it ought to be invisible beyond the earth's dip to Iceland. Its appearance on the farthest rim is caused by atmospheric refraction. North Rona is a National Nature Reserve, holding the same relation to seal as St. Kilda to gannet. Its population of Atlantic grey seal is the world's largest. Nearly 7,500 arrive in the last four months of each year, and haul out to calve, to mate, and to change their coats. Some 2,500 calves are born there annually. The island is famous too as a breeding station for storm petrel. Our detection of these far-off islands is a minor triumph needing not only good weather but an absence of haze. Most often one will look out only to grey sea fading into grey sky. And that too is appropriate to the place. One may then face due north and know that there is no land between the cape and the Pole. Cape Wrath is the end of all things.

Appendices

National Trust for Scotland

An important activity of the Trust on the west coast is its organization of annual cruises: these enable you to see remote islands and mainland coasts that are seldom visited because hard to reach by other means, and to do so in the company of an expert staff from whom you can learn much about the regions and islands seen—their history and geology, their wild life and human life. These cruises are open to everyone.

The National Trust for Scotland was founded in 1931 to preserve for the nation places of natural beauty and of historical and architectural worth, and at the same time to encourage people to know them. The Trust receives no exchequer grants and depends for support on its members, yet it owns more than sixty properties, which are visited by more than half a million people a year. Entry to Trust land is free, but non-members are asked to pay small charges for entry to the great houses, gardens, and castles, in order to help meet the costs of maintenance. You may find it worth while joining the Trust. Ordinary membership costs only a few pounds. Apply to the Secretary, 5 Charlotte Square, Edinburgh 2.

The Trust has a beneficient influence on the Highland scene in the high standard to which its properties are maintained, the good example it sets to other owners and to local authorities, and the help it gives to visitors, not only in such important matters as litter disposal but also in guidance on the attractions of all surrounding country given from a chain of infomation centres sited on its properties.

Every year at least two cruises are run, each of 7 to 12 days. The spring cruise is expensive—£180 to £500 according to class of accommodation chosen. The food and service are excellent. The late summer 'adventure' cruise is relatively inexpensive—£90 to £330—and the ship then carries a much larger complement of passengers. Both cruises visit the Hebridean islands, the west and north coast bays and ports, and go as far afield as St Kilda, the Orkney and Shetland Islands, Fair Isle, or the Irish and continental ports.

A feature of all these cruises is their wide range and the frequent opportunities given for landing at remote places.

Ski-ing

Scotland has an abundance of snow-holding mountains affording cross-country ski-ing and downhill running. Close approach by road being difficult, only three mountain areas have (in 1977) facilities fully developed for ski-ing holidays with high access roads, chairlifts, ski-tows, hill-chalets, and ski-schools, supported below by hotels providing night entertainment. These three areas are Glencoe, Strathspey, and Glenshee. The development of other centres is certain to follow in the near future. In the west, Glencoe has the field to itself.

Ski-ing in Glencoe, or to be more exact, on the north face of Meall a' Bhuiridh, differs from that of the Cairngorms and Glenshee in the greater steepness and variety of its downhill runs. Those of Cairngorm and Glenshee are more open and even, those of Glencoe more restricted and testing. Meall a' Bhuiridh has at least seven runs. These are more appreciated by the skier of some experience than by beginners, who have suitable nursery slopes at hand but tend to find the longer runs frightening in icy conditions. Icy pistes are common in Scotland. Glencoe, with its more frequent thaws and frosts, provides them more often than the Cairngorms. The Cairngorm and Glenshee tops offer better opportunities for cross-country ski-ing. At Glencoe, access to the White Corries chairlift is unimpeded by the snow-drifts that often, after blizzard, stop access to Cairngorm.

The Scottish season normally starts in mid-December and lasts till the beginning of May. Only in exceptional years like 1965 does it start in early November. At the height of the season in February, March, and April, and in the best conditions, Scottish ski-ing compares well with Alpine, but you must come to Scotland prepared for bitter wind. When foul weather makes ski-ing impossible or unpleasant, Strathspey is the region best supplied with alternative sports—skating and curling rinks, a swimming pool, and indoor games. But Glencoe offers at Kingshouse a bowling alley, curling rink, film-shows, concerts, and at Clachaig dancing.

The White Corries, Glencoe

The access road leaves the main road south of Kingshouse and at 950 feet crosses the moor past Blackrock Cottage to the chairlift car-park. The chairlift takes you to the plateau at 2,090 feet. Two successive T-bar ski-tows then drag you from 2,250 feet to 3,600 feet close under the summit.

364

In good conditions the run from the summit to the car-park is probably the best in Scotland. A third and lower tow has been added for beginners.

At the foot of the chairlift, a heated chalet provides hot drinks and an equipment hire service.

The chairlift and tows operate in winter only at weekends and holidays, but they may be chartered for mid-week service. Charges are irrespective of numbers using the uplift. The chairlift is open for summer tourists from June to 10th September.

The railway station has direct sleeper connection with King's Cross and the hotel a ski-shop with equipment for hire.

Glencoe (Loch Leven end), 20 minutes by car.

Ballachulish, 25 minutes by car.

Royal Hotel, Tyndrum, 25 minutes by car.

Further information can be obtained from the booklet *Winter Sports in Scotland*, published by the Scottish Tourist Board (see over).

Scottish Tourist Board

The Board will give you information about Travel in Scotland if you apply to the principal office at 2 Rutland Place, Edinburgh EH1 2YU (*Tel.* 031-229 1561), or to the Inverness and Loch Ness Tourist Organisation, at 23 Church Street, Inverness (*Tel.* 34353).

The Board publishes the following booklets, obtainable direct or through booksellers:

Where to stay in Scotland. A national register of accommodation published annually	75p
Hotels, Guest Houses and B & B in Highlands and Islands	25p
Self Catering Accommodation	45p
Self Catering in the Highlands and Islands	25p
Scotland Home of Golf	50p
Walks & Trails in Scotland	60p
Camping & Caravan Sites	45p

Other titles are seasonably available on fishing, sea angling, winter sports, castles and historic houses, and public holidays. Prices and titles change from one year to another and inquiries should be made of the Board or booksellers.

Hotels

The list below is a selection, graded according to price-range and set down in order of districts and itinerary as these appear in the book.

* means that the price of room and breakfast can vary between £2 and £2.50 (figures correct for 1977)
** between £3.50 and £6
*** between £6 and £8
**** between £6 and £15
No star means under £2

In several instances, the lower price charged by a hotel is less or more (but the higher price should not be more) than that stated above for its grade. Hotel charges are much open to fluctuation. Always ask quotations in advance. The lower charges generally refer to out-of-season periods.

A full list of hotels with details of accommodation and prices is published annually by the Scottish Tourist Board under the title *Where to Stay in Scotland* (see page 366). It lists also guest houses, "bed and breakfasts", hostels. The Board does not arrange accommodation or make any other reservations. That should be done direct or through a travel agency. In July and August book in advance. You cannot arrive at any Highland village or hotel and expect to find a bed empty at the height of the season. At the very least telephone ahead the day before. Be warned that it will often be difficult to get a meal after 7.30 p.m. *Where to Stay* gives a list of local tourist information centres, who in any difficulty will help you to find accommodation if there is any.

Abbreviations

U	Unlicensed	F	Fishing	PT	Pony-trekking
GH	Guest House	R	Riding	DS	Deer stalking
Sk	Ski-ing	S	Shooting	WSk	Water ski-ing

ARGYLL

ARDUAINE	*** Loch Melfort Motor Inn 28 rms.
ARDNAMURCHAN	** Glenborrodale House 8 rms.
	*** Kilchoan 11 rms.
ARDRISHAIG	* Anchor 10 rms.
	* Auchendarroch 10 rms.
	** Royal 20 rms.

BALLACHULISH	*** Ballachulish 35 rms.
	* Laroch House 7 rms. U
BENDERLOCH	** Lynn of Lorne 10 rms.
BRIDGE OF ORCHY	** Bridge of Orchy 12 rms.
	* Inveroran 8 rms. F
CAMPBELTOWN	** Argyll Arms 48 rms.
	** Ardshiel Hotel 14 rms.
	* Hall 9 rms.
	** White Hart 21 rms.
CONNEL	** Dunstaffnage Arms 11 rms.
CRINAN	**** Crinan 24 rms. S
DALMALLY	*** Dalmally 57 rms.
DUROR	** Duror 9 rms.
FORD	* Ford 13 rms
GLENCOE	** Chachaig Inn 12 rms.
	** King's House 22 rms.
KILFINAN	** Kilfinan 7 rms.
KILMARTIN	* Kilmartin 6 rms.
LOCH AWE	** Carraig Thura 23 rms. F
	** Loch Awe 73 rms. F
LOCHAIRESIDE	*** Taychreggan 22 rms. F S
LOCHGAIR	*** Lochgair 21 rms. F
LOCHGILPHEAD	* Argyll 10 rms.
	** Stag 25 rms.
	* Victoria 10 rms.
MINARD	** Minard Castle 38 rms.
NORTH CONNEL	*** Loch Nell Arms 13 rms.
OBAN	* Achnamara Private 12 rms. U
	** Atholl 11 rms. U
	** Balmoral 18 rms. WSk
	** Barriemore 14 rms. U
	** Columba 57 rms.
	** Commercial 12 rms.
	* Corran House 22 rms. U
	** Esplanade 24 rms.
	** Glenburnie Private 15 rms. U
	* Heatherfield Private 10 rms. U
	* Kilchrennan 12 rms. U
	** King's Knoll 18 rms.
	* Oban 9 rms. U

	*** Marine 39 rms.
	* Sutherland 10 rms. U
	* Thornloe Private 8 rms. U
	* Wellpark 14 rms. U
	* Woodside 7 rms.
PORT APPIN	** Airds 17 rms.
PORTSONACHAN	*** The Hotel 23 rms. F R
SALEN	* Salen 6 rms.
SOUTHEND	** Argyll Arms 14 rms.
TARBET	* Columba 14 rms.
	** Tarbet 20 rms.
TAYNUILT	** Netherlorn 18 rms.
	** Polfearn 13 rms.
TIGHNABRUAICH	** Tighnabruaich 10 rms.
ARINAGOUR	** Isle of Coll 9 rms. F
ISLE OF IONA	** Argyll 20 rms. U
	** St. Columba 30 rms. U
BOWMORE	** Bowmore 10 rms.
BRIDGEND	** Bridgend 9 rms.
PORT ASKAIG	** Port Askaig 10 rms.
PORT ELLEN	** Ardview 8 rms. R
	** Machrie 33 rms. F S
	** White Hart 22 rms.
ISLE OF JURA	** Jura 16 rms. F
CRAIGNURE	** Bayview 7 rms.
PENNYGHAEL	** Kinloch 5 rms.
SALEN	** Glenforsa 14 rms. F
	** Salen 18 rms.
TOBERMORY	**** Western Isles 50 rms. F
SCARINISH	** Scarinish 17 rms.

CAITHNESS

CASTLETOWN	* Ponderosa Motel 4 rms.
	* St. Clair Arms 8 rms.
DUNNET	* House of the Northern Gate 10 rms.
	** Northern Sands 15 rms.
JOHN O'GROATS	* Caver-Feidh House 10 rms. U
	* John o' Groats 27 rms.
	* Seaview 10 rms.

THURSO   * Central 10 rms.
                           * Holborn 14 rms.
                           * Park 16 rms.
                           ** Royal 83 rms.
                           ** St. Clair 13 rms.
WICK   ** Nethcliffe 10 rms.
                           * Queen's 8 rms.

INVERNESS-SHIRE

ARDERSIER   * The Ship Inn 7 rms.
ARISAIG   ** Arisaig 19 rms.
                           ø Cnoc-na-Faire 10 rms.
AVIEMORE   ** Alt-Na-Craig 10 rms.
                           * Aviemore Chalets Motel 80 rms.
                                U F PT Sk
                     **** Badenoch 81 rms.
                     **** Coylumbridge 133 rms. F PT Sk
                         ** Dell 14 rms. U
                      *** High Range 25 rms.
                     **** Post House 103 rms.
                     **** Strathspey 90 rms.
BOAT OF GARTEN   *** Boat 28 rms.
                           ** Craigard 20 rms.
CANNICH   * Glen Affric 18 rms. F
CARRBRIDGE   * Struan 18 rms.
DALWHINNIE   ** Grampian 25 rms.
DAVIOT   ** Meallmore 19 rms. F
DRUMNADROCHIT   ** Benleva 12 rms.
                           * Lewiston Arms 8 rms.
                           ** Polmaily House 10 rms. F
FORT AUGUSTUS   Caledonian 13 rms.
                           ** Lovat Arms 25 rms.
                           ** White Gates 8 rms. U
FORT WILLIAM   *** Alexandra 34 rms.
                           ** Clan MacDuff 50 rms.
                           ** Croit-Anna 90 rms.
                           * Cruachan 14 rms.
                           ** Grand 35 rms.

ø terms on application

	** Highland 59 rms.
	** Imperial 37 rms.
	*** Milton 44 rms.
	* Milton Motor Inn 60 rms. U
	** Nevis Bank 20 rms.
	** Station 19 rms.
BANAVIE	* Glen Loy Lodge 7 rms.
CORPACH	** The Hotel 7 rms.
INVERGARRY	* Craigard Private 7 rms.
	** Glengarry Castle 30 rms. F
INVERSMORISTON	** Glenmoriston Arms 15 rms. DS F S
	* Tigh-na-Bruach 9 rms.
INVERNESS	* Albert 20 rms.
	* Ardconnel 7 rms. U
	* Ashvale 11 rms. U
	**** Caledonian 120 rms.
	* Carlone 7 rms. U
	** Columba 54 rms.
	* Corriegarth 14 rms.
	* Craigmonie 11 rms.
	*** Cummings 35 rms.
	** Douglas 88 rms.
	* Eastlyn 7 rms. U
	* Elms Private 12 rms.
	* Felstead 8 rms. U
	* Gellion's 6 rms.
	* Glenmoriston 15 rms. U
	* Larchfield 8 rms. U
	** Lochardil 10 rms.
	* Millburn 12 rms. U
	* Moyness Private 9 rms.
	** Muirtown Motel 40 rms.
	** Ness Castle 22 rms. U
	* Ramasaig House 7 rms. U
	** Rannoch Lodge 14 rms.
	** Redcliffe 8 rms. U
	** Riverside 11 rms. U
	**** Royal 45 rms.
	** Springfield House 5 rms.

ø Station 70 rms.
** Tower 9 rms.
* West End 8 rms. U
* Windsor House 13 rms. U
KINCRAIG   ** Ossian 11 rms.
KINGUSSIE   ** Duke of Gordon 72 rms.
** Royal 29 rms.
* Scott's 10 rms.
* Silverfjord 8 rms.
* Star 26 rms.
LOCHAILORT   * Glenshian Lodge 7 rms.
* Lochailort Inn 7 rms.
MALLAIG   ** Marine 25 rms.
** West Highland 30 rms.
NETHYBRIDGE   * Grey House 10 rms. U
* Heatherbrae 7 rms.
* Mount View 9 rms. U
NEWTONMORE   * Badenoch 14 rms. U
** Balavil Arms 30 rms. F PT S Sk
* Braeriach 16 rms.
** Craig Mhor 30 rms. F Sk
** The Glen 10 rms.
** Truim 35 rms.
NORTH BALLACHULISH * Loch Leven 12 rms.
ONICH   * Allt-Nan-Rhos 24 rms.
** Creagdhu 24 rms.
** Onich 25 rms. F
ROY BRIDGE   * Kinchellie Croft Motel 10 rms. U
* Stronlossit 10 rms. F
SPEAN BRIDGE   * Spean Bridge 25 rms.
* Corriegour Lodge 9 rms. U
TOMDOUN   * Tomdoun 12 rms.
TOMICH   * Tomich 6 rms. U
WHITEBRIDGE   ** Whitebridge 13 rms. F
CREAGORRY   ** Creagorry 6 rms.
TARBERT   ** Harris 23 rms. F
ARDVASAR   ** Ardvasar 8 rms.
BROADFORD   *** Broadford 30 rms.
** Dunollie 20 rms.

ø terms on application

DUNVEGAN	ø Atholl House 12 rms. U
	** Dunvegan 18 rms. F PT S
	* Ose Farm 7 rms. U
ISLE ORNSAY	** Duisdale 25 rms.
	** Isle Ornsay 10 rms.
	** Kinloch Lodge 15 rms.
KYLEAKIN	* Dunringell 18 rms. U
	** King's Arms 23 rms.
	** Marine 25 rms.
	* White Heather 21 rms. U
PORTREE	** Coolin Hills 29 rms.
	** Graylor House 10 rms. U F
	* Pier 5 rms.
	** Rosedale 20 rms.
	** Royal 28 rms.
SCONSER	** Sconser Lodge 8 rms. F
SKEABOST	** Skeabost House 25 rms. F
SLIGACHAN	*** Sligachan 26 rms. F
STRUAN	* Ullinish Lodge 9 rms. F S
UIG	** Uig 25 rms. F
LOCHMADDY	**** Lochmaddy 16 rms. F
LOCHBOISDALE	ø Lochboisdale 19 rms. F S

ROSS & CROMARTY

ACHILTIBUIE	** Summer Isles 13 rms. DS F
ACHNASHEEN	** Achnasheen 9 rms.
	** Ledgowan 25 rms.
APPLECROSS	* Applecross 5 rms. U
ARDGAY	* Lady Ross 10 rms.
AULTBEA	** Aultbea 24 rms.
	** Drumchork Lodge 22 rms.
BALMACARA	** Balmacara 27 rms.
CONTIN	** Achilty 12 rms. F
	** Craigdarroch 19 rms. F
DINGWALL	* Lisliard 7 rms.
DUNDONNELL	** Dundonnell 15 rms.
FORTROSE	* Oakfield 9 rms. U
	* Rosevale Private 7 rms. U

ø terms on application

373

	** Royal 17 rms.
GAIRLOCH	** Badachro Inn 5 rms.
	** Gairloch 53 rms.
	*** Gairloch Motor Inn 20 rms.
	* Myrtle Bank 12 rms.
	** Shieldaig Lodge 14 rms. F S
	** The Old Inn 10 rms. U
GARVE	** Garve 42 rms. F
	*** Inchbae Lodge 13 rms.
	*** Strathgarve Lodge 20 rms. F S
GLENSHIEL	* Ratagan House 7 rms. U
KILDARY	** Jackdaw 20 rms.
KINLOCHEWE	** Kinlochewe 18 rms.
	*** Merlinwood 8 rms.
KYLE OF LOCHALSH	ø Lochalsh 47 rms.
LOCH BROOM	*** Leckmelm Chalet 12 rms. DS F
LOCHCARRON	** Lochcarron 14 rms.
	** Rock Villa 14 rms.
MUIR OF ORD	** Ord Arms 11 rms.
MUNLOCHY	* Munlochy 5 rms.
NIGG	Nigg Ferry 7 rms.
PLOCKTON	ø Seaforth 5 rms.
POOLEWE	** Poolewe 18 rms.
	** Pool House 22 rms. F
ROSEMARKIE	** Marine 50 rms.
	* The Plough Inn 2 rms
STRATHPEFFER	** Ben Wyvis 92 rms.
	** Highland 100 rms. F
	** Holly Lodge 9 rms.
	* MacKay's 20 rms. U
	** Richmond 18 rms.
	** Strathpeffer 37 rms
TAIN	* Mansfield House 10 rms.
	* Morangie House 8 rms.
	** Royal 22 rms.
TORRIDON	*** Loch Torridon 28 rms. DS F WSk
ULLAPOOL	ø Altnaharrie 2 rms. F
	ø Argyll 10 rms.
	*** Caledonian 47 rms.

ø terms on application

	* Riverside House 19 rms. U
	**** Royal 56 rms. F
	** Tir Aluinn 19 rms.
CARLOWAY	** Doune Braes 10 rms.
STORNOWAY	** Newton House Hotel & Motel 14 rms. U
	** Royal 17 rms.

SUTHERLAND

ALTNACEALGACH	** Altnacealgach 14 rms. F
ALTNAHARRA	* Altnaharra 14 rms. F
BONAR BRIDGE	** Caledonian 26 rms. F
BRORA	** Links 31 rms. F
	** Sutherland Arms 11 rms.
DORNOCH	** Burghfield 50 rms.
	** Dornoch Castle 20 rms.
	** Dornoch 93 rms.
	* Eagle 5 rms.
	** Royal Golf 43 rms.
DRUMBEG	ø Drumbeg 10 rms. F
DURNESS	** Far North 18 rms. U
	* Parkhill 10 rms. U
FORSINARD	** Forsinard 13 rms.
GOLSPIE	** Sutherland Arms 19 rms. F
HELMSDALE	* Navidale House 24 rms.
INCHNADAMPH	** Inchnadamph 33 rms. F
INVERSHIN	* Invershin 16 rms.
KINBRACE	* Garvault 10 rms. F
KINLOCHBERVIE	** Garbet 24 rms.
KYLESKU	* Kylesku 7 rms.
LAIRG	**** Aultnagar 29 rms.
	*** Sutherland Arms 38 rms.
LOCHINVER	** Culag 45 rms. F
OVERSCAIG	** Overscaig 16 rms. F
ROGART	* Rogart 4 rms.
SCOURIE	** Scourie 22 rms. F
STRATHY POINT	* Strathy Inn 7 rms.
TONGUE	** Ben Loyal 20 rms. F

ø terms on application

375

ø Tongue 20 rms. F

ORKNEY

KIRKWALL	** Kirkwall 42 rms.
	** Lynnfield 6 rms.
	ø Queen's 8 rms.
STENNES	** Standing Stones 21 rms. F
STROMNESS	ø Royal 5 rms.
	** Stromness 40 rms.

SHETLAND

BALTASOUND	** Springfield 10 rms.
FAIR ISLE	ø Fair Isle Bird Observatory 11 rms.
LERWICK	** Grand 22 rms.
	** Hayfield 8 rms.
	*** Lerwick 26 rms.
SUMBURGH	** Sumburgh 17 rms.
UYEASOUND	* Maundeville 8 rms.
VOE	** Voe Country House 5 rms.

DUNBARTONSHIRE

ARROCHAR	** Lynwood House 9 rms.
BALLOCH	** Glenroy 6 rms.
ARDLUI	** Ardlui 12 rms.
	* Inverrarman House 15 rms.
ARROCHAR	*** Ardmay House 23 rms. F
	**** Arrochar 65 rms.
	** Cobbler 23 rms.
	** Loch Long 53 rms.
BALLOCH	** Balloch 7 rms.
	** Lennoxbank House 5 rms.
TARBET	** Tarbet 60 rms.

ø terms on application

376

A Short Bibliography

GENERAL

1768 MACINTYRE, DUNCAN BAN. *The Songs of Duncan Ban MacIntyre.*
Oliver & Boyd, 1952. Gaelic text and English rendering are set on
facing pages.

1774 PENNANT, THOMAS. *A Tour in Scotland: 1772.* A pioneer traveller
in then little-known country, this Welsh zoologist found the mountains emotionally overwhelming. His account of them is often false,
but his observation of detail elsewhere is accurate.

1775 JOHNSON, SAMUEL. *Journey to the Western Islands of Scotland.*
Johnson has nothing of value to say about the Highland scene, but
much about men, their talk, character, and custom. The same may
be said of Boswell.

1785 BOSWELL, JAMES. *Journal of a Tour to the Hebrides with Samuel
Johnson.*

1824 MACCULLOCH, J. *The Highlands and Western Isles of Scotland.* Dr.
MacCulloch, a geologist, was one of the first serious travellers to
appreciate every physical aspect of the Highlands. He is garrulous
(in three volumes), general descriptions have a 19th-century
romantic style, but he is most lively.

1909 GILLIES, PATRICK H. *Nether Lorn.* Historical incidents and
topography.

1920 DONALDSON, M. E. M. *Wanderings in the West Highlands.* One of
the most sensitive and informative writers on the region, especially
on its archaeology, district history, and natural beauty. A fiery
damner of philistinism.

1923 MACCORMACK, JOHN. *Island of Mull.* The best book on its
subject.

1924 MACKENZIE, OSGOOD. *A Hundred Years in the Highlands.* Bles,
1949. A 19th-century classic on the Gairloch district, its people and
natural history.

1926 DONALDSON, M. E. M. *Further Wanderings mainly in Argyll.* By far
the best descriptive book on the county.

1935 GORDON, SETON. *Highways and Byways in the West Highlands.* A
comprehensive and reliable guide to the west coast from Cape
Wrath to Argyll.

1947 CARMICHAEL, IAN. *Lismore in Alba.*

1949 DWELLY, EDWARD. *Illustrated Gaelic Dictionary.* Maclaren, Glasgow. The world's best Gaelic glossary. Records 100,000 words (as against 70,000 in the most comprehensive Irish Gaelic glossary), to which it gives more meanings than any others, including the obsolete.

1949 ROBERTSON, R. MACDONALD. *Wade the River, Drift the Loch.* Oliver & Boyd. Mainly fishing and legends.

1952 HALDANE, A. R. B. *Drove Roads of Scotland.* Nelson.

1955 STEVEN, CAMPBELL. *The Island Hills.* Hurst & Blackett. The Inner Hebrides, including the Isles of the Sea, Lismore, Handa, and other inshore islands.

1960 MAXWELL, GAVIN. *Ring of Bright Water.* Longmans. Glenelg and Sound of Sleat.

1962 MURRAY, W. H. *Highland Landscape.* National Trust for Scotland. A report, designating 21 regions of outstanding natural beauty, and assessing landscape changes there and in 31 other regions over the last 20 years.

1964 COWAN, MAY. *Inverewe.* Bles. The garden in the North-West Highlands.

1966 MURRAY, W. H. *The Hebrides.* Heinemann. The most comprehensive account of both the inner and outer islands.

ARCHAEOLOGY

1856 & 1867 STUART, JOHN. *Sculptured Stones of Scotland.* 2 vols

1881 DRUMMOND, J. *Sculptured Stones of Iona and the West Hihglands.* Society of Antiquaries of Scotland.

1903 ALLEN, J. ROMILLY. *The Early Christian Monuments of Scotland.*

1961–62 CAMPBELL, MARION. and MARY SANDEMAN. *Mid Argyll.* Reprinted from Proceedings of the Society of Antiquaries of Scotland. Vol. 95. A field survey of historic and prehistoric monuments. Sites listed: 125 pp.

1964 RICHARDSON, JAMES. *The Medieval Stone Carver in Scotland.* Edinburgh University Press.

1965 SIMPSON, W. DOUGLAS. *The Ancient Stones of Scotland.* Hale. A non-technical account from the Stone Age to the 18th century.

CHILDE, V. GORDON and W. DOUGLAS SIMPSON. *Ancient Monuments in Scotland.* HMSO. A brief account of a chosen few. Illustrated.

ARCHITECTURE

1887–92 MACGIBBON, D. and T. ROSS. *Castellated and Domestic Architecture of Scotland.* 5 vols. The fullest work. Each fortified house and castle described in detail with history where known. For more recent discoveries refer to Transactions of the Glasgow Archaeological Society, New Series, and to the Proceedings of the Society of Antiquaries of Scotland.

1960 CRUDEN, S. H. *The Scottish Castle*. Nelson. A general survey of the subject (without detailed listings).

ECOLOGY

1965 DARLING, F. FRASER and J. MORTON BOYD. *The Highlands and Islands*. Collins. A revision of Dr. Darling's *Natural History in the Highlands and Islands*, 1947. The most comprehensive and interesting book on the subject.

ECONOMY AND GEOGRAPHY

1793 THE STATISTICAL ACCOUNT OF SCOTLAND. *Argyll. Invernesshire. Ross and Cromarty. Sutherland.* Detailed accounts are given parish by parish by the parish ministers. They include much local history, not always reliable.

1845 *NEW STATISTICAL ACCOUNT OF SCOTLAND. Argyll. Invernessshire. Ross and Cromarty. Sutherland.* See above.

1955 DARLING, F. FRASER. *West Highland Survey*. Oxford University Press. Essential reading for an understanding of the region's economic life and problems. Includes the Hebrides.

1962 O'DELL, A. C. and KENNETH WATSON. *The Highlands and Islands of Scotland*. Nelson. Detailed description of the physical and historical geography of the Highlands, Eastern Lowlands, and Islands.

1964 THIRD STATISTICAL ACCOUNT OF SCOTLAND. *Argyll.* Collins.

GEOLOGY

1865 GEIKIE, A. *Scenery of Scotland*. 1901 edition.

1907 PEACH, B. N. and J. HORNE. *The Geological Structure of the North-west Highlands of Scotland*. HMSO.

1914 PEACH, B. N. and J. HORNE. *Guide to the Geological Model of the Assynt Mountains*. HMSO. 32 pages with 12 diagrams.

1936 PHEMISTER, J. *British Regional Geology: The Northern Highlands*. Geological Survey of Scotland. HMSO. 93 pp. with maps, memoirs to districts, and list of references to bigger books.

1937 MACGREGOR, M. and J. PHEMISTER. *Geological Excursion Guide to the Assynt District*. Edinburgh Geological Society.

1941 HARKER, ALFRED. *The West Highlands and the Hebrides*. Cambridge University Press.

1964 RICHEY, J. E. *British Regional Geology: Scotland: The Tertiary Volcanic Districts*. Geological Survey. HMSO. 3rd edition revised. Deals with Ardnamurchan, Mull, Skye, etc.

HISTORY AND BIOGRAPHY

c 685 ADAMNAN. *Life of St. Columba*. Nelson, 1961. Latin text with English translation. Style anecdotal. Adamnan was Abbot of Iona from 679 to 704.

1746–75 FORBES, ROBERT, Bishop of Ross and Caithness. *The Lyon in Mourning*. Scottish History Society: 3 vols., 1894–96 Henry Paton, editor. The foundation of our knowledge of the '45 rising. Every piece of information was severely tested by the author before inclusion. Now a rare book.

1782 FLATEGAN and FRISIAN MSS. *Haco's Expedition against Scotland, 1263*. 13th-century Norse text with English translation. A bare account.

1816 ANONYMOUS. *Account of the Depredations committed on Clan Campbell, 1685 and 1686*. In the Scottish National Library, Edinburgh (under CAMPBELL). The losses suffered in the Atholl Raid are presented as a financial account.

1842 BROWNE, JAMES. *History of the Highlands*. 4 vols. A most important work. Includes an appendix of *Stuart Papers*.

1876–80 SKENE, W. F. *Celtic Scotland*. 3 vols.

1880 GARNETT, T. *The Highlands of Scotland*.

1881 GREGORY, D. *History of the Western Highlands and Islands of Scotland*. An indispensable study of inter-clan feuds and history.

1885 CAMPBELL, LORD ARCHIBALD. *Records of Argyll*. The author roves at random, recording bits and pieces of Argyll's history (much of which might have been lost to us).

1897 BLAIKIE, W. B. *Itinerary of Prince Charles Edward Stuart*. A good map shows the prince's movements, which are given day by day in the text.

1899–1904 NORIE, W. D. *Life and Adventures of Prince Charles Edward Stuart*. 4 vols. The best life of the prince, but does not cover his later years. Written with compassion. Contains valuable photographs of places and relics.

1906 MACKENZIE, W. C. *Short History of the Scottish Highlands*.

1908 TULLIBARDINE, MARCHIONESS OF. *Military History of Perthshire, 1660-1902.* The book is listed here only for its useful references to the Jacobite risings of 1719 and 1745.

1928 BUCHAN, JOHN. *Montrose.* A scholarly biography—not for popular reading.

1930 NICOLSON, A. *History of Skye.* Popular rather than scholarly history. A good and thorough work.

1935 CHILDE, V. GORDON. *Prehistory of Scotland.*

1946 CHILDE. V. GORDON. *Scotland before the Scots.*

1950 MACDONALD, COLIN M. *History of Argyll.* Holmes, Glasgow.

1959 MCNEILL, F. MARION. *Iona.* Blackie. Brief, but a good account for the summer visitor.

1962 DOMHNULL GRUAMACH. *The House of Islay.* Graham Donald, Port Charlotte, Islay. A short history of Somerled and the Lords of the Isles. 108 pp.

1963 PREBBLE, JOHN. *The Highland Clearances.* Secker & Warburg. Dispassionate and reliable. Not easy reading.

1965 MACDONALD, DONALD J. *Slaughter Under Trust.* Hale. The massacre of Glen Coe. A trustworthy and scholarly account with full evidence brought in support.

1965 DOMHNULL GRUAMACH. *The Foundations of Islay.* Graham Donald, Port Charlotte, Islay. A valuable commentary on Celtic history. 99 pp.

1966 PREBBLE, JOHN. *Glencoe.* Secker & Warburg. A vivid account of the massacre, imaginary in dialogue and in some of its detail but with main events and motives fairly stated and documented.

1966 LINKLATER, ERIC. *The Prince in the Heather.* Hodder & Stoughton. A plain narrative of the prince's escape after Culloden. Excellent photographs.

1967 MONCREIFFE of that Ilk. *The Highland Clans.* Barrie & Rockcliff. Dynastic origin of the clans and history in brief.

MOUNTAINEERING

1947 MURRAY, W. H. *Mountaineering in Scotland.* Dent, 1962.

1951 MURRAY, W. H. *Undiscovered Scotland.* Dent. Both books describe rock, snow, and ice climbs in the West Highlands.

1952 HUMBLE, B. H. *The Cuillin of Skye.* Hale. A history of mountaineering in Skye.

The Companion Guide to the West Highlands of Scotland

SCOTTISH MOUNTAINEERING TRUST

District Guides: Southern Highlands. 1951

West Col	*Western Highlands.* 1964
Productions	*Northern Highlands* 1953
	Central Highlands. 1968
	Island of Skye. 1954
	Islands of Scotland. 1952
	Munro's Tables. 1969

Rock-climbing Guides: Arrochar 1954

West Col	*Glencoe and Ardgour.* 2 vols. 1959 and 1965
Productions	*Ben Nevis.* 1969
	Cuillin of Skye. 2 vols. 1969
	Northern Highlands. 1969

Wholly reliable, handsomely produced, and up-to-date guides written by members of the Scottish Mountaineering Club. The information given is wide-ranging and comprehensive with every needed map, diagram, and photograph.

NOVELS

1817 SCOTT, WALTER. *Rob Roy.*

1886 STEVENSON, R. L. *Kidnapped.*

1899 MUNRO, NEIL. *John Splendid.* Blackwood. Historical novel.

1905 MUNRO, NEIL. *Doom Castle.* Blackwood. 18th century romance set around Inveraray.

1914 MUNRO, NEIL. *The New Road.* Blackwood. Historical novel.

1925 BROSTER, D. K. *The Flight of the Heron.* Heinemann. A Jacobite romance.

1931 GUNN, NEIL. *Morning Tide.* Faber.

1937 GUNN, NEIL. *Highland River.* Faber.

1962 MURRAY, W. H. *Maelstrom.* Secker & Warburg.

These nine novels are suggested for their faithful painting of scenic background, or of historical incident, or of human life in the West Highlands.

Index

Index

Wolf, 69, 82, 90, 165, 347, 356
Wood of Eredine, 81
Wordsworth, William, 21, 84, 189
Wrath, *see* Cape

Yachting, 34, 41, 48, 58, 71, 72-3,

88, 97, 98, 108, 136, 140, 143, 179,
212, 281, 307
York Buildings Company, 80
Younger Botanic Gardens, 39
  H.G., 39
Youth Hostels, *see* Scottish